Writing Environments

Writing Environments

Edited by

Sidney I. Dobrin
and
Christopher J. Keller

STATE UNIVERSITY OF NEW YORK PRESS

Published by
State University of New York Press, Albany

For information, address State University of New York Press,
90 State Street, Suite 700, Albany, NY 12207

Production by Michael Haggett
Marketing by Michael Campochiaro

Library of Congress Cataloging-in-Publication Data

Writing environments / edited by Sidney I. Dobrin and Christopher J. Keller
    p. cm.
    Includes bibliographical references and index.
    ISBN 0-7914-6331-1 (alk. paper) — ISBN 0-7914-6332-X (pbk. : alk. paper)
    1. Authorship.   2. Authorship—Psychological aspects.   3. Place (Philosophy)
  I. Dobrin, Sidney I., 1967–   II. Keller, Christopher J.

PN145.W754 2005
808.'.02—dc22   2004018763

10 9 8 7 6 5 4 3 2 1

This one's for
Asher Miekal.
Welcome my son,
Welcome to the machine.

For my mother and father,
Robert and Jean Keller.

Contents

Acknowledgments

One of the most exciting parts of putting *Writing Environments* together has been the number of people we have had the opportunity to work with. We cannot begin to express our gratitude to those who have invested their time and energy into helping us complete this book. First and foremost, we are grateful to those who participated in the interviews themselves and then helped us make the interviews into the versions found here. We could not have put this book together without the kind participation and collaboration of Annette Kolodny, Rick Bass, David Quammen, Janisse Ray, Max Oelschlaeger, Simon Ortiz, Scott Russell Sanders, Cheryll Glotfelty, Ann Zwinger, and Edward O. Wilson. We are deeply grateful, too, to Ann, Herman, and Sophie Zwinger for having us up to Constant Friendship for a day to conduct the interview with Ann. We are grateful to all of these interviewees not just for their continued support of *Writing Environments* but for the friendships and professional relationships that have evolved with many of them since we met during the interviews. Likewise, we are indebted to those interviewees who wrote responses to the responses in this book.

We are also deeply grateful to the scholars who have responded to each of the interviews. Their contributions to *Writing Environments* give substance to the collection of interviews within a conversation about writing and environment.

We would like to acknowledge and thank Carla Blount for her never-ending support; without her efforts *Writing Environments* would never have been completed. Similarly, we are grateful for the transcription work provided by Dean Swinford and indebted to the departments of English at both the University of Florida and the University of Hawaii, Hilo, for their support of this project and our work in general. We gratefully acknowledge Bonnie Lorenz for her hospitality (particularly the bourbon and steaks!) when we traveled to Denver for one of the interviews. We are also grateful to Robert, Jean, and Daisy Keller for their support of this project.

We offer particular gratitude to our friend and frequent collaborator Christian Weisser, whose own work greatly influenced *Writing Environments* and for whose friendship and scholarly guidance we are deeply grateful (congratulations, too, to Christian and Traci on the recent birth of their first son, Cole Weisser).

We offer our never-ending gratitude to Teresa and Cindy for their patience, support, and love. We could not do the work we do without them, and, in fact, more often than not, we do the work we do specifically because of them. They are our strength.

Finally, we offer thanks, gratitude, appreciation, and gratefulness to Priscilla Ross for her faith in this project, her lenience with deadlines, her editorial advice, and her friendship. She is not just our favorite editor, she's one of our favorite people. Thanks, Priscilla.

Why Writing Environments

An Introduction

Sidney I. Dobrin and Christopher J. Keller

Can the extrinsic forces of earth, water, and sky alter the intrinsic elements of language, rhetoric, and imagery?

—William Howarth, "Reading the Wetlands"

This collection looks broadly at the relationships between writing and places, or textuality and places: for instance, how the production of texts and discourse is influenced by the places and environments in which and for which they are produced; how texts and discourse construct places and environments and in turn how these texts influence, affect, and persuade readers; how different cultural and sociopolitical factors affect the production and interpretation of texts that focus on places and environments; and how, in short, writers in various disciplines and professions write when they write about places and environments.

Much practical and theoretical work in English and writing studies already asks similar questions about texts and place, and a good deal of it harnesses work in other disciplines, including but not limited to philosophy, geography, architecture, anthropology, social theory, and history. And much of this work has entered English and writing studies from a variety of critical directions, such as Marxism and other materialist-oriented approaches, feminism, postcolonial studies, popular cultural studies, ecological studies, and so forth. Thus, it is commonplace to suggest that studies of textuality and place are in most cases highly interdisciplinary and highly diverse in their critical methodologies and approaches. Additionally, no one umbrella term exists that adequately characterizes the diversity of such studies, though one often comes across phrases and terms such as spatial criticism, critical or cultural geography, postmodern geography, ecocomposition, or cognitive mapping, just to name a few. Although it is not possible here to summarize all of these scholarly arenas of criticism, a good deal of this work examines not only how place-related metaphors and concepts function but also how various kinds of texts are able to shape places (and vice versa), and, additionally, how different models of place and space limit or expand our understandings of diverse texts, disciplines, peoples, cultures, and the world in general. In a number of disciplinary conversations, furthermore, it is not uncommon to come across studies of how places are conceived as sites of politics, conflict, and struggle; how productions of fictional places occur in novels and how these productions circulate across "real" space; how narratives might endow readers with a heightened sense of place; how discussions of nationalist literatures must attend closely to how these literatures negotiate global places and contexts; and, in short, how places are not static, reified things but instead are open-ended, contradictory processes.

Scholarly criticism that examines places and environments is quite dynamic, complex, and diverse, to say the least. While much of *Writing Environments* taps into these sorts of conversations, this book, however, approaches many of these scholarly and important topics from a slightly different angle and perspective. And it does so with a unique structure and format. *Writing Environments* includes ten original interviews with an array of important writers, most of whom do not work in the field of English or writing studies but whose work is deeply entrenched in the project of better understanding relationships between texts and places, texts and environments. The interviewees are individuals who are concerned with environment from the standpoints of activists, scientists, naturalists, teachers, and visible writers: Rick Bass is a well-known writer of fiction and nonfiction, who is often labeled a "nature writer" and who is known as a vocal activist. Cheryll Glotfelty is best known as one of the founding scholars of ecocriticism, an ecologically based literary criticism that has greatly affected the evolution of English studies and ecocomposition. Annette Kolodny is unquestionably one of the most important contemporary literary critics, contributing greatly to work in feminist critical theory. Max Oelschlaeger's work has changed how we understand concepts of wilderness, asking us to rethink wilderness in historical and philosophical perspectives; his work has earned a Pulitzer prize nomination. Simon Ortiz has earned the reputation as one of the most important Native American writers and poets writing today. David Quammen is best known for his articles that appear in outdoor magazines, such as *National Geographic* and *Outside*. Janisse Ray's book *Ecology of a Cracker Childhood* won numerous awards including the American Book Award. Scott Russell Sanders's work has become some of the most frequently anthologized of our time, work that often centers on the importance of place. Two-time Pulitzer prize winner E. O. Wilson has changed the way the world thinks about science and, particularly, its relationships to larger public audiences. And, naturalist Ann Zwinger's books about natural history have given audiences new insight into the way we understand our relationships with places. These are all writers and thinkers whose work often centers on concepts of place and environment, whose work is influenced explicitly by particular places and environments, and whose work influences the way readers see and understand the environments they read about.

Each of the interviews is followed by two short responses written by individuals whose profession is in writing and rhetoric studies; these responses are meant to help draw the interview discussions into the realm of English and writing studies and, in turn, to help develop important lines of thought for these disciplines. We also provided each interviewee the opportunity to respond to the responses to further encourage dialogue among English and writing and those working in other areas who are interested in questions of place and environment. Some of those who participated in interviews chose to write, others did not. Nonetheless, *Writing Environments* contains several important conversations that produce larger dialogues about how issues of environment and place are important to those of us who study discourse and texts of all kinds.

The interviews and responses in this collection take up a number of issues and concerns that are relevant to writers and readers both inside and outside of academia, those who are generally interested in how we come to understand places and environments—and how texts play a role in this understanding. The interviewees in *Writing Environments* represent a diverse range of voices, voices that speak lucidly and captivatingly about topics such as place, writing, teaching, politics, race, and culture, for instance—and how these overlap in many complex ways. Yet these contributors to the book are individuals who—despite their differences—all recognize the importance of contextualizing these interview conversations within particular understandings of place and environment. Thus, the writers we interviewed are people who not only write *about* certain kinds of places and environments but also consider how different environments have influenced them and the production of their texts, and how their writing (and all writing) affects environments and the ways readers experience environments. We chose to interview these ten particular individuals because many of them are writers whose work is anthologized in composition and literature textbooks and readers (it is becoming uncommon to find a reader that does not include essays and excerpts by, for instance, Rick Bass, Scott Russell Sanders, and E. O. Wilson), or they are writers whose work has been discussed in a variety of scholarly conversations in English and writing studies. The interviewees are all prolific and fascinating writers who have much to tell us about environments, politics, cultures, history, teaching, and, most important, they have much to tell us about writing.

We would like to cite a few qualifications about *Writing Environments*. These qualifications, however, might first need a bit of background about the production of this book. Interviews were conducted either in person or over the phone, and they were recorded on cassette tape to be transcribed later. After transcription, the interviews were sent to the interviewees for initial editing; however, we did ask the interviewees to try not to edit out the conversational tone of the interviews. Most made minor changes only to clarify their positions and to make the interviews more readable. After receiving the edited interviews from the ten interviewees, we solicited scholars in English and writing studies to write responses to these interviews. This, however, is something that warrants careful, honest, and candid attention. To put it bluntly, as Sid Dobrin and Randall Roorda have addressed in detail in their responses, these responses are a bit unfair. The interviewees in this book participated in conversations about environments and about writing, but we only asked them to talk with us informally, to respond to our questions without preparation, without drafting and revising answers. Their answers are impromptu not rehearsed. In contrast, the responses are usually more academic, and contributors have been given time to carefully craft their responses. Randall Roorda says it perfectly in his response to the Ann Zwinger interview: "It's unfair to transcribe what Zwinger treats as a conversation and scrutinize it as if it were a composed, deliberate performance, from which compositionists might expect to elicit insights and applications" (p. 314). It is unfair to do this to any of the interviews; yet, this is specifically what we have asked the respondents to do. It is perhaps even more unfair that we then ask the interviewees to respond to the responses after we put them in the position that necessitates they defend themselves through response.

The concept of interview responses (and the interviews themselves) grows from the interviews and responses that Gary A. Olson published in *The Journal of Advanced Composition* (*JAC*) over the past dozen plus years and the subsequent books he published with SUNY Press. Prior to

Roorda's critique of this format, there has been little, if any, question of the viability of the interview/response format. There should have been. And yet, we specifically have asked the respondents included in this collection to address these informal interviews as though they had been written in anticipation of response. Likewise, it was probably unfair of us to ask the kinds of questions we repeatedly ask in these interviews, hoping to get the interviewees to give the respondents something to respond to. But what we hoped to develop was specifically a sense of conversation, one that stretched between the academic world and the world of nature writers, biologists, ecologists, activists. We wanted these "conversations" to transcend the unfortunately rigid borders among different academic disciplines and perspectives.

Importantly though, it is not a stretch to say that this book is composed of two different kinds of texts—interviews and responses—that themselves manifest the different places and environments in which discourses and writings are shaped and produced. In short, we might suggest that the responses are a bit unfair to the interviewees because they were produced on different ground, in different environments, which made for these disparities. With this said, however, the numerous and diverse voices in this collection do in fact speak with, to, and against one another in various productive and beneficial ways. The "apples-and-oranges" nature of the interviews and responses, we believe, makes not for a terminal impasse but for further investigations into how environments and places are in fact linked closely with textuality. *Writing Environments*, then, itself is a text that derives from and was shaped by a hodge-podge of environments that to no small degree influenced its production and its conversations.

Taking Back the Language

An Interview with Annette Kolodny

Elaine Showalter has described Annette Kolodny as "the most sophisticated theorist of feminist interpretation." Similarly, Cathy N. Davidson, writing in the *Centennial Review*, explained that Kolodny is "one of the few contemporary critics" to link "those who attempt to revise critical stances towards theoretical issues of textuality by reference to a traditional literary canon and those questioning of the function and ideology of a literary canon." Simply put, Annette Kolodny has been one of the most important literary critics of recent time. Her work in feminist literary criticism is landmark. Her essays "Some Notes on Defining a 'Feminist' Literary Criticism," "Dancing through the Minefield: Some Observations on the Theory, Practice, and Politics of a Feminist Literary Criticism," and "A Map for Rereading: Gender and the Interpretation of Literary Texts" are some of the most important works in establishing feminist literary theory and practice. What makes Kolodny's work in feminist literary criticism so crucial is that she situates feminist literary criticism within political thought and tries to offer practical solutions to pressing social problems.

What makes Kolodny's work even more intriguing is her devoted attention to environmental concerns and her recent attention to the structure and politics of higher education. Her books *The Lay of the Land: Metaphor as Experience and History in American Life and Letters* and *The Land Before Her: Fantasies of the American Frontiers, 1630–1860* most directly reflect her engagement with feminist thought and politics as they connect to issues of environmental concern. Her book *Failing the Future: A Dean Looks at Higher Education in the Twenty-First Century* explores the role of higher education and its intersections with the political and the environmental.

Kolodny has served on the faculty at a number of institutions, including Yale, University of British Columbia, University of New Hampshire, University of Maryland, Rensselaer Polytechnic Institute and, currently, the University of Arizona. Kolodny faced problems within the university system when the University of New Hampshire denied her tenure. In an ensuing lawsuit, Kolodny charged the university with sexual discrimination and anti-Semitism. The lawsuit was settled out of court, and Kolodny used a good portion of her financial award to establish the Legal Fund of the Task Force on Discrimination within the National Women's Studies Association. Kolodny refers to this case here and to her ongoing activism and political work. She is well suited to discuss the role of university systems, and she does so in depth.

What is crucially apparent is Kolodny's attention to the role of the political within university systems and the political within writing and discourse systems as well. She asks, for instance, "how do we exercise our right to clean air and pure water if we cannot choose non-polluting technologies and protect the aquifers through legislation? In other words, we must reconstitute a wholly new set of definitions for what we mean by the words *rights* and *choice*. This must all be done as teachers and as public intellectuals." Kolodny also discusses not only her perspectives on the production of discourse and discourse studies in the university system but also the numerous struggles over discourse both inside and outside academic institutions, suggesting that "any kind of progressive discourse is being drowned out by the discourses of profit, biotechnology, and cost-benefit analysis. Cost-benefit analysis is a convenient phrase for obscuring the fact that we are trading long-term survival for short-term corporate profits. We need to intervene and take back the language." Thoughts on intervention, discourse, environment, and feminism are certainly at the core of the following interview.

Q: At the beginning of *The Lay of the Land,* as you are discussing early exploration of North America, you write, "All the descriptions of the wonderful beasts and strangely contoured humans notwithstanding, the published documents from explorers assured the reader of the author's accuracy and unimpeachable reliability. No mere literary convention this; an irrefutable fact of history (the European discovery of America) touched every word written about the New World with the possibility that the ideally beautiful and bountiful terrain might be lifted forever out of the canon of pastoral convention and invested with the reality of daily experience." You seem to be making some interesting connections between the act of writing and the notion of experience and the presentation of literary image and experience. What is the relationship between experience and the written account of that experience?

A: That's an interesting question, and the answer is somewhat complicated. In my view, no written account simply tells an experience raw, or captures it whole, but instead, in the very act of writing there is a shaping and a reshaping. In other words, the final written account is inevitably partial and contrived, a shaping and reshaping of whatever the actual raw experience might have been. For the historian or literary critic, it is essential to remember that the reconstruction of experience that we find recorded even in so-called authentic diaries or personal journals is itself the product of narrative patterns that have been previously available to the writer. Nobody writes without having some sense of what has been previously written, and what kind of generic patterns, story shapes, or stylistic possibilities already exist. And so, even in trying to get at what has been the "real" experience, in effect, narrative conventions take over. Thus, the writer is never writing about what truly happened; no matter how hard writers try to capture what they understand as reality, in a sense, they are writing about the process of writing. They are writing about how they understand reality *in the terms and language and story patterns made available to them by their culture.* But the reader doesn't know that. What comes out, finally, is the writer writing about what he or she has been able to understand of their experience through the narratives that have been available to him or her through culture. And if the reader shares that culture, then what has been written will be wholly comprehensible and seem authentic. But if the reader is outside the culture—and has learned a different set of narrative conventions—then the same writing may be incomprehensible or seem inauthentic or unbelievable.

Q: Do narrative conventions then also affect the experience that writers had even before they wrote about it?

A: Absolutely. I'm inclined to believe that there is no innocent experience. By that, I mean that all experience is mediated through culture, and that when one reports an experience, either to yourself, in a personal journal, or to an external audience, what you're really reporting is the way in which whatever happened was given meaning through the narratives and belief systems that your culture made available in the first place. After all, it isn't as though we hold our culture but, rather, that our culture holds and wholly embraces us. It informs the way we think and know the world.

Q: You write, "When America finally produced a pastoral literature of her own, that literature hailed the essential femininity of the terrain in a way European pastoral never had, explored the historical consequences of its central metaphor in a way European pastoral had never dared, and, from the first, took its metaphors as literal truths." It is an interesting point to make that American pastoralism holds more of a kinship with the feminine than European pastoral traditions, and of course, this has been an important argument of yours in much of your work. We are curious as to how you would apply such an argument to contemporary nature writers. That is, does the contemporary movement in nature writing—including writing that uses elements of the pastoral, science, natural history, experiential, or personal narrative—and contemporary nature writers, such as Ann Zwinger, Terry Tempest Williams, Barry Lopez, and Rick Bass, somehow hold and utilize a greater feminine kinship?

A: No. It seems to me that what marks all of their work is that they are searching for alternate metaphorical patterns. What each of them is doing in his or her own unique way is trying to forge some kind of language that is not burdened by the errors and depredations of our historical past. Because each of the writers you mention is acutely aware of how language—especially symbolic language like metaphor—influences the way we conceptualize and act upon the natural world, they are all trying to escape the legacies of a feminized natural world. Each one keeps searching; no one's found it yet. We haven't yet found any powerfully consistent language for nature that has been popularly adopted, but it's a searching process that distinguishes their work.

Q: You have written that "Colonization brought with it an inevitable paradox: the success of settlement depended on the ability to master the land, transforming the virgin territories into something else—a farm, a village, a road, a canal, a railway, a mine, a factory, a city, and finally an urban nation." Undoubtedly, eco-colonization has remapped not only the new world frontiers, but the entire world, and now stands to potentially redraw the borders in space as well. How much of a role in this colonization, this mastery of land, has writing played? That is, is there a relationship between writing and colonization?

A: One couldn't take place without the other. In the Western tradition, if you look at the etymology of the verb *to name*, it means to know and to own at the same time. The dual concept works like this: Because I know (or understand) this land, I also know what the right name for it must be—and that gives me a sense of ownership. At the same time, because I own (or possess) this land, I have the right to name it—and thereby declare its meaning for others in the future. Thus, naming becomes a means of inscribing one's presence and beliefs and values on the land. Therefore, the very act of writing about the land is a process of inscribing and re-inscribing over and over again the fact that you know and own this land. I think that colonization could never have taken place in the Western tradition without the writing process. Every one of the early explorers, even if he was unable to write himself, had with him a secretary who chronicled that exploration and, most important, the naming process. Once the explorer named this land, that recorded act meant that, basically, Europe owned it, and claimed to know it, and had renamed it or wrested it from its previous native inhabitants.

Q: One of the most provocative statements you have made is that "I fear that the human species is hell-bent on self-annihilation, with the United States rather blindly leading the way. We pollute our minds with trivia and our environment with carcinogens. The political and moral awakenings of the nineteen-sixties are now being dismissed—to our peril; and the current women's movement may run out of energy before it achieves the changes it envisions. The nation as a whole is in the hands of the blind, the selfish, and the mediocre." Because of the forum in which it will be published, many of those who read this interview will agree with your statement to some degree or another. And so our question here is twofold: first, how do those of us who agree with you work to change this, and second, how do we encourage the rest of the country, in fact the world, to reverse these charges?

A: This is a key question, and I have tried to respond to it in several conference papers this year. I tried again in my remarks at the biannual conference of the Association for the Study of Literature and Environment (ASLE), held this year in Flagstaff. First, I think we must heed U.N. Secretary General Kofi Annan's observation that "We do not face a choice between economy and ecology." As he said, "In fact, the opposite is true. Unless we protect the resources and the earth's natural capital, we shall not be able to sustain economic growth." This means that it is now time for all of us to put our considerable skills in analysis and exegesis in service of deconstructing the deceptive antienvironmental rhetoric that would exploit and destroy *all* our natural resources and claim to be saving jobs in the process. All that is really being saved are short-term corporate profits. And we must do this analysis and exegesis both inside and outside the classroom: inside the classroom as teachers of rhetoric and language analysis, and outside as public intellectuals.

Second, we can unravel the rhetoric that equates conservation exclusively with private virtue by examining most of the other major industrialized nations that have made conservation a linchpin of public policy through things like subsidies for low-cost public transportation and tax incentives for the construction of energy-efficient housing. In short, private virtue *must* become public policy if we are to have livable, sustainable communities. It simply isn't enough for a private individual like me to decide to use solar panels for heating my home's water. We need a national program—like substantial tax incentives for builders, home owners, and businesses—to encourage *everyone* to use solar if they live in an area with many days of sunlight. In other words, conservation must become a national and community priority. The vision of renewed and constantly renewing community is thus the rhetoric we must now advocate.

Third, we can address the often facile rhetoric of rights and free choice by examining how truly limited our choices really are. In most of the United States, the infirm and the elderly—let alone the hale and the hearty—cannot choose public transportation because it simply isn't available. As a result, millions are virtually trapped in their homes and immediate neighborhood—whether for work, for shopping, or for recreation. And how do we exercise our right to clean air and pure water if we cannot choose nonpolluting technologies and protect the aquifers through legislation? In other words, we must reconstitute a wholly new set of definitions for what we mean by the words *rights* and *choice*. Clean air, potable water, and uncontaminated soil should be seen as inalienable human rights—for everyone on the planet and not just for the wealthy few. And no one should have to choose between having a job and protecting the rain forest. That's *not* a meaningful choice.

As teachers and as public intellectuals, we have to take back the language. How do we do this as teachers? Taken together, the essays collected in the book Sid [Dobrin] did with Christian Weisser, *Ecocomposition: Theoretical and Pedagogical Approaches*, suggest that all of these are appropriate topics for most required first-year composition and rhetoric classes. After all, do we not try to teach our students in these classes how discourse functions in specific domains and how to analyze those discourses?

And whether we teach in urban or rural environments, we can also introduce our students to the growing movement loosely called "greening of the campus." These comprise efforts across the country to introduce energy conservation strategies, recycling, and new modes of transportation systems to the campus. In doing so, we respond to Lawrence Buell's good advice that was published in the June 1, 2001 issue of the *Chronicle of Higher Education* that we give our students a more "complex under-standing of what counts as environment, environmentalism, and environmental writing"—an understanding that includes the campus itself as an environment.

As public intellectuals, however, we must get out of the classroom and write for audiences other than the readers of the *Interdisciplinary Studies in Literature and Environment (ISLE)* or the *Chronicle of Higher Education*. We must "out-fax" big oil interests, transnational nuclear conglomerates, and the right wing by assiduously faxing our own op-ed pieces to local and national newspapers. Our students should be encouraged to investigate these issues and compose their own opinion pieces for publication, too. You'd be surprised how eager newspapers are to get well-written free copy for their editorial pages—and especially when the writer has some mark of authority that commands attention, like a publication record or a university affiliation. And when your piece is published in one local paper, you'd be surprised how quickly other papers will pick it up and reprint it on their own editorial page. It is surely a painless way to gain influence. And when your local paper asks you for another piece—maybe even a full article—you can be sure they'll also offer a fee. As a result, you may even get paid for helping to save the planet. But even more important, you'll help to disseminate new ideas and new language for protecting our shared and very fragile environment.

I do think, alas, that we are still in the hands of the blind, the selfish, and the mediocre. Any kind of progressive discourse is being drowned out by the discourses of profit, biotechnology, and cost-benefit analysis. Cost-benefit analysis is a convenient phrase for obscuring the fact that we are trading long-term survival for short-term corporate profits. We need to intervene and take back the language.

Q: Essentially speaking, we could (as many critics have) say that your work has focused on two primary emphases. Your articles and essays often address literary criticism from a feminist perspective and work to identify the roles political contexts play in feminist literary criticism and practice. In addition, you often write of powerful environmental concerns and ask readers to question the ways in which European Americans have imposed their beliefs onto the physical/natural world. For many working in the areas of ecocriticism, ecofeminism, and ecocomposition, these are both crucial and critical projects, and they stand as foundational to the work in these areas. Your book, *The Land Before Her*, in many ways combines these two projects and offers "some alternative metaphorical design . . . that would lead us away from our destructive capacities" while examining a tradition of women's writing from the west. Though a rather large question (with its own minefields), but one of deep interest, we were wondering if you would take a moment to envision an amalgam of these two projects and offer an outline for what you might see as a feminist-environmental literary criticism.

A: I don't know, in any large sense, what a feminist-environmental literary criticism would look like. I appreciate the fact that feminists have in very different ways approached the ecological crises of the twentieth and twenty-first centuries. Some have gone the spiritual route and advocated worshipping nature as a sacred space. Some have become Wiccan and advocated ways of living in harmony with natural rhythms. Others have joined Greenpeace and tried to influence political policies on a global scale. Others have found their way through the Nature Conservancy or the Sierra Club. Others, like me, have interrogated language and its political consequences. There are so many different approaches, and I think all of them are valuable, so I don't see a single feminist-environmental discourse emerging; what I see are several complementary discourses but with different kinds of emphases, some on the spiritual, some on the activist, some on rethinking the language. If we have anything in common it's the attempt to give voice to a voiceless natural world and to speak or act on behalf of a fragile environment that has too few advocates. For the most part, we all also speak out of deep love and respect for a world that can so easily be destroyed. Hopefully, we will eventually all work together in a complementary way.

Q: In "A Map for Rereading," you take Harold Bloom to task for his notion of literary influence and write that "whether we speak of poets and critics 'reading' texts or writers 'reading' (and thereby recording for us) the world, we are calling attention to interpretive strategies that are learned, historically determined, and thereby necessarily gender-inflected." While we agree with you regarding the ways in which such reading is historically conducted and constructed, we are also curious about the act of production, the notion of writing, the idea of recording that you allude to in this statement. Of course, writing is also inextricably linked with the kinds of historical readings you refer to, but we'd like to know if you see writing as having the power to resist some of these historical constraints, and if so, what effect that ultimately has on interpretive strategies.

A: Yes, writing always has the power to resist the historical constraints and popular paradigms of the moment. Just as an example, you can think about women's private journals as an act of resistance. For a woman on the overland trail in 1850, for example, her private journal was a space in which she could construct an oppositional self—often oppositional to this westward journey that she had never chosen but her husband had. Here is the place where she can invent language to challenge the popular notion that the frontier west is always a land of opportunity, or the notion of the Indians as savages. So, if you look at things like women's overland diaries and frontier journals, you will discover a very different set of voices about what this journey means, what it will entail for the family, and how these women want to interact with the native people en route and with the landscape that they are eventually brought to. Thus, writing is always a space in which, potentially, resistance can take place. Moreover, because we are such a heterodox and diverse country, there are always multiple competing value systems, multiple competing discourses, and multiple competing belief systems. As a result, you can always break out of and resist certain kinds of historical constraints because they're never homogenous, they're never overarching. The view that the frontier West was a place of economic opportunity was powerful and popular in the nineteenth century. But there were also writers who presented that same terrain as threatening, lawless, even uncivilized. In this way, differing images and discourses competed with one another for dominance and influence.

Q: Part of your argument in *The Land Before Her* is that women need "to find some alternative set of images through which to make their own unique accommodations to the strange and sometimes forbidding New World landscapes." This quote seems reflective of, if not prophetic of, current conversations regarding both alternative discourses and also arguments from many of the French feminists that women need to develop their own discourses, outside of, removed from, resistant to traditional phallocentric discourses in order to have a more authentic means of expressing feminine experience. We'd like to ask, first, whether you have seen a move toward the kinds of alternative discourses you call for here, and second, if you see a relationship between the work of French feminists, such as Luce Irigaray or Hélène Cixous, and contemporary feminist/environmentalist thinking?

A: First of all, I have to confess that I do not find much of the French feminist writing either interesting or useful. Perhaps that is because the French have a tendency to think on the left but act on the right, and that always bothers me. I prefer consistency between the way that you think and the way that you act in the world. But, it is the case that, at least in the United States, women writers have always experimented with tropes and symbolic systems different from the reigning systems constructed by men. One might even argue that the sentimental novel is a peculiarly female discourse in nineteenth-century America. None of this is unusual, though. All subdominant groups, whether they be women, or racial minorities, or ethnic minorities, are always inventing, just for their own survival, oppositional or subversive discourses. That's the way they survive and find a means of undermining the dominant culture and, at the same time, reaffirm their connection to their own culture or their own group. What happens over time is that the dominant group usually co-opts the subdominant group's discourse, whether it's rap or hip-hop, and that becomes the new popular mode of expression. Then, the subdominant group has to go on and invent, yet again, an alternative oppositional discourse that marks itself as different and unique, and undermines what it still sees as a dominant, or homogenizing culture around it. Right now, I would argue that environmentalists are in that subdominant group, where what we need to do is forge a discourse that can be adopted and co-opted by the general public, by the dominant culture, so that the dominant culture comes to own and believe in an environmental discourse of its own.

Q: Does that homogenization remove the radical edge from the discourse?

A: Always. It has to. It's unfortunate, but it has to. Because, in order for the ideas, the discourses, the oppositional stance of the subdominant group to become popularized, a certain edge must be taken off so that the rest of the culture can live with it, and then feel that it invented it. That's certainly been the case with the women's movement. And that is, in part, an explanation for why the women's movement, which was so expressive and creative, and had such an incredible impact in the sixties and seventies, then looked as though it was not as energetic in the eighties and the nineties. People began to talk about a postfeminist era. But, of course, it wasn't a postfeminist era. It's just that so many ideas previously advocated only by feminists were now so much a part of the general culture that they no longer seemed "feminist." It's true that the kinds of changes we all had envisioned in the sixties and seventies had only made a dent in altering the larger culture. Nonetheless, enough ideas and pieces of language got co-opted that they became popularized to the extent that, for example, *equal pay for equal work* is a phrase that no one even blinks at any more. Well, of course, it took us a long time to get that kind of phrasing into the popular imagination, but it did finally become both law and practice. Whereas government-subsidized, round-the-clock, high-quality child care, which we also fought for, we haven't gotten yet. The discourse of *national* responsibility for the care and rearing of every child remains in competition with a discourse of exclusively *parental* responsibility. So, you get some things into the popular imagination, and you make some social changes, but in the process you do lose part of your radical edge. Always. But that's why any subdominant group remains organized and keeps working.

Q: In the Preface to *The Land Before Her*, you make the important statement "Our actions in the world are shaped by the paradigms in our head." We'd like to ask, from where does that paradigm come? What influences it, creates it?

A: Well, language is learned, and therefore all of the metaphors and symbolic patterns that we know are learned from the culture into which we were born. It's very hard to escape those. The advantage we have in the United States is that there are so many cultures at work here, side by side, that individuals can, if we are conscious, begin to change and reorganize metaphors and symbolic patterns, and pick and choose among the many different ones that are available to us.

Q: Your essay "Dancing through the Minefield" has been noted as one of the most important works in feminist literary criticism, and the numbers of times it is anthologized seems to reflect its prominence. What makes this work so crucial is that it was one of the first articles to both survey and analyze a large period of feminist literary inquiry. In this piece you offer three propositions that you have argued "if handled with care and intelligence, could breathe new life into now moribund areas of our profession." Your three propositions were, of course, "(1) literary history (and with that, the historicity of literature) is a fiction; (2) insofar as we are taught how to read, what we engage are not texts but paradigms; and finally, (3) since the grounds on which we assign aesthetic value to texts are never infallible, unchangeable, or universal, we must reexamine not only our aesthetics but, as well, the inherent biases and assumptions informing the critical methods which (in part) shape our aesthetic responses." Taking these three propositions as guidelines, how would you ascribe them to an ecological literary criticism, ecocriticism? And can we also translate these propositions into a better understanding of how we produce texts/paradigms?

A: Well, that is a big question. But it seems to me that with a little paraphrasing, I could apply those same three propositions to ecocriticism, and apply them to the ways in which we respond to the environment and the physical world around us.

1. Any history of the land and the environment is, to some extent, a fiction that we constantly reinvent in order to explain what our present relationship is—either in terms of how we came to this relationship, or in terms of how awful the present relationship is, and we need to return to some prior golden age. The histories that we have are responses to land, landscape, and environment in terms of what we *believe* to be true or what we *want* to be true. They are always historically inaccurate, but they have explanatory power and influence (or justify) the situation of the present moment.

2. Insofar as we engage or interact with our environment, what we engage is not a raw physical reality, but the symbolic structures that we inherit from our culture that tell us what that physical reality is about, and how we are to relate to it. So, we do not really engage our environment per se; we engage paradigms about our environment. That explains why one culture may worship a tree and carefully tend to it, while another culture cuts down the very same tree and sends it off to a sawmill. One culture sees divinity or spiritual capital in the tree; the other culture sees the tree merely as an instrument for economic capital.

3. The grounds on which we assign any kind of value to our physical environment are never infallible, unchangeable, or universal. At different times, we ascribe aesthetic value, we ascribe spiritual value, we ascribe economic value—even to the same place or landscape. So, we need to reexamine our art, our language, our politics, our inherent biases and assumptions that inform the ways in which we decide whether a physical environment is spiritually valuable, or aesthetically valuable, or economically valuable. And we need to rethink what it is that we mean when we talk about value. Valuable in what sense, and to whom?

Q: Your career has been marked by an intense attention paid to the political, and your experiences at the University of New Hampshire involved a denial of tenure and promotion and ultimately a lawsuit in which you charged the university with anti-Semitism and sex discrimination. You won the landmark lawsuit, and with some of the monetary award you established the Legal Fund of the Task Force on Discrimination within the National Women's Studies Association.

A: I need to correct that. I didn't win the lawsuit; it was settled in my favor out of court just two weeks before we were to go to trial. But what happened in the process of getting to trial was that we set important legal precedents, because mine was one of the earliest Title VII cases. And what I won in the settlement was a number of stipulations that changed the university, and the largest financial award to date in a Title VII discrimination suit. I also used some of the money for the Reproductive Rights Project within the Massachusetts Civil Liberties Union because they were then fighting the landmark case on reproductive rights and a woman's right to choose. What ties together my willingness to take on a Title VII discrimination suit and my commitment to environmental justice is the word *justice*. I advocate respect, regard, and appreciation for all human beings equally; and I want the same for the environment that embraces and supports us. I call that justice.

Q: Thank you for clarifying that. When you resigned from the task force it was noted that "in fighting your own battle so courageously, and in assisting numerous other women past, present, and future to fight their own, you have made a permanent difference in the lives of feminist teachers and scholars." And as tribute to your work, Annis Pratt's column in *Concerns*, the newsletter of the Women's Caucus for the Modern Languages, is titled "Dancing through the Minefield." Such tributes mark an amazing devotion to your activism. Of course, your activism in this instance grew from an unpleasant scenario, but for many of our readers, this instance of activism is of extreme interest. We were curious as to how you view the role of activism in the academy and if you see faculty, particularly those in English departments, as being in positions to enact activism.

A: I don't believe in a schizophrenic existence; there's got to be harmony and consistency between what one believes and how one acts in the world. In Judaism, the highest accolade you can render is to say that someone is a "just" person. My grandmother's repeated admonition was "You need to be a *mensch*," and what she meant by that was that you have to act forthrightly and justly in the world. For me, that's a profound guiding principle. I don't see how the teaching of literature—which is essentially the examination of discourses, the unearthing of power relationships, and the development of a regard for the power of language—

can be divorced from the ways that discourses and language work in the political realm.

Of course, I respect the fact that different people have different temperaments, and therefore not everybody wants to work for César Chávez, as I did in grad school, and stand on the United Farmworkers picket line in Bakersfield against the union busters. Some of the growers hired thugs and goons to threaten and rough up those of us on the picket lines—and it was a really frightening experience. But, there are other ways to be politically active. You can work within political parties or neighborhood groups, you can write editorial pieces, you can contribute a substantial portion of your expendable income to organizations that you think are going to make a positive difference in the world, you can volunteer your time in the office of Greenpeace, even if you don't want to join them on a boat to go out and stop illegal whaling. There's lots of different ways to be an activist. And that includes English department faculty, too. I think it's probably easier for those of us who teach American literature and American studies to combine our activism with our literary and scholarly pursuits, because what we study is our national culture, whereas those who teach other literatures and other national cultures sometimes feel divorced from the capacity to act effectively in those national cultures that they know best; and they are not often as well informed as they should be about what is going on in their home culture. So, maybe it's Americanists, like me, who have the easier time of it. On the other hand, those who study other cultures have the advantage of an educated perspective from which to measure and evaluate what is happening here. They can make useful comparisons and alert us when other societies solve problems with which we are still struggling.

To answer your question more directly, though, I think that there's no excuse for trying to suggest to our students that literature often offers a critical appraisal of our society, a way of examining its faults or dilemmas, but then evade that knowledge or insight by not acting on it. At the same time, professors often suggest to our students that literature invites a certain kind of activism in the world, so that it will become the world you want it to be. Professors then have a moral obligation to model that same activism—in some form or other.

Q: Because you have spoken out about anti-Semitism, we'd also like to ask as to the relationship between Judaism and environmental activism and why we do not see more Jewish engagement of environmental politics and theory, either from a literary standpoint or an activist standpoint.

A: I think that we do, but that we haven't identified it as such. My friends and colleagues, both in the environmental activism community and in the feminist community—which has very much been involved in issues of environmental justice—include many people whose background is Jewish, and many people who are observant and active Jews. What unites them—whether they consider themselves secular Jews or observant or orthodox or conservative or reform or whichever brand of Judaism they practice—is this sense of acting justly in the world. They share a belief that social justice and economic justice must be equated with, and are inherent in, environmental justice, because you can't have one without the other. But they identify themselves publicly as feminists or environmentalists or ecocritics, not as *Jewish* feminists or *Jewish* ecocritics.

Q: In your landmark article, "Some Notes on Defining a 'Feminist Literary Criticism,'" you write, "I think we need to make clear that what women have so far expressed in literature is what they have been *able to express*, as a result of the complex interplay between innate biological determinants, personal and individual talents and opportunities, and the larger effects of socialization, which, in some cases, may govern the limits of expression or even perception and experience itself." You wrote that more than twenty-five years ago, and the statement is an important one regarding not only the limits of expression placed on women but on the process and act of socialization as well. As compositionists we are interested in the ways women express themselves in nonliterary writings. Are the constraints on women somehow different in the realms of the literary and nonliterary?

A: Only in degree. The woman who chooses to write novels or poetry may benefit from the larger vocabulary or from the wide range of conceptual patterns that she has gleaned from her reading (assuming she has been permitted to read widely, of course); and she may more self-consciously employ these wider possibilities in her writing than may her nonliterary sister. But the two still live within certain cultural parameters and societal constraints.

The woman who chooses to compose a private journal solely for her own benefit may feel freer to experiment with language and form than her literary sister who wants her novels and poems to be accepted and read widely. But even if she is unaware of it, the journal writer too has models, generic conventions, and paradigms in her head that influence not just how she writes but what she chooses to write about. None of us ever entirely escapes our culture.

Q: In your article "Honing a Habitable Languagescape: Women's Images for the New World Frontiers," you introduce the concept of *languagescape*, a term you intend to use to describe the relationship between physical places and consciousness. In some ways the concept refers to an idea that places are bound up, or at least our knowledge of places is bound up, in a language that defines that place. We are very interested in the relationship between language and place, and are curious as to how you would articulate that relationship. That is, what role does language play in a place, in defining, making that place, in our knowing a place?

A: Language creates a relationship between people and space, and then the language, the paradigm, the symbolic structure, guides our action in that space. Think of the papers that we just heard [at the ASLE Conference in Flagstaff]. Chadwick Allen examines N. Scott Momaday's work and the way that their language binds the Kiowa people to certain sacred spaces through various kinds of narratives, various kinds of stories. In a very different way, as Vermonja Alston was pointing out, the language of ecotourism promises a particular set of experiences as though it were possible, for the right amount of money, to return to some kind of Edenic paradise. And, as Jared Aragona was pointing out, the language of El Dorado and the lust for gold predisposed people to basically destroy California. So language is always a powerful determiner of how we physically act on a landscape, because language is the mediator between our consciousness and the physical world around us.

Q: You conclude that article by writing that women need to "assert their right to a languagescape of their own." Have there been decidedly female languagescapes?

A: There have been attempts. Seventeenth- and eighteenth-century women tried to develop a language of gardening, and of responsible stewardship of the garden. I talked about that in *The Land Before Her*. Nineteenth-century American women have often used the language of home, and the language of child care, or of caring for a child, as a way of describing their relationship to the land around them. In more recent decades, those from the women's movement who joined Wiccan groups tried to develop a powerful language of mother-spirit relationship to the land. But none of these have ever become dominant, and none of these attempts at alternative paradigms and symbolic structures have become powerful outside of that realm, culture, or region in which they were used.

Q: In your well-known Introduction to *The Lay of the Land*, you write about the battle over People's Park at UC Berkeley. You suggest, "the advocates of People's Park had asserted another version of what is probably America's oldest and most cherished fantasy: a daily reality of harmony between man and nature based on an experience of the land as essentially feminine." We are wondering, in short, whether this "cherished fantasy" still exists and, if so, in what discursive structures is it manifested?

A: The fantasy of harmony between the natural world and the human world still exists. Unfortunately, we need the fantasy because most Americans still see the *human* and the *natural* as separate and separated. In other words, we don't see ourselves as *part* of nature. Therefore you need some kind of harmonizing relationship, and that harmonizing relationship is inherent in most utopian structures. But, when I wrote *The Lay of the Land,* the dominant imaging was through a fantasy of the feminine—mother Earth or virgin land. That particular fantasy structure is less prevalent now. I like to think that the book had something to do with it, but I suspect that the women's movement had more. What we have not figured out is a way to develop a language of relationship in which the human is not apart from nature, but is not only a part of it but responsible for it. That's the nonexploitive, nondestructive fantasy structure we haven't been able to invent.

Q: In this same introduction, you ruminate, "Perhaps, after all, the world *is* really gendered, in some subtle way we have not yet quite understood." In what ways have you come to better understand such questions?

A: Are you familiar with the Gaia hypothesis that the Earth is a living being, and that if you destroy any part of it, you can hurt the whole? Interestingly enough, Gaia is gendered female; I don't know how to think about this. I wonder still if the world is really gendered. I wonder about it and I also worry about it, because gender is so powerfully marked a category in every society. There is no society in which gender doesn't carry baggage. It's potentially very destructive. So, I'm not sure I know how to think about that, beyond what I've already written.

Q: At the end of *The Lay of the Land*, you quote Gene Marine and his discussion of those with an "engineering mentality" who are "in every section of every state, ripping, tearing, building, changing," that is, facilitating, "a rape from which America can never, never recover." As both a professor of comparative cultural and literary studies as well as a former dean of the College of Humanities at the University of Arizona, could you comment about the current state of the "engineering mentality"? That is, is Marine's almost apocalyptic vision an accurate one?

A: Absolutely, and even more so today than when I wrote *The Lay of the Land*. The engineering mentality still dominates. We see the physical world almost exclusively as an instrument for our use and manipulation. That is at the heart of the engineering mentality: the physical world *can* be altered for our use and is, in fact, *there to be altered* for our use. As soon as you begin thinking in those terms, you do not think of wholes or integrated systems. You think in terms of a discrete project, a discrete region, a discrete river that needs to be dammed, a discrete power supply that needs to be exploited, but you never think in terms of the consequences of any one of those actions for the whole system, because we aren't taught to think in terms of systems. As a result, we engineer livestock by pumping them with antibiotics in order to increase beef or milk production. But we never stopped to consider how those antibiotics, passed along to children in their food, then lowers these drugs' effectiveness in combating disease. The routine use of antibiotics in agriculture produces more drug-resistant strains of bacteria. We thus subordinate health concerns to productivity and agribusiness profits. We ignore the delicate interlinkages. The engineering mentality is not a mentality that considers the whole; it considers the instrumentality of a discrete act, and that's very dangerous.

Q: You contend, "My abiding concern for landscape as a symbolic . . . realm derives from the conviction that, in addition to stringent antipollution measures and the development of wind, water, and solar energy sources, we also need to understand the unacknowledged fantasies that drive us either to desecrate or to preserve the world's last discovered Earthly Paradise. . . . Our actions in the world, in short, are shaped by paradigms in our head." These paradigms, you have argued, need to be brought to "conscious awareness" in order to pick and choose among them. How do you respond to critics who suggest that psychoanalytic theories and methods—those dealing with fantasies and dreams—are esoteric and ineffective in the face of our growing environmental dilemmas. That is, can you elaborate on how psychology can fight environmental degradation?

A: We need to find every means possible of fighting environmental degradation. It's almost too late. We have so jeopardized the health of this planet, that there is almost no course of action that can stop the ongoing pollution and destruction. The best we can do is slow down the course of the destruction in hopes that, in slowing it down, we can, in the course of time, find ways of reversing the destruction we have set in motion. But, it seems to me that what the Western world especially lacks is a psychology of community and the communal. We need a psychology and symbol system that embraces the human and the world around us in a single interconnected and interdependent whole. We need to think of the planet—and everything in and on it—as a huge, complex, integrated community. But that's difficult because we don't advocate—especially in the United States—the satisfaction of sharing; we're a very individualistic and self-centered society. We live in abundance and waste the world's resources without even realizing it. We're a very unhappy culture, as well. I mean, we're a culture that sees one atrocity story after another on the evening news, unlike many other industrialized countries. The Scandinavian countries, for example, have public policies for encouraging the use of wind energy and ecologically friendly farming. They also have less poverty and less crime. So, that suggests that the American psychology of rugged individualism has not, in fact, been entirely successful, and that we need to come up with a psychology of community, communality, and sharing, and learn to discover that, in sharing resources with one another, and with the rest of the planet, we would actually end up being healthier and happier.

Q: In *Failing the Future* you suggest that "the students we educate in the twenty-first century must be taught to comprehend systems, patterns, and interconnections." This is a very important line of thought that many compositionists now argue as well. In particular, we are interested in the interconnections between writers, discourse, and environments. As a writer and an educator can you offer any thoughts about these connections?

A: Because our students grow up in a culture and a discourse system that equates capitalism with democracy, our students don't even see the ways in which we commodify the world around us. They don't see that the accumulation of massive wealth, or capital, in the hands of a few really undermines democracy because political power can be purchased—and that leaves out the poor and the middle class. They also don't see that natural resources—which should belong to everyone for the common good—are actually reduced to commodities whose sale brings profits to a few but whose use may not benefit many people equally. Let me explain what I mean by sharing some personal observations.

Whenever I teach undergraduate courses on Literature and the Environment, the best of my students go off for a time and become docents in national parks or they train as guides for the white-water rafting tours and still-water floats down the Colorado River. Of course, I applaud what my students are attempting to accomplish as they find their own version of Henry David Thoreau's Walden Pond retreat; and I applaud their reverence for the sheer beauty and fragility of this landscape, a reverence they earnestly try to convey to the many Grand Canyon tourists who purchase the river trip experience.

Young and idealistic, these undergraduates are desperately trying to do their part in preserving nature unspoiled. They want to believe—along with Thoreau—that a sojourn away from civilization and an immersion in nature will call out their spiritual capacity for what Ralph Waldo Emerson termed "moral Reason." They want to believe, along with Aldo Leopold, that in wilderness is the preservation of themselves and the preservation of the world.

But when these students return to school and take more courses with me, it is my obligation to remind them again of ecocriticism's sobering truth that there are no pristine wildernesses remaining, that the entire planet has been altered by eons of human interventions; and that the very means that they have used to escape culture—or civilization—has turned nature *into* culture. What my students resist admitting, but finally come uncomfortably to understand, is that the woods, the meadow, the river that they sit and take in are transformed, in that very process, into instruments for a specifically defined and culturally situated experience. And those who enable the paying tourists to float down the Colorado River—despite all the best intentions in the world—have helped turn the river into a highly defined and purchasable experience, in effect, another commodity in our capitalist, consumer culture.

This doesn't mean that I want my students to refrain from hiking in the woods. Nor do I want to stop people from enjoying the beauty of the river. But I do want us all to understand that such activities turn nature into an instrument for our pleasure; and that our pleasure too often introduces damage or pollution to the very places we love. I also want my students to recognize how the poor are often prohibited from these experiences; it takes money to raft the Colorado.

My point here is very simple: In any society where profit making supersedes all other goals, no matter how innocent our individual motives nor how well-meaning our intentions, in the end we are all inescapably both victim and collaborator. And the natural world around us is consumed in and by our Utopian fantasies.

Q: You write that *Failing the Future* is "a book about higher educa-tion . . . [and] it is consequently a book about social responsibility." In particular, you reject the "notion that colleges and universities are merely training vendors, that students are end products or interim consumers, that the professoriate is a quantifiable human resource, or that prospec-tive employers represent higher education's ultimate customers and most important constituency." Teachers and theorists of composition and rheto-ric studies have often come to blows over the ways writing should be taught—as courses that facilitate "nuts and bolts" and "skills and drills" exercises or as courses that emphasize social, political, and cultural inves-tigations by students. As someone who has spent time working in English departments, can you comment on what you see as the place of compo-sition studies in the university?

A: I think that you have to do both. There is no way that you can ask students to pursue important social, political, and cultural investigations unless you give them the nuts and bolts, the skills and drills, that allow them to do that. One of the reasons our students can't act effectively in the world is that they can't articulate what the problems are. And they can't articulate what the problems are because they have poor analytical skills, they have impoverished vocabularies, or possess only limited grammatical systems. Thus, they can't even construct an intelligent and complex thought. What I say to my students is that if you can't say it or write it clearly, then that means you can't think it clearly, and you must be able to do both.

At the same time, students will resist a boring rote memorization of skills and drills if these are not attached to some exciting larger project that really grabs their imagination. That's why social, political, and cultural investigations are such a vital aspect of composition courses. After all, skills have to be put to a worthy purpose—or else, why master those skills?

Q: Could you speak for a moment about how your work in environmen-talism and feminist literary criticism has affected your approach to uni-versity administration?

A: I see the university as a complex interplay of many different environ-ments—intellectual, financial, political, national, and local. At its heart, though, the campus is a human environment and a physical environ-ment. My work in feminist literary criticism led me to conclude that, because power structures in the university are always contingent and provisional, they are available to change. "The way things always were," in other words, did not mean the way things had to be in the future.

After many years as a faculty member at a number of very different institutions, I had decided that the university was a pretty vicious place. One of the things that we needed to do was to make the campus more humane and to make it more welcoming for faculty, students, and staff. So, as dean, I worked with faculty, staff, and students to put in place paid leaves for family care, for example, and improved mentoring and advising for students. I think these are human environmental issues. Part of what we need to do is take care of the world around us, and that includes the people around us. I also tried to encourage the university recycling policy, and to develop architectural plans for a new building for the humanities that would foster many different kinds of human interactions—as well as saving energy. Altogether, I tried to make the College of Humanities feel like a place where people would feel like they were part of a community, rather than separate competing entities. If we did that in a national way, this would be a very different country.

Q: You spend a good deal of time examining concerns over academic freedom in the modern university, particularly as it relates to female scholars. As scholars interested in questions about the relationships be-tween discourse and place—or environment—we often come across those who see this kind of work as just "more trendy nature stuff." In short, much work on nature and environment is regarded as illegitimate—or "flash in the pan" scholarly work. This, no doubt, is beginning to change, but we are wondering if you could comment on where you see this kind of work moving in the future, the work of ecocritics, the kind of work taking place at this ASLE conference. What forces serve to help make this scholarship appear illegitimate?

A: I don't think this vast range of scholarship on the relationship between culture and environment appears illegitimate any more. I think that more and more, citizens of the United States understand that what is at stake right now is the air we breathe, the water we drink, the pollutants and dangerous toxins in our food supply. And while I think most folks in the United States don't yet see us at the crisis edge where survival of the planet is at stake, they do understand, at least subliminally, that there's a connection between the depletion and degradation of our environment and the skyrocketing incidences of childhood asthma, the epidemic num-bers of cancers, or the increasing numbers of debilitating chronic dis-eases. So, it seems to me that an organization like ASLE is crucially important because it puts the stamp of a serious professional organization on this work and also provides a forum for all this new scholarship to be openly discussed, disseminated, and published. When our students come to us, they have some sense that something is really wrong in this nation's relationship to its physical environment. By providing these students with copies of ASLE's journal, *ISLE*, or with books that have been written by ASLE members, we can give them ways of thinking about what's wrong, and let them know that they're not thinking in a vacuum, that their suspicions are, in fact, grounded, solidly grounded. More important, we can give them a sense that there's a movement to change things. That's why I would like to see ASLE continue its emphasis not only on the scholarly but on the activist. As I said in my remarks today, we need to become public intellectuals, and we need to change the public discourse.

Q: You comment numerous times in *Failing the Future* about the need for universities to begin tearing down old boundaries and establishing new interdisciplinary departments. In order to better understand our connections with landscapes—our fantasies and dreams, our degradations and preservations—what kinds of interdisciplinary work do you see at the forefront of solving such problems?

A: The interdisciplinary areas that I see at the forefront unfortunately aren't working together, and that is the main problem. But if I had to list them, I would include programs in ethics, evolutionary biology, history of science, environmental studies, ecocriticism, science and technology studies, planetary sciences, cultural geography, and cultural studies. Because cultural studies examines how a society establishes its value systems, it is crucial to all the rest, from intellectual history to comparative literary studies. The great crime is that all of these interdisciplinary studies, alas, aren't working together—collaborating on research, developing joint curricula, even reading one another's articles—in some kind of coherent way. The coherent connectedness of these areas should be the future curriculum of the American university.

Where Writing Takes Place

A Response to Annette Kolodny

Lynn Worsham

Over the years, I have occasionally toyed with the idea that the process of composing a text involves a kind of spatial thinking—thinking in terms of space, place, and location. I typically return to this idea when, in the process of composing a piece, I find myself picking dejectedly through the apparent wreckage of what I had hoped would be a strong and compelling conceptual structure, searching for the necessary corner-stones to begin the work of redesigning and rebuilding. My efforts to think the relation between discourse and place have been encouraged, of course, by a long tradition of Western rhetorical theory and philosophical thought, including, for example, Quintilian, Cicero, Martin Heidegger, Kenneth Burke, Richard McKeon, and Michel Foucault. This tradition urges us to think of composing architectonically, as a structuring of a space of meaning, a meaningful place that opens up particular possibilities of thought, feeling, and action while at the same time foreclosing other possibilities. To this tradition, I would add Annette Kolodny. In "Taking Back the Language," Kolodny makes a number of provocative statements that should lead to renewed reflection on the fateful relationship between space, place, language, and identity—between words and habitation. As Kolodny puts it, "Language creates a relationship between people and space, and then the language, . . . the symbolic structure, guides our action in that space." In the space afforded me here, I want to take up Kolodny's provocation and reflect on what has become, in my view, a rich and compelling analogy between the composition of places and the composition of texts. I want to go further than she does, however, along the path that leads to the intersection where language constitutes power.

Especially useful in any endeavor to think about the relationship between language and place is Donlyn Lyndon's and Charles Moore's

Chambers for a Memory Palace, a book that explicitly treats architecture as a kind of language or rhetoric. Lyndon and Moore open their meditation on the architecture of places by recalling Cicero's practice of making ideas memorable by locating them in space, in an imagined palace whose rooms and furnishings represent those ideas. Working from Cicero's insight into what makes ideas memorable, Lyndon and Moore identify and explain key concepts that architects throughout the world have used in their composition of memorable places. In their view, the task of the architect is to transform "space" into "place"—into meaningful, habitable, and therefore memorable places. As Lyndon and Moore explain, places are those physical spaces that you remember, care about, and make part of your life. Places are necessary to what they call "the good conduct" of life. That is, places, through their distinctive grammar of design, have the potential to help us to "better understand ourselves and how we relate to others," including our relationship to nature (xii). Lyndon and Moore develop this perspective in the context of, and as a way of counteracting, the contemporary world of actual buildings and landscapes that have not been crafted with wisdom and care and thus carry little significance for those who must live and work within and among them. In their view, the world of actual buildings and landscapes—more nearly "space" than "place"—is not benign in its impact on human life and imagination; it actively creates and perpetuates alienation, apathy, and thoughtlessness. Clearly, the composition of places is, from this architectural perspective, a work of meaning-making and a profoundly ethical practice, one that seeks, as Kolodny might say, a harmonizing relationship between physical world and built environment. This perspective is not only quite distant from what Kolodny calls the dominant "engineering mentality" in the West that with impunity desecrates the physical environment for material profit; it is also entirely opposed to any purely instrumental use of space.

More specifically, Lyndon and Moore offer a series of observations on the composition of places, observations cast metaphorically as chambers of a memory palace. Each chamber is composed of "elements" (or nouns) and "actions" (or verbs) that form the focus of their discussion. Lyndon and Moore explain: "Elements are ones we have found to be present in architecture throughout the world; the actions describe how these elements shape the experience that a place affords" (xiii). Thus, they explicitly treat architecture as a language comprising nouns and verbs, elements and actions, that when combined in different ways compose unique places that have the power to shape experience, impose perspective, convey meaning, and direct action. In their view, language does indeed define place, as Kolodny suggests; however, place also mediates, when it does not determine, human thought, feeling, and action.

Some of the elements and actions that Lyndon and Moore discuss include "axes that reach" and "paths that wander"; "openings that frame" and "portals that bespeak"; "borders that control" and "walls that layer"; "ornaments that transmit, transform, and encode." In their discussion of these and other elements and actions, the authors take their readers on a tour of the world's most memorable architecture, offering example after example of just how to "read" the language of place. In doing so, Lyndon and Moore provide what Kolodny might call a "languagescape," a language for understanding the relationship between space, place, language, and identity. This languagescape is especially useful in constructing an analogy between the composition of place and the composition of text. No mere expressive detail, this ornament, this analogy, provides a framework, a structure for understanding an important truth about our ways of world-making. In the following discussion, I offer what is at most a highly allusive blueprint for constructing this analogy, one that treats only the elemental concepts of axes, paths, openings, and borders. Let me first clarify the architectural sense of these terms.

In the process of composing a place, an architect constructs an axis that takes material shape as a line of vision in physical space. An axis, as Lyndon and Moore explain, reaches "across space to draw together the important points in a place. [Axes] are mental constructs that help us to position ourselves and make alliance with things, buildings, or spaces" (5). In reaching across space to draw together the important points in a place, an axis connects threshold to horizon and, in effect, traces the boundaries of that place and suggests its scope. An axis realized as a line of vision in physical space gives coherence to space and transforms it into a meaningful, memorable place. Although an axis is, as Lyndon and Moore suggest, a mental construct in the sense that each visitor to a place must construct it for him or herself, an axis is nonetheless realized in physical space through the thoughtful placement of buildings or other structures, through the creation of paths or roads, and through landscape design. Lyndon and Moore derive the concept of axis from the experience of being face to face: "when you want to be certain to give your full attention to someone, or signal that you're doing so, you position yourself opposite them, your bodies roughly aligned, your eyes attending to theirs" (7). In much the same way, an axis in physical space marshals attention and regulates movement in that space in a particular way and for a particular end. The organizational power of the axis is especially apparent in religious architecture where the architecture works to draw all eyes to a particular focal point, usually the altar, and thus works to impose an attitude of worship. Whereas an axis positions you in space, directs interest and attention, and provides possibilities for movement, paths are, as Lyndon and Moore explain, "where your feet actually trod, so that what happens along the way becomes the important thing. In some of the most interesting places, axes and paths interweave, with the axis allowing the mind to do the connecting, and the path allowing the feet to wander, explore, make choices, and put things in sequence" (5). Interesting places are created where axes and paths interweave to create depth, dimension, orientation, and alliance. Interesting places beckon you to move into and through them, wandering and exploring, putting things in a meaningful sequence.

The creation of borders and the character and placement of openings (such as doorways, windows, and gates) are also important elements in the composition of places. As Lyndon and Moore observe, borders serve to demarcate inside from outside, establish the edges of a domain, enclose a privileged place, and control access:

> If they [borders] are simple, they make it clear where we are; if they are complex, encompassing distinct pockets of space, they afford choices or the chance to change. Since the ancient Egyptians built their temples, one of humankind's most potent devices for achieving mystery, distance, and the setting apart of a special place has been to build layers of walls—buildings within buildings, wall around wall like the successive skins of an onion. In architecture, as in thought, simple tight boundaries are most often too confining. (81)

Borders may be simple and abrupt, demarcating what we take to be grand and absolute differences, such as the city and the sea, or the sacred and the profane. Borders may also be "layered and interwoven, thick with opportunities for reconsideration" and negotiation (96). Whatever their character, borders are as necessary to the composition of a place as is the suggestion of their possible transgression. Just as enclosure is a very powerful action, providing a sense of security, location, and orientation, openings are equally powerful. They are portals that draw us into a place and, as Lyndon and Moore explain, "bid us welcome": "Doorways and gates cultivate expectations of the places that lie beyond. Windows in a wall, like the eyes of a person, allow us to imagine the life within. From inside, windows and other openings can frame a view, editing out unwanted parts, emphasizing the wanted ones. A well-framed view brings the world close; clumsy muntins thoughtlessly push it away" (101).

The language that Lyndon and Moore employ to elucidate the composition of places is helpful in understanding the process of composing a text, where, in my view, many of the same elements and actions are also at work. For example, the coherence given to the composition of a place by an axis is not unlike the coherence worked into a text in the process of composing it. Indeed, the process of composing a text is the process of composing a meaningful place for writer (and reader) to grasp, or to move toward grasping, a subject or theme in a particular way according to particular interests. Much of the early and most arduous work of composing involves the discovery or creation of an axis of thought that will reach across the space of what ultimately will be the text-as-meaningful-place. Ideally, an axis of thought exerts a kind of gravitational force in the process of composing, drawing together all the elements of a text into a meaningful, coherent statement and thereby creating a line of vision or perspective. The more complex and nuanced the thought, the more axes and paths interweave to give greater density and texture to the text and to the experience of reading it.

Thus, an axis of thought worked into and through a text is more than a superficial stringing together of key points. It is more than the enumeration of minor claims and their subsumption in the major claim forming a text's overall argument. It is more than the sum of key words and topic sentences. An axis of thought, working together with other elements, creates the texture that constitutes a text as a text. That is, texture is the defining attribute of a text, the necessary element that transforms a set of sentences and words into a text, into a meaningful discursive place rather than an assortment of unrelated, disconnected sentences and words. Texture can be defined, then, as the underlying semantic relations within, among, and beyond a given set of sentences and words, relations that are not necessarily realized through explicit surface-level markers of cohesion and coherence. Texture results in part from the way in which layers of meaning are built into a text through what linguists call reference and co-reference: reference to a world or worlds outside the text; co-reference to multiple elements in different parts of a text that depend on each other for their interpretation. Through reference and co-reference, for example, a writer builds semantic relations within, among, and beyond a set of sentences that constitute the text as text. Again, these semantic relations may or may not be realized explicitly through surface-level markers that, in effect, mark explicit paths that writer (and reader) may take in constituting meaning. These semantic relations may also be established indirectly and obliquely through other discourse strategies (including elements that we have captured metaphorically through concepts of tone, voice, and style as well as through punctuation), and through the background knowledge and the interpretive disposition that a reader may be presumed to bring to a text. In the process of composing a text, a writer moves back and forth between different elements of a text, creating semantic relations and resonances between and among words and sentences that will form a textured discursive place. Thus, texture, and the many elements that go into creating it, undercut the apparent linearity of discourse production and interpretation—that is, the seemingly incontrovertible fact that a writer produces, and a reader interprets, one word at a time, building (or rebuilding) a structure of meaning by placing words, bricklike, one after another.

Yet, a text does begin somewhere. Indeed, much of the hard work of composing involves creating an appropriate opening; it involves deciding just where to place the threshold that will most effectively frame the desired view and indicate its horizon. Certainly, this concept of the function of introductory sentences or paragraphs is a familiar one: the idea that an introduction serves as a kind of portal that beckons a reader into the world of the text. Understanding something about the rhetoric of composition, Kenneth Burke once wrote that form results from the arousal and fulfillment of desire. His formulation foregrounds the sense in which a critical element in the creation of discursive form is the carefully crafted opening, one that arouses desire by creating expectations that draw the reader into the text, expectations that the text must then fulfill. In setting up expectations, an introduction provides a kind of lobby—that is, the initial textual context that will influence the staging of everything that follows it. It provides, in other words, a point of departure that projects the relative prominence of various elements of the text and thereby creates an almost palpable sense of a three-dimensional place where the mind is invited to wander in the light of foregrounded elements and in the shadows cast by backgrounded ones.

The introductory sentences or paragraphs of a text are not the only kind of opening to be found in a meaningful discursive place. Transitional sentences and words also function as doorways or gateways into new pockets of discursive space. As *transitional* sentences and words, they provide *transit*: they transport the writer (and reader) to a different place in the text, to a cognate set of relations, or to a different level of meaning in the discursive space articulated by the text. Serving as windows, transitional sentences and words may refine the view that is framed in a text, or they may be clumsy, artless places that as a consequence push the reader away and obscure the view that the text desires to frame.

Implied in what I have said thus far is the suggestion that any given word is itself a kind of portal or opening, a suggestion that makes diction an issue of great consequence in the composition of texts. To clarify more precisely just how important word choice may be, I want to draw on V. N. Vološinov's view of the relationship between language and power. According to Vološinov, the word—or what he calls the ideological sign—is "the most sensitive index" of social existence and social change. Actual existence—one element of which is the materially produced hierarchical relationships between individuals and groups—determines multifarious discursive performances; likewise, discourse "reflects and refracts existence in its process of generation." There is, in other words, a dialectical relationship between the world and the word. As Vološinov puts it, the "domain of ideology" coincides with the "domain of signs": "They equate with one another. Whenever a sign is present, ideology is present, too" (10). More specifically, a given word becomes invested, through usage, with a group's attitudes, interests, and values and is nuanced by the affective valences of those interests. It is not composed of a neutral content or meaning that can be divorced from what Vološinov calls its evaluative "accentuations." Because different social groups with different interests and values use the same language, the same words, a given word will acquire multiple, conflicting accents and thus become the key place where competing interests intersect. While it is through this intersection of accents that a word maintains its vitality and dynamism—its power to both reflect and refract social existence—the "multiaccentuality" of the word also and more importantly makes language the preeminent arena for social struggle.

Words, then, are portals, as Lyndon and Moore might say, bespeaking social existence, portals opening on to and framing particular interests. Words are pockets of social space where hegemonic struggle takes place, pockets into which are tucked competing interests and values. A choice of words, therefore, is never innocent, is always implicated in social struggle, and is too often unwittingly complicitous in maintaining regimes of privilege. When Kolodny calls on us to "take back the language" that has been used to frame a disastrously instrumental and exploitative relationship to the physical environment, she is reminding us of the nature of hegemonic struggle and of the power of language to take possession of physical space. Commenting on the relationship between writing and colonization, Kolodny reminds us that "colonization could never have taken place in the western tradition without the writing process." She focuses in particular on writing as a process of naming and owning: "naming becomes a means of inscribing one's presence and beliefs and values on the land." Here, she calls attention to the fact that historically writing has served primarily as a boundary-producing technology, an indispensable tool in the creation and maintenance of a world system governed by a very powerful act of enclosure: the concept of the modern nation-state. In effect, she calls attention to "the West" as a portal opening on to a world, a languagescape whose boundaries are imposed, for example, by possessive individualism, instrumental rationality, and an engineering mentality. Capitalism, imperialism, racism, sexism, classism—these form the axes of thought and action that reach across the space of many centuries to trace the horizon of modernity. Operating together and in historically specific ways, they have installed the material and symbolic boundaries that compose the lives of untold millions of people who misrecognize the ideological terms in which they are placed in the world.

At issue, therefore, in every act of composing is the nature of the boundaries that words will inevitably impose: texts (worlds) with simple, narrow boundaries that arrogantly sacrifice complexity and conflict for the sake of self-serving answers or single-minded truths; texts (worlds) with complex, multilayered boundaries, generous boundaries that remain genuinely open to different axes of thought even while they may inscribe a particular view. Kolodny reminds us that because "there are always multiple competing value systems, multiple competing discourses," we can "break out of and resist certain kinds of historical constraints" inasmuch as they are never homogenous or overarching. Thus, she reminds us that although there are values and interests at stake in every choice of words—although we may also know that a choice of words is never freely and individually chosen, and although our choices are always conditioned (even determined and overdetermined) by a history of social struggle—we can nonetheless become conscious of the boundaries imposed by a given languagescape. We can become conscious, and we can "pick and choose," to use Kolodny's terms, among the different words available to us and thereby locate a different portal opening on to a better, more "just" world. Certainly, it should be the world that Kolodny envisions: a world in which both human will and desire harmonize, in nonexploitative, nondestructive ways, with all of the elements of the natural world to make "a single interconnected and interdependent whole." It should be a place that is capacious enough for truly humane habitation for all the world's peoples, not just the privileged few.

The task of making ourselves conscious, of taking back the language, is as urgently necessary as it is impossibly difficult—difficult because, as Louis Althusser observes, "ideology has very little to do with 'consciousness' " (233). Indeed, its existence and operation are profoundly unconscious, structuring identity and existence in ways that largely escape conscious notice. While there is no single, overarching ideology, there is also no existence outside of ideology (and, paradoxically, no consciousness) and thus no habitation beyond the multiple, conflicting, interwoven boundaries of discourse. Precisely for this reason, I am drawn, again and again, into the act of composing, into the friction of contending words. Here, where writing takes place, I wrestle with what is and what might be.

WORKS CITED

Althusser, Louis. *For Marx*. London: Verso, 1977.

Lyndon, Donlyn, and Charles W. Moore. *Chambers for a Memory Palace*. Cambridge: MIT P, 1994.

Vološinov, V. N. *Marxism and the Philosophy of Language*. Trans. Ladislav Matejka and I. R. Titunik. Cambridge: Harvard UP, 1986.

Developing Feminist-Environmental Rhetorics

A Response to Annette Kolodny

Elizabeth A. Flynn

Annette Kolodny is an excellent choice for inclusion in *Writing Environments*, as the interview with her, "Taking Back the Language: An Interview with Annette Kolodny," demonstrates. In addition to having devoted much of her career to writing books and articles about the environment from a feminist standpoint, the time she spent in the interdisciplinary Department of Language, Literature, and Communication at Rensselaer Polytechnic Institute no doubt gave her a better understanding of the field of rhetoric and composition than is available to most specialists in literature. She was an excellent mentor of RPI graduate students of rhetoric as evidenced by the publication of *Reclaiming Rhetorica*, a collection that arose out of one of her graduate seminars and that includes essays by six of the students in that seminar. Kolodny has been an important foremother. In the late 1970s I made a contribution to the fund in support of her lawsuit against the Department of English of the University of New Hampshire. In the early 1990s I alluded to her "Dancing through the Minefield" in the title of a session I coordinated at the Modern Language Association convention sponsored by the Women's Caucus for the Modern Languages, a session that Kolodny attended. In the late 1980s and early 1990s I also heard stories of her controversial deanship at the University of Arizona, including her wonderful idea that only individuals who have met the current criteria for tenure and promotion should evaluate untenured faculty. *Failing the Future* is a moving description of her troubled experience as an administrator as well as a compelling analysis of challenges higher education faces in the twenty-first century. My having served as interim chair of an

41

interdisciplinary department for three years, two of which coincided with pregnancy and childbirth, enabled me to read her discussions of academic administration and the need for the creation of family-friendly policies with considerable attention. I have seen Kolodny from time to time at the MLA convention; each year she is more crippled with rheumatoid arthritis. I found it interesting that there is no reference to her disability in the interview, an indication of the considerable success she has had in moving beyond it.

The interview makes evident the need for the development of a subfield within rhetoric and composition that attends to relationships among rhetoric, feminism, and the environment, a variation on the feminist-environmental literary studies mentioned in the interview. At present, no such subfield exists. What attention has been paid to environmental concerns within rhetoric and composition has generally not been feminist in orientation.[1] Although a number of the essays in Craig Waddell's groundbreaking edited collections *Landmark Essays on Rhetoric and the Environment* and *And No Birds Sing: Rhetorical Analyses of Rachel Carson's Silent Spring*, for instance, are written by women or are about women, none takes an overtly feminist stance. Rhetoric is also visibly absent from the list Kolodny provides in the interview of areas that could contribute to the interdisciplinary study of feminist and environmental problems—ethics, evolutionary biology, history of science, environmental studies, ecocriticism, science and technology studies, planetary sciences, cultural geography, and cultural studies.

Embedded in the interview, however, are the beginnings of a feminist-environmental rhetoric, especially as Kolodny stresses relationships between language and the environment. For her, language is the mediator between our consciousness and the physical world, and she speaks of attempts to create female languagescapes. Many of the strategies she mentions are common in both rhetorical and feminist analyses—examining metaphors, examining names, deconstructing the rhetoric of others, advocating visionary rhetoric, reclaiming language, critiquing discourses, giving voice to the voiceless. She observes that language influences how we think, feel, and act, speaks of writing as a space within which resistance can take place, and finds that differing images and discourses compete with one another for dominance and influence. She sees the need for the development of oppositional or subversive discourses. Her's is an optimistic vision in that she finds that it is possible to begin to change and reorganize metaphors and symbolic patterns toward the goal of improving the environment and that we can select from among the many different metaphors available to us.

Kolodny's emergent feminist-environmental rhetorical approach is a kind of feminist ecocriticism that recognizes that gendered histories of the land and the environment are fictions that can be constantly reinvented. It also recognizes that when we interact with the environment we are engaging not with raw physical reality but with symbolic structures that we inherit from our culture. It assumes that the grounds on which value is assigned to the physical environment are never infallible, unchangeable, or universal. She sees that we need to reexamine our inherent biases that inform the ways in which we decide whether a physical environment is valuable spiritually, aesthetically, or economically, and value for Kolodny is always contextual and rhetorical. It is a question of how it is valuable and to whom. She includes writing editorial pieces in her discussion of possible forms of activism; feels that professors have a moral obligation to model activism in some form or other, to become public intellectuals and change public discourse; and understands the importance of social, political, and cultural investigations in composition courses.

Extending Kolodny's observations, feminist-environmental rhetorics might attempt to determine what a feminist-environmental nonliterary text is. The description Lawrence Buell provides in *The Environmental Imagination* could easily be modified to serve feminist ends. Buell provides a brief checklist of ingredients that might be said to comprise an environmentally oriented work: (1) The nonhuman environment is present not merely as a framing device but as a presence that begins to suggest that human history is implicated in natural history; (2) The human interest is understood to be not the only legitimate interest; (3) Human accountability to the environment is part of the text's ethical orientation; (4) Some sense of the environment as a process rather than as a constant or a given is at least implicit in the text (7–8).

Feminist-environmental texts would have as their central focus the gendered nature of interactions between the human and the nonhuman environment. They might be descriptive, historical, theoretical, ethical, or methodological, but they would attempt to examine relationships between gender and the natural world. Rhetorical analyses of such texts would examine the language and arguments of such books, pointing out ways in which the gendered human world is related to the nonhuman world. Or they could recuperate the gendered nature of environmental texts that do not deal explicitly with women's issues. The work of Rachel Carson would certainly lend itself to such analysis.

An example of an overtly feminist-environmental nonliterary text is Carolyn Merchant's important work *The Death of Nature: Women, Ecology and the Scientific Revolution*. Merchant explores commonalities between the egalitarian perspectives of the women's movement and the environmental movement, both of which emerged in the 1960s and 1970s. Central to her argument is an association between the premodern organic cosmology that placed female earth at its center and the present-day environmental movement, finding that the Scientific Revolution and the rise of a market-oriented culture in early modern Europe undermined this gynocentric cosmology (xx). A rhetorical analysis of her work would analyze the strategies she employs in accomplishing her goal of examining "the values associated with the images of women and nature as they relate to the formation of our modern world and their implications for our lives today" (xxi). She is attentive, for instance, to linguistic images of nature as nurture, devoting some attention to literary images as well as those in philosophical texts.

Kolodny's *The Lay of the Land* and *The Land Before Her* are also good examples of overtly feminist-environmental nonliterary texts. In *The Lay of the Land*, she describes a uniquely American pastoral impulse and vocabulary motivated by a yearning to know and to respond to the landscape as feminine (8). The discovery of America, she suggests, revived the linguistic habit of assigning gendered characteristics to the land (8). She sees that in the American pastoral, metaphor and the patterns of daily activity refuse to be separated (9). In *The Land Before Her*, she charts women's private responses to American frontiers and traces a tradition of women's public statements about the West in letters and diaries. She is concerned with women's developing literary response to the fact of the West (xi). Her main concern is the imagery through which the landscape is rendered and assimilated into meaning (xii).

Feminist-environmental rhetorics could also make productive use of descriptions of recent rhetorical traditions. James Berlin in *Rhetoric and Reality* and *Rhetorics, Poetics, and Cultures* and Lester Faigley in *Fragments of Rationality*, for instance, in the process of promoting what is sometimes called "social-epistemic rhetoric" or "postmodern rhetoric," provide useful overviews of the major rhetorical traditions that have arisen within the field of rhetoric and composition. In *Rhetoric and Reality* Berlin distinguishes social-epistemic rhetoric from both current-tradition rhetoric and expressionist rhetoric (sometimes called expressivist rhetoric). As I will suggest, all three traditions could be deployed toward the goal of developing a feminist-environmental rhetoric, though social-epistemic or postmodern rhetoric, which most closely resembles the approach Kolodny takes in the interview, is probably the most useful. Although the three perspectives are usually described as discrete traditions, in fact they are often inextricable, as I observe in my forthcoming book *Feminism Beyond Modernism*.

Current-traditional rhetoric derives from Enlightenment thought and is positivistic, seeing meaning as contained within the text and meaning-making as a process of extracting that meaning with accuracy. According to this view, the successful language user encodes meaning in a value-neutral way so as to approximate the author's intention. The goal of the rhetorician in the current-traditional view is to read as objectively as possible by attempting to suspend idiosyncratic perceptions and emotions that might interfere with an understanding of the text's true meaning. Communication is seen as relatively unproblematic once the bias of the interpreter has been eliminated. Pedagogical strategies rooted in current-traditional assumptions include attention to textual forms, which are represented as relatively static, and to the rules of grammar.

Feminist rhetoricians are often critical of Enlightenment rhetoric, emphasizing its androcentrism and what Miriam Brody calls "manliness." Rooted in positivist perspectives on language and in Cartesian commitments to rationality and empiricism, it is often linked to the exclusion of women from the scientific enterprise and philosophy and to a denigration of the work women have traditionally been assigned, such as homemaking and the rearing of children. It is the scientist or rationalist philosopher who has the authority to determine what is true and what is not because only the professional has been trained in methods that insure that bias will not taint perception. It is not difficult to document that scientists and philosophers have traditionally been men. From a feminist perspective, then, what passes for objectivity and the suspension of bias is actually the bias of those in positions of power. The authority that derives from Enlightenment thought and also from current-traditional rhetoric, therefore, is especially dangerous from a feminist perspective. It poses as value neutral while in actuality masking values that guarantee the maintenance of the status quo and the exclusion of groups that have been marginalized. The Enlightenment, however, also gave rise to democratic political structures and to emancipatory movements, such as liberal feminism. This form of feminism constructs women and men as having fundamentally the same capacities but finds that women have been excluded from the world of men as a result of discrimination. The emphasis here is on individual rights and on action necessary to rectify past wrongs. Kolodny's discrimination suit against the University of New Hampshire most closely resembles this form of feminism.

A current-traditional rhetorical feminist approach to the environment would be liberal feminist in orientation and would construct the human and the nonhuman as separate and distinct and would establish a hierarchical relationship between the two, placing human concerns and issues above those of the environment and emphasizing ways in which language can name and hence control nature. It would place faith in scientific and technological development as ways of solving environmental problems and in the creation of rational policies and procedures for adjudicating disputes in environmental matters. It would also emphasize the importance of education in instilling respect for the environment in children and young adults, a respect that would be rooted in the assumption that humans have a responsibility to contain nature. Carolyn Merchant in *Radical Ecology* describes the liberal feminist approach to environmental problems in terms of better science, conservation, and laws (189).

Expressionist or expressivist rhetoric directly opposes current-traditional rhetoric. Rather than emphasizing authorial and textual authority and the desirability of arriving at a single and correct interpretation of a text, it emphasizes the openness of texts and the inevitability of multiple interpretations. Deriving from the Romantic movement, it makes emotion and perception central to the rhetorical process. Verbal expression is seen as a manifestation of an authentic, private self, and social, political, and educational institutions are often seen as impeding that expression. Language takes on a healing function, allowing individuals to externalize their private sorrows and problems thereby lessening their grief and pain. Pedagogical expressivist approaches take the form of journals and writing assignments that encourage students to explore their private lives and emotional responses to their worlds.

Feminist expressivism is rooted in radical or cultural feminisms, identifying male domination as the cause of women's problems and calling for the elimination of patriarchal rhetoric and institutions as the solution to those problems. Within patriarchy, men dominate speaking situations while women are relegated to passive listening roles. They dominate discourse by attending only to male experience and through the promotion of the discourses of dominant groups. Those in positions of power and authority are permitted to become assertive writers while women are relegated the role of uncritical readers. Such domination will only be eliminated when patriarchal discourse and patriarchal institutions are overthrown. Cultural feminists also sometimes emphasize the positive aspects of women's different discourse, seeing that the roles women have been assigned in patriarchy, such as childbearing and rearing, have enabled them to develop nurturing roles and abilities to communicate interpersonally and nonhierarchically. Whereas men's discourse is seen as competitive and aggressive, women's is seen as communal and collective. Kolodny's reference to the woman writer's competent reading community being composed only of members of her sex in "Dancing through the Minefield" is cultural feminist in impulse.

Feminist expressivist approaches to the environment are often Romantic approaches. Nature is worshipped and seen as a spiritual text that can cleanse the soul of impurities that result from urban and industrial culture. Merchant observes that cultural ecofeminists often celebrate the relationship between women and nature through the revival of ancient goddess worship (191). From a feminist expressivist perspective, the environment is seen as a pristine embodiment of order and harmony that has been untainted by human projects or by discourse. Nature must be protected at all costs, and urban and industrial encroachment must be resisted. Nature writing is seen as giving voice to an environment that otherwise could not speak and defend itself and as giving verbal expression to spiritual communion with nature. Antiscientific and antitechnological approaches to the environment can take the form of radical rhetoric and resistant forms of activism.

Postmodern rhetoric recognizes the central role that language plays in all human endeavors and questions claims of value neutrality and objectivity made by current-traditional rhetoricians and by scientists and rationalist philosophers. Observation is always mediated through language, and interpretation is always involved in description and analysis. The authority that derives from employment of scientific and rationalist procedures is viewed with skepticism. Furthermore, interpretation derives from and is conditioned by culture and hence is social rather than individual. Science and rationalist discourse are not rejected but are seen as inherently rhetorical, hence, the claims of scientists and philosophers are seen as provisional and contingent. Objectivity is seen as a goal that is ultimately unattainable. From a pedagogical perspective, students should be introduced to forms of public discourse and to traditional academic forms of writing, but they should also be taught that they are always situated, hence, biased. A goal of such pedagogies is to identify the political and cultural biases of such discourses.

Postmodern feminist rhetoricians question the value neutrality and objectivity of dominant discursive formations and are critical of scientific and rationalist enterprises without rejecting them completely. They recognize that science and philosophy have been dominated by men but attempt to develop alternatives to androcentric methods and procedures that are inclusive while remaining rigorous. Some postmodern feminists attempt to broaden the scope of medicine to include folk medicine and herbal cures, approaches that have traditionally been employed by women and other marginalized groups. Other postmodern feminists redefine objectivity by insisting on inclusion of many and diverse perspectives rather than the monocular view of a single white male. Some postmodern feminists also point out ways in which traditional scientific and rationalist discourses have been oppressive to women. Postmodern feminism insists that women do not form a culture that is separate and distinct from that of men but interact with dominant culture in complex and often contradictory ways. Warning of the dangers of essentializing and decontextualizing women's situations, they insist that gender is only one factor in a matrix that must include other factors, such as race, class, and sexual orientation.

A postmodern feminist approach to the environment emphasizes that the human and the nonhuman are necessarily connected in complex ways and that any change to one necessarily affects the other. It is futile to attempt to dominate nature: it can be contained but not controlled. It is also futile to attempt to describe nature with complete accuracy because the bias of the interpreter can never be entirely eliminated. Policies that are developed to attempt to solve environmental problems, therefore, are thoroughly rhetorical—arguments that must be understood and adhered to and that will always be contested. Postmodern solutions to problems such as environmental degradation and pollution, therefore, call not for eliminating scientific investigation or developing rational policies but rather for recognizing their serious limitations and the extent to which their findings can and probably will be challenged. Unlike the Romantic who calls for the destruction of industrial and urban threats to the environment and idealizes a premodern matriarchal past when women and nature were one, the postmodern feminist environmentalist cautiously attempts to determine what sustainable development might mean and attempts to use scientific and rationalistic methods in support of improving the environment.

There are numerous possible feminist-environmental rhetorics. These are but a few, and good cases can no doubt be made for all of them; multiple strategies are necessary in such a crucial matter as saving the planet from destruction. The postmodern perspective that Kolodny's comments would seem to point toward, however, is especially compelling because it places language in such a central position and because it encourages the development of policies, educational structures, and scientific methods that would work to improve the places where we live and work. Hers is not a conception of nature as remote and pristine. Rather, the environment includes cities, parks, and university campuses in addition to national parks and uncultivated forests. As a literary historian, she recognizes the value of looking not only at trees and plants but also at archival materials and noncanonical and canonical texts. She also recognizes that problems of environmental degradation cannot be divorced from the problems of women—both have histories of abuse, and the mistreatment of both are closely interconnected.

The personal preface Kolodny appends to *Failing the Future* suggests that her five years as dean at a major state research university were enormously challenging. She emerged, however, with a feminist perspective that is not naïve and that moves toward an expansive interdisciplinarity and an ecological conception of the environment broadly defined to include the many habitats in which we live. I find all of Kolodny's work to be extraordinarily insightful and hopeful, a testament to the ways in which rhetorical facility and feminist commitment can converge toward the goal of saving both the natural and the cultural environment.[2]

NOTES

1. An essay that does deal with rhetoric from a feminist-environmental perspective is Connie Bullis's "Retalking Environmental Discourses from a Feminist Perspective: The Radical Potential of Ecofeminism." Some attention is also paid to the environment in *Feminist Rhetorical Theories* edited by Sonja Foss, Karen Foss, and Cindy Griffin.

2. I made good use of the extensive library on environmental issues of my late husband, John F. Flynn, in preparing this essay. He taught courses and published essays on nature writing and the environment, was a member of the Association for the Study of Literature and Environment (ASLE) until his death in the fall of 2000, and was being encouraged by an editor of a university press to transform an ASLE conference paper on nature writing into a book when he was diagnosed with a rare, congenital bile duct disorder and bile duct cancer in the summer of 1999.

I wish to thank my colleague Craig Waddell for providing helpful comments on a draft of this essay, lending me a copy of *And No Birds Sing*, reminding me that *Reclaiming Rhetorica* originated at RPI, and providing me a copy of the Bullis essay. I also appreciate the helpful feedback provided by members of my writing group, Vicky Bergvall, Heidi Bostic, Steve Pluachek, and Patty Sotirin.

WORKS CITED

Berlin, James A. *Rhetoric and Reality: Writing Instruction in American Colleges*, 1900–1985. Carbondale: Southern Illinois UP, 1987.

———. *Rhetorics, Poetics, and Cultures: Refiguring English Studies*. Urbana: NCTE, 1996.

Brody, Miriam. *Manly Writing: Gender, Rhetoric, and the Rise of Composition*. Carbondale: Southern Illinois UP, 1993.

Buell, Lawrence. *The Environmental Imagination: Thoreau, Nature Writing, and the Formation of American Culture.* Cambridge: Harvard UP, 1995.

Bullis, Connie. "Retalking Environmental Discourses from a Feminist Perspective: The Radical Potential of Ecofeminism." *The Symbolic Earth: Discourse and Our Creation of the Environment.* Ed. James G. Cantrill and Christine L. Oravec. Lexington: U of Kentucky P, 1996. 123–148.

Faigley, Lester. *Fragments of Rationality: Postmodernity and the Subject of Composition.* Pittsburgh: U of Pittsburgh P, 1992.

Foss, Sonja K., Karen A. Foss, and Cindy Griffin, eds. *Feminist Rhetorical Theories.* Thousand Oaks: Sage, 1999.

Flynn, Elizabeth A. *Feminism Beyond Modernism.* Carbondale: Southern Illinois UP, June, 2002.

Kolodny, Annette. "Dancing through the Minefield: Some Observations on the Theory, Practice, and Politics of a Feminist Literary Criticism." *Feminist Studies* 6.1 (Spring 1980): 1–25.

———. *Failing the Future: A Dean Looks at Higher Education.* Durham: Duke UP, 1998.

———. *The Land Before Her: Fantasy and Experience of the American Frontiers, 1630–1860.* Chapel Hill: U of North Carolina P, 1984.

———. *The Lay of the Land: Metaphor as Experience and History in American Life and Letters.* Chapel Hill: U of North Carolina P, 1975.

Lunsford, Andrea, ed. *Reclaiming Rhetorica: Women in the Rhetorical Tradition.* Pittsburgh: U of Pittsburgh P, 1995.

Merchant, Carolyn. *Radical Ecology: The Search for a Livable World.* New York: Routledge, 1992.

———. *The Death of Nature: Women, Ecology and the Scientific Revolution.* 1980. New York: HarperCollins, 1990.

Waddell, Craig, ed. *And No Birds Sing: Rhetorical Analyses of Rachel Carson's* Silent Spring. Carbondale: Southern Illinois UP, 2000.

———, ed. *Landmark Essays on Rhetoric and the Environment.* Mahwah: Lawrence Erlbaum, 1998.

Response to Flynn and Worsham

Annette Kolodny

Both Elizabeth Flynn and Lynn Worsham offer very kind remarks about my work on language and environmental studies, remarks for which I am deeply grateful. Even more important, however, each employs her own considerable expertise to lay important theoretical groundwork for introducing issues of feminism and ecocriticism into the composition classroom. When, for example, Flynn argues that "a postmodern feminist approach to the environment emphasizes that the human and the non-human are necessarily connected in complex ways," she opens the door for some fascinating exercises in comparative linguistics. Here, I am thinking of the fact that in ancient Hebrew the word for earth is *adama*, while the word for man is *adam*. At the level of basic vocabulary, therefore, Hebrew (like many older languages) reminded its speakers daily of the intimate connection between the world and the human, emphasizing etymologically that one (man) was contained in the other (earth) inseparably. At least in part, this may help to explain why the texts that comprise the Hebrew bible tend to suggest a reciprocal and stewardship (rather than instrumental and ownership) relationship between humans and the physical earth out of which they are created. Unfortunately, in the rewriting and reassembling of these texts into a so-called old testament for the Christian bible, with subsequent translation into English, much of this nuanced language gets lost. How interesting it might be, therefore, to ask students to examine the cognitive consequences of precisely this kind of language change and its implications for cultural attitudes and actual behavior. In this way, students might better grasp that environmental dilemmas are inherently rhetorical and that, in Flynn's words, "policies that are developed to solve environmental problems" must themselves be "thoroughly rhetorical."

Because Flynn concentrates on "postmodern *feminist* rhetoricians" (my emphasis), her analysis insists on the examination of gendered categories in environmental language. In her splendid overview of postmodern feminist rhetorics, Flynn avoids any kind of essentialist assumption. Still, she suggests how fruitful a gender-sensitive discussion of environmental vocabulary might prove. For example, what shall we make of the fact that the usage *virgin forest* is fast being replaced by locutions like *old growth*? If I am not mistaken, because her analysis *is* so wide-ranging, Flynn would see both phrasings as interpretive and thus inescapably rhetorical. Her analytic framework would require at least some historical account of this shift and lead students to investigate how (or whether) either phrasing is finally compatible with "sustainable development . . . and scientific and rationalistic methods in support of improving the environment." Her analysis and its potential applications, in other words, strike me as at once engaging and provocative.

Similarly with Lynn Worsham's approach: where environmental issues are the subject, she is absolutely correct to assert that "language constitutes power." For the developer intent on siting a large housing project or another shopping mall, an overgrown *swamp* is something to be drained and paved over. But to the scientist and the environmentalist, what is about to be destroyed may well be fragile *wetlands* that support a variety of endangered species, allow migrating ducks annually to nest and reproduce, and provide necessary drainage for underground springs or seepage for aquifers. If the developer can persuade the local zoning board and the general public that it's *only a swamp*, then he will prevail. But if the environmentalists and biologists can explain how species diversity and even our own survival require *wetlands*, then a sustainable future may prevail. At the moment, however, sustainability hangs in the balance because in 2001 the administration of President George W. Bush allowed developers to build on wetlands without replacing them.

This reinforces the importance of Worsham's invaluable insight that different groups within the same society—that is, groups with different agendas and value systems—may use exactly the same words for different, and even diametrically opposed, purposes. Thus, as Worsham puts it, "words are pockets of social space where hegemonic struggle takes place, pockets into which are tucked competing interests and values." An example that immediately comes to mind is the characteristic debate over locating a potentially hazardous chemical or nuclear waste facility. Because wealthy communities (and countries) enjoy both the political and economic clout to keep such facilities out of their backyards, new plants are typically located in poorer, low-wage areas. Local people are urged to see the plant as an economic *benefit* that will bring in new jobs, maybe higher wages, and a tax base to support local public schools. Opponents argue that the only real benefits accrue to the corporation, which gets cheap land on which to build, a low-wage local labor pool, and tax incentives from the state. In recent years, what has been added to such discussions is the need for long-range health insurance benefits for those who might one day suffer from polluted air, water, or soil emanating from the plant. Ostensibly, as Worsham's analysis makes clear, the public discourse hinges on competing *benefits*—and competing meanings of that term.

For those of us in the environmental social justice movement, however, these debates are empty of real meaning because they obscure fundamental questions about the political and corporate processes by which potentially polluting facilities are located in poor communities to begin with; and they obscure the lack of stringent environmental regulations that make these facilities profitable for their owners and shareholders (because they are inexpensive to build and run) but, at the same time, hazardous for their workers and near neighbors. To get past this impasse, environmentalists seek alternative nonpolluting solutions to social problems, advocating government investment in wind, solar, and water technologies. In addition, ecocritics attentive to language and committed to social justice ask what we mean by benefits in such debates. And instead of benefits, we ask who *profits*—and at what cost to whom?

Flynn and Worsham provide vital theoretical underpinnings for practical and workable applications that can make theory come alive for our students. They convince me, yet again, that all of these are issues for the undergraduate rhetoric and composition classroom, and that the social construction(s) of nature is possibly the most important topic that we can raise for our students.

Writing Activism

An Interview with Rick Bass

Rick Bass, according to one critic, is "a writer remarkably able to put people in nature in a way that enhances our understanding of both." This ability comes in large from Bass's position as both a fiction and a nonfiction writer as well as a leading environmental activist—and he has been amazingly prolific in all of these endeavors. His writings include short-story collections, such as *The Watch* (1989), *Platte River* (1994), *Fiber* (1998), and most recently, *The Hermit's Story* (2002); a novel, *Where the Sea Used to Be* (1998); and numerous collections of essays about wilderness, advocacy, and activism, such as *Winter: Notes from Montana* (1991), *The Book of Yaak* (1996), *Brown Dog of the Yaak: Essays on Art and Activism* (1999), and *The Roadless Yaak: Reflections and Observations about One of Our Last Great Wilderness Areas* (2002).

Despite the abundance of Bass's important works—fictional and nonfictional—he cautiously notes in the interview below that "You can do worse as a friend than as an enemy. We love nature to death, and that sometimes causes greater problems than when we view nature as just a resource." In addition to his comments about the relationship between nature and humans, scholars in composition studies and literary studies will be especially interested in some of the distinctions Bass makes between fiction and nonfiction, particularly nonfiction that serves as environmental advocacy. And such readers will also find of interest the conversations about the role of writing in constructing environments and the role of writing in responding to environments.

The phrases *nature writing* and *nature writer* have been criticized by scholars and critics as confusing and reductive labels that should not be attached to texts and authors. In the interview below, however, Bass embraces the label: "Well, I am a nature writer. Absolutely." And commenting on his role as a writer and activist who has gained much attention in the public eye, Bass speaks candidly and interestingly about how environmental issues are often misunderstood by larger public audiences,

55

remarking that he is often "made uncomfortable by what I perceive to be a lack of depth. They're saying the right thing, but they don't know what they're saying. They believe it, they sense politically that it is right, but they just don't know how to engage it, or arrive at the knowledge that engagement can bring." This is perhaps one of the root problems in environmental education today—in English departments and elsewhere—and is no doubt a crucial question and concern that has shaped much of this entire book.

Q: In *Where the Sea Used to Be*, Old Dudley says that "book-reading was usually the kiss of death for the kind of geologist he was searching for" and that book readers want "to keep things nice and safe and comfortable, all imagined, at arm's length." Yet many of your books, like *The Book of Yaak*, seem conceived to make readers uncomfortable, to bring the plight of the Yaak to them, instead of keeping it at a distance. Of course, Old Dudley's statement is that of a fictional character, but we are curious about the act of reading when it comes to issues like those addressed in *The Book of Yaak*, *Where the Sea Used to Be*, and much of your other writing. Do books like yours help collapse the at-arm's-length safety of reading?

A: Yes, the short answer to that question is yes. I do want there to be a significant difference between my fiction and my nonfiction. My nonfiction is, for the most part, for environmental advocacy, so I know right from the beginning that I would be asking the reader to collapse that arm-length distance, that I want to bring that issue to the reader, or bring the reader to the issue, or to bring both to some middle ground of action. When you're asking about the traditional role of the reader, though, I don't want to speak only in terms of environmental advocacy. There are other forms of literature, like the creative essay, where you want the reader to have whatever comfortable distance is best suited to the story. You want the reader to be comfortable, at least for part of the narrative, so that, when it's necessary, you can bring the reader in closer or bring the subject in closer, depending on whether the writer is trying to persuade the reader to diminish that safe arm-length distance. With environmental advocacy, though, yes, you want to crush that safe arm-length distance.

Q: You write in a variety of genres: novels, short stories, and nonfiction essays, to name a few. Yet, in all of theses forms, your primary agenda of environmental awareness—particularly awareness of protecting the Yaak—seems clear. As a writer, how do you approach writing in different genres, for different audiences, while maintaining some rather core goals in most of your writing?

A: That's a hard one for me to answer because it may not be for me to even address. I do perceive a significant difference—of night and day—between my fiction and nonfiction. There appears to be, particularly in my environmental advocacy nonfiction pieces, core themes suggesting the idea that what is rare is often valuable. Wild, unmanaged country is a nonrenewable natural resource that we have a dwindling supply of. It is a very valuable supply. I try to address these ideas from a variety of perspectives: biological, social, cultural.

Q: We're interested in thinking about this genre of nature writing. The term itself has been used to refer to so many different approaches. Books of nature writing include stories, speeches, expository essays, etc. We were wondering if you approach these various genres differently.

A: Yes, I do. There might be a core value of my beliefs in all of these, that of my values as a human. My fiction is about people, and it's true that in my fiction, the people are often exploring rivers, trees; sometimes they encounter animals.

Q: Do you like being categorized as a nature writer, or do you think that label is too narrow?

A: Well, I am a nature writer. Absolutely. The majority of my fiction takes place in nature. Using this criteria, any story I've written could be considered nature writing.

Q: In *Where the Sea Used to Be*, Mel may have been "shaped not so much by her blood lineage as by the land itself." There are some interesting suggestions couched in this statement about genetics versus environment, but more specifically we'd be interested in hearing about what role you see environment playing in constructing individuals, selves, and cultures. Hippocrates, for instance, made similar claims (though rather racist claims) about environments' effects on people's temperaments, health, and physical characteristics. Does environment make us who we are?

A: That is pretty much what the novel is about in a lot of ways: what shapes us, what shapes nature, what shapes culture; how much of it is genetic, how much of it is landscape, how much of it is based on combinations of these factors.

How much of these combinations are, in fact, expressions and mani-festations of the landscape that supports these individuals? I don't know. When it comes down to a question of contrasting scale, sure, you rely on time scales versus cultural or geological scales, and I certainly don't have an answer for that, but I'm very interested in how it is different for every individual, every society, every community to answer that question. It sounds like an easy out to just say "I don't know," but I really don't, and I don't expect to know, and I'd be suspicious of anyone who claimed to have absolute answers to such questions about individuals and cultures.

Q: A question like that comes out of frustration over the complexity of such issues. We try to look at how things like race, class, gender are constructed in individuals, but very few people look at environments and their impact at constructing identity.

A: Well, good. I agree. I think that culture is constituted by multiple factors. I think our culture is just starting to realize that forces outside the culture, physical forms and forces, spiritual forces, are stronger than our individual lives. These are stronger than our individual communities. I consider that as a truth evident through the diversity of landscapes. These diverse landscapes give life, and their diversity controls the components that make up our own communities.

Q: In your short story "Mexico," you write "You can't control some things, and that's what makes them the best." The argument has been made that writing, like ecology, developed to help humans have better control over environments. That is, early recordings of crop cycles, herd migrations, and flood seasons in early writings were attempts to better manage nature for human needs. Do you see writing as giving us control over nature in any way?

A: I don't remember the context of that statement, which character made it, or whether it was made by the narrator, but I'd agree with that. What I've come to understand with regard to what I believe outside of the realm of fiction, I would say that writing, like ecology, was developed as a way to order the outside. I don't think it was developed exclusively to give us greater control of our environments. Writing is, for me, a way to make order out of disorder. And certainly not just the disorder of knowl-edge or the unknown in the physical world, but also the inner world. Yes, more so for the inner world than outer world.

I don't know about the origins of writing, whether it is related to control of the physical world. From my experience with writing, I'd be surprised if that's how it developed. I would think that it is more an art, and not a science or a mechanical tool, and that it is used to convey our emotions, our fears, and our hopes.

Q: There's a book called the *Spell of the Sensuous*. The author looks at how the Greek alphabet came about. The *w*, for instance, was originally a symbol for water, meant to depict the up-and-down movement of a wave, for instance.

A: Perhaps. But those elements of nature carry an impact to the heart that is not conveyed otherwise. The wave is not a mechanical construction of water. The wave makes your heart feel in a certain way. I think writing comes from attempts to respond in a deeper way to where the wave came from. The words in the text or the script—these symbols were an attempt to convey that it is the heart that matters most. I don't think writing is so much about control as understanding. The cave paintings, for example, were attempts to understand the environment, and the emotions it evokes. They were attempts, maybe, to add emotion, or to celebrate an emotion, or to respect an emotion.

Q: Each of the stories in *The Watch* seems to locate nature or the wild as an escape. In "Mexico," the wildness of the bullfights becomes the escape and even Kirby's pool is set as a place different than the surrounding neighborhood. In "Choteau," it's the hunt. In "The Watch," it's the primitive life at Buzbee's camp colony. "Mississippi" has the woods and water. And it's the desert in "In Ruth's Country." This is an interesting positioning of nature and wild as something separate from daily lives. We were wondering if you could talk about the position nature has been given in contemporary America and why you chose to place it in the position you have in these stories.

A: As for your observation, it is really six of one and half a dozen of the other. Your question appears to be closed to me. It really is the other side of the coin. I would probably perceive nature, wild nature, as a constant and it is not. I guess that's just the way the question is phrased. The civilization or developed area is the aberration from what had previously been constant. It is an escape, a fantasy, isn't it? It's a return to lifestyles that were more comfortable, in a social and biological sense.

The last couple centuries and the industrial revolution, almost exclusively, aided in the separation of nature and its perceived role in our lives. The sad irony is that nature is this vast reservoir of selective grace and design and experimentation, and it exists as the ultimate determining factor, even as the anxieties and dreams of our civilization grow greater, and dig deeper and deeper—this graceless old mechanical system that just daily implements its own rhythms and values. I'm not very well qualified to speak about the position of nature. But, we tend to stereotype things. All cultures do. It is our selective advantage to make quick decisions, to see trails and patterns, and to recognize how something will be. I'm sure that nature writers grow tired of the countless repetition of images of nature as villain, as nature forced and conquered, or nature as this torturous realm, as something that attempts to keep us from greater achievements.

Q: In *Winter*, you write about ouzels: "In a hundred years—in this narrow canyon in extreme northwest Montana, anyway,—ouzels haven't changed. I feel spirited back in time, whisked away into the past." Others, such as Thoreau, have felt taken back in time when encountering parts of the natural world. In addition, the media often construct nature as a separate, prehistorical space. Does this separation of nature from "culture" or "civilization"—as most people see it—through temporal spaces make nature an "other"? That is, do such depictions leave nature open for conquest, justified by our attempts to bring places "up to date"?

A: Absolutely. I don't think it's a fiction to think of nature as another place, or fiction, rather, to think of man as the other, separate, forced wanderer— the hungry wanderer, searching always for more of everything. I don't think that fiction renders nature any more or less open to conquest. If anything, I'd argue that an artificial representation of nature as accommodating, or as an accomplice awaiting our mutual benevolent partnership, can be far more destructive to wild lands. You can do worse as a friend than as an enemy. We love nature to death, and that sometimes causes greater problems than when we view nature as just a resource.

I certainly agree with philosophers like Wendell Berry who advocate a benevolent, sustainable relationship with the land. And Berry comes across less as an advocate, and more as a nonfiction writer, as a nature writer. We've got how many tens of thousands of square miles on which to experiment, as the last shreds of untouched land are dwindling fast? So, while we might think we've got it all figured out now, as we start tinkering, we go back to places that have been ravaged, and we try to practice our labor of love, and restore these damaged spaces, and continue to do for nature the best we can. Maybe wild nature will be the better for it now that we understand, or at least we understand in a different way than we used to, what environments need to survive.

Q: In *Winter* you write, "Everyone back east wants me to send them pictures, but very few of them sound serious about wanting to visit [Montana]. This is fine with me. I will send them pictures." This passage reminds us greatly of our students. That is, many of them enjoy talking and writing about the land, but few actually care about "visiting" it, about cultivating a connection with it. We're speaking here specifically about young people. In what ways, if any, do you see young people—mainly teenagers—in our society and culture caring less or caring more in some cases about the natural world and environmental issues?

A: I like the distinction you make, or that I infer, through your place-ment of the word *visiting* in quotes. Everybody loves to visit places. I mean, that's one of our current ways of doing things. Anywhere we go, there's nowadays this implicit assumption about visiting, that if someone doesn't have something to give us, we don't want to visit. We like to visit places, and it is connected to how things are sold to us. There's the ten best beaches, the ten best wilderness trails, the ten best restaurants. Anywhere you go to visit, you're going there to take something, and that's a different kind of visitation than what I'd like to see. I'd like to see the kind of visitation where, and this is what I think I mean as far as becom-ing a member of the community, there is giving to both the human and natural community. You know, you can never give more than you take, but you can at least be respectful, and aware of that imbalance, that debt. That's the kind of visiting I was talking about.

Regarding young people, I see young people in our society and cul-ture caring more and more about the natural world and environmental issues, far more than in the last several years. It's not just a one-year fad; awareness has increased in the past several years, and it continues to increase. I think that more have been encouraged to care. For a long time, environmentalists would comment on the general apathy in regard to environmental matters. They would say things like, "well they don't know nature because there's not any left to bond with," and that argu-ment, while understandable, always has simply bothered me, because I've met a lot of folks who first get interested in environmental matters, and then physically encounter nature.

It's not a thing you gain, this so-called appreciation for nature; it's more a way of changing your perception of the world as you encounter it. So, it's with surprise that I see the current stretch of young people feeling passionate about wild nature. They seem to have somehow come to the knowledge, within them, perhaps based on the dire set of circumstances threatening nature.

Q: We ask this because we tend to mention nature frequently in the classes we teach. There seems to be this stigma associated with the word *environmentalist*. Very few who are eighteen or nineteen years old feel comfortable admitting their concern or interest for environmental matters and even fewer would claim to be an environmentalist. So, perhaps the distinction we're making is that they don't like taking on the label.

A: Certainly there has, but I really think there's something far greater at work. So many social injustices are linked together, and we are realizing the inequities underlying the entire system in relation to nature. How much is it costing? These costs are just beginning to become apparent. Basically, things have gotten so bad that such students probably are not so afraid to be called environmentalists anymore because, even in the midst of incredible privilege and affluence, they're being denied that thing most needed by humans, what they need the most, which is respect.

Branded as "Generation X" or "Generation Y," as a "twenty-something" or a "thirty-something," threatens their individuality just at the time they need it most. This is more true now than it has ever been. Our culture thrives by oppressing individuality, and by manufacturing identities, values, and desires. That contagion is so rampant. And again, there's the idea of nature being where these practices are not conducted, and their identities are not controlled. How could that not be attractive to the younger generation?

Q: In "On Willow Creek" you write, "A scientist will tell you that it's all connected—that if you live in Texas, you must protect the honor and integrity of that country's core, for you are tied to it. It is as much a part of you as family—but if you are a child and given to daydreaming and wondering, I believe that you'll understand this by instinct. . . . You can know of the allegiance you owe it, can sense this in a way that not even the scientists know." Many suggest that care and love for the natural world is something taught. In what ways is or isn't the opposite true, that we are actually taught destructive habits? That is, are we taught as we grow older not to care for the land?

A: That's a good question. I suspect that many people are born with a deep allegiance to wild landscapes, to the woods, and are born with a shoulder turned to the crowded world. This isn't to say with a shoulder turned to the world of humans, but to the crowded gatherings of people. That said, I do believe that care of the natural is something taught. I don't think that, as a species, we automatically care for nature. Instead, we have innate tendencies to grasp for, to acquire, to control what we perceive to be a resource.

I see it often in children who will kill a fly because it's moving, or will kill small mammals, or anything that they can corner. Certainly, this is part of us as a species. I do believe both characteristics are coded by culture.

Chris: I grew up in Texas, and the woods were always there. Until about age twelve, that's where I was every day, out in the woods. But at about age twelve or so, I could just care less about anything related to nature. I had to relearn that "instinct"; perhaps at some point I must have been taught not to care.

A: I think you're right. I think there may be two forces at work, one overlaying the other, and these forces have a destructive engagement. I wonder if there's not some biological rhythm there, in terms of development, and caring selectively. As a child, it is to your benefit to have those areas as places of safety and security. At the time of adolescent development, it is to your advantage to have that kid go away for a little bit. You harbor contempt for that and seek territories previously unavailable. I don't mean just new places, but new values, too. Values that will help you adapt in a social environment. Then, you can return to nature as a sanctuary.

I think there's probably that bedrock pattern to life. That certainly works in this culture. But there's no responsibility to go back. I'd say this lack of responsibility exacerbates the problem. With that fundamental life pattern established in adolescence, it is going to be very hard to come back because mass popular culture does not turn you back to where you came from.

Q: That might be typified by the bumper sticker that says "Whoever dies with the most toys wins." In *Winter* you note that you were "a writer in a valley of workers." And you often speak of having to gain respect from others because you were new, an outsider at first. You write, in addition, "I don't know how to write about this country in an orderly fashion, because I'm just finding out about it. If a path develops, I'll be glad to see it. . . . I know *nothing* about this valley. Everything I see is new, and I understand nothing." In some ways it might seem odd that an outsider, a newcomer, could devote such time and effort to writing a book about Montana. However, in what ways was being new to the area a benefit for you? That is, does being the newcomer, or beginner, allow one to see things in a different light than the others? How does the mystery of a place affect your writing? And, how did this help or hinder your writing?

A: That one I've spent a lot of time thinking about. A new place that captures your imagination can be really beneficial. There can be a real benefit to knowing next to nothing about a place or a situation or a relationship, because there's something that, if you're a creative person, a writer or an artist, helps you to slip into this position where the input, the stimuli, engage with your imaginative powers and they work back and forth. One nurtures the other, engages the other, back and forth, and *Winter* addresses that. In this kind of situation, you don't really create. Instead, you just read what is around you.

It's good because your ability to explore knows no bounds. It's like how your outdoor adventure can be hindered by a handbook. This is the place where, without realizing it, you will find yourself writing success-fully based only on your keenness of observation where there's that nice balance between knowledge and imagination.

Q: Also in *Winter* you make a distinction between *learning* and *being told*: "This year I have been seeing rabbits come out of hiding after the sun goes down, white rabbits hopping across the logging roads as I come down off the mountain with a load of wood—trying, with the windows rolled down, to listen and feel for myself, and to learn rather than always having to be told. I think that I can learn." The distinction you make is particularly relevant for teachers who want their students to learn about and care for the land through writing. However, one concern many such teachers have is that *being told* is a kind of forced indoctrination into certain political positions. When it comes to *learning* about the land-scape, does *being told* often work against learning?

A: Again, I don't mean to generalize, but I'm a teacher and a student. But I do see that as an environmentalist, I'll be at some function, at some discussion about some issue in which some of the participants share the same political position or party-line stance as me, and yet I will be made uncomfortable by what I perceive to be a lack of depth. They're saying the right thing, but they don't know what they're saying. They believe it, they sense politically that it is right, but they just don't know how to engage it, or arrive at the knowledge that engagement can bring.

I'm not saying they're right or wrong. I'm just saying it can be disconcerting because you realize that they don't know why they believe the way they do, and this is much the same way that people on the other side of the issue haven't thought through their rationale for taking a particular position.

On the other hand, I know a lot of teachers, particularly in higher education, who are attempting to address such issues by taking students out into the landscape and conducting interdisciplinary courses, and I think those are huge success stories, and good places to help solve various problems.

Q: We go to conferences sometimes, and when we talk about issues like this, how we teach nature, there's nearly always someone who has to pop up and say, "Well, you're just indoctrinating the students; you're just giving them manipulative rhetoric, and you're trying to persuade them of the validity of your own political position." So, it's hard to answer and say, "Of course. Why else would we teach these issues if we weren't interested in persuading people of their importance." There's always the opposite too that might happen, that by focusing so intently on environmental matters with students, that we're going to make students resistant to the messages, even as we are trying to persuade.

A: Yes, but I don't worry about that anymore because it is a self-selective process. If there's such intellectually unchallenged individuals who are going to oppose something simply because they're bored, then you don't want them on your side anyway.

Q: One anthology of nature writers we came across mentions that you "ended up majoring in petroleum geology, but along the way [you] took a workshop on writing nature essays." In what ways can or cannot the classroom be an effective space for teaching nature writing?

A: In many ways, the classroom really can't teach nature writing. You're not in the woods, you're not in that environment. You are going to be removed from the environment that you are going to be studying. While this is an understandable factor, it still is important. On the other hand, and more so than with other kinds of writings, nature writing has this requirement that must be fulfilled in the classroom because it is such a deep and enduring tradition in this country.

Indeed, nature writing provides the first literary tradition in this country. Of course, there are other literary traditions, too. But nature writing features such a vast range of writers and styles, themes and subjects. You've got to look at native culture, too, which has this great culture of storytelling. I remember when I was first beginning to write, and it struck me as such a novel idea that I might not have read a certain writer, but I did read a writer who read that writer. That's a really important thing to consider in terms of establishing a tradition of nature writing. I use this as a stepping stone for such a tradition.

Q: In "Cats and Students, Bubbles and Abysses," your narrator is rather cynical about freshman composition—a course he seems "stuck" teaching—and he says of it, "I teach at the junior college—Freshman Comp, Heroes and Heroines of Southern Literature, Contemporary Southern Literature, Contemporary Northern Literature, that sort of crap." But, he is particularly dismayed by composition. He talks about not bothering to grade papers, about using them to start fires, and generally about how awful the papers are. As people who occasionally teach freshman composition, and who are certainly invested in training those who teach first-year writing, we have to ask: Is teaching Freshman comp crap?

A: In general, in the story, it was for this guy. It's kind of strange trying to teach writing as an art to a classroom full of people who don't want to be there. In that sense, "crap" is probably too kind.

In the story, I'm trying to portray a narrator who just wants to focus on writing. To him, anything that gets in the way of writing, or of working on writing, is crap. Certainly, I understand that freshman composition or any higher education course has benefit to students who accept the course gratefully. With this character, anything that prevented him from working on writing was crap.

Q: One of your most cited lines occurs in "On Willow Creek": "When we run out of country, we will run out of stories. When we run out of stories, we will run out of sanity." Can you explain in more detail what you mean, ultimately, by connecting our sanity to the landscape?

A: Again, that character is referring to the notion of logic and order in previously random or unutilized developments: the absence of confusion, the presence of meaning, the presence of grace through the elegance of nature. She doesn't mean a slapdash concoction of elements but just graceful dignified order.

Q: In "Creatures of the Dictator" you make the quick comment, "It's so easy to be an eco-warrior in the States." Is it?

A: That was said because of my bitterness and sarcasm. Everyone's an eco-warrior—anybody who writes about nature. Fewer—like Wallace Stegner, Terry Tempest Williams, Doug Peacock—are traditional activists. What I mean is that it is too easy to be perceived as an eco-warrior. I guess what I'm criticizing is the perception that simply writing about the environment will take care of the problem, so others in the larger public don't have to engage.

Q: What about the reactions you get from audiences like the one you describe in "Thunder and Lightning"? That doesn't seem easy. You suggest that you're often seen as a zealot—not an easy role to occupy.

A: You know, I feel ashamed for our culture when that happens. I don't think we'd know a zealot if we saw one. It's frustrating to me as I advocate wilderness protection for a five- or ten-thousand-acre parcel. I see extraction companies whose public relations firms overwhelm the media with a viewpoint that is more extreme than what I'm advocating. But their viewpoint is never construed as extreme or overzealous.

Avenues of Activism

A Response to Rick Bass

Christian R. Weisser

> It's interesting to think about and consider what art lies out there
> waiting to be released—not yet written, not yet painted—but
> enmeshed in a culture's foundation, as if within the soil, awaiting
> its release.
>
> —Rick Bass, "Postwar Paris: Chronicles of a Literary Life"

In the world of creative nonfiction, Rick Bass seems to be more widely
read than just about anyone. A quick look at the composition readers in
my office proves that his work has been anthologized in practically every
new textbook published in the last ten years—or at least those that made
it to my already crowded bookshelves. In recent conversations with campus colleagues, I found that faculty across campus and across disciplines
knew of Bass, and many of them were familiar with specific books, citing
The Book of Yaak, *Where the Sea Used to Be*, and the recently published
The Hermit's Story as among their favorites. I discovered that Bass's writing is recognized and valued in such seemingly diverse disciplines as
geology and art. To be sure, those faculty appreciated his writing for
different reasons; the geologists seemed to appreciate Bass's keen eye for
detail and vivid descriptions of natural places, while the Art faculty saw
in his work their own appreciation for representations of modern life and
the questions that only art (be it in text, oil, or clay) can address. Quite
simply, I was amazed by the number and variety of faculty who had
something good to say about Rick Bass.

In hindsight, it is easy to see why so many faculty appreciate his work: much of it represents the ideals that bring many educators to teaching, regardless of whether their classroom work focuses upon writing, geology, or some other discipline. Like most educators, Bass is concerned with helping students to develop a critical awareness and understanding of environmental, cultural, and social issues. In this interview, Bass suggests that he sees "young people in our society and culture caring more and more about the natural world and environmental issues, far more than in the last several years." Bass does not see environmental issues as solitary topics; however, he sees them connecting with practically every important area in the typical university curriculum and in society in general, arguing that he tries to "address these ideas from a variety of perspectives: biological, social, and cultural," which suggests a connected, interdisciplinary approach to understanding our world and our knowledge of it rather than a discrete, specialized focus on natural or wild places. Bass emphasizes his commitment to critical and sustained public debate, suggesting that "so many social injustices are linked together, and we are realizing the inequalities underlying the entire system in relation to nature." In short, Bass makes it clear that his primary agenda is to help reshape and disrupt public conversations about crucial environmental and social issues, making readers "uncomfortable," as the interviewers suggest, in order to "crush that safe arm-length distance" that those readers might have from public debate.

We can learn a lot from authors like Bass, Quammen, and the other essayists and authors interviewed in this book, whose work (though different from traditional academic work) constitutes an important component of civic dialogue about the world in which we live. By offering perspectives that often run counter to dominant political and social perspectives on the environment, they help to transform public opinion, and in the process, help to maintain and create a more healthy, dynamic public sphere. At the essence of a thriving public sphere is dialogue and debate; these create the sort of disruption and negotiation that is necessary for progressive social change. In *The Dialogic Imagination*, Mikhail Bakhtin suggests that meanings unfold through what he calls a "dialogizing of the word." By this he means our language use (written or spoken) constantly enters into dialogue with the language used by our interlocutors. By interacting with the meanings of directly or indirectly addressed individuals, we help to create new possibilities and interpretations. We construct meanings that are not wholly ours and not wholly others', but which can bring both, as Bass suggests, "to some middle ground of action."

This process of reshaping, redefining, and reconstructing meaning forms the basis of public discourse. Conversation and negotiation determine the meanings of words, concepts, and ideas in contemporary culture. It is important to note that public spheres are not physical locations or structures but are discursive constructs, "immense, ongoing set[s] of open conversations carried on through a variety of media" (Smith 62). While public spheres may be accessed through a number of avenues, such as printed text, face-to-face discussion, or electronic media, it is language that forms their basis. Unique public spheres are constituted wherever and whenever two or more participants engage in discussion or debate. As Gerard Hauser writes, "Each context provides a space in which the confluence of history, society, psychology, and culture creates a turbulence unlike any that has existed before or will follow" (8). In other words, publics emerge in the spaces between perspectives, at the points in which we cocreate meaning. A healthy public sphere requires above all else diversity; multiple avenues, multiple voices, and multiple perspectives ensure that the discussion will never reach stasis.

While few college and university faculty have the broad public influence of Bass and his contemporaries, we have access to audiences that are equally diverse—those found around campus. Universities play a vital role in public discourse; they provide both an institutional framework and a training ground for the conversations and interactions that comprise the public sphere. In fact, academic institutions provide some opportunities for participating in and creating public discourse that may not be so readily available to Bass and other authors who are not closely tied to a university. Public discourse arises through a variety of institutionally sponsored outlets, including speeches, colloquia, conferences, debates, and other forms of dialogue. Universities support the exchange of information and ideas through journal subscriptions, library acquisitions, and research support. Universities also provide place and opportunity for discourse that is often both more personal and more sustained than that found in most media outlets. Perhaps most important, public spheres are created thousands of times each day between students and teachers as they interact, debate, and create new knowledge. As Woodruff Smith points out in "Higher Education, Democracy, and the Public Sphere":

> Universities and colleges are particularly important in constituting, shaping, and maintaining the American public sphere, and they play this role to a large extent because of the existence of public institutions of higher education. For better or for worse—mostly for better—American public higher education, the American public sphere, and American democracy are closely linked. (69)

In other words, the American university system is a primary component of the American public sphere; whereas coffeehouses and newspapers served as primary sites of public discourse in the seventeeth and eighteenth centuries, classrooms and conference centers serve similar purposes today. Few authors have the discursive opportunities and audiences that are available to most faculty every day. While there are certainly some restrictions on what can be said (and by whom) in university-sanctioned events and courses, avenues for critical engagement of social, political, and environmental issues are readily available through the American university system.

Though avenues to the public seem to be quite different for university faculty than they are for Bass and his contemporaries, the lines between them are often indistinguishable; there is no clear dichotomy between the "in here" of the university and the "out there" beyond its walls. Ultimately, the university is deeply enmeshed with the public-at-large and vice versa. When faculty communicate with students or colleagues, they connect with individuals who are members of the academic community and also members of many other social and political groups. Our deliberations with others, even if they are within the physical or political confines of the university, are also connecting with multiple other public spheres. Likewise, though Bass may not be affiliated with any particular university, in many respects, he is a part of the American university system. As I mentioned earlier, his writing is highly anthologized in collections designed for university consumption, and many of his speaking engagements occur in academic contexts. Few other contemporary authors are as widely read and discussed in academic settings. Ironically, though Freshman Comp may be "crap" for his narrator in "Cats and Students, Bubbles and Abysses," Bass's own work is as much a part of university writing courses as practically anyone's. Ultimately, the goals of Bass and many university faculty are the same: to help shape public opinion, to keep the conversations open and ongoing, and to encourage people to critically engage in debates about important issues. It is no wonder, then, that Bass is widely recognized by many of my colleagues because his primary objectives seem to run parallel to many of our own.

WORKS CITED

Bakhtin, M. M. *The Dialogic Imagination: Four Essays.* Ed. Michael Holquist. Trans. Caryl Emerson and Michael Holquist. Austin: U of Texas P, 1981.

Bass, Rick. "Postwar Paris: Chronicles of a Literary Life." *Paris Review* Spring 1999. 27 May 2003 <http://www.parisreview.com/history/bass/bass1.htm>.

Hauser, Gerard A. *Vernacular Voices: The Rhetoric of Publics and Public Spheres.* Columbia: U. of South Carolina P, 1999.

Smith, Woodruff C. "Higher Education, Democracy, and the Public Sphere." *Thought and Action* Summer 2003: 61–73.

The Active Voice

Sid Dobrin

Let's be honest about it; these responses are a bit unfair. Chris and I have invited the interviewees in this book to talk with us about environment and about writing, but in doing so we only asked them to talk with us, to offer their responses to our questions without the benefits afforded them should they have been able to write their responses, without drafting and revising answers. Their responses are often off-the-cuff, conversational, impromptu. The responses to the interviews, however, are more academic. They address the interviews more deliberately. Randall Roorda says it perfectly in his response to the Ann Zwinger interview: "It's unfair to transcribe what Zwinger treats as a conversation and scrutinize it as if it were a composed, deliberate performance, from which compositionists might expect to elicit insights and applications" (p. 000). It's unfair to do this to any of the interviews; yet, this is specifically what Chris and I have asked the respondents to do. It is perhaps even more unfair that we then ask the interviewees to respond to the responses after we put them in the position that necessitates they defend themselves through response.

There's no doubt that these responses grow from the tradition of interview responses that Gary A. Olson developed in his scholarly interviews for the *Journal of Advanced Composition (JAC)* and his subsequent books with SUNY Press that reprint the *JAC* interviews. I don't recall anyone ever questioning this format in the way that Roorda has pointed that we should. I wish they had. And yet, Chris and I have asked the respondents included in this collection to do just that: to address these interviews, these conversations, these informal dialogues as though they were a different kind of text, as though they had been written in anticipation of critique, of response. Perhaps, too, it was unfair of me and Chris to ask the kinds of questions we repeatedly ask in these interviews, hoping to get the interviewees to give the respondents something to respond to, something we wanted them perhaps to say. But part of what we hoped to develop here was specifically a sense of conversation, one

75

that stretched between the academic world and the world of nature writers, biologists, ecologists, activists. Certainly those demarcations of difference are convenient and often don't hold (how could we not consider Annette Kolodny, E. O. Wilson, or Max Oelschlaeger academics?). And let's face it, the "academic" responses offered by Lynn Worsham, Elizabeth Flynn, Chris Schroeder, and the others are magnificent. But are they fair?

Despite that, and given the fact that I say so in the introduction to my own response to the Rick Bass interview, it would only seem fair that I now talk about the Rick Bass interview in a manner that doesn't translate it into an academic discussion, that doesn't scrutinize Bass's words as though he presented them for such scholarly (or even public) critique. It would be easy to write about Bass's avoidance of more scholarly issues in this interview, such as the moment when Chris and I ask him about the origins of writing as an early form of control and he has the sense to tell us, "I don't know about the origins of writing, whether it is related to control of the physical world. From my experience with writing, I'd be surprised if that's how it developed. I would think that it is more an art, and not a science or mechanical tool, and that it is used to convey our emotions, our fears, our hopes." What a brilliant move. He takes our obviously leading question and refuses to play our game. This isn't scholarship, it's a conversation. Call it a "scholarly" interview if you'd like, but that's not the arena in which Bass works. He is an advocate and a writer. His agendas are geared toward a different public audience; his motivations toward action are focused on more important things than whether Chris Keller and Sid Dobrin (or anyone else) have theorized that writing controls nature or is even related to nature. Bass is one of those writers who reminds me that once in a while (and never often enough) we need to put aside the academic theory and get out in the thick of it, even if the thick of it is just a conversation with Rick Bass. Sure, I think the theory, the academy, the teaching, the reading, and the writing all affect and are affected by "getting in the thick of it," but you have to get your hands dirty with the experience of the places you want to translate into that academic language. Thanks, Rick, for reminding me.

That said, though, what we cannot overlook in this interview is what Bass does say about writing and environment. Bass is without a doubt one of the most important writers writing in the United States today. I am able to say this not because he's turning out books that are streaking to the top of best-seller lists or that are being nominated for Pulitzer prizes (though some should be), but because his work regularly appears in a variety of magazines, his books are in demand in bookstores and libraries, and his fiction and nonfiction are often reprinted in first-year readers and anthologies. I'm amazed at how those in English departments, particularly in composition studies, who are so bound up in studying the "politics" of language and writing tend to overlook all of the writing produced by those working to protect the world in which those politics are played out. In saying so, what I admit is that when I go home at night, I want to put down the theory and pick up Bass, or Ray, or Sanders, or Zwinger, or any of the other writers out there writing about the natural world. I am specifically enraptured by folks like Janisse Ray and Rick Bass because they write not just to tell fun stories but to elicit response, to get things done. Their writing is active. Bass is clear in this interview that he sees a difference between his fiction and nonfiction and that his primary goal in writing nonfiction is to promote environmental advocacy. Sure, we could say that anyone who writes does so to elicit some sort of response, but that's not the same as turning to writing as a form of activism.

I've heard Rick Bass speak and give readings a number of times. He's one of those writers I want to hear, whom I want to connect with beyond the standard writer–reader relationship specifically because his writing evokes action. Each time I hear Bass read and speak, I catch a glimpse of his Yaak Valley, a place I have never been. I know it only through his words and the slides he shows sometimes when he speaks; yet, the power of Bass's writing makes me want to help him protect his place. That fascinates me—not necessarily Bass's ability to evoke such a response, but the powerful way in which he is able to do so through writing. When I read magazines such as *Florida Sportsman*, *Sport Diver*, *Smithsonian*, *National Geographic*, and other publications that depict places, I often find myself wanting to go to those places. John McPhee's *Coming into the Country* has driven me back to Alaska time and time again; Archie Carr sends me to my home's beaches, springs, and swamps. But, Bass's writing about the Yaak makes me want to stay away in a reverent respect. Would I go should the opportunity arise? Certainly, but to what end? In 2000, I published a book called *Distance Casting: Words and Ways of the Saltwater Fishing Life*, a book about the connections between writing, fishing, and the places where fishing happens: rivers, streams, lakes, ponds, and oceans—mostly oceans. In this book I consider the relationships that are bound up in fishing and writing about fishing, and in doing so I hope to get my readers to think a bit more about protection waters and about protecting fish populations. One of my concerns is how fishing magazines and other texts have aided in the overcrowding of many of Florida's waterways (and other aquatic places around the country) by making public not just their locations but tactics for fishing those areas. I argue that the very writing that exposes such places, also makes the places vulnerable and ultimately is damaging those places. And so, when I read Bass, I find myself wanting to honor his places in the same way—by not going to them, but by thinking about them, because, as Bass explains in this interview, visiting a place is much different than being a member of the community of that place: "Anywhere we go, there's nowadays this implicit assumption about visiting, that if someone doesn't have something to give us, we don't want to visit. We like to visit places, and it is connected to how things are sold to us. There's the ten best beaches, the ten best wilderness trails, the ten best restaurants. Anywhere you go to visit, you're going there to take something, and that's a different kind of visitation than what I'd like to see. I'd like to see the kind of visitation where, and this is what I think I mean as far as becoming a member of the community, there is giving to both the human and natural community. You know, you can never give more than you take, but you can at least be respectful, and aware of that imbalance, that debt. That's the kind of visiting I was talking about."

There's a great moment in E. L. Doctorow's *Billy Bathgate* when Billy, having never been outside of the Bronx, is taken into the country and sees "nature" for the first time. Upon gazing out at this new world, Billy makes the interesting statement, "I mean you don't really appreciate a phrase like *natural resources*, you have to see the trees on the mountains, and the stream, and the lumberyard beside the stream to begin to get the idea, to see the sense of everything made" (116). Of course, Billy then admits that the country life, where he can see all of these resources, is not the life for him. But, I remember when I first read *Billy Bathgate* thinking about the power of this claim, that to really understand a place or its resources, one has to see it to make the connections between a place and its conservation or protection. In a lot of ways, Bass is a writer that disrupts this idea of "seeing" a place (or an issue) to find connection to it or to understand the value in its protection. Rather, Bass makes evident that writing is itself a way of seeing, and that writing allows the promotion of a kind of advocacy and activism through writing: "My nonfiction is, for the most part, for environmental advocacy, so I know right from the beginning that I would be asking the reader to collapse that arm-length distance, that I want to bring that issue to the reader, or bring the reader to the issue, or to bring both to some middle ground of action." The problem, of course, is the role advocacy and activism have taken on in contemporary America.

Let's face it, the United States is not populated by activists. In fact, activism is cast more often than not in negative light. Being called an activist carries baggage of disruption and nonconformity, and for the status quo those are not good things. Activism is a necessary function of democracy, yet activism has been redefined in contemporary America as an antidemocratic activity. Activism, that is, often gets conflated with progressivism, and as Sharon Crowley notes in her book *Composition in the University: Historical and Polemical Essays,* "Cold-war rhetoric simply conflated progressivism with socialism, the ideology whose agenda for the world reputedly involved the eradication of democracy" (166). Caught up in this rhetorical move against progressivism, activism was also pinned (penned) as an antidemocratic endeavor. Orwell's Hyde Park agitator comes to mind. Crowley goes on to identify through Gary Miller that cold war rhetoric began to recast the very understanding of democracy from a process allowing for and encouraging change into one of a definable, unchanging political paradigm that stands not as a system for change and voice but as a system opposed to communism. Crowley quotes Miller:

> In the post war and Cold War years, people began to define democracy differently. Democracy was no longer seen as a *process* that encouraged change; it was a political ideal that was to be *preserved* in the face of the communist threat. The focus was not on the individual's right to change society but on the individual's responsibility as a citizen to protect democracy, which was now identified with the status quo. (Miller 117 qtd in Crowley 166)

Hence, activism is seen as a threat against democracy, against a democratic political paradigm, not a necessary function of it.

Activism is a doctrine that dictates energetic action, that demands participation, the very thing that contemporary democratic thought seems to find frightening. Think, for instance, of the image projected of antiwar demonstrators, of environmental activists, of antiglobalization protestors. Many wish these agitators would simply be quiet. No activism means silence. A silent democracy is something we should all fear. And, let us face it, activism has a strong tie to fear. As Rabbi Marshall T. Meyer explained in an address to the students and faculty of Dartmouth College on October 17, 1991, "One must understand that fear is the inevitable concomitant of activism. But one must know how to live with fear. Both the activist and the coward know fear. They know it intimately. The difference is that while the coward allows the fear to paralyze him or herself, the activist learns how to function despite the fear that makes you quake." Meyer went on to say: "If we are to guarantee a democratic process, if we are to guarantee a democratic society, we must reeducate ourselves to respond to the injustices of our society. We must commit ourselves to the welfare of the polis within which we live. In short, we must be responsible citizens of our society. We must vote, we must become candidates and leave our soft tranquility. We must maintain civilized discourse with those who hold contrary views. We must not slap and punch when we get angry. We must learn how to live with the drama of existence which is no easy task." No easy task, indeed. Perhaps this is why I find Bass's activism so important, not only for what he does and says but for how he makes his voice heard: through a conscious active writing.

Deciding to act, to be active is a rhetorical choice.[1] Rhetoric is itself active. To act requires that one understand the rhetorical strategies of acting: toward whom does one act? What is one's audience? Why does one act? What is one's purpose? In what ways does one act? What is one's ethos, logos, and pathos of action? There is no singular form of activism, and no singular approach to activism can initiate change within a particular event, especially when dealing with environmental issues: active lawyers are needed, active scientists are needed, active parents are needed, active politicians are needed, active community leaders are needed, and yes, active writers are needed—no matter how or what they write. Bass makes this evident. And so, Bass gets his hands dirty with the activism of writing, and as he makes clear in this interview, that kind of activism is what gets things done, not necessarily the theoretical speculation about the relationship between writing and activism, but the actual active work of writing: "Everyone's an eco-warrior—anybody who writes about nature. . . . I guess what I'm criticizing is the perception that simply writing about the environment will take care of the problem, so others in the larger public don't have to engage."

In his book *Essays on Heidegger and Others: Philosophical Papers, Volume 2*, Richard Rorty makes a similar argument. He posits that theory work can only go but so far. He responds to Paul de Man's argument that literary theory and critical linguistic analysis do have an active role in moral and political movements and instead argues that for political (and moral) reform to occur there need to be active participants working to make changes, not merely analyzing and criticizing. He writes:

> It does not take any great analytical skills or any great philosophical self-consciousness to see what's going on. It does not, for example, take any "critical-linguistic-analysis" to notice that millions of children in American ghettos grew up without hope while their U.S. government was preoccupied with making the rich richer—with assuring a greedy and selfish middle-class that

it was the salt of the earth. Even economists, plumbers, insurance salesmen, and biochemists—can recognize the immersion of much of Latin America is partially due to the deals struck between local plutocracies and North American banks and governments. (135)

What I understand Rorty to be saying is that the theory, in this case literary criticism, can only go but so far; in order for any real change to take place, there must be action, activism. Reformers, Rorty argues, need not be caught up in intellectual movements, but in what he calls "campaigns." As Ray Linn writes, Rorty "believes that thought can only be justified in the realm of action, and, specifically, that it can only be justified by successful action in a democratic society" (42–43).

Bass has made his campaign known and his method of campaigning is through writing. And so, while I do see the translations of these conversational interviews into more academic kinds of discussions a bit unfair to the interviewees, I also see a need to read an interview like the one with Bass as a call to activism, as an act of activism itself. Bass's is an active voice, one campaigning, one working to encourage change.

Notes

1. I am actually a bit hesitant in calling someone "an activist" and using the term as a label of identity in the same way that I hesitate to call someone who writes "a writer." Writing is an active function. One writes; one is not one who writes, a writer. One is active; one acts. One is not defined by that action in label—an activist.

Works Cited

Crowley, Sharon. *Composition in the University: Historical and Polemical Essays.* Pittsburgh: U of Pittsburgh P, 1998.

Doctorow, E. L. *Billy Bathgate.* New York: Random House, 1989.

Koestler, Arthur. *The Invisible Writing.* 1954. Reprinted by Olympic Marketing Corporation, 1984.

Linn, Ray. A Teacher's Introduction to Postmodernism (NCTE's Teacher's Introduction Series, 5). Urbana, IL: NCTE, 1996.

Meyer, Marshall T. "Why and How to be an Activist." 30 July 2003. <http://www.bj.org/kh_00october/mtm.html>.

Rorty, Richard. *Essays on Heidegger and Others: Philosophical Papers,* Volume 2.

Writing Nature, Making Connections

An Interview with David Quammen

"Nature is a dauntingly difficult word to define," David Quammen muses in the following interview. Quammen, however, has spent a great deal of time tackling this difficult endeavor, lucidly and imaginatively describing nature in his various written works. Former editorialist for *Outside Magazine*, Quammen has also published and edited numerous books, including *The Song of the Dodo, The Flight of the Iguana, Natural Acts, Wild Thoughts from Wild Places, The Boilerplate Rhino*, and *The Best American Science and Nature Writing*. Quammen's writing uniquely and adeptly mixes and blurs genres to afford his audience greater insights into the natural world, or, in Quammen's own words, his writing utilizes *synergy*: "just as you mix metals into alloys," he suggests, "I like to mix types of literary strategy and different kinds of elements into a given piece." Quammen's discursive mixtures, no doubt, offer theorists and teachers of writing a number of astute and important ways to rethink and remap the direction of composition studies—both theoretically and pedagogically.

Quammen's ideas about *constructive disorientation* should certainly appeal to those interested in language and writing, the notion that "By putting together certain facts, certain people, certain historical events, certain ideas, certain creatures, with other elements that seemed unrelated, you could generate insight, some new ways of seeing the world and of seeing particular parts of the world." In addition, Quammen perceptively sees composition studies and the teaching of writing as one area of study that might help bring together diverse fields in the humanities and the sciences, "the old two cultures in limbo," as Quammen describes them. As a writer of articles and books—both fiction and nonfiction—Quammen is particularly interested in thinking about audiences, about the ways in which he addresses readers and the way readers address his texts. He believes it is the job of the writer "not just to talk to the reader in a companionable, conversational tone, but to think about, wonder about and imagine what the reader is thinking, where the reader is, what

83

the reader wants, whether the reader is bored or lost or confused." Quammen, without a doubt, is a writer of nature who is concerned about how nature is read, perceived, and ultimately cared for by his audiences.

In the interview below, recorded on election day 2000, Quammen admits that "in a half-serious way" he aspires "to being a moral philosopher" and that acts of writing for him are "partly about teaching." Quammen's writings—his teachings—have resonance for those of us in both the humanities and sciences, but they manifest particular importance for those of us interested in the ways environments are produced and captured in discourse and the ways certain environments need to be saved. Quammen admits that he is "pessimistic" about our prospects for saving much of the natural world; however, he makes clear that he is "not despairing because despairing is an emotional response and pessimism is an intellectual response." Readers will find in this interview both spaces of pessimism and optimism, and the words of a gifted writer who has much to teach us about the relationships between writers and audiences, people and nature, and discourse and place.

Q: You write in a range of genres, on an array of subjects, in a variety of fora, and for a medley of audiences. Why has writing become the primary medium for you to teach about nature?

A: Writing was always my greatest interest. From the age of ten I was writing stories and poems and plays and skits, and found myself through college interested in becoming a novelist if I could do that. So, the first thing I ever published, essentially, was a novel that I wrote while I was a junior in college and I thought that by disposition as well as by education I was a literary guy. And then I discovered—after I moved to Montana in 1973, having had the good fortune of publishing that first novel fairly young—that despite that good start I couldn't make a living as a novelist. So, I gradually transformed into a magazine writer, but I had always been interested in the natural world. So, when I started doing nonfiction in order to make a living, it was natural for me to do nonfiction that was focused on the natural world, on forests and jungles and rivers and swamps. It became sort of a journalistic beat for me.

Q: Do you see your writing as instructional?

A: Yeah, the secret concession that I suppose I should make on that is that deep down inside, in a half-serious way, I aspire to being a moral philosopher, so that I'm always interested in entertaining the reader, in keeping the reader engaged, in being interesting rather than didactic. There's also a serious point that I want to get across and sell and promote. And in that sense, certainly, it's . . . I fancy the enterprise as being partly about teaching.

Q: You are a magnificent storyteller, both in fiction and nonfiction. Often your stories blend different types of writing—say, for instance, adventure stories and natural history writing. For example, "Swamp Odyssey" is a great nonfiction story with fun characters and adventure, but at the same time your audience learns a good deal about the natural history and ecology of the Okeefenokee. That is to say, most of your writing, even when you're storytelling, attempts to teach your readers something about the natural world. We'd like to ask about this blending of narrative and natural history: As a writer what do you see such a discursive hybridity ultimately producing for the written work and for your audience?

A: A *discursive hybridity*, wow, let me try and answer that one first. And I'll do it with another big word: *synergy*. I think storytelling, narrative, combined with a certain amount of humor, combined with explication of interesting but obscure ideas can create a stronger, more energized, and more engaging literary work than if something is all of one type. So just as you mix metals into alloys, I like to mix types of literary strategy and different kinds of elements into a given piece. I started as a fiction writer and then in my second and third novels I found myself mixing a lot of history and a certain amount of science into what, ostensibly, were spy thrillers. And about the same time I was turning into a magazine journalist specializing in science, and I found there on the other side of the coin that mixing humor and narrative and human portraiture in with science writing created something that seemed more able to engage people.

Q: What about the relationship between how you convey narrative and how you convey natural history.

A: Is there a relationship? Well, there is in this sense. I'm interested in all the bizarre creatures, in all the strange species that exist on the surface of the planet, and I try to cater to readers who are also interested in those creatures or can be made interested in them. But I admit at the same time that the most amazing, most peculiar, most interesting species on the planet is *Homo sapiens*. By telling stories of individual humans you can enliven what might otherwise be a dry, expository treatment of a scientific subject. People like to read about other people. Even when they are engaged in reading about the natural world, or in reading about obscure scientific concepts, or great movements of history. I can still remember David Halberstam's *The Best and the Brightest*, one of the earliest really good serious books that came out about the Vietnam War, and the thing that energized that book so much was that it had these mini-biographies of the players. Of Robert MacNamara and Maxwell Taylor and the Rostow brothers and the people who had essentially been the architects of the Kennedy-Johnson Vietnam policy. It was a book that came alive in these little biographies, these human portraits, and I tried to do something similar in *The Song of the Dodo*, not consciously copying Halberstam but with that in the back of my mind.

Q: That's the same kind of effect that people like Krakauer have started to use also with the adventure stories giving glimpses of mountaintops but more focused on the individual character sketch, too; this seems to becoming much more popular.

A: Yeah, I think so. You know Jon is a friend and a colleague of mine, he's a friend and a colleague that I value and respect very much, and we both come out of this background of being magazine journalists. Making a living writing for what, impolitically, would be called slick magazines like *Outside*. And we both did that because we had to make a living as writers, but I think having to make a living is something of a salubrious dilemma. You know, shared in the past by such good role models as Shakespeare and Leonardo da Vinci. And one of the salubrious things about having cut your teeth in magazine writing is that you're likely to have written profiles. Little, mini-biographies, where you're sent out to follow an eminent biologist or a famous athlete and to spend three or four or five or ten days with this person and then write a character study. Jon Krakauer and I and others who work in magazines have, I think, benefited from that kind of on-the-job training in terms of having a desire and maybe a certain knack for bringing human portraits into the stories.

Q: You are very conscientious of what form your writing takes. For instance, in the Author's Notes to both *The Flight of the Iguana* and *Natural Acts*, you point out that many of the included essays were written for magazines but that the potential of placing them in a book also affected how you wrote those pieces. In addition, you are quite aware of the role of your reading audience in your writing, and you have noted that you keep preeminently in mind your readers, whom you imagine as "an interesting and mentally vigorous group of folks." You mention in the Introduction to *The Boilerplate Rhino* that the readership of *Outside* magazine is about 500,000, and that "Most of those readers were people who neither knew nor cared much about the difference between a barnacle and a limpet, the difference between a meadow and a savanna, the difference between an ecosystem and 'the environment.'" You also discuss the relationship between yourself as a writer and the audience, stating that "I loved the particular audience to which *Outside* gave me access" and that your writing holds "conversations" with readers. "Good writing," you suggest, "sounds like talk, not oratory." We're very interested in audiences of nature writing—both conventional and unconventional. When you sit down to write, in what ways do you envision your audience? That is, can you in any way pinpoint how it is that you have managed to write so successfully to an audience that, in your own words, doesn't know much or seem to care about the topics of your prose?

A: Well, I can say one very specific and heartfelt thing about the way in which I think about the audience. I think about audience in the second person singular. And I frequently write in the second person. I say, "*you*, the reader, the book that *you* hold in your hands, whether *you* care about this or not," and address the reader that way. The English language does not happen to, unfortunately, distinguish between second person singular and second person plural. Except in the south where it's "y'all." But up here we Yankees don't have any way of distinguishing between talking to *you*, one person, and *you*, 500,000 people. But, when I think about the reader, and when I use the second person, I'm thinking about talking to one person. I'm thinking about a conversation in a quiet room. A room quiet enough for someone to be reading, but instead of one person reading there's two people: a writer talking to a reader. And listening carefully—but in a sense always futilely—for the reader to say something back, for the reader to respond. And I care very much about the relationship with the readers. I feel that one of the most important parts of my job is not just to talk to the reader in a companionable, conversational tone, but to think about, wonder about, and imagine what the reader is thinking, where the reader is, what the reader wants, whether the reader is bored or lost or confused. Whether the reader wants a joke now, or just a clear, straightforward explanation of something that I've mentioned. So, it's a big part of the writing process for me to think about the reader, to imagine the reader at all moments, and to work hard with every paragraph to try to bring the reader along and keep the reader connected.

Q: One of the overriding agendas of this book is to explore the relationships between writing and nature, and to some extent, we've begun to discuss those relationships. But, let us ask more directly, do you see a relationship strictly between writing and nature? That is, when you write about nature do you consider that you may actually be "writing nature"? Do writers construct nature? And, what effect does nature and/or environment have on writing?

A: Well, nature is a dauntingly difficult word to define. So, I won't say flat out that I don't feel like I'm constructing nature. I think, in the Introduction to the new book from Houghton-Mifflin, *The Best American Science and Nature Writing* (2000), I say something—at the beginning of that Introduction—about how nature is not just things that are green or furry and grow and reproduce. Nature is—and this is obvious—nature is also the physical universe. You can't say that a high-rise housing project on the South Side of Chicago is not nature. It certainly is. And human history, human behavior, as I say there, is a subset of primate behavior, which is a subset of biology, which is a subset of nature. But when I write I don't think of it as constructing nature, I think of it as constructing culture, constructing very conscious acts of communication, literary artifacts. And I'm not even positive I understand exactly what you mean by the proposition that a writer is constructing nature. Except maybe in the postmodern sense of *constructing*—constructing and deconstructing—and I tend to be sort of tone deaf in that realm of discourse.

Q: That's essentially what we are getting at. Along the same lines, does it worry you that your readers might only have access to these environments through your writings and through the pictures and other writings in nature magazines, that it constructs for them some particular portrait of nature.

A: Well, I'm very worried that many people out there only have access to nature through electronic media. Through film and video and documentaries on TV, and also related to that is the concern that a lot of people only have access to nature in the form of zoos. Both of those things—videos and documentaries about the natural world and zoos—have their merits but they also have their dangers, their pernicious effects. I've written about that in one or two essays, I think, including the one titled "The White Tigers of Cincinnati," where I go after zoos. And I suppose the title piece in *The Boilerplate Rhino* is also on that track.

Q: We actually have another question about that. In your essay "The Boilerplate Rhino," you write, "You can pick out a handful of rare and prodigious species, tote them home in your grocery bag or brief case. . . . Obviously I'm not talking about the flesh-and-blood creatures but about what passes in our age for the phenomenological equivalent: their images, expertly captured, potently edited, and preserved with the permanence of plastic, which surpasses the permanence of life." We now don't even need to go to the video store; cable companies often include in their standard packages both *The Nature Channel* and *Animal Planet*. Thus, nature has become "popular," a source of entertainment in the home, not outside of it. These images can misguide understandings of nature, but does this proliferation of images in any way actually help insulate nature from the dangers of overvisiting, overcrowding, and over-exposure by the human presence? That is, can the simulation of nature actually protect the real thing?

A: Well, certainly they have a benefit. They have various benefits includ-ing the ones you mentioned. There is a danger of overvisiting and over-crowding in some of the most fragile corners of the natural world. There is the factor of needing to recruit a constituency for these places and these creatures, and reaching out to people who are never going to have the chance to get on a plane to Central Africa and go walking through the Congo Basin. And so it's good if magazines and TV documentaries and radio enterprises—like the thing that Alex Chadwick does on NPR, the radio expeditions series—do what they do. It's good if those things bring people into awareness of and appreciation of these wondrous places and creatures. Absolutely. And zoos, of course, serve to a certain degree that function, too. But there are also these very definite dangers. There's the danger that because people have seen a certain place or a certain creature portrayed on the *Discovery Channel* they think, "That's fine, that creature's out there; that creature exists." When, in fact, that habitat may be in the process of being bulldozed away while people sit in their living rooms and watch the flamingoes and the cranes feeding in their great piece of habitat. Another danger that exists is that skillfully made video documentaries persuade people that there's something happening all the time. That there is a great level of drama and a great ease of seeing wondrous creatures. For instance, in tropical rain forests. It's really an extreme version of the way that art focuses and belies the lack of focus and the mundane tedium of most of the real world. What I mean by that is, as I'm sure you well know, if you go to a natural rain forest, if you go to the Amazon or to the Congo Basin and walk through a pristine stretch of forest, you will not see monkeys except very rarely at a distance. If you work hard at it. You will not see birds. You will not see snakes eating chicks out of their nests. The wildlife in a tropical forest is really sparse, far between, and difficult to see. When you get the video version everything is right there, in your face—reproductive activity, predatory activity, drama. Because all of the nine hundred and ninety-nine points out of a thousand that are boredom and waiting have been edited out. It sort of spoils people and gives them a false sense of what exists and what can be expected from those places.

Q: You've been writing for *Outside* magazine for some time now, as well as for other magazines. *Outside* is one of many magazines that reach audiences interested in interactions with nature: *Outdoors, Field and Stream, Sports Afield, Florida Sportsman,* and countless others that are subject specific to hunting, fishing, skiing, boating, camping, kayaking, and so on. In addition, there are many magazines that explore human relationships with nature from a more scientific or natural historical approach: *Audubon, National Geographic, Scientific American,* and so on. Why do you suppose the outdoor/nature magazine is so popular? That is, is there something about the magazine essay that makes it accessible as a genre? Follow up: Does the popularity of these kinds of magazines also suggest something about the corporatization and capitalization of nature?

A: Yes, I'm sure they do. I'm a little bit more concerned about the mercantilization of travel than the mercantilization of nature itself that those magazines represent, because we as a species are traveling more and more. There are more human air miles being flown every year by a large margin; I'm not sure what that margin is, but I know there is a boom there, and that leads toward . . . well, it's good in the sense that ecotourism is the last resort of every conservation project and every conservation situation around the world. How to save a particular species or a particular habitat against the economic pressures that are exerted on it? Everybody always says, "Oh, ecotourism," and it does work in certain places. It doesn't work in other places, and it probably causes harm in still other places. But still it's being promoted by magazines like those you mentioned, including those which I write for and feel that ambivalence about each time I do, or each time I receive my own copy of one of those magazines. I guess that's true of nature, too, and it's part of this difficult bargain, the reality of six billion people on this planet and eleven billion people projected to be on this planet 100 or 125 years from now when perhaps the population peaks. There is just not any vestige of the natural world that's going to survive on this planet unless it has economic justification as well as legislative protection. And so the race is on to see how we can perhaps reach some sort of arrangement that brings about a balance and allows people to feed their children, allows economic activity to continue, allows this garish population increase to continue to its peaking point, and yet allows a few wild places, maybe, to survive.

Q: Again, from *The Boilerplate Rhino,* you mention in this same introduction that you wanted to "depart distantly from conventional nature writing, of which I have never much cared to be either a reader or an author. The editors [of *Outside*], for their part, didn't want conventional nature writing either—no sensitive descriptions of wildflowers or babbling brooks . . . no hushed piety in the presence of Mr. Woodchuck and Mrs. Deer. They let me monger scandal about the secret life of spoon worms. They let me say tasteless things about bedbugs. They let me digress into history and culture." You write here a slightly sarcastic description of "nature writing"; is nature—or natural environments—burdened in any way by these stereotypical, sensitive understandings of writing about nature?

A: Well, I don't think the natural world is burdened by misunderstandings. I think the world of readers is burdened. It doesn't hurt any of those meadows or any of those deer to have people speaking sweetly and without edge and without irony and, to me, without much interest about them. But . . . except in a sense that trees die to make paper. But it's, I think, unfair to readers out there, particularly unfair to that group of readers who care about landscape, who care about the natural world, but who just have no tolerance for writing that is sweet and pious and righteous and curious and—in the sense that it's gentle writing about the natural world—therefore it *must* be good and valuable and even holy. No. Those more demanding or more acerbic readers deserve to be served by nature writing that recognizes their own sorts of critical capacity.

Q: A good deal of your writing could be characterized as retreat narrative, writing that you produce while wandering into and about wild places. That is, you go places and write about those places. Do the places in which you write affect how you write?

A: That's an interesting question, and I don't know exactly how to answer it. I mean, I'm sure the answer is yes but beyond that I don't know what to say.

Q: Let us add to it a little bit to maybe clear it up. Do the attitudes you see toward nature in various places affect or change your own attitude toward nature, and in turn, affect what you write about?

A: Well, I travel enough to see a lot of different surfaces, a lot of different pieces of the surface of this planet. And one effect of that is that it increasingly makes me a pessimist as to how much of the natural world and how many wild places we're going to be able to save. I'm not despairing, because despair is an emotional response, and pessimism is an intellectual response. But I don't believe that the prospects at this point are very good for us to save very much for very many more generations. I don't harp on that fact because I don't think it's useful for people to give up. I think that even if the cards are stacked against the prospect of conserving much in terms of biological diversity for the next 100 or 200 years, still there's no enterprise on earth that's more important, more worth trying. I think that—changing gears slightly—the places that I travel to are as much a *reflection* of my interests, and my beliefs about what is important, as they are factors that *shape* those tastes and beliefs. To a great degree I choose where I'm going to go, and I go there because I think that I really will be interested in finding out about brown bears in the Carpathian Mountains in Romania or about the state of the forests in the Congo Basin. It's not like I am an employed journalist who is sent to places and then has epiphanies of necessity when I'm in this or that place at the dictation of my editor with his cigar and his green eyeshade at his home office.

Q: Let us shift gears a little bit here. One of the clichéd responses given when discerning between humans and nature is that language is the thing that sets us apart from nature. In "Talk is Cheap" you write about Washoe and a few other chimpanzees who learned American Sign Language and you theorize as to what makes a person a person. That is, you ask important questions about the separation of person from nature. You write of people's perceptions of these "talking" chimps that "some people said at the time—and a few might still say—that by crossing the language barrier Washoe had irreversibly blurred the boundary between her species and ours." This notion of bringing language to nonhuman realms, be they natural or artificial, has long been a subject of interest for authors and philosophers. Writers such as Isaac Asimov have addressed anointing artificial intelligent beings with the label *person*. What are the ramifications of anthropomorphizing to the point of making the nonhuman into person?

A: Well, anthropomorphizing is a danger, but it's also a form of metaphor, and writers depend on metaphor. Scientists hate anthropomorphizing, biologists hate anthropomorphizing, and they're always hard on science journalists when we commit anthropomorphizing. But that's because science hates metaphor, and science has reasons to hate metaphor and it needs to. It's something that lies outside of the rules of science and the dimension of science. But it's very much within the rules and the dimension of the literary enterprise. So as far as I'm concerned, writers don't need to apologize for anthropomorphizing per se. It's a form of metaphor. But it can go beyond that, and people can sentimentalize other creatures and can become blurry in their thinking about other creatures. And rather than follow that thought out much further, I want to jump sideways and say something about language. I think that it's arguable that language is a categorical distinction between humans and other species. I mean, obviously written language is. Spoken language, no, because there's all sorts of communication between individuals of other species. I don't think it's really very important whether or not other species can acquire language in a human sense. What I do think is important and was trying to get out in that piece about Washoe is the extension of the concept of personhood. I don't think it constitutes dangerous anthropomorphizing to contemplate the personhood or the potential for being recognized as a *person* in other creatures. I think that that word is a bigger and more resonant word. So by saying that Washoe was a person, we're not blurring the lines between *Homo sapiens* and . . . what's the species of chimpanzee . . . *Pan troglodytes*? We're just saying that the concept *person* suggests a value, a fullness of physical and psychological life, a potential for being interacted with that shouldn't be completely limited to *Homo sapiens*.

Q: You write in the Introduction to *Natural Acts: A Sidelong View of Science and Nature* that "My ambition has been to offer some small moments of constructive disorientation in the way nature is seen and thought about. Along the way I have been drawn in particular toward certain creatures that are conventionally judged repulsive, certain places that are conventionally judged desolate, certain humans and ideas that are conventionally judged crazy." Could you elaborate more on your ideas of "constructive disorientation"?

A: I think that one of the worst offenses any writer can commit is to be predictable and boring. Piety is another bad offense. So that one of a writer's most important tools is surprise, is bringing in the unexpected. To some extent that means bringing in content that is unexpected, and to some extent that means presentation, juxtaposition, a combination of things that are unexpected. And that's what I mean by *constructive disorientation*. During the whole time that I was doing my column for *Outside* magazine, I thought that part of my job was to make connections between things that other people hadn't seen as connected or hadn't appreciated as connected. By putting together certain facts, certain people, certain historical events, certain ideas, certain creatures, with other elements that seemed unrelated, you could generate some insight, some new ways of seeing the world and of seeing particular parts of the world. And that's what I mean by constructive disorientation.

Q: After graduate school in English, you gave up the expected continuation of a Ph.D. and ultimately of becoming a professor of English. Contemporary English departments are seeing a growing interest in ecological literacy, ecocriticism, and nature writing—your work, in fact, is being taught in English classrooms as literature, nature writing, and ecological literature. You also often use literary analogy in making your arguments ("The Siphuncle," for instance). As one who gave up on the academic life but whose work is part of academic work, do you see a role for ecological literature in contemporary English departments? What about in writing classrooms specifically?

A: I do. I mean I'm openly surprised that there are hearty and persistent groups of you guys out there who are saying, "Let's use landscape nonfiction, let's use nature writing, let's use literary ecological exposition, whatever you want to call it. Let's use that in classrooms that are devoted mostly to helping people learn to use and savor the English language." To me it's completely unexpected. I think it's great. I think it's certainly good for writers to be blessed with that kind of close reading and that kind of scrutiny, and I think it's really good for the students to be exposed to factual content as well as careful, graceful prose. To get beyond the notion that you have to go to fiction and poetry to find careful, graceful, musical, satisfying prose.

Q: That answer in some ways references English departments and literature classes in general. How would you respond to that same question about a classroom designed to teach writing specifically?

A: The teaching of writing has always been a big mystery to me. To me, it's sort of metaphysical, and I view it from the disposition, from the viewpoint essentially of a materialist. An agnostic materialist. So, if it can be done, if you guys can do it, great. I don't know how. I don't want to try. But I wish you well (laughter).

I do want to note too that my life as a writer has been pretty much shaped by that fact that in 1966 I went off to Yale to study English, wanting to be a writer, and came under the wing of Robert Penn Warren. One of the main reasons I went to Yale was because a brilliant Jesuit who had taught me in high school told me that I should not just think of going to Jesuit colleges, but maybe I should think about this place called Yale, sort of thought of as a "pagan university." I asked, "Why?" and he said because it's got a great English department. When I asked, "What's so great about it?" he said, "Well, Penn Warren is there for one thing." And I asked, "Who's Penn Warren?" And then he explained to me. And I started reading Robert Penn Warren and eventually took a class from him and got to know him very well and became his protége to a certain degree. I lived with his family in Vermont, and he helped me get my first book published. He was the great shaping teacher/mentor in my life, or one of the two. He and this Jesuit. And one of the things that I learned from him, not because he told me this, but by example, is that a writer doesn't have to be only one kind of writer. Warren had won a couple of Pulitzers, one for fiction for *All the King's Men*, one or maybe two, I can't recall, for poetry. He had written social criticism; he had written history, biography, and he had written essays. And that was an inspiration to me that sort of gave me permission to turn into a magazine science journalist when I had started out very consciously as a literary guy who wanted to write novels. To do various sorts of writing and *combine* various sorts of writing, sometimes in the same short piece, I suppose. I can't overstate the importance that spending time at the elbow of Robert Penn Warren had on me.

Q: In the Introduction to *The Flight of the Iguana*, you write that frequently humans look at various organisms and view them as oddities, more as freaks than as natural. You write, "If we ourselves can fathom them only in the context of carnival canvas and hootchy-kootchy music, the problem is probably our own." You go on to say that "One name for that problem is xenophobia: fear or hatred of what is foreign or strange. The term is applied most often in connection with attitudes toward folk of the wrong skin color, but it's applicable also to non-human characters with the wrong number of legs or eyes, the wrong shape of face or jaws, the wrong sexual or alimentary deportment." Scholars, such as Robert Bullard in his book *Dumping in Dixie*, argue that the same ideologies that oppress peoples of color and other groups are the same sorts of

ideologies that oppress and abuse nature. It would seem that the xenophobia toward organisms that you discuss suggests a larger intolerance of
difference. Do you see a relationship between, say, speciesism and racism?

A: Oh, I see some relation but I agree with your premise or your hypothesis that this reaction to strange creatures is even larger than racism. I
don't know exactly where it comes from, maybe it's a natural human
instinct, but just the whole tendency to squeal and cringe when you see
something that has the wrong number of legs and the wrong number of
eyes. Ed Wilson has written about this in *Biophilia* and other places, and
I've written about it and about him writing about it, in one or two essays.
I have admitted, as he has admitted, that each of us is an arachnophobe
with that same cringe response to something that has the wrong number
of legs and the wrong number of eyes. Mainly eight of the former and
more than two of the latter. Why do humans do that? Even humans who
are sort of liberal in disposition and would like to think that they don't
judge people by the color of their skin. It's related but not synonymous.
I don't think one is just an extension of the other. I think this xenophobia
in terms of other creatures, and particularly creatures that are not easily
sentimentalized, with two legs or four legs, brown eyes, feathers or fur.
That kind of human xenophobia or speciesism is really deep and complicated, and it's something that we should keep thinking about and researching and wondering about. Any human who walks through a swamp and
comes out on the far side and finds that he or she may have a leech on his
or her crotch is going to manifest more than a rational level of annoyance.
And why? I don't know. But I think it's an important question.

Q: Let us follow up on that. In that same Introduction you also write that
"almost nothing bears more crucially upon the future of this planet than
the seemingly simple matter of human attitudes toward nature." Similarly, you have asked in "The Face of a Spider," "How should a human
behave toward the members of other living species?" It is interesting that
you should frame this question both in behavioral terms and as attitudi-
nal. Of course, you are speaking of human action toward nature, but
we're also curious as to how you might answer the question, "How should
a human think about the members of other living species." That is, is our
relationship with other species epistemological? And what might that
epistemology be?

A: I once sat with Warren in his office, and I was supposed to do a long
paper for a course I was taking from him on a given author and a given

subject, and I said that I wanted to write about Faulkner's epistemology. He kind of scrunched his jaw and said, "Hmm. It's a big word. Let's talk about what it means." So . . . I think that I know what that word means, but I want to be careful in answering this. I don't think it is [epistemological]. I don't think we have *an* attitude toward nature. I think we have a whole panoply or spectrum of probably sociobiologically influenced *reactions* toward different *aspects* of the natural world. I think there are researchers who have gone some way toward establishing that, for instance, humans feel very soothed, very comforted, very positive, when they gaze out on a savanna-like landscape from a slightly elevated viewpoint. When they gaze out from their trophy house across grass with a scattering of trees in it, then they feel great. And if they gaze out across a frozen arctic landscape, somewhere around the tree line at 12,000 or 13,000 feet, then they might feel awestruck, but they won't feel comfortable in the same way. They'll feel inspired but at the same time menaced and scared and just a little bit chilly. And if they gaze into thick rain forest on all sides of them, most people will have a different response. If they gaze at a young grizzly bear, a cub-of-the-year grizzly, they'll have a very particular reaction. A big, full-grown sow grizzly with a snarl on her face, they'll have a very different reaction. I think all these things are to some degree pre-cultural and sociobiological. But there's just a whole variety of different reactions that package together to form something that can be labeled— but probably *shouldn't* be labeled—*a* reaction to nature.

Q: In "Swamp Odyssey," you make mention of some of your political activism in the 1960s and early 1970s. Are you politically active now? Is your writing—or any writing, for that matter—a form of activism?

A: Oh, yes. I certainly hope so. I would like to believe that most if not all of my writing is a form of (a) entertainment and (b) conservation activism, and I suppose (c) teaching. That is, I suppose, a lot to claim. That's my hope, it's not necessarily my assertion. But yeah. I believe that, even when writing is not delivering a polemic or even a clear but subordinate conservation message, I think that it's a form of activism to write about the natural world in a way that makes people say, "Hey this stuff is interesting; this stuff is valuable. Let's continue to have that around."

Q: One final question for you. You write that when you stopped going to school, "trout were the indicator species for a place and a life I was seeking." You explain what you mean by this in "Synecdoche and the Trout." What would be your indicator species now?

A: Oh, right now I suppose an indicator species for the greatest concerns that I have and the things that I'm most interested in is the lowland gorilla in the Ogooué River Basin, where I've been spending some time and where I'll be going back in a couple of weeks. In particular, there is a forest called the Minkebe Forest, in eastern Gabon, where the habitat is still wonderful, it's filled with forest elephants; it's filled with ungulates, and it's nearly completely vacant of gorillas. And the question is why. And the answer seems to be—there is a *suspicion* that the answer is—that they died from Ebola virus at the same times as Ebola hit a number of human villages along the periphery of this big block of forest. This is kind of a complicated and roundabout answer, but I've really been thinking about this forest of missing gorillas a lot. I've written a piece recently for *National Geographic* and am writing three pieces in all about this part of the world. The second of those is focused mainly on this forest of missing gorillas. And the relationship between nonhuman primates, human population, and landscape conversion, and the increasingly menacing problem of emerging viral diseases. It's a really scary subject. I think it's a really important subject. And it's a subject I'm getting more and more interested in and seem to be devoting more and more of my time and energy to.

Natural Diversity

A Response to David Quammen

Christopher Schroeder

How strange, I thought, that I would be asked to respond to David Quammen, one of the nation's foremost nature writers, someone who in addition to winning an award from the American Academy of Arts and Letters, recently gave the Bradley Lecture on Darwin's *On the Origin of Species* at the Library of Congress. Though not antinature, I much prefer the concrete jungles of metropolitan New York where the theaters, restaurants, universities, and hospitals offset the obnoxious people and endless ribbons of traffic of urban life. Especially after reading *Deliverance* and watching *The Blair Witch Project*, I firmly believed that my distaste for nature was based not upon predilection and persuasion but upon empirical evidence. Green acres are not the place to be. City living is the life for me. Give me regular news, ethnic foods, *and* busy avenues.

So, I wasn't prepared to see Quammen argue that even a housing project on the South Side of Chicago is nature. (Could the clogged arteries of the Long Island Expressway (LIE), with its millions of cars, be nature, too?) Nature is the physical world, he insists, and suddenly, I find myself drawn across an ironic divide.[1] As you already know, Quammen is *writing nature* (not *nature writing*), as in foregrounding the presence of place and space in meaning. Such a move makes me think about how much the spaces I have occupied and the experiences I have had in them (e.g., moving from St. Louis to rural Illinois as a young child) have given rise to my perspectives on nature, as well as to every other belief that I have about the world, and how these figure significantly in what counts as legitimized meaning, naturalized meaning-making processes, and authorized forms of intellectual work in the places where I have some power, such as the classroom. Place figures significantly in the selves we construct and the narratives we tell ourselves to make sense of the world.

Place is also important to meaning, as meaning is contingent upon the meaning-maker's position in time and space. These positions—both diachronically, as in intellectual history, and synchronically, or cultural context—become important pieces in the interpretive puzzle. From my perspective, the argument over nature and civilization is less over the natural condition of the South Side of Chicago or the LIE and more over the belief that the physical world is always nature, which makes more sense when I can place Quammen (or any writer, for that matter) in a particular context, such as the one that this interview provides. Knowing, for instance, that many of the essays in his *The Flight of the Iguana* and *Natural Acts* were written with an awareness of "the potential for placing them in a book" even as they originally appeared in magazines leads me to read them differently.

Though disciplines like to pretend that knowledge and meaning can be removed from context, some of them, at least, have tacitly recognized the importance of place by institutionalizing research narratives within a section in the conventional genre form that recounts researchers' efforts to collect and interpret evidence and data even as these stories are often narrated in what Clifford Geertz has called author-evacuated prose. Feminists, such as Gesa Kirsch and others, however, have long advocated the importance of context for knowledge and meaning. As part of a larger movement in the academy toward alternative discourses,[2] the role of these narratives of place and experience is not to display personal events, as Victor Villanueva is careful to clarify ("Personal"), but to foreground what Daniel Mahala and Jody Swilky call the politics of location, or our relations to the communities, from families to disciplines and institutions, that have constructed and constrained us (379). Such narratives require an alternative discourse,[3] as it is never easy, if at all possible, to tell these stories in the argumentative discourse of the academy, which is based on a monologic model of discourse that legislates against the self-conscious shift from the conventional to the narrative.[4] Beyond a range of functions, from investigating the circulation of cultural capital in the bodily reactions to producing and consuming discourse as "material evidence" of the ways that culture is inscribed to establishing and maintaining relationships between researchers and participants through "self-reflection and active nostalgia" and " 'problematizing the existential' " with critical autobiography,[5] these narratives and other alternative discursive practices can provide an escape from the alienation of academic discourse by disrupting traditional literacies and cultures in the academy and authorizing new ones. As avant-garde academic writers continue to explore the interrelations between narrative and conventional discursive practices, they will generate what Quammen and his interviewers call "hybrid" texts although *hybridity*, like *nature* and *civilization*, are often in the eye of the beholder. Given this contingency and other problems with the notion of hybrid texts that Patricia Bizzell ("Basic") and Sid Dobrin ("Problem") examine, the term that I prefer is *constructed*, as this designation foregrounds the ways that these linguistic collages are assembled from different discourses and discursive practices, from the materials of the spaces and places inhabited by those who produce them.

Given my claims about contingency and context, I should reveal that I have argued for rereading what critics have called the contemporary crisis in literacy as part of larger crises in meaning and education in the United States that many, from bell hooks to Jean-François Lyotard, have critiqued. As part of these growing crises, literacy instruction has become increasingly decontextualized, a process that Jan Nespor has documented, in a way that authorizes purportedly context-free literacies that mask an enculturation that some, such as J. Elspeth Stuckey, have characterized as acts of violence. From the position that I have assumed, instruction in literacy amounts to imposing an illegitimate discourse and culture upon communities, an imposition that occurs, more often than not, in English departments. According to the best-selling textbooks in composition and literature, the cultural literacy of the academy consists of discursive practices based on elaborated syntactical and sequential relations, substantial amounts of new information, and truth values instead of rhetorical conditions. As being literate in a discourse amounts not only to mastering discursive practices but also assuming particular subject positions and demonstrating solidarity with particular metanarratives, the discursive practices of academic culture also authorize essentialized rational minds communicating with other objectified rational minds and a version of the world in which a completely accessible reality is entirely expressible in texts.[6]

Given the limitations of conventional academic cultural literacies, David Quammen's efforts "to mix types of literary strategy and different kinds of elements into a given piece" is, in part, an attempt to legitimize *constructed literacies*, or an agenda of self-consciously integrating different discursive practices.[7] By bringing together literary and nonliterary traditions, Quammen authorizes an alternative that goes beyond what his interviewers describe as blending "adventure stories and natural history writing" into "a great nonfiction story with fun characters and adventure," and even beyond what he justifies as merely a technique "to enliven what might otherwise be a dry, expository treatment of a scientific subject." Such moves are more than the attempt, which he cites, to appeal to shared human experience—"People like to read about other people. Even when they are engaged in reading about the natural world, or in reading about obscure scientific concepts, or great movements in history"—and they're definitely more than palliatives for a declining level of concentration in the U.S. American reading public. From the perspective I've described, such acts, themselves, are acts of cultural negotiation and intellectual work that authorize legitimate alternatives to the alienation of conventional academic literacies and discourse that academics—both minority and mainstream—encounter and that students experience.[8] In the example cited in the interview, Quammen's efforts to integrate competing discursive practices challenge two distinctly cultural traditions— European literary traditions with their shift from learning to taste and the rise of national identities and nature writing in the United States with its focus upon wilderness and the mythical symbolism of virgin land[9]—and that reconfigures these traditions in such a way as to offer a distinctly third position for readers and writers.

More than ever, these constructed alternatives are necessary in order to address the widespread cultural differences that exist within colleges and universities in the United States and to obviate the loss of the difference that occurs when critics misread these conditions as a crisis in literacy. Significantly, literacy crises and enrollment increases have coincided.[10] From the perspective I have described, such correlation suggests that critics declare a crisis in literacy rather than confront the crisis of legitimacy in academic culture brought on by the dramatically increased discursive and cultural differences. At the present, colleges and universities are immersed in another dramatic upsurge in enrollment. Between 1995 and 2015, the combined undergraduate enrollment in the United States will increase by 19 percent from 13.4 million to 16 million students, and in addition, more than 2 million of these additional students will be African American, Hispanic, and Asian Pacific Islander, thereby increasing the total number of minority students from 29.4 percent in 1995 to 37.2 percent in 2015 (ETS). Perhaps less obviously, the legitimacy of conventional academic literacies and cultures is suspect for students generally, even more so in this increasing era of difference in which conventional academic discourses, as Jackie Jones-Royster and Peter Elbow ("Vernacular") point out, are no one's mother tongue. At the same time, the legitimacy of conventional literacies is even more problematic for minority students, who will experience these literacies and cultures as hurdles to overcome or values to resist depending on, John Ogbu argues, whether they are voluntary (e.g., immigrant) or involuntary minorities.

Having a writer with the stature of David Quammen authorizing alternatives that bring together competing discursive practices and cultural traditions can only increase the chances that constructed literacies

will have an increasing legitimacy. There is some sense that constructing
literacies and negotiating cultures are more the norm than the exception,
at least outside the academy,[11] and even within the academy, constructed
literacies are consistent with post-process theories and practices of Thomas
Kent, Sid Dobrin, and others. Nevertheless, such a perspective represents
a substantial challenge to institutional practices. For example, colleges and
universities still labor under monologic models of discourse despite increasing criticism.[12] Simply exchanging monolithic models of discourse for more
dialogic models would require widespread change, including our standards
for assessment, the way that we respond to writing, and our models for
intellectual work, not to mention the kinds of discourse that we authorize
through our syllabi and assignments and the kinds of textuality that promotion and tenure committees regard as legitimate.

Although I hope the options available to David Quammen for making meaning will become available to more academics and students, I
recognize that substantial institutional and political changes must occur
before such discursive practices are seen as legitimate. Nevertheless, there
is a growing awareness of difference in the professional discourse of academics—both their conference presentations and their scholarly writing[13]—and several recent collections of essays—*Alternative Rhetorics*
(Gray-Rosendale and Gruber), *Elements of Alternate Style* (Bishop), and
ALT DIS: Alternative Discourses in the Academy (Schroeder, Fox, and
Bizzell)—have begun to legitimize the discursive hybridity that the interviewers cite in their conversation with Quammen. More to the concerns
I've outlined here, discursive hybridity and constructed literacies not only
serve the increasing diversity within academic institutions but also could
make intellectual work more engaging, and the irony in being asked to
respond to a nature writer writing nature is that discursive and cultural
differences depend on differences in place—rural and urban, country and
city, and all of the spaces in between. We city mice who define going
natural as a long subway ride to the Bronx zoo nonetheless need our
country cousins who prefer traveling to the Carpathian Mountains of
Romania or the forests in the Congo Basin (interview). Together, we can
teach each other what it means to write nature. And such an environment would be a natural world to which I'd want to belong.[14]

NOTES

   1. Nevertheless, Quammen seems to invoke the pervasive nature-civilization binary later in the conversation when he dismisses the "pernicious effects" of nature films,

videos, documentaries, and zoos, which for many who live in the housing project on the South Side of Chicago and elsewhere, are the physical world.

2. For experiments in language studies, see Brodkey, Foss, Fox, Gilyard, Rodriguez, Rose, Villanueva (*Bootstraps*), and many of the essays in collections edited by Bishop, Gray-Rosendale and Gruber, and Schroeder, Fox, and Bizzell, and for experiments outside of language studies, see Cochran-Smith (Education), Johnson (Comparative Literature), Thaiss and Zawacki (various disciplines), and Williamson (History). For more theoretical considerations of these alternatives, see Bizzell ("Hybrid"), Bridwell-Bowles, Elbow, Gale, Lyons, Owens, Schroeder, and other essays in Bishop, Gray-Rosendale and Gruber, and Schroeder, Fox, and Bizzell.

3. See Schroeder ("From"), as well as Miller.

4. See also, Bizzell ("Basic") and Dobrin.

5. See Miller and Brandt et al.

6. The cultural literacies of the academy are essayist literacies, as Faigley and others have also argued. In describing the cultural literacies in this way, I have drawn extensively from Scollon and Scollon (41ff.). For more on English departments and the history of literacy instruction in U.S. colleges and universities and for an extended discourse analysis of best-selling textbooks in literature and composition, see Schroeder (*ReInventing* 39ff.).

7. See Schroeder (*ReInventing* 126ff.).

8. Much has been written about the alienation of minority intellectuals (e.g., Gilyard, Villanueva, and Rodriguez). For more on the alienation of mainstream intellectuals, see, for example, Brodkey, Elbow ("Illiteracy"), Foss, Miller, and Schroeder (*ReInventing*). For more on the alienation of students, see Chiseri-Strater's ethnography of students at the University of Rhode Island.

9. See Williams (45ff.) and Rea (760).

10. See, for example, Russell (35) and Hourigan (3 ff).

11. See, for example, Duranti and Ochs.

12. See, for example, Bizzell ("Basic"), Dobrin ("Problem"), Farmer, Gale, Schroeder ("From"), Schuster, Villanueva ("Personal"), and Ward.

13. See, for instance, Johnstone (59ff.) and Thaiss and Zawacki.

14. I thank Sid Dobrin and Chris Keller for the opportunity to respond to David Quammen's comments about hybrid texts, and I thank Edmund Miller for his feedback on this response. Many of these ideas also appear in Schroeder, "Academic," "From," and *ReInventing*.

WORKS CITED

Bishop, Wendy, ed. *Elements of Alternate Style: Essays on Writing and Revision*. Portsmouth, NH: Boynton/Cook Publishers, 1997.

Bizzell, Patricia. "Basic Writing and the Issue of Correctness, or, What to Do With 'Mixed' Forms of Academic Discourse." *Journal of Basic Writing* 19.1 (2000): 4–12.

———. "Hybrid Discourses: What, Why, How." *Composition Studies* 27 (1999): 7–21.

Brandt, Deborah, Ellen Cushman, Anne Ruggles Gere, Anne Herrington, Richard E. Miller, Victor Villanueva, Min-Zhan Lu, and Gesa Kirsch. "The Politics of the Personal: Storying Our Lives against the Grain." *College English* 64.1 (2001): 41–62.

Bridwell-Bowles, Lillian. "Discourse and Diversity: Experimental Writing within the Academy." *College Composition and Communication* 43 (1992): 349–68.

Brodkey, Linda. "Writing on the Bias." *College English* 56.5 (1994): 527–47.

Chiseri-Strater, Elizabeth. *Academic Literacies: The Public and Private Discourse of University Students.* Portsmouth, NH: Heinemann-Boynton/Cook, 1991.

Cochran-Smith, Marilyn. "Blind Vision: Unlearning Racism in Teacher Education." *Harvard Educational Review* 7 (2000): 157–90.

de Certeau, Michel. *The Practice of Everyday Life.* Berkeley: U of California P, 1984.

Dobrin, Sidney, I. *Constructing Knowledges: The Politics of Theory-Building and Pedagogy in Composition.* Albany: State U of New York P, 1997.

———. "A Problem with Writing (About) 'Alternative' Discourse." *ALT DIS: Alternative Discourses and the Academy.* Ed. Christopher Schroeder, Helen Fox, and Patricia Bizzell. Portsmouth, NH: Heinemann-Boynton/Cook, 2002.

Duranti, Alessandro, and Elinor Ochs. "Syncretic Literacy: Multiculturalism in Samoan American Families." *Research Report 16.* Santa Cruz, CA: National Center for Research on Cultural Diversity and Second Language Learning, 1997. 1–15.

Elbow, Peter. "Illiteracy at Oxford and Harvard." *Essays toward a Hopeful Theory of Writing and Teaching Writing.* New York: Oxford UP, 2000. 5–27.

———. "Inviting the Mother Tongue: Beyond 'Mistakes,' 'Bad English,' and 'Wrong Language.' " *Essays toward a Hopeful Theory of Writing and Teaching Writing.* New York: Oxford UP, 2000. 323–50.

———. "Vernacular Rhetorics and Grammars in Teaching Writing: Probing the Culture of Literacy." *ALT DIS: Alternative Discourses and the Academy.* Ed. Christopher Schroeder, Helen Fox, and Patricia Bizzell. Portsmouth, NH: Heinemann-Boynton/Cook, 2002.

ETS. "Soaring Number of Qualified Minority Students Poised to Enter College." 18 May 2001. <http://www.ets.org/textonly/aboutets/news/00052401.html>.

Faigley, Lester. "Going Electronic: Creating Multiple Sites for Innovation in a Writing Program." *Resituating Writing: Constructing and Administering Writing Programs.* Ed. Joseph Janangelo and Kristine Hansen. Portsmouth, NH: Boynton/Cook, 1995. 46–58.

Farmer, Frank, ed. *Landmark Essays on Bakhtin, Rhetoric, and Writing.* Mahwah, NJ: Hermagoras Press, 1998.

Foss, Megan. "Love Letters." *Creative Nonfiction* 9 (1998): 13–33.

Fox, Helen. *Listening to the World: Cultural Issues in Academic Writing.* Urbana, IL: National Council of Teachers of English, 1994.

Gale, Xin Liu. *Teachers, Discourses, and Authority in the Postmodern Composition Classroom.* Albany: State U of New York P, 1996.

Gee, James Paul. *Social Linguistics and Literacies: Ideologies in Discourses.* 2nd ed. London: Falmer Press, 1996.

Geertz, Clifford. *Works and Lives: The Anthropologist as Author*. Stanford: Stanford UP, 1988.

Gilyard, Keith. *Voices of the Self: A Study of Language Competence*. Detroit: Wayne State UP, 1991.

Gray-Rosendale, Laura, and Sibylle Gruber, eds. *Alternative Rhetorics: Challenges to the Rhetorical Tradition*. Albany: State U of New York P, 2001.

Hindman, Jane E. "Making Writing Matter: Using 'the Personal' to Recover[y] an Essential[ist] Tension in Academic Discourse." *College English* 64.1 (2001): 88–108.

———. "Special Focus: Personal Writing." *College English* 64.1 (2001): 34–40.

Hourigan, Maureen. *Literacy as Social Exchange: Intersections of Class, Gender, and Culture*. Albany: State U of New York P, 1994.

Johnson, Lemuel. 22 Aug. 2000 <http://www.westafrica review.com/war/vol1.2/vol1.2a/lemuel.html>.

Johnstone, Barbara. *The Linguistic Individual: Self-Expression in Language and Linguistics*. New York: Oxford UP, 1996.

Jones-Royster, Jacqueline. "Academic Discourses or Small Boats in Big Seas." *ALT DIS: Alternative Discourses and the Academy*. Ed. Christopher Schroeder, Helen Fox, and Patricia Bizzell. Portsmouth, NH: Heinemann-Boynton/Cook, 2002.

Kent, Thomas. *Paralogic Rhetoric: A Theory of Communicative Interaction*. Cranbury, NJ: Associated UP, 1993.

Kirsch, Gesa. *Ethical Dilemmas in Feminist Research: The Politics of Location, Interpretation, and Publication*. Albany: State U of New York P, 1999.

———. *Women Writing the Academy: Audience, Authority, and Transformation*. Carbondale: Southern Illinois UP, 1993.

Lyons, Scott. "A Captivity Narrative: Indians, Mixedbloods, and the 'White' Academy." *Outbursts in Academe: Multiculturalism and Other Sources of Conflict*. Ed. Kathleen Dixon, William Archibald, and Jane Varley. Portsmouth, NH: Heinemann, 1998. 87–108.

Lyotard, Jean-François. *The Postmodern Condition: A Report on Knowledge*. Minneapolis: U of Minnesota P, 1984.

Mahala, Daniel, and Jody Swilky. "Telling Stories, Speaking Personally: Reconsidering the Place of Lived Experience in Composition." *JAC: A Journal of Composition Theory* 16.3 (1996): 363–88.

Miller, Richard E. "The Nervous System." *College English* 58.3 (1996): 265–86.

Nespor, Jan. "The Construction of School Knowledge: A Case Study." *Rewriting Literacy: Culture and the Discourse of the Other*. Ed. Candace Mitchell and Kathleen Weiler. Westport, CT: Bergin & Garvey, 1991. 169–88.

Ogbu, John U. "Minority Education in Comparative Perspective." *Journal of Negro Education* 59.1 (1990): 45–57.

Owens, Derek. "Composing as the Voicing of Multiple Fictions." *Into the Field: Sites of Composition Studies*. Ed. Anne Ruggles Gere. New York: Modern Language Association. 159–75.

Rea, Paul W. "Nature Writing in the U.S." *Benét's Reader's Encyclopedia of American Literature*. Ed. George Perkins, Barbara Perkins, and Phillip Leininger. New York: HarperCollins Publishers, 1991. 760.

Rodriguez, Richard. *Hunger of Memory: The Education of Richard Rodriguez*. New York: Bantam Books, 1982.

Rose, Mike. *Lives on the Boundary: A Moving Account of the Struggles and Achievements of America's Educational Underclass*. New York: Penguin, 1990.

Russell, David. "American Origins of Writing-Across-The-Curriculum Movement." In *Writing, Teaching, and Learning in the Disciplines*. Ed. Anne Herrington and Charles Moran. New York: Modern Language Association, 1992. 22–42.

Schroeder, Christopher. "Academic Literacies, Legitimacy Crises, and Electronic Cultures." *Journal of Literacy and Technology* 1.2 (2001): <www.literacyandtechnology.org>.

———. "From the Inside Out, or From the Outside In, Depending." *ALT DIS: Alternative Discourses and the Academy*. Ed. Christopher Schroeder, Helen Fox, and Patricia Bizzell. Portsmouth, NH: Heinemann-Boynton/Cook, 2002.

———. *ReInventing the University: Literacies and Legitimacy in the Postmodern Academy*. Logan: Utah State UP, 2001.

Schroeder, Christopher, Helen Fox, and Patricia Bizzell, eds. *ALT DIS: Alternative Discourses and the Academy*. Portsmouth, NH: Heinemann-Boynton/Cook, 2002.

Schuster, Charles I. "Makhail Bakhtin as Rhetorical Theorist." *College English* 47.6 (1985): 594–607.

Scollon, Ron, and Suzanne B. K. Scollon. *Narrative, Literacy, and Face in Interethnic Communication*. Norwood, NJ: Ablex, 1981.

Spigelman, Candace. "Argument and Evidence in the Case of the Personal." *College English* 64.1 (2001): 63–87.

Stuckey, J. Elspeth. *The Violence of Literacy*. Portsmouth, NH: Heinemann, 1992.

Thaiss, Christopher, and Terry Meyers Zawacki. "Questioning Alternative Discourse: Reports from across the Disciplines." *ALT DIS: Alternative Discourses and the Academy*. Ed. Christopher Schroeder, Helen Fox, and Patricia Bizzell. Portsmouth, NH: Heinemann-Boynton/Cook, 2002.

Villanueva, Victor. *Bootstraps: From an American Academic of Color*. Urbana, IL: National Council of Teachers of English, 1993.

———. "The Personal." *College English* 64.1 (2001): 50–52.

Ward, Irene. *Literacy, Ideology, and Dialogue: Toward a Dialogic Pedagogy*. Albany: State U of New York P, 1994.

Williams, Raymond. *Marxism and Literature*. Oxford: Oxford UP, 1977.

Williamson, Joel. "Wounds Not Scars: Lynching, the National Conscience, and the American Historian." *Journal of American History* 83 (1997): 1221–53.

Of Gardens and Classrooms, Plants and Discourse

A Response to David Quammen

Christopher J. Keller

> The garden has always been a place to experiment, to try out new hybrids and mutations. Species that never cross in the wild will freely hybridize on land cleared by people.
>
> —Michael Pollan, *The Botany of Desire*

I've always been intrigued and pleased to see scholars in composition studies—and scholars in the humanities in general—utilize concepts and terms that derive from what are often termed the "hard sciences." I find that we in composition and in the humanities too quickly shy away from—if not rebel outright against—the work done by those in these sciences, important work that could perhaps help and inform our own methodologies, theories, and pedagogies. In the Introduction to their edited collection *Ecocomposition*, Christian Weisser and Sid Dobrin suggest accurately that "only recently have compositionists begun to significantly inquire into scientific scholarship to inform work in their own discipline" (1). Ecocomposition, in particular, explores the interdisciplinary connections between composition studies and ecological studies. Such scholarship not only lays out some of the groundwork to open up other interdisciplinary conversations between composition and the sciences but also manifests the need to examine more thoroughly the connections that already exist, those that we rarely recognize or question as such.[1] I'm particularly excited and interested to see where all of composition's recent talk about *hybridity* will take the field in the long run.[2] Much work about hybridity in composition studies, however, might be complicated by a phrase Quammen uses in the interview above, a phrase he offers in lieu of hybridity—*synergy*. Many in composition and rhetoric often theorize and debate about hybridity but rarely provide enough terminological scrupulousness to this concept—a concept derived in large part from biology and the life sciences as well as a concept that developed as part of the vocabulary of scientific racism in the nineteenth century (see Young). That is, when composition studies borrows phrases such as *hybrid* and *hybridity* and applies them to the workings of discourse, I question whether these words' usages and meanings have been adequately theorized, and whether their original contexts have been thoroughly studied in order to avoid oversimplifying these difficult and complex terms. I do not wish here to offer Quammen's synergy as a simplistic solution to the dilemmas brought forth by hybridity but as a way to help us rethink our conversations and carve out new and fruitful directions.

It is also not my intention to turn this response into an etymological review of terms in the sciences, but it is necessary to take a closer look at the word hybridity, to look more closely at its places in the sciences, and then, perhaps, rethink the use of the word in composition studies. Biological encyclopedias and dictionaries consistently suggest that hybrid might best be defined as *a plant or animal that has been produced from two different types of plant or animal, especially to get better characteristics.* Such a definition might easily be transferred into composition studies to create theories of hybrid discourses and texts—types of discourse that have been produced from two different parent discourses, especially to get "better" characteristics than could have derived from either discourse by itself.

Patricia Bizzell defines hybrid academic discourses: "Previously non-academic discourses are blending with traditional academic discourses to form the new hybrids. These new discourses are still 'academic,' in that they are doing the intellectual work of the academy—rigorous, reflective scholarship. . . . they have combined elements of traditional academic discourse with elements of other ways of using language that are more comfortable for the new academics [non-male and non-white]" ("Hybrid" 11). Bizzell offers examples of hybrid discourse texts in her examination of *Lives on the Boundary* by Mike Rose, "an Italian American of working-class background," *Voices of the Self* by "African American Keith Gilyard," and *Bootstraps: From an American Academic of Color* by Victor Villanueva, a "Puerto Rican American." Importantly, for Bizzell, "None of these authors is a white male from the upper social classes . . . [which reflects] the relatively recent advent into the academy of people from more diverse communities" ("Hybrid" 12). This advent differs from the "upper-class white male paradigm" that has for so long constructed academic discourse.

Bizzell's version of hybrid academic discourse has responded to and facilitated important conversations in composition studies; importantly, she points out many of the deficiencies of traditional academic discourses while theorizing new forms of discourse production for both students and scholars. She contends, furthermore, that "a hybrid form [of discourse] that borrows from [two other discourses] is greater than the sum of its parts, accomplishing intellectual work that could not be done in either of the parent discourses alone" ("Hybrid" 13). Hybrid discourses for composition studies are those that disrupt traditional academic discourses to accomplish intellectual work that could not be achieved otherwise. Hybrid academic discourses in this sense, therefore, are new, experimental, disruptive, and innovative.

Bizzell clearly points out the immeasurable value of hybrid discourses, suggesting that they may include a nontraditional range of cultural references, variant forms of English, personal experiences, humor, indirection, and offhand refutation, just to name a few. Bizzell also offers ways that hybrid academic discourses can be taught in the composition classroom. Her goal is to "help students develop a range of experimental discourses. . . . I am encouraging a sort of craft-person attitude toward writing, in which various tools are developed and students learn to deploy them with greater facility" ("Hybrid" 20). Because there are few models on which students can base their experimental discourses, Bizzell suggests that instructors spend a lot of class time emphasizing process and revision. "It will not be easy for students to control such hybrid experiments," she argues, "and their texts will probably need a fair amount of revising; but the students will probably be able to go far beyond the usual, rush-to-closure 'this is my opinion.' In attempting to inter-weave rigorous responses to their reading and their own reflections, it could be said that they are devising a new version of the essay genre for the academic setting" ("Hybrid" 19). These pedagogical goals allow students to experiment, to get away from the traditional academic essay, and to connect experiences among a wide range of texts, therein allowing students to recognize the complexity and variety of argumentative positions.

In *Opening Spaces: Critical Pedagogy and Resistance Theory in Composition*, Joe Marshall Hardin to some extent follows Bizzell's lines of thought in discussing the importance of hybrid discourses in writing classrooms, but Hardin more specifically argues that hybrid discourses can pave the way for student resistance against hegemonic structures and for greater empowerment:

> The concept of hybridized discourse . . . is not about a mix of cultures; nor is it about a place where all ideas are magically given equal opportunity. Instead, it arises from the notion that it is hegemonic struggle itself that constitutes culture within the politics of a social democracy. Discourse, text, and rhetoric become sites where writers negotiate the spaces between their own values and the values of other writers in a way that exposes and critiques the power imbalances of that particular moment and space. . . . By concerning ourselves with teaching students to see that their own writing is an intervention into academic and cultural discourse that reconjugates that discourse and that participates actively in the hegemonic struggle that constitutes the culture of social democracy then we might finally give real meaning to the project to empower them. (112)

For Hardin, composition teachers and scholars must resist teaching and theorizing "fixity," the ways in which texts, discourses, and values are fixed and rigid—the ways they are naturalized. If teachers and students, that is, do not resist fixed discourses, they are unlikely to question received values and beliefs, therein accepting and spreading dominant and oppressive ideologies. Rather, Hardin contends, teachers and scholars of writing must commit to teaching "discourse and rhetoric that are open, available, malleable, interested, and endlessly political. . . . We are called upon more and more to address the seemingly irreconcilable goals of teaching students to critique and resist the unthinking acceptance of hegemonic values while at the same time providing them with the tools they need to succeed in the academy and in society" (113). Hardin's version of hybridity is less concerned with the construction of new and experimental texts per se than it is interested in the intervention and critique of old, hegemonic ones: "Each such intervention into discourse presences a new voice in the political din and forges a new hybrid text that rearticulates rhetoric in a new political space" (111).

Bizzell and Hardin each complicate the term hybridity for composition studies in meaningful, critical, and important ways, but the ways the term hybridity has been theorized in composition studies might be more problematic and less simplistic than accounted for here. My purpose is not to critique specifically how compositionists such as Bizzell and Hardin have used the (scientific?) term hybridity but to examine in more detail compositionists' uses and assumptions about hybridity in order to pinpoint some of the oversimplifications, pitfalls, suppositions, and difficulties associated with the word. In particular, if we in composition are to borrow terms from the sciences—and I believe that we should just as they in the sciences should be comfortable borrowing from us—we must not pretend that we can rip these terms out of their (scientific) contexts without looking closely at the problems these terms facilitate in their original contexts. In other words, the term hybridity raises a number of problems, issues, and concerns in the sciences that might be equally important and problematic in composition studies, issues and problems that perhaps follow hybridity as it moves from the sciences to composition studies.

The epigraph I use above from Michael Pollan's *Botany of Desire* provides an image of the garden as a space cultivated for experimentation, hybridity, and domesticity (the domestication of plants). The garden is a place cleared away by humans—deliberately—for experimentation and hybridity. Gardens are controlled places where pesticides and chemicals are used to protect the fruits and vegetables from predators and from the *wild*. The classroom too is an environment like the garden, an environment cleared away by instructors for the growing of discourse. In some cases, teachers, like gardeners, experiment and try to grow hybrids: new, experimental discourses. The word hybrid, however, brings with it connotations of *selective breeding,* a product grown and transformed by the crossbreeding of two parents. Hybrid discourse too appears to be a mixture of different parent discourses that produce a unique offspring. Hybrids are distinct from their parents, but we must remember that they are not completely novel; they still manifest traits of both parents. For composition studies, then, one cannot assume that theories and pedagogies of hybrid discourses are entirely revolutionary, critical, empowering, or radical. Bizzell suggests in "The Intellectual Work of 'Mixed' Forms of Academic Discourses," "The biological metaphor of hybridity implies that what mixes in the new forms . . . are two distinct 'parents,' that is, distinct, well-defined, and culturally independent linguistic and discursive practices. It is not at all clear that this is the case, however" (4). In most cases, in other words, parents—whether animals, plants, or discourses—are themselves some form of hybrid. Furthermore, though, we must keep in mind that hybrid experiments—whether in the classroom or the garden—are still *experiments*, often prone to failure as much as success: success, however, depends on social, political, and cultural ideals of *success*. Pollan writes about how to rethink cultural expectations of growth, "Like the other canonical flowers . . . the tulip has been reinvented [hybridized] every century or so to reflect our shifting ideals of beauty" (61). Hybridization no doubt is necessary for nature and humans to bring about newness and change. Compositionists, too, in their theories of hybrid discourses should not only consider deeply hybridity itself, but the purposes and goals behind this hybridity, this breeding. In the case of discourses, that is, equal attention must be given to the kind of intellectual work that these new discourses are supposed to accomplish. We should scrutinize the meaning of intellectual work as much as we scrutinize hybrid discourses.

No doubt, there are cautionary tales, dangers, and great complexities for hybridity in composition studies just as there are in the sciences. If we see the composition classroom as a space for experimentation of hybrid discourses, then we must realize that as instructors we play the role of cultivator. We are plowing fields, planting seeds, spraying pesticides, and harvesting crops. In his discussion of different potato hybrids, Michael Pollan reminds us that "Any given type of potato reflects the human desires that have been bred into it. One that's been selected to yield long, handsome french fries or unblemished, round potato chips is the expression of a national food chain and a culture that likes its potatoes highly processed" (195). Composition scholars and teachers are in a large sense controlling these experiments, no matter how much we like to think our students are experimenting on their own. We as composition teachers are selective breeders—those in control of this domestication process—in that we are introducing many of the discourses to our students that will, essentially, be bred, or hybridized. And the desire for hybridity is often rampant. Thus, we must be aware of the consequences of such experiments as well as recognize what is missing from our theories and pedagogies.

Compositionists might first ask whether attempts to have students hybridize, for example, *academic* and *home* discourses do not in some ways neutralize or domesticate some of these discourses. As Sidney I. Dobrin warns in "A Problem with Writing (about) 'Alternative' Discourse," "The very notion of hybrid discourses serves to fold all other 'parent' discourses into the hegemony and master narrative of academic discourse" (46). That is, rather than empowering students and their discourses through hybridization are we in composition not making them even more domesticated and controlled? And, second, by theorizing hybridity for composition studies, have we examined adequately one of the most crucial components in the outcome of hybridity: environment?

Pollan discusses the various hybridized forms of the apple in American history and the resulting consequences in American culture: "The domestication of the apple has gone too far, to the point where the species' fitness for life in nature (where it still has to live, after all) has been dangerously compromised. Reduced to a handful of genetically identical clones that suit our taste and agricultural practice, the apple has lost the crucial variability—the wildness—that sexual reproduction confers" (52). Many of the discourses and texts that compositionists ask students to experiment with in their writing may be considered wild in relation to traditional academic discourses. However, compositionists must wonder to what degree these discourses will lose this wild flavor once they are hybridized with traditional academic discourses and brought into the academy. Pollan contends, "To domesticate another species is to bring it under culture's roof" (56). In this case, we might argue that to hybridize discourses in the composition classroom is to domesticate them, and domestication here means bringing these discourses under the academy's roof.

Second, and related, many who theorize hybrid discourses do so without looking closely at the environments in which this hybridity takes place. In nineteenth-century America, Pollan shows, Americans conducted a vast experiment in hybrid apples:

> By planting so many apples from seed, Americans . . . conducted a vast evolutionary experiment, allowing the Old World apple to try out literally millions of new genetic combinations, and by doing so to adapt to the new environment in which the tree now found itself. Every time an apple failed to germinate or thrive in American soil, every time an American winter killed a tree or a freeze in May nipped its buds, an evolutionary vote was cast, and the apples that survived this great winnowing became ever so slightly more American. (44)

Apples that have become noted as the great American apples, such as the Red Delicious or the Granny Smith, are not *American* apples simply because Americans like them. Rather they became powerful symbols of America because they were hybridized experiments that turned out as such because of the American (natural) environments in which they were bred. Red Delicious and Granny Smith Apples could only have become what they are by being hybridized on American grounds—in specific environments.

Those interested in hybrid discourses should take account of the fact that discourses don't hybridize or clash in empty space. The resulting outcome of hybridization is determined in large part by the particular environments in which these experiments are conducted. Deepika Bahri writes, "If the concept of hybridity is useful in undoing binaries and approaching the complexities of transnationalism, as many would find in composition studies, I would warn that it tends to avoid the question of location because it suggests a zone of nowhere-ness, and a people afloat in a weightless ether of ahistoricity" (39). Thus, as theorists and teachers of hybrid discourse, one of our absolute goals must not only be to teach students how to utilize various discourses but to recognize the effects of (garden) environments in which these experiments take place. That is, compositionists need to be more aware of environments we have created for students as well as the environments in which the various discourses they experiment with have derived. Sharon Crowley declares, for instance, "composition teachers have still not begun to account satisfactorily for our own and our students' location in physical and ideological space" (221). This line of thought, no doubt, has ties with Dobrin's theory of ecocomposition, that it is important for scholars and teachers alike to consider the sites and places of writing, including "classroom environments, electronic environments, writing environments, and textual environments" ("Writing" 13). Ecocomposition, Dobrin continues, must turn "to the conversations that composition and rhetoric provide us with for understanding how discursive construction interacts with those places, builds those places, maps those places, defines those places, and ultimately controls those places" ("Writing" 24). Hybrids not only result from parents but also from the environmental conditions in which the act of (re)production takes place. In theorizing and teaching hybrid academic discourses, then, compositionists cannot neglect to account for the cultural, political, social, and economic forces that help construct the environments in which this hybridization occurs.

There is no easy way out of such dilemmas. The term hybridity brings with it to composition studies from the sciences a lot of baggage that has often been overlooked. Hybridity needs a closer look, more theoretical and practical inquiry, and perhaps more suspicion. Although the term needs to be debated, theorized, and tested more in the discipline, we might begin to turn our attention elsewhere for a moment to help us rethink some of our ideas about experimentation with various discourses. Namely, we might look more closely at what David Quammen calls "synergy." In the interview above, Quammen responds to Keller and Dobrin's question about whether he sees his writings as types of *discursive hybridity*:

A *discursive hybridity*, wow, let me try and answer that one first. And I'll do it with another big word: synergy. I think storytelling, narrative, combined with a certain amount of humor, combined with explication of interesting but obscure ideas can create a stronger, more energized, and more engaging literary work than if something is all of one type. So just as you mix metals into alloys, I like to mix types of literary strategy and different kinds of elements into a given piece.... And about the same time I was turning into a magazine journalist specializing in science, ... I found there on the other side of the coin that mixing humor and narrative and human portraiture in with science writing created something that seemed more able to engage people.

Quammen's *synergy* suggests there is a combined power in a group of things—discourses, genres, audiences, for example—when they work together, a power that is greater than the total power achieved by each working separately: perhaps exemplified by the notion that $1+1 = 3$ not 2. No doubt this notion of synergy is similar to that of hybridity, thus I'm wary of simply trying to replace one metaphor with another, thereby simply covering up the multitude of problems brought up by the former. By contemplating and theorizing synergy more closely, however, we might not simply do away with hybridity altogether, but we may be able to better understand its shortcomings and problems.[3]

Synergy like hybridity deals with the coming together of elements that produce a different offspring, but synergy perhaps allows us to widen the scope of our playing field. Rather than examining the interplay of different discourses and what new hybrid they yield, synergy is concerned with the interplay of various agents: synergy is the interaction of discrete agencies, agents, or conditions such that the total effect is greater than the sum of the individual effects. Synergy perhaps allows compositionists to think in more depth about relationships, connections, and mixtures that comprise discourses and texts. By understanding synergy as the interaction of various diverse types of agents rather than the interaction of similar (species of?) discourses, compositionists might then better see a new world of relationships and hybrids: texts that derive not simply from the interaction of parent discourses but the interactions of various discourses, places, audiences, cultures, beliefs, markets, economies, and politics, for instance. In this sense, all texts—student or otherwise—are synergistic in one way or another, but perhaps we are limiting our understanding of these various, complicated relationships when we attribute experimental texts only to the clashing of different discourses and their resulting hybrids.

Synergy, though, is not simply meant to serve as a marker of certain textual forms but more so as a certain type of power—a power of accumulation. This power effects a different approach to thinking and writing rather than simply a new genre or process for students to master. Synergy is not necessarily a cure to any of the ills brought about by the problems of hybrid discourses. It no doubt brings up its own set of complexities and problems. What synergy does, however, is expand on our understandings of hybridity rather than supplant them. Texts may be constructed by discourses but synergy reminds us to look deeper into the larger make-up of discourses themselves. Synergy perhaps complicates our task of theorizing and teaching hybrid (academic) discourses but only through this complication will we come to any better understanding of how discourse functions, changes, constructs, and travels—how and where it is domesticated and how and where it is wild, and if it's not too much to say, how and where it is bred and cultivated.

NOTES

1. Stephen Jay Gould's posthumously published book, *The Hedgehog, the Fox, and the Magister's Pox: Mending the Gap Between Science and the Humanities* (New York: Harmony, 2003), offers a nuanced study of disciplinary "ways of knowing" and seeks to heal the conflicts between the sciences and the humanities.

2. The number of articles that take up questions about hybridity in composition studies are too numerous to cite here; however, for a thorough study of hybrid—or alternative—discourses, see Christopher Schroeder, Helen Fox, and Patricia Bizzell's collection of scholarly articles on the topic, *ALT DIS: Alternative Discourses and the Academy.* (Portsmouth, NH: Boynton/Cook, 2002).

3. A brief qualification is in order here: Quammen brings up this notion of synergy "off the cuff" in the interview, so one might argue it is a mistake to make too much of it, to run away, so to speak, with a concept that is briefly discussed and described by Quammen. Given the prevalence of discussion in composition theory and discourse studies about hybrid discourses, however, and given the importance of interdisciplinary studies between the sciences and humanities, this notion of synergy—like that of hybridity—is ripe for further exploration by those of us in fields other than the sciences.

WORKS CITED

Bahri, Deepika. "Terms of Engagement: Postcolonialism, Transnationalism, and Composition Studies." *JAC: A Journal of Composition Theory* 18.1 (1998): 29–44.

Bizzell, Patricia. "Hybrid Academic Discourses: What, Why, How." *Composition Studies* 27.2 (1999): 7–21.

———. "The Intellectual Work of 'Mixed' Forms of Academic Discourses." *ALT DIS: Alternative Discourses and the Academy.* Ed. Christopher Schroeder, Helen Fox, and Patricia Bizzell. Portsmouth, NH: Heinemann-Boynton/Cook, 2002. 1–10.

Crowley, Sharon. *Composition in the University: Historical and Polemical Essays*. Pittsburgh: U of Pittsburgh P, 1998.

Dobrin, Sidney I. "Writing Takes Place." *Ecocomposition: Theoretical and Pedagogical Approaches*. Albany: State U of New York P, 2001. 11–26.

———. "A Problem with Writing (about) 'Alternative' Discourse." *ALT DIS: Alternative Discourses and the Academy*. Ed. Christopher Schroeder, Helen Fox, and Patricia Bizzell. Portsmouth, NH: Heinemann-Boynton/Cook, 2002. 45–56.

Hardin, Joe Marshall. *Opening Spaces: Critical Pedagogy and Resistance Theory in Composition*. Albany: State U of New York P, 2001.

Pollan, Michael. *The Botany of Desire: A Plant's-Eye View of the World*. New York: Random House, 2001.

Weisser, Christian R., and Sidney Dobrin. "Breaking New Ground in Ecocomposition: An Introduction." *Ecocomposition: Theoretical and Pedagogical Approaches*. Albany: State U of New York P, 2001. 1–10.

Young, Robert C. *Colonial Desire: Hybridity in Theory, Culture, and Race*. London: Routledge, 1995.

Writing with Intent

An Interview with Janisse Ray

Blending social history, natural history, and family history into a stimulating portrait of life in southern Georgia, Janisse Ray's *Ecology of a Cracker Childhood* (1999) has become one of the most important and respected books in recent times that narrates the complex and destructive relationships among humans, their institutions, and natural worlds.

Ray grew up in the Georgia countryside amid her family's junkyard, within a tradition of Christian Fundamentalism, and among the beauties of the longleaf pine forest ecosystem in the American South. *Ecology of a Cracker Childhood* takes us into Ray's world—her family life, her Southern heritage, and her landscape—not only to show readers environmental problems but also, as she says in the interview below, to "create a picture of how life could be different, . . . how we could live, how we have lived in the past, and what parts of that we are all yearning for." Ray's work, then, focuses on how forces of change must struggle against the forces of tradition.

Focusing primarily on the Deep South, Ray offers insight into what sorts of environmental movements, thinking, and writings take place in an area of the country that many of us do not consider as "environmentally literate" or "active." In doing so, Ray shatters dangerous stereotypes about people in the South and their relationships with and understandings of natural places. Ray discusses how her writing embodies a certain type of activism for the South and how her writing "intends" to and does achieve positive effects for environments in this region of the country. Her work and words, however, have echoed well beyond her childhood homeland, and resonated with those in all parts of the United States and the world who are concerned about the various tensions among natural environments and human cultures and societies.

Q: You suggest in the Introduction to *Ecology of a Cracker Childhood* that you "carry the landscape inside like an ache." Why did you choose writing as the medium through which to express the landscape, this ache?

A: You know, I'm not even sure I had a choice. I started reading early, and reading was the way that my imagination got fired. Honestly, before I knew I wanted to, I was doing nature writing. I went to Florida State and got an undergraduate degree in creative writing. That's what I wanted to do from the start. But at the same time, I was an environmental activist. I was homesteading out in the woods of North Florida. It wasn't until I was divorced, had a two-year-old, and was in South America teaching English that I realized I could no longer be divided between writing and my love of nature. The two trunks of passion for me had to come together. I had to put the two elements of my life into one thing— it was that overarching attempt to find wholeness. I found mine. I remember walking with my son on my back in the Andes, and I remember thinking, as I walked, this is exactly what I have to do when I get back to the United States. It feels like one of those moments. Some people go their whole lives and don't know what their calling is, their mythological path. That time in the Andes would be the moment that I realized my path. What I do now is always ask myself, "Am I on the path? Am I doing as much as I think I can do?" Another part of the answer to this question is that I think there's no better way to make change than through literature. We see that clearly with Marjory Stoneman Douglas and the Everglades. We wouldn't be where we are with restoration without *River of Grass*. I think that if Rick Bass hadn't done so much to bring attention to it, we wouldn't have got where we got with the Roadless Initiative. I absolutely believe in the power and strength of words.

Q: Let us ask you about two terms you are using there. You mention the term *nature writing* in reference to what you do. What does that term mean to you? What constitutes nature writing?

A: What it means is a chance to write about this thing, this feeling I have way deep in my body, this compassion I have for landscape. Honestly, I suppose in the old controversy about being known as nature writers or as plain writers, I suppose that I too am simply a writer. But, I think that the great work of the twenty-first century is for us to figure out how we are to live on the earth, how and where we are to live sustainably, functionally, and well. I think there's no bigger task ahead of us than figuring this out. So, I think nature writing is the great work of our time. Because I'm a writer first, and because this is the great work, I naturally tend toward what is called "nature writing." I want to quote my friend Jan DeBlieu, who said, "Nature writing is not marginal. We are writing the human story now." I tell you, I think nature writing is probably an unfortunate label. I don't think it's what we're doing at all. I think we are writing the course of literature, and people like you and me, and our friends and colleagues, we will probably go down, and maybe this is too egotistical to even say, we'll go down in history as being part of a movement saying we'd better stop and pay attention, or we'd better name what we have now, because we're not going to have it forever. We better provide a template now for living, because we're going to need it in this century.

Q: You used the word *literature* there twice. We're interested in this concept of change through literature. That word *literature* has always had a privileged cultural connotation. How do you conceive of literature as capable of producing change?

A: I think literature is an attempt, on the part of the author, to do something great. I know that's a vague definition, but to me, it implies intent as much as anything. I'm not sure if there was ever an author who intended to entertain, who accidentally approached literature. You know how eager we are in this culture to name stars: Michael Jackson and Magic Johnson, and whoever else. We are enamored of stars at the expense of furthering an entire culture. To me, that's what literature is, too: the furthering of our culture. Modern literature is archives of society, the present society, now, and of the earth, but intent figures into this. I think literature happens with intent.

Q: In another interview in this collection, natural historian Ann Zwinger talks about the importance of naming, of knowing scientific names in order to better understand places, environments, natures. You have written about reading the names of places on bottles you'd collect to trade for money, "We'd finger the names of those far away places we knew nothing of, marveling that a name could tell so little." Yet, your writing seems very name oriented. You are careful to explain names of family, friends, places, plants, animals. You provide lists of names, explain their origins. Are names important? Does the act of naming affect a place? Our perception of that place?

A: One time in the mountains of North Georgia, my high-school English teacher and I were hiking, and I wanted to know the names of the wildflowers, and he said that the names were unimportant. What was important was the flower itself. Knowing its name was unimportant to enjoyment of it. But at a much later date, I was in South America, in Colombia, birding with an ornithologist. In the Southeastern United

States, we have primarily one species of hummingbird, the ruby-throated hummingbird, but in Colombia, there are over thirty species. I cannot tell you how magnificent they are. One had a beak on it about eight inches long, entirely adapted to pollinate this one tubular flower; the flower itself was about eight inches long. The bird was called the "shimmering gold." If you just put those names together, you would have a poem: shimmering goldwing. It was music, it was poetry, it was everything you needed to know, to know how glorious the hummingbirds of South America are. And that's what I've done in naming things. It's an invisible power, and probably not even one that could be understood, but somehow knowing the name of a thing adds so much substance to your understanding of it. To know something's name—or someone's name—gives it identity, gives it visibility, gives it presence, gives it voice. Naming admits a thing into the circle of life.

Q: In a recent review of *Ecology of a Cracker Childhood* in the *Atlanta Journal-Constitution*, the author closes by writing, "Consider the effectiveness of *Ecology of a Cracker Childhood* as an argument for all of us to think beyond our lives." As people who spend a great deal of time thinking and writing about writing, we were particularly interested here in this concept of *argument*. How argumentative is your writing and in what ways? Do you envision a certain kind of audience to whom you are making a form of argument?

A: When the book first came out, I was on the "Forgotten Language Tour" in the Northeast, and people were buying the book, and walking away, and I thought, with a sinking feeling, that the wrong people were buying the book. Over the course of the one-and-a-half years it's been out, I've seen many Southerners buy it, and that's been its biggest audience. That is its intended audience. When I first wrote it, William Kitteredge was one of the first people who read it, and he thought it had some wider audience. He thought its theme was honor—how we honor or what we do to honor our place. Eighty to ninety percent of the land across the South is privately owned, so we are the ones responsible for what we do to the land in the South. Given that scenario, I don't want to be argumentative. I want to create a picture of how life could be different and also try to show people how we could live, how we have lived in the past, and what parts of that we are all yearning for, whether we recognize it or not. How easy it would be to live closer to the land, human communities sustained by wild communities, recognizing interdependence. Sometimes we have been so addled by what society offers us: satellite TV and big cars, it goes on and on. I think we're sold on this idea of progress, and we don't realize, as human beings, how important something like connection to a place is. What I wanted to do was to point out that culture is inextricably tied to the landscape. For Southerners to recognize that, knowing how much most of us value where we came from, the land, and our sense of place, we wouldn't be so quick to have it destroyed. That was my hope. I didn't intend to be argumentative, and I tried never to offend.

Q: Toward the end of *Ecology of a Cracker Childhood*, you make one of the most daring and profound calls for environmentalism, mirroring a familiar Southern call, that we'd like to quote here at length:

> We don't mind growing trees here in the South; it's a good place for silviculture, sunny and watery, with a growing season to make a Yankee gardener weep. What we mind is that all of our trees are being taken. We want more than 1 percent natural strands of longleaf. We know a pine plantation is not a forest, and the wholesale conversion to monocultures is unacceptable to us.
>
> We Southerners are a people fighting again for our country, defending the last remaining stands of real forest. Although we love to frolic, the time has come to fight. We must fight.
>
> In new rebellion we must stand together, black and white, urbanite and farmer, workers all, in keeping Dixie. We are a patient people who for generations have not been ousted from this land, and we are willing to fight for the birthplace of our children's children and their children's children, to be of a place, in all ways, for all time. What is left is not enough. When we say the South will rise again we can mean that we will allow the cutover forests to return to their former grandeur and pine plantations to grow wild.

Let us ask about your rhetorical strategy here. You have made an important call for more than sustainability, for growth. You make this call in a way that calls on Southern pride, a thing that many Southerners will listen to, admire. However, the South is also now populated with others who hear the call of Southern pride as echoing a dangerous history. Could you talk about why you chose to make this call in this way, what are you saying to Southerners, and what your response is to non-Southerners who might read this call differently in your book—a text that has, obviously, earned a good deal of non-Southern readership?

A: Probably it was mere ignorance on my part. My two faults are, first, that I was not thinking about non-native Southerners and, second, that I took the liberty of putting my views in terms of the universal. I used the word *we*, which is, honestly, just a fighting strategy, and not a fair one, you know, because it is pretty subtle.

Q: Does this have to be a fair fight? This seems to me to be the one place where we don't want a fair fight.

A: We don't want a fair fight. I know that I got the idea for this strategy from Rick [Bass]. We were trying to keep a rural school open here, the school my mother attended. Our school board had voted to close the two rural schools and bus the children into town. They thought they would consolidate, that the children in town were not getting as much attention as the children in the rural schools. They wanted to make everything fair. They wanted to build a new school in town, and the people in the county went into an uproar, and we demanded the schools stay open; we got enough signatures for a county referendum. It was during the course of that struggle, and my writing about it, I remember Rick telling me, just write *we* as if everybody thinks the way you do. Assume it. Five years ago or ten years ago, I would have done readings, anywhere in these little libraries across the South, and when I said *A pine plantation is not a forest*, like I do now, people would have stared blankly, with their mouths open. I think the book came in good time, because in the South, people are seeing what we are losing, and we're losing it so quickly. I think people are ready for an environmental awakening. The people who have been here, and their parents, and their grandparents, they see what's gone, and I think a huge part of them mourns it. When I describe what I see happening to the Southern landscape, people sit in the audiences and weep. I am *we*. That's all I need to say about that.

Q: In another interview in this collection, Cheryll Glotfelty makes the statement that "there was some sense that the West might be more receptive to a place-based approach or an environmental approach, nature-oriented approach, than the East" when asked as to why schools like University of Nevada at Reno have become such prominent places for those wanting to study literature and environment. Similarly there is a sense that places like California, Oregon, and Washington are hotbeds for environmental activism. Rarely do we hear the South being touted as an environmentalist's location. Why do you suppose the South is only recently finding an environmentalist voice? And, why hasn't the

South become a hotbed for, or initiator of, environmental activism, research, policy?

A: You know, since we lost the Civil War, we've been dealing with big social issues. I believe it's set us back. I think that over the past decades, people would go away from the South to get an education, or leave the rural South and go into bigger cities, where they got introduced to other, more rational, ways of living, and they could not come back to the South in good faith. What has happened over the years is that the South has bled large numbers of thinking people. Who immediately comes to mind is a dear friend of mine named Franklin Burroughs, from the low country of South Carolina. He's a nature writer, and writes about the South, but he's spent his entire adult life in Maine (he teaches at Bowdoin). He attends our Southern nature writing gatherings, and he identifies with this landscape more than any other. I think because of the direness of the problems we face, and how overwhelming they seem, a lot of people have not been able to stay and tackle them. Myself, I thought for years I'd die if I came back, and I'd die if I didn't come back. Georgia was so much a part of me, and so deep inside me—and yet, 40 percent of the people in my county never finished high school. Since I've been back, I've been lonely, but I feel like people have been hungry to make changes and hungry for answers. Sometimes, I feel like a pioneer, in this part of the country, because I'm one of the people who has decided not to let the South fall by the wayside because of lack of education, and poverty, and racism, and classism, and environmental injustice.

Q: Environmental sociologist Robert D. Bullard, in his book *Dumping in Dixie: Race, Class, and Environmental Quality*, writes, "The environmental movement in the United States emerged with an agenda that focused on such areas as wilderness and wildlife preservation, resource conservation, pollution abatement, and population control. It was supported primarily by middle- and upper-middle-class whites. Although concern about the environment cut across racial and class lines, environmental activism has been most pronounced among individuals who have above-average education, greater access to economic resources, and a greater sense of personal efficacy." He goes on to say that "mainstream environmental organizations were late in broadening their base support to include blacks and other minorities, the poor and working-class persons." Many others, including ecofeminists such as Dorceta Taylor, have noted a relationship between racial oppression and environmental oppression. You also write about the ways in which social problems affect land, as we've just discussed. Similarly, in her poem "Sorrow Home," Margaret Walker laments how she is kept from her roots in the South because of the various symbols of racial hatred: "O southland, sorrow home, melody beating in my bone and blood! / How long will the Klan of hate, the hounds and the chain gangs / keep me from my own?" Can you explain in greater detail the relationship between land abuse and racial hatred, or racial injustice?

A: I don't think that land abuse and racial hatred come from the same place. I think one comes from greed, and one comes from fear. I think that the ways to contradict both of them have to be different. To me, to contradict racism, people in power, by which I mean the white people, are going to have to, in their daily lives, be friends with people of color, and work through the issues, in all ways, so that nothing stands between you and another person because of color. I think the work there has to be done on a personal level, although it has to be political as well. With land abuse, I think the answer is action, activism, courage, ferocity, doggedness. No child is born a hater. Of course with both, education makes a difference, so you can say that the land ethic is taught. So, in that, part of the answer is going to be the same. People of color often have had few to no resources, and being polluted upon made them victims in many cases. I would say it's not just people of color, but also poor whites. When I came here, I had in mind that I would do so many things, you know, and I guess I have done a lot, but there were so many visionary things I wanted to do. As I started trying to organize people back here in my homeland, I realized we were going to have to start on the level of self-esteem. People who had no college education, no high-school education, no money, thought very poorly of themselves, and they were going to be the last people to speak out against the nuclear plant being here. It is not that people who lack education are stupid; they very well understand that our cancer rate likely has increased because of Plant Hatch on the river, or that once we cut all our trees, with this cycle of cutting, we're never going to have old good lumber anymore, or that the water's got a higher pesticide content now.

Q: As a follow-up to this last question, Donald Worster writes in *The Wealth of Nature: Environmental History and the Ecological Imagination* that "We are facing a global crisis today, not because of how ecosystems function but rather because of how our ethical systems function." Your writing weaves together a discussion of natural history, human history, politics, economics, race, class, religion, and education, for instance.

Human ethics and ecosystems are bound together tightly in your writing. Along these lines, do you see a particular ethical crisis over the horizon as we move into the twenty-first century?

A: A particular ethical crisis? I think that we are going to have to go back and redo our Bill of Rights, so that we extend human rights to the nonhuman. I think our individual rights to "life, liberty, and the pursuit of happiness" end where another's rights begin, or where the rights of a wild species or landscape begins. We're smack in the middle of a profound ethical crisis.

Q: Harry Crews, who also grew up in southern Georgia, in Bacon County, concludes his book *A Childhood: The Biography of a Place* by writing, "I had already done what, in Bacon County, was unthinkable. I had cursed the sun. And in Bacon County you don't curse the sun or the rain or the land or God. They are the same thing. To curse any of them is an ultimate blasphemy. I had known that three years ago, but in three years I had somehow managed to forget it. I stood there feeling how much I had left this place and these people, and at the same time knowing that it would be forever impossible to leave them completely. Wherever I might go in the world, they would go with me." Your book, *Ecology of a Cracker Childhood,* also addresses the relationships between people and nature—the land, the sun, the rain—and people and God. Could you talk about this cultural link between nature and God, the ways in which the small-town Southern living contributes to this culture, the ways that cultures, particularly lower socioeconomic, Southern cultures, foster a dependence on God and Nature as inextricably linked?

A: I guess you're right. Because God is creation, because God created everything, then everything is God. I don't remember Crews writing that in the book. That is a fascinating idea. So, I think that typically the rural Southerner has been so dependent on the land for survival that much of his or her life has been praying to God for benevolence so that the crop may grow, or that there are enough trees to be cut, that there's good fishing, good crabbing that year. What I can absolutely see: there is a definite link between God and natural resources and also a pious spirit in the face of that connection, and I'm not sure I can add much to Crews's thinking.

Q: Let's talk for a moment about the pinelands of south Georgia and north Florida and about aesthetics. The eminent Florida naturalist Archie

Carr writes in his essay "Eden Changes" that "Some people don't like the look of flatwoods anyway. Jacob Rhett Motte, an army surgeon of Charleston, South Carolina, who arrived in Florida during the Second Seminole War, was appalled by the appearance of the pinelands around the Georgia-Florida line. They seemed to him a 'dull, insipid pine barren, where the listlessness of a blank vacuity hung upon the flagging spirits.' Motte was probably just prejudiced. Most naturalists would give a lot for a chance to see what those pinelands looked like before they were cut down. But later on the flatwoods were cut over, most of them more than once, and the Crackers burned them into blackened, bare-floored semi-desert, devoid of animal life except for razorback hogs that plowed up the bayheads and thin sooty cattle that stood around in the road or wandering through the unfenced country foraging morosely for scattered sprigs of wire grass." He goes on to say, "now the ritual burning has stopped. In some cases, protection is overdone, but a new and pleasantly lush look has come over the land." Of course, here Carr is addressing some of the same loss of pine forests that you address in your work, but we'd like to talk for a moment about nature and aesthetics, a subject both you and Carr touch on. You have written, "My homeland is about as ugly as a place gets. There is nothing in south Georgia, people will tell you, except straight, lonely roads, one-horse towns, sprawling farms, and tracts of planted pines." You go on to say "Unless you look close, there's little majesty." But, you tell us, "It wasn't always this way." Both you and Carr seem to be addressing a kind of aesthetic in nature, and we were wondering if you could comment on how such a natural aesthetic is created and perhaps why you and Carr make these similar statements.

A: I think that the natural aesthetic is created with maturity, with age, with time. I think we evolve with the landscape, and so, what is beautiful, I believe, has come from generations of people believing that it is beautiful. I don't see any way around that, really, and it's what E. O. Wilson concludes when he talks about our inclination to inhabit savannas, those forested grasslands.

Q: His Savanna Hypothesis is one of the most exciting things we've seen recently. He tells us he's writing a new piece on it.

A: He's a brilliant man. I think that is where our aesthetic comes from, from a long-evolved, biologically necessary affinity. Once an editor came to visit me here. He was a manager at Milkweed. He was raised in Brunswick, then left, and he didn't have an idea in his mind about what the original landscape was like. So, when he came to visit me, I remember us sitting at the kitchen table, and he said, "Janisse, I don't know what you're talking about, all the trees getting cut. All the way from Brunswick to here I passed trees. There's trees everywhere." What he didn't see was that the trees are only five, ten, or fifteen years old, and he passed through maybe two several-acre pieces of natural forest between here and Brunswick. My fear is that, as we lose more of it, we forget what our native landscape was like. I suppose our aesthetic changes, but I can't imagine it changing to love a pine plantation, although it has changed to love a lawn, or the insides of a well-designed mall. I'm not sure we're going to retain our natural aesthetic.

Q: You have mentioned in your writing how important a book *The Yearling* is to you, so we'd like to turn for a moment to Marjorie Kinnan Rawlings. In *Cross Creek*, Rawlings writes so profoundly, "There is of course an affinity between people and places." She continues, "We were bred of earth before we were born of our mothers. Once born, we can live without mother or father, or any other kin, or any friend, or any human love. We cannot live without the earth or apart from it, and something is shriveled in a man's heart when he turns away from it and concerns himself with the affairs of men." Would you speak for a moment about the influence Rawlings's work has had on you and, in particular, how you respond to the words we've just quoted?

A: I read it when I was very young. She's a model to me, of a woman living alone in a rural place, paying close attention to what was happening around her. I absolutely love her work. I love *The Yearling* and *Cross Creek*. I love them all. I think it was because she was a woman, and because most of the time she lived there without her husband, and because she paid attention, and she honored a place in its local glory. Both she and Harry Crews wrote about the place I belonged to as a girl. Another author I admired was Caroline Miller, a woman whose book—which won the Pulitzer Prize in the late 1930s—is a phenomenal book of this landscape. She lived in my county. Maybe their work affected me because those people were writing about things I knew about. I remember being young—fifteen or sixteen— a young girl reading Rawlings as she described watching a chameleon, an anole, on her porch in the sunlight flashing its moneybags. I remember just being so thrilled that the mating ritual was on paper, you know, something that I'd seen, and do you know that when I get letters from people, that's what people say the most, that I've told the story of their childhood. Or that they've lived that life. I think it's wonderfully reaffirming.

Q: Are you familiar with Steve Chapple's concept of the eco-redneck? Well, Author Phil Caputo has described Chapple's agenda in *Confessions of an Eco-Redneck* as an attempt to "reconcile the redneck killer and the spirit of Thoreau that divides the hearts of American outdoorsmen." Chapple himself makes the argument that "A strange new animal stalks the woods of North America: the eco-redneck. *Ecce homo.* It is obvious irony to some, an unintentional one to others, but these days sporting persons and environmentalists are apt to be one and the same." That is, Chapple is calling for an environmentalist movement from the very folks who spend a good deal of time engaging nature, in finding a place in nature. In a lot of ways, his eco-redneck seems reflective of and reflected in your concepts of Cracker ecology (though we want to be clear to our readers that we Southerners make clear distinctions between Crackers and rednecks). Why do you suppose environmentalism is making its way into the lives of groups like rednecks and Crackers?

A: There's a man named James Holland, who was born in Cochran, Georgia. He spent the past twenty-five years as a crabber off the coast of Georgia. When he first started crabbing, he could go out for the day, and check traps, and come home with 1,500 to 1,600 pounds of crabs in a day. Now, he goes out, and can bring in 150 to 200 pounds. He decided to do something about it. What I have heard him say is that we are watching our way of life go down the drain, and we are tired of it. He doesn't have a high-school education. He does not look like an environmental activist, but he's the best environmental activist I've ever seen. He is coming from the ranks of working-class people, who depend on the earth, and whose lives are diminished by industrialism and the effects of pollution, and are tired of it. He is absolutely tired of it. He started this group, knowing that the crabs spawn in the river deltas and that the crabs are absolutely dependent on good water quality for spawning. So, he's taken on the Altamaha Rivershed, and started the group the Altamaha Riverkeepers, which is how the original riverkeeper group, the Hudson Riverkeepers, started. It was fishermen who saw their catches going down, and saw even what they were catching had sores—the fish had sores. James sees that, too. He brings in photographs of fish with lesions on them. This is sobering stuff that he sees out there, being on the water, every day.

These issues affect working-class people both directly and immediately. I've heard James say, "We want jobs, but dammit give us jobs that are worthwhile. Give us jobs that we deserve." I think that there's a wave of environmentalism rolling across the South. You know how it might have come from upper-class Southerners. I think now it is coming from lower- and working-class Southerners.

I'm so happy to be a part of it. Maybe it was coming twenty years ago, when John McPhee traveled through Georgia with Carol Ruckdeschel, and Carol was looking at native ecosystems, and naming things, along with Charles Wharton, but it's really happening now. When I moved back here a few years ago, below Macon, there was not a single environmental group. Maybe Savannah had a couple, and I think there was a small Audubon Society on St. Simons. Then when James started Riverkeeper, he got a bunch of us together for the first board meeting; and within three months, we had 300 members, and now, we've hired an executive director and a full-time Riverkeeper, and have an office in Darien. Even foundations are realizing they've neglected environmental projects in the Southeast and they're sending money like crazy. And thank God for Ted Turner.

Q: Several times throughout *Ecology of A Cracker Childhood*, you make reference to the idea that people are afraid of nature. We note, for instance, people's fear of your grandfather because of his attachment to the outdoors. Are people afraid of nature, of people who are in touch with nature?

A: You know, I guess so. Unfortunately, it's just a matter of being taught that way, and not knowing. But once you see someone pick up a non-venomous snake, once you know the difference between venomous and nonvenomous, that changes your view toward snakes. I know that E. O. Wilson writes that snakes are afraid of bipedal creatures, and we're afraid of slithering creatures, but I've seen in my life that it can be overcome. I think that if you get children soon enough, they don't have that kind of fear. They don't have it, or they get over it really quickly.

Q: In her essay "Teaching my Class," compositionist Lynn Z. Bloom relates an anecdote that seems evocative of a story you tell in your book. Bloom writes: "On the pretext of telling the neighbor kids—even towering third and fourth graders—a story they'd never heard before, I would lure them to the row of Campbell's soup cartons I'd arranged as desks under the pines in our New Hampshire neighborhood. I'd hand out the bright Crayolas, fist-fat pencils from my Detroit grandfather's print shop, and to write on, empty bluebooks discarded by my father's students. Then I'd proceed to impart the lesson de jour. I do not remember the substance of a single one of these impromptu discourses, but there were enough occasions, with pupils lured by shameless bribes of jellybeans and chocolate chip cookies smuggled from home, to let me know from the age of six on that teaching would be the great love of my life." You tell a similar story of playing teacher to outdoor classes filled by your brothers and sister and your dolls. You also make it clear that reading, education, became an important avenue in your growth and your becoming environmentally conscious. Do you see a relationship between teaching, education, and environmentalism? And, do you see children's outdoor, playtime classes, like those Bloom and you describe, as making an impact on children's approaches to education?

A: To both those questions, I'm going to say yes. I do see a relation between education and environmentalism and, yes, I see that playtime and outdoor time will have an impact. I heard an educator once say, "How can we expect the child to protect the tree, if they don't know what a tree is, have never climbed one or hugged one?" I also want to say, however, that in the beginning of this environmental movement that began twenty to twenty-five years ago, we thought that we had time, and that if we just educated the children about our environmental and ecological issues, that we could catch up, and we now know it has not worked, and that we no longer have the time to depend on children changing the world.

It has to be that we head for the adults. We must tell our neighbor that we don't want—and this just reminded me of Barbara Kingsolver's book *Prodigal Summer*—that we don't want his spray coming over into our organic garden. I have to tell my neighbor who, with the chickens, and with the broiler house here, that I don't want his broiler house polluting the creek that comes through my land. That's the way I think it has to be, now. It has to be that we're reaching out to the people who we can affect, who are around us, and not around us. I think it has to be adult-to-adult now, and thank God for the teachers who are doing it in the schools. I'll tell you this. There was a survey done not very long ago, and the children of Georgia knew more about the rain forest than they did their own homeland—the pine flatlands or the Appalachians. I'm not sure environmental education in the schools has been working.

I do think, though, that the South has a special place in its heart for literature. We have produced phenomenal writers, and continue to do so. I think that so much change can come through that medium. I have all the hope in the world that how we write in the South can really make a difference. That's why I have been so involved in getting Southern nature writers together. Three years ago, we did the first gathering of Southern nature writers. This year, it's being done at the University of

Georgia. If we can get our writers to pay attention to environmental issues, and start incorporating that in their work, I think we can really start making deep change.

Q: Referring to times when you and your brothers and sister would play school outside, you have written, "I would leave the board filled with writing, knowing that a thunderstorm loomed and rain would do the work" of washing the board clean. Though you were being literal here and not making metaphoric claims about the relationship between nature and writing, this relationship is something we are keenly interested in addressing in this collection. Your statement, if we played some metaphor games, could be seen as giving nature a power over writing. Many have argued, also, that writing has a direct effect on nature, more often than not having the ability to erase nature more than the other way around. Your writing, for instance, seeks to have profound impact by encouraging protection of the pine forests of southern Georgia and northern Florida. Could you speak to how you see the ecology of writing and nature?

A: This question is harder for me to understand. If I didn't believe in the power of literature, and the strength of words, I wouldn't be writing now. I absolutely believe in this power, and I guess the best way to answer this is with a couple of stories. When the book *Ecology of a Cracker Childhood* came out, people wrote to me. One man said to me that his family was meeting to decide whether to cut their tract of timber or not. He photo-copied the four pages from that chapter "Clearcut," that you better be praying if you clear-cut a forest, and handed them out to the family. They decided not to cut. That story speaks most clearly that there is a power in what you put out in the world, and what you say. Just the fact of writing a book gives you such authority, because of how we in the South feel about books. We really feel that they are sacred things. Most of us still believe, from growing up with books from the local library, that you don't dog-ear the pages, and that you don't write in the book. You don't leave a book out in the rain, and, honestly, you don't throw them away. A book is so pow-erful, that once it's made, it's not even something that can be destroyed. Because we believe that, I think we are willing to believe what they say. (I think that's changing, though. There are so many changes in the publishing industry. Today, books are becoming more secular and commonplace.)

Q: You have said, "I want a life constructed of books." Is life constructed by books? Can nature/is nature constructed by books? What are the ramifications and/or implications of having a life constructed by books?

A: I think yes, our lives can be. I think of Wendell Berry. He is a person I started reading when I was young. Wendell Berry is a prophet to me. He is a brilliant man; he's done some really good thinking about being an agrarian, and taking care of the land. If it weren't for Wendell Berry in my life, where would I be? I wouldn't be back in Georgia. I wouldn't have returned. I wouldn't have thought about racism the way I do, since I read *The Hidden Wound* when I was a young woman. So, I think, yes. On a recent backpacking trip out in Montana, we read *The Tracker*; my friend found it, and said, "Let's read this every night." Every night, we were either in the tent or around the campfire, and we'd read it out loud to our three boys. I noticed how they listened to the book, and how they talked about it afterward. The stories of Tom Brown Jr. as a young man, and not just tracking animals, but enduring cold, and doing all kinds of wild things, had a definite impact on them. I know their lives were changed by some of the things he said. Now, they came to the point where they also didn't believe all his stories. But they believed enough of them to stay mesmerized. So my answer is yes.

Q: Books can affect our lives in that way, but how do they affect nature?

A: I like the idea, spiritually, of books having an effect. I like the idea that somewhere the lonely pine forest knows that I am working toward its protection, or that when I was fighting DuPont to keep the company from mining titanium in Okefenokee Swamp, that there was someplace where the black bears of Okefenokee knew that I was working desperately to protect their environment. It would be wonderful, wouldn't it? Wouldn't it be amazing if there was that kind of transcendental knowledge between places and people? It's absolutely possible that yes, I do think that a book can save a place. What I've seen, and I know that the book is not responsible for everything that's happened to longleaf since it came out, but it was part of a movement to take care of our coastal plain uplands, so many positive changes have happened. I'll tell you about one: we saved Moody Swamp here in Appling County; that's 3400 acres of land, two to three miles long along the Altamaha River. The Altamaha is a wild river. It probably would not have happened if the book hadn't been out, and there hadn't been all kinds of attention focused on our area. But it did.

Making Arguments

A Response to Janisse Ray

Julie Drew

I read with much pleasure Sid Dobrin's and Chris Keller's interview with Janisse Ray—much pleasure because she reminded me, powerfully, that words do things. "Literature happens with intent," she says and, later, that as a Southerner she knows books as "sacred things." Her apparent love affair with the act of writing and with books, and the reverence she feels for the power of the written word sits quite comfortably with her success as a writer. Ray exudes an appealing mixture of confidence and humility that leaves no doubt about her ability to produce literature that does real work in the world.

One of the most interesting aspects of Ray's discussion in "Writing with Intent"—especially interesting to compositionists, I suspect—is her take on argumentation, some of the most important work that writing can do. When the interviewers ask if she thinks *Ecology of a Cracker Childhood* is a form of argument, however, Ray leaps in with a swift apology, assuring readers that she "didn't intend to be argumentative." The pejorative understanding of argumentation—that is, to be argumentative, to deliberately seek out disagreement as a matter of course—is a very different thing than to craft an argument in order to persuade. This unfortunate misunderstanding on Ray's part prohibited her in the interview from discussing the ways in which she crafts her writing—the deliberate rhetorical choices she makes—in order to persuade her readers to view the world as she does, and to act on those views.

Ray is undoubtedly making an argument: her book is about memory, about childhood, about landscape, and about belonging. It is about understanding the human value in the nonhuman places we occupy, because those places in so many ways define our humanity. Ray persuades us to remember the landscape of our childhood and its meaning, to look around at what used to be and no longer is, and to do something about it. She reminds us, she paints vivid landscapes familiar to those of us who know North Florida, she *inspires*, and this is an incredibly effective form of argument, one that gets too little consideration when we teach students to compose arguments. Her writing is inspirational because it's about love—it invokes the love of home, of humidity, of dry pine needles pricking, crunching under bare feet.

Inspiration in nature writing goes way back—look at Wordsworth, at Gerard Manley Hopkins, for example. They wrote poetry, beautifully crafted, inspiring words and images that made arguments about the meaning of progress and humanity in the industrial age, about the value of nature for a spiritual human life, about where to find God in a world that had seemingly replaced him with science. Literature does indeed happen with intent, and Ray's intent is found in her argument. I'd like to go back and ask her that question again to find out something about her writing process, how she goes about this business of persuading her readers. The only little tidbit offered is that strategic use of *we* she learned from Rick Bass.

There's a spiritual element to Ray's remarks that is striking, though not unexpected. One of the hallmarks of green writers is their attention to the interrelatedness of themselves and the world around them, and to living deliberately with an eye toward a holistic existence—an "overarching attempt to find wholeness," as Ray puts it. She speaks of her calling, her path, and concludes "there's no better way to make change than through literature." She's doing work with her writing, trying to create a better world, composing a romanticized past to shed light on an impoverished present, in the hope that it will inspire readers to create a better future.

Ray is making other arguments in this interview, however; arguments I've had to work with a bit to try to identify. She claims that "we don't realize . . . how important something like connection to a place is." I think we *do* realize it, but it's hard in the South, maybe *precisely* because the land is owned by individuals: too often those individuals are other people, not us. Private ownership of land is, for Ray (a landowner) a good thing; there's a stake in preserving and rejuvenating what we own. But there's a real class issue here: most of the land in the Southern United States is not public, and is therefore unknown and inaccessible to most people.

I'm a Florida native, third generation; I lived for thirty-five years in central and northern Florida, and while I spent a lot of time on the land, it was always somebody else's. All land is posted land, in my experience, and you can get through the barbed wire but you might get shot at. In short, you have to know someone, or you're trespassing. There's an alienation that occurs in such circumstances, circumstances in which public referendums don't decide the fates of trees and waterways; in which paid, trained professionals don't keep an eye on and maintain the health of the land. When you have no say and very little access, the fights over land become a developers' war you read about in the newspaper as you watch the coastline disappear. I think we *do* get it, but I think there's a feeling of helplessness that's very real, and that helplessness is reinforced by generations of experience: the inevitability of what gets termed "progress" and the loss that always accompanies it.

Ray says that "in the South, people are seeing what we are losing, and we're losing it so quickly." This is not a revelation; in the South, particularly in Florida, we're used to losing things. Losing shoreline, losing wetlands and forests, losing marine populations, losing *species* for god's sake, losing farmland to golf courses and gated-community developments, losing the ability of an entire economic class to live on native soil because it's been bought up and built over with million-dollar pink mini-mansions. Ray says, "The people who have been here, and their parents, and their grandparents, they see what's gone, and I think a huge part of them mourns it." Indeed. I spent more hours of my childhood than I could ever begin to count in a small Chris-Craft with my father, fishing at John's Pass in St. Petersburg or racing the afternoon thunderstorms back from Egmont Key; skiing with friends in the intercoastal waterways off Indian Rocks Beach; playing with my brother and sister on Sand Key or Sanibel Island, letting the tiny wedge-shaped clams in coquina shells tickle our hands as they tried to dig down and hide when we scooped them up from the wet sand. Today John's Pass is a collection of tourist bars and Jet Ski rentals, the surface of the water a trout-skin's rainbow of gasoline and engine oil. Indian Rocks hasn't got a square inch of sand that doesn't have a stilt house or motel on it—all privately owned, making the beach unreachable. Sand Key is one big condo—you can't even see the water if you're not a paying customer, and Sanibel Island's shells have been depleted beyond hope from too many tourists carrying them home glued to tacky lamp bases for too many years.

It's no wonder that "people sit in the audience and weep" when Ray describes what's happening to the Southern landscape. She is an artist with the language of childhood, of sensory experience, and of loss. For those who are of the South, but living as though they have no right to coexist with its bounty, consciousness-raising and pleas for activism may not be enough; when there are no more public, unclaimed spaces, what is the stake for those who are not property owners? A better world? Sure. But this is the most likely population to be struggling economically, to be holding down two jobs, or to have already given up on a brighter future for themselves, let alone everybody else.

The challenge to enlist local workers of every economic class in activism seems at times insurmountable, but Ray may be shooting herself in the foot *despite* her persuasive storytelling. She notes that "culture is inextricably tied to the landscape," and I couldn't agree more. Economic forces drive massive, seemingly overnight changes in the landscape— witness the pine plantations she speaks of—but in her enthusiasm, in her efforts to motivate and inspire, she makes what I believe to be a grave misjudgment, both ethically and practically. In reclaiming the phrase "the South shall rise again," Ray attempts to alter its meaning, referring instead to a regrowth of the region's wild pine forests. But this phrase cannot but conjure a rebel-flag-waving, defiant South unwilling to condemn its own past as an agrarian society built on the backs of African slaves. She should know better. Ray notes that her audience is a regional one; she speaks to the memories of those who have shared the same landscapes, the same aesthetic. Her specialized audience, and, more important, any potential larger audience, is unlikely to ever be able to replace this phrase's weighted meaning with a new, far less controversial and historically important meaning. To tie such language to a more hopeful future seems counterproductive at best, and suspect at worst.

Issues of race are certainly difficult and complex, perhaps especially so for multigenerational Southerners. Ray's discussion of race in this interview is no exception, particularly when compared to her comments about environmental activism and the ethics of that endeavor. She is *vehement* about recreating the decimated landscapes, claiming that "With land abuse, I think the answer is action, activism, courage, ferocity, doggedness." When it comes to human abuse, however, white folks have to just start being nice, have to "be friends with people of color." The work has to be done on a "personal level," rather than a public, political level. This all-too-typical Southern acquiescence to the times, to the rightness of being against racism, appears too often to be mere lip service. I'm reminded of my Great-aunt Gwen who often told me when I was a little girl (during the late 1960s and early 1970s, mind you) that a lady never leaves the house without a slip on; that I should always endeavor to "be sweet"; and that I should be "friendly" to the little colored children in my class at school. At the same time, black voter drives, girls who smoked or chewed gum, demonstrations for civil rights, and the violence often visited upon those who participated in public political actions earned a distinct frown of disapproval from her. It just wasn't necessary to be so *ill-bred*. It wasn't nice, was what she said; but it's uncomfortable, and I don't want to face it because I'm implicated, is what was really going on. No, we should all just go about our business quietly, and do what's right in a personal, private, and mannered sort of way. No need to be fierce or active, courageous or dogged when it comes to racism.

Ray's ability to acknowledge the multitudes of good people who have left the South to get an education and who, subsequently, have been introduced to "other, more rational, ways of living" does her great credit, as does her conclusion that "the South has bled large numbers of thinking people." This acknowledgment makes it difficult for me to understand the subtle but insistent way Ray suggests in this interview that since culture is tied to landscape, cultural history is somehow rendered apolitical, a natural occurrence, and in order to embrace one the other must also be embraced. I believe, even for Southerners who love home with everything we've got, there are ways and there are ethical reasons to divorce ourselves from an easy acceptance of that region's history; to fail to do so is tantamount to an erasure history. A small but necessary part of that intellectual and ethical separation of place from culture is to mark certain language as unacceptable because of the cultural baggage it will always bring with it. To speak of Southern pride with the words "the South shall rise again," despite Ray's intended new meaning, will most certainly evoke a stand from which many, if not most, Southerners of the ilk Ray longs for in rebuilding and protecting her beloved landscape will wish to disassociate themselves.

My favorite bumper sticker reads, "If You Want Peace, Work For Justice." This seems so obvious, so self-evident in both international and domestic matters, and so particularly poignant these days. In much the same way, it's possible that the impoverished South will become more environmentally active when the economic fortunes of its average citizens improve—and this is very much about race and gender, not just class— when more Southerners are able to claim a personal stake in the future of the land they live on or near.

Whether we think it should be true or not, environmental activism is a luxury for those who struggle to maintain a roof and provide food for themselves and their families. I was struck this past year, while teaching in Beijing, by the very astute comments of a Chinese graduate student to a Yale professor delivering a paper on environmental work in developing nations. The speaker had just given a very informative and not uninspiring talk on raising the consciousness of villagers in remote areas of China to the long-term effects of their decisions to allow clear-cutting and strip mining, as opposed to the short-term benefits of immediate economic windfalls. How, asked the student, will you persuade people to look to the long-term benefits, when the short-term benefit offered them is literal survival? His answer indicated that he would not, or could not, grasp that for many—particularly those who live on and with the land—choices about protecting or endangering the landscape can mean life or death for an individual, a family, or an entire community.

Although Ray says that we need to start with self-esteem, I'm not convinced that's what it's about at all. It's about justice, first. If feminism has taught us anything, it's that abuses of people, animals, and ecosystems are a part of the same human enterprise. To stake out a political and activist position against one designated Other and not all Others is to cripple efforts to create a more humane and livable future. If you want to save the landscape, work to improve the lives of its inhabitants and neighbors.

Ecocomposition, Activist Writing, and Natural Ecosystems

A Response to Janisse Ray

Eric Otto

Marjory Stoneman Douglas's *The Everglades: River of Grass* generated public interest in protecting the Florida Everglades at a time when the barons of industry were about to further their exploitation of the sensitive wetlands. Rachel Carson's *Silent Spring* attracted unprecedented attention to the irresponsible and dangerous use of pesticides, leading to an eventual banning of DDT. And Janisse Ray's *Ecology of a Cracker Childhood* has influenced grassroots movements to protect southern Georgia's longleaf pine and swamp ecosystems. As Sid Dobrin and Chris Keller note in one of their questions to Ray, ecocomposition studies is interested in exploring the "concept of change through literature," the idea, as Ray says, "that there's no better way to make change than through literature" and, I will add, through writing in general. That Douglas's, Carson's, and Ray's works have not only brought about changes in public and personal opinion and in environmental policy but also, and as a result, have positively affected the health of natural ecosystems substantiates this interest and opens important avenues of inquiry for ecocomposition.

Writing is not a stable concept in composition studies, and as current-traditionalism, expressivism, process theory, and post-process theory each view writing in different ways, so does ecocomposition. Current-traditionalism is concerned with the rigors of expository writing, expressivism and process theory with personal writing and individual cognition, respectively, and post-process theory with the non-codifiable, social dimensions of written discourse. Ecocomposition follows and extends the direction of the latter—post-process theory—by examining the relationship between writers and their surroundings. As Joseph Harris writes from the position of post-process theory, "We write not as isolated individuals but as members of communities whose beliefs, concerns, and practices both instigate and constrain, at least in part, the sorts of things we can say. Our aims and intentions in writing are thus not merely personal, idiosyncratic, but reflective of the communities to which we belong" (261). Marilyn Cooper expresses a similar view in "The Ecology of Writing," grounding composition in an "ecological model of writing, whose fundamental tenet is that writing is an activity through which a person is continually engaged with a variety of socially constituted systems" (367). Ecocomposition draws from such theories, but it moves composition theory further forward by looking not only at the social environments within which writing takes place but also at the physical environments that we write and that write us.

Because ecocomposition examines the ways in which writing and language compose environments as well as the effects of physical environments on writing and on us, the discipline is well suited to study and promote environmental activism. Like ecocomposition, environmental activism attends to physical space—specifically, to the health of natural space—as it also understands the influence of language on perceptions of place, on public and personal opinion, and ultimately on natural ecosystems. In *Natural Discourse: Toward Ecocomposition*, Sid Dobrin and Christian Weisser claim, "one of ecocomposition's very reasons for being is to inquire into ways to bring about political, social, and/or environmental change" (86). Further, Dobrin and Weisser "argue for activist intellectuals—intellectuals who take their work to the streets" (87). If ecocomposition wants to move in such a direction—to probe into how writing and activist writers can bring about change—then it serves the discipline to look at and teach works, like Douglas's, Carson's, and Ray's, that have brought about real change. Rhetorical studies of such works would help us theorize what exactly effective discourse is within the context of environmental activism. On top of this type of study, though, we must also pay close attention to the stories and theories of writers who have produced successful pieces of activist environmental writing. In doing so, we learn about activist writing from the inside. Autobiographical and theoretic statements—like those included in the interviews in this book—teach us about the places and experiences that contributed to crafting the discourse of activist writers and about how such writers conceive of their craft as capable of bringing about tangible environmental change. In short, and to borrow the language of ecocomposition, we learn ways the natural world constructs activist writing as well as ways activist writing affects the natural world.

In *Ecology of a Cracker Childhood*, Janisse Ray remembers the influence the natural world had on her growing up: "I slept under the stars and ventured out alone to hunt a certain place where lady's slipper and trailing arbutus was said to bloom. It was as if my spirit had suddenly been let free. Nature was the other world. It claimed me" (262). As she relates in the above interview, later in her life Ray fused this passion for the natural world with her passion for writing. Within the context of ecocomposition, which aims to understand the role of the natural world in constructing our writing and our discourse, the moment of this fusion becomes as important as the fusion itself. For, Ray's realization of her "mythological path," her moment of self-realization and growth as an environmentalist writer, occurred in a natural setting—in the Andes. This experience in the Andes not only constructed her as a writer of environmental literature but also constructed her writing to involve pertinent issues of ecology and environment, and further, formed her effective activist discourse.

Besides the conditions of Ray's realization, that she fuses writing and nature is another important point when studying discourse from the perspective of ecocomposition. While we learn from Ray that nature writes us and that the natural world inspires activist writing, we also learn that writing about nature shapes our perception and treatment of the natural world. We get to know and understand nature through writing, through giving the natural world the same discursive value we give to other important aspects of our lives. Hence the value of writing for environmentalism. As Ray teaches us, writing benefits environmental activism in several ways. First, "by telling our stories and naming our vision" we articulate scenarios for a more sustainable future, as we also put our hopes and worries into language, making our agendas available for all to understand. Without doing so, we risk the kind of unawareness that Ray felt as a child: "I knew the Dewey decimal system inside and out, could calculate the force of gravity on a ten-pound block sliding down an incline, had read Dumas and Chekhov and Brontë but couldn't tell a weasel from a warthog. I never knew a naturalist or that there was such a thing as an environmentalist" (*Ecology* 211).

Similarly, writing, and more specifically naming, allows us to know a place and its inhabitants. Asked "Are names important? Does the act of naming affect a place? Our perception of that place?" Ray responds in the affirmative: "To know something's name—or someone's name—gives it identity, gives it visibility, gives it presence, gives it voice." Indeed, to write "*Sandhills clubtail dragonfly. Pine snake. Tiger salamander. Florida mouse. Mitchell's satyr. Henslow's sparrow. Sand skink. Bobwhite quail. Buchholz's dart moth. Gopher tortoise. Ground dove. Indigo snake. Sandhill scarab beetle. Southeastern kestrel. Flatwoods salamander"* composes a place as a community of recognized nonhuman interactors (*Ecology* 142). Naming signifies the living components of local ecosystems using language, the means by which we construct and understand the world; and understanding is certainly a vital step in changing perceptions of the often-feared and misunderstood natural world.

Finally, as Ray mentions, writing is the means by which we compose "a template now for living," drawing upon the ideas of thinkers who promote views of the natural world alternative to those of exploitive economic systems and the ideology of material progress. Ray believes we need these alternative views and, in fact, suggests that we "redo our Bill of Rights, so that we extend human rights to the nonhuman." Certainly another significant step in providing a reworked template or model for living with, rather than against, the natural world, Ray's proposal to rewrite the Bill of Rights is interesting for ecocomposition. Not only does it reflect Aldo Leopold's land ethic, which "enlarges the boundaries of the community to include soils, waters, plants, and animals, or collectively: the land," but it aims to add the natural world to a document that writes certain human rights into existence (Leopold 239). "[F]reedom of speech," "the right of the people peaceably to assemble," and "the right of the people to keep and bear Arms" are not intrinsic to being human. Rather, they are language-constructed rights that have real value within the context of American society. Ray's "template for living" is, like the Bill of Rights, a construction of language and written ideas, one that will ideally yield real results within natural systems.

"Writing with Intent: An Interview with Janisse Ray" thus contributes to the work of ecocomposition by confirming the claim that "environment is as much a construct of discourse as discourse is a product of environment" (Dobrin and Weisser 14). Ray highlights and proves the importance of experiencing the natural world and blending these experiences into writing. It is of great consequence for us, as activist ecocompositionists and as teachers, to perform our acts of writing about place in those places about which we are writing, to incorporate our experiences in those places into our writing, and to encourage our students to do the same. Ray also suggests that activist writing must give voice to natural ecosystems, promote an understanding of environmentalist visions, and thereby work toward protecting the natural world. Again, we can match Ray's attention to these aspects of environmental activist writing by helping our students and the public to understand, to

name, both the interrelated components of local natural ecosystems and
the environmental policies and philosophies we support. Writing helps us
accomplish all of these things.

To conclude on a speculative note, a note that Ray's comments inspire, the circularity of the relationship between activist writing and the
natural world—between Ray's *Ecology of a Cracker Childhood* and Georgia's
pine forests and swamps, for example—interestingly parallels the circulation of matter that occurs within any healthy ecosystem. But this symbiotic relationship between writing and environment does not only
metaphorically parallel the complex dynamic of a natural ecosystem—of,
for example, the relationship between ruddy daggerwing butterflies and
the undergrowth of a tropical hardwood hammock, where each needs the
other to ensure continued fitness. Rather, as evidenced by the tangibility
of the changes Douglas's, Carson's, and Ray's books have initiated, writing *is* an essential part of ecological health. Likewise, the natural world
is essential to constructing writing, language, and us as members of larger
human and nonhuman communities.

It would take the combined work of evolutionary biologists and
psychologists, linguists, anthropologists, literary scholars, ecologists,
compositionists, and more to investigate fully the claims that language
evolves in natural environments and that discourse is yet another mechanism by which ecological systems preserve their own integrity. Such claims
make up the visionary, interdisciplinary motives of ecocomposition. Like
Janisse Ray, who hopes "that somewhere the lonely pine forest knows that
[she is] working toward its protection" and that there is "a kind of transcendental knowledge between places and people," ecocompositionists
interested in activist writing and natural ecosystems endeavor to find
deep scientific and cultural connections between writing and environments in an effort to promote positive change in the ways we write,
understand, and treat the natural world. Indeed, Ray gives us hope that
such change is possible.

WORKS CITED

Carson, Rachel. *Silent Spring.* Boston: Houghton Mifflin, 2002.

Cooper, Marilyn M. "The Ecology of Writing." *College English* 48.4 (1986): 364–75.

Dobrin, Sidney I., and Christian R. Weisser. *Natural Discourse: Toward Ecocomposition.*
    Albany: State U of New York P, 2002.

Douglas, Marjory Stoneman. *The Everglades: River of Grass.* Sarasota, FL: Pineapple Press,
    1997.

Harris, Joseph. "The Idea of Community in the Study of Writing." *On Writing Research: The Braddock Essays, 1975–1998.* Ed. Lisa Ede. Boston: Bedford, 1999. 260–71.

Leopold, Aldo. *A Sand County Almanac, With Essays on Conservation from Round River.* New York: Ballantine, 1966.

Ray, Janisse. *Ecology of a Cracker Childhood.* Minneapolis: Milkweed, 1999.

The Quest for Truth

An Interview with Max Oelschlaeger

In 1991 Max Oelschlaeger was nominated for both the Pulitzer Prize and the National Book Award for his *The Idea of Wilderness*. In this book, Oelschlaeger examines the relationships between humans and nature from a historical perspective. What makes this historical examination so intriguing is that Oelschlaeger grounds his critique in the history of intellectual thought. That is, he articulates the relationships between humans and nature as an intellectual relationship. In the interview below, Oelschlaeger talks extensively about this relationship and about the ways that intellectual thought has shaped how we as humans engage nature. What is most fascinating is that Oelschlaeger is quite literal in his explication of this relationship, identifying that even reading the words of a poem while standing in a wild setting can affect how we encounter that setting and that poem. He says, "Poetry, which is meant to be read aloud, in an oral way, moves me into a position where I can begin to sense and appreciate more readily my affiliation with the earth and all that is going on."

Oelschlaeger's writing blends elements of science, literature, philosophy, religion, and environmental studies, and the interview here reflects his broad knowledge of those fields. For those of us interested in discourse studies, Oelschlaeger's attention to how language affects these areas of study is critical. Oelschlaeger says, "I am a lover of language, so I'm always reading about language," but that is a bit of an understatement. His love of language translates into a serious attention to theories of discourse and language and the ways in which the production and interpretation of language function as a bonding element between intellectual work and human interaction with wilderness. Oelschlaeger is as much a scholar of language and discourse as he is a natural historian, a philosopher, or a scientist.

Many readers will be interested to hear Oelschlaeger identify the importance of the "postmodern turn" in understanding current thinking about nature and wilderness. Perhaps more important, though, Oelschlaeger is clear that "With the advent of twentieth-century critical rhetorical inquiries that are not the province of any one discipline—like philosophy or literature—but open to all, we have started to think more about wildness and wilderness, and what this means in what might be a more traditional philosophical question, what this means in terms of our humanity, who we are, where we're going, where we have been. That certainly was the impetus for me." He explains here that his own intellectual development grew from an intense study of Greek rhetoricians and that he has always been critically aware of the relationships between rhetoric and philosophy, rhetoric and literature, rhetoric and science, and the role of rhetoric in his own work on wilderness and environment. And furthermore, in curbing our current environmental dilemmas, Oelschlaeger believes, "critical rhetorical work is absolutely essential." The interview below is testament to Oelschlaeger's range of understanding environmental discourses throughout Western history.

Q: You suggest in the Preface to *The Idea of Wilderness* that your work refers "elliptically to Heidegger's observation that human beings never come to thoughts; thoughts happen—out of historical and linguistic inevitability—to us. To allow thought to be bounded by social context is not to think philosophically. And yet to be human is to be linguistically and historically enframed. Consequently, philosophical discourse must affirm the presence of what can never be revealed through words." As scholars with backgrounds in rhetoric, we often study the ways that words do reveal and construct, particularly something like wilderness. This may be an age-old and large question, but is it possible for you to comment on the relationship or differences between philosophy and rhetoric as they affect our examinations of wilderness?

A: It's a good question. As I look at the history of Western philosophy, I feel as if the best part of philosophy—which is critical theory, critical study, architectonic rhetoric and the like—was lost in the shuffle with the Greeks about two thousand years ago, and philosophy turned in a direction of searching for immutable foundations for knowledge, for certitude, for universals which would be good for all people in all places at all times. Rhetoric was largely ignored by the philosophical community. That's changed, of course, in the twentieth century with the advent of postmodernism, and critical theory, in philosophers like McKeon, Rorty, and others. Philosophers are far more open now to the realization that they themselves are embedded within social, historical, linguistic circumstances and that attention to these circumstances helps us to overcome the illusions of superiority that the philosophical community has always had. I think the reason that philosophers per se, as a professional community, have typically had little to say about wildness or wilderness is that it basically defies their attempts to fashion rigorous philosophical schematisms. With the advent of twentieth-century critical rhetorical inquiries that are not the province of any one discipline—like philosophy or literature—but open to all, we have started to think more about wildness and wilderness, and what this means in what might be a more traditional philosophical question, what this means in terms of our humanity, who we are, where we're going, where we have been. That certainly was the impetus for me.

I grew up, philosophically speaking, in a very traditional way, and thought the Greeks hung the moon, and that the unexamined life was not worth living, you know, the Socratic dictum. But, as I went further with this, I began to discover that most of life was not being examined at all, that philosophy was a project of looking within the artifice of human civilization and of particularly intellectual achievements. It was kind of a neck-up philosophizing and so the rest of the world disappeared. After I finished my philosophical studies, for many years, I was trying to catch up, and I was reading everything from anthropology to zoology, a lot of biology, a lot of natural history, trying to fill in this large part of the world that I had totally neglected in my philosophical studies. I think that what's going on right now, as we begin to see all different kinds of people, such as Janisse Ray talking about her childhood in Georgia as a "Cracker," as she puts it herself, we're beginning to see that these kinds of inquiries that begin to confront the linguistically perpetuated circumstances into which we all are flung, simply by the fact of being human, and to rediscover this large living chaos of the biophysical world in which we are embedded, to call that exclusively philosophical does violence to people like Janisse Ray, whose work is extremely interesting for me.[1] I would like to do away with distinctions like *philosophy* and *literature*. We are storytelling culture dwellers, and we're embedded in a Western narrative that has deluded itself in many ways, one of which is that we, as human beings, are above nature, that we're in control of the wild earth, and that, really, the only thing that counts is us and our own narrow human projects.

Q: It sounds as though, in that distinction between philosophy and rhetoric, what you just articulated was leaning toward a more Burkean concept of rhetoric, in that notion of biological life and intellectual life are inseparable, and we cannot make that distinction.

A: I think that distinction between philosophy, as dealing with surety and certainty, and providing foundational knowledge, and methodologies as over and distinct from the various forms of rhetoric, as dealing with this frothy surface of knowledge, of the way that we persuade people to believe in things, or manipulate people, is an untenable distinction—which, in some ways, mirrors the untenable distinction, or the unsustainable distinction, between wilderness and civilization.

Q: You have also said, "As many hermeneutists and critical rhetoricians suggest, the intellectual interprets in order not to be deceived, a process without end." Could you speak to the need for critical rhetorical work when exploring environmental and ecological pursuits and how those never-ending processes might proceed?

A: Let me give you an example or two that begin to get to this question. In about the last ten years, since I finished *The Idea of Wilderness*, I have been reading a number of philosophers, but I've found the work of Charles Taylor particularly inspiring, particularly the two volumes of collected essays, volume one being *Human Agency and Language*, which is a masterpiece, and then also his major work, *Sources of the Self*, which shows the many different narrative traditions that have contributed to, shall we say, a somewhat confused sense of who we are and where we're going as we enter into postmodernity. Taylor talks about the importance of moral maps. If you think of the horizon of human possibilities, as we move on into the twenty-first century, you begin to get some sense that what Taylor is seeking is the ability for diverse groups of human beings to draw upon all the different kinds of resources that are available to us, whether this might be Jewish resources, Christian resources, Enlightenment resources, or Greek classicism, or whatever, in an effort to get some sense of the directions in which we progress. He calls this effort "strong evaluation," and he distinguishes it from "weak evaluation." Weak evaluation is, in one sense—Taylor doesn't say this; this is more my interpretation of it—weak evaluation is not evaluation at all. It means simply going with the currents of the time. This parallels Ortega y Gasset's notion of the mass man, who seeks only to be like everybody else. Taylor suggests that we have the resources available to us to make far better inquiries into the human condition and better possibilities to draw these maps of human possibility and then to begin to compare and contrast these different routes. Certainly, when you begin to think about wilderness and civilization, we see that we have created a civilization that is simply not sustainable. We are perilously close to some bifurcation points, such as the collapse of the climate as we have known it. We have been living in this wonderful climatological period. If we look back at some other civilizations that have experienced climatological permutations, like the Roman Empire during the Roman climate optimum, we discover the Romans had no choice, in terms of the next decade or the next century. In contrast to them, in relation to atmospheric phenomena, such as levels of carbon dioxide, we do have very real choices. So, critical rhetorical work is absolutely essential to making good choices. There's some remarkable theoreticians out there who have been doing that. I might also add that some of these people are scientists, rather than rhetoricians or philosophers. I think particularly of the work of John Firor who was the Director of Research at the National Center for Atmospheric Research. He wrote a remarkable book called *The Changing Atmosphere*. In that book, he deconstructs the prevailing viewpoint that these problems will be solved entirely through technology and scientific research and the application of that research, and concludes the book, after deconstructing that thesis, by demonstrating that such an approach simply will not work, that it is not a viable possibility, even from the standpoint of scientific analysis. He indicates that we will not find our way into a sustainable future until we seriously consider the human project, who we are, where we're going, and why we're doing it. So, from both sides of the street, the natural scientist who dared to be reflective and critical, as well as the humanities perspective, I think that we are beginning to see a resurgence of interest in criticism, which is enormously more informed than earlier critical projects.

Q: In your essay "Wilderness, Civilization, and Language," you contend, "if it is through language that we have been alienated from nature, then reconciliation might also be affected through language." Such a statement resonates with the work of others, such as David Abram and, perhaps, Neil Evernden. As part of this "reconciliation" process, you turn to the writings of "the great wilderness thinkers and poets," such as Aldo Leopold, Henry David Thoreau, Gary Snyder, and John Muir who "penetrate the vocabulary and rhetoric of the modern age." Does the language in written texts somehow hold greater potential for reconciliation (or alienation) than do other forms of language?

A: I'll tell you a story. I still get out for day hikes and occasionally backpack, and when I go backpacking or hiking, I'll always take something with me, and sometimes it's something very short, like a poem by W. S. Merwin, like "Witness." It goes roughly like this:

I want to speak for the forest,
I will have to recover a forgotten language.

Let's say you go into the Sangre de Cristo Mountains right outside of
Santa Fe, or you go into the San Francisco peaks, and you go up in the
fall, about mid-October. You sit in the middle of an aspen forest that has
changed, but the leaves are still on the trees. The wind hasn't beaten them
off yet. You read that poem aloud, and it becomes almost like a Zen
meditation. Some very strange and powerful things have happened to me
when I have done that. I don't even think about this as weird anymore,
but all of a sudden, the brain chatter stops, and I know that, somehow,
I'm part of all this. That there's an enormous continuum of time. There's
been this evolution in the local vicinity of space and time, of the carbon
complexity. I'm part of it, but so are those aspen. Poetry, particularly,
helps me begin to overcome the divide between egoic consciousness and
the rest of nature. Now, my appreciation of poetry, the nature poets like
Merwin, or Roethke, or Snyder, or Jeffers, or Emily Dickinson, or some
others, is probably reinforced by reading people like David Abram or
Martin Heidegger, and Charles Taylor and others who have theorized
about language. Poetry, which is meant to be read aloud, in an oral way,
moves me into a position where I can begin to sense and appreciate more
readily my affiliation with the earth and all that is going on. I will also
say that most of the things I've done which I'm proud of intellectually
have come to me, almost instantaneously, which sounds strange, but like
The Idea of Wilderness, the idea for that book came to me almost instantaneously about four or five in the morning outside of Pagosa Springs,
Colorado, in October when a bull elk bugled. I must have rocketed up
about a hundred feet into the sky, and in the next two days, I produced
about a twenty-page single-spaced overview which, with just a few exceptions, became that book. It was just an instantaneous *shazam*, and that's
happened on multiple occasions. It's not a process of "okay, I'm going to
grind something out here." Instead, it's this total gestalt of intellective
and affective being. Its not that I am privileged or gifted in any sense.
Maybe the only advantage I've had is, as a philosopher, to become a bit
heretical about a lot of things, including rationality, and to open my
affective sensibilities.

Q: In that description of poetry providing this connection, there seem to
be two things going on: one is that writing, that text, whether it is poetry
or not, is engaged in an ecological relationship with you and the aspen
grove. It is creating an awareness there. My question following that would

be: we talk a lot in postmodern wilderness studies about nature and wilderness as constructs, as things that we discursively create. In that example you have just given, there seems to be a very tight relationship between the construct of the environment and that text. Suddenly, the text you brought with you, through recitation, has given you the opportunity to see this aspen grove in a different way. What, either personally or philosophically, is that ecological relationship between that text and that construct of nature?

A: I know that one of the other people you are interviewing is Ed Wilson, who is a friend of mine, and who I respect enormously. You had mentioned reading *The Naturalist*. I wrote a review of that book. That book tells a lot about his childhood. He'd go out and wander around, and he'd see real things. He became fascinated with the ants, and he'd get down on his hands and knees, and see the ants. There's what a Heideggerian might call a "givenness to the world." Yet, there's also a tendency for us to believe in the fallacy of the immaculate perception, as if seeing, for example, the sun going around the earth. Obviously, the sun's going around the earth, but think again. And so, interpretation of this givenness is part of the human condition, and interpretation, of course, occurs within linguistic communities. I think Ed is aware of that himself. So, then, the other person I wanted to mention was Neil Evernden, the Canadian, who has two remarkable books, *The Natural Alien*, and *The Social Creation of Nature*. He's doing a lot with continental language philosophy, not so much with Wittgenstein, and some of the Anglo-Americans, such as Rorty, although he's aware of them in his second book. He sees that there is a stubborn facticity to the world, there's a givenness to the world. Yet the world doesn't interpret itself. We bring to the world our narrative, or, in the case of the aspen example, a very short and powerful poem, and that poem, to me, opens up the aspen grove, so that it's no longer scenery, and something pretty and something I want to take photos of, but it's, to speak loosely, it's as though all of a sudden I've been reattached to the cosmos by some sort of umbilical cord of being here, now in that aspen grove, and that energizes me. I will confess to needing those fixes, and it's not by accident that I'm living here in the mountains. So, I'm very comfortable with those experiences. Literature is the catalyst. It's not like a slot machine, where you just pull the handle and that good thing happens, but I'll go up there and say that poem, and be saying that poem, and then just shut off for awhile, and all of a sudden, *shazam*, it happens. You can't say when it is going to happen, but it happens almost every time for me. There's a few places where I can go that are pretty reliable, like the Windsor Trail that takes you into the aspen forest just outside of the Santa Fe National Forest in the Sangre de Cristos. I lived in New Mexico for four years, and I've hiked that trail probably two hundred times. Every October I'd go on Saturdays and Sundays continuing for two or three weeks. I'd do that as long as the leaves were on the trees.

Q: Coming back to your essay "Wilderness, Civilization, and Language," as in other areas of your work, you often seem to use the words *wilderness* and *nature* synonymously, though *wilderness* is typically used in your titles. Is there a difference?

A: I think that words have a history, and this history extends through certain communities. The word *nature* in the late nineteenth and twentieth centuries has been appropriated largely by scientific communities. With that appropriation of the word comes some baggage; in part, the baggage is that *nature* becomes an objective phenomenon to be methodologically studied, subject to experiment, so that we can determine causal relationships, and then intervene in nature to control the world. *Wildness* and *wilderness* belong to different communities than *nature*, and these are the treehuggers, and the conservationists, and lovers and poets of nature. You might say there's always a contest going on, in what I'm writing. I'm trying to free nature up, and create a more expansive notion of what constitutes nature, but I'm certainly, because of my own experiences, more comfortable with nature as known from the inside. This ability to get out of your own psyche and, again, become *soma*, become body, become earth, to know nature from the inside. Heidegger talks about dwelling, and Heidegger is like cheesecake, a little bit goes a long way. Bruce Foltz recently published one of the single best books on Heidegger called *Inhabiting the Earth*. This piece brought me to a new understanding of dwelling. The dweller is one who has become psychologically, subjectively, comfortable with the notion that you are part of this place, and that this place is fundamentally intertwined with your own being, and with the possibilities of your own humanity. There's no distinction between *psyche* and *soma* and *geos*. Being here on the southern Colorado plateau, with such powerful biophysical features, brought this home to me. There's a twenty-two-acre conservation easement behind my house, and I never realized that elk stink, but I've become adept at knowing when the elk are back there because I can smell them. Remember the first time you went to Barnum and Bailey [circus] and smelled the elephants?

Elk are just a pinch down from elephants. I get that smell, and the world goes away; it's just wonderful.

Q: Is the word *nature* itself so broad, complex, and misunderstood that it itself is what alienates us?

A: There's a book called *Key Words of the English Language*, and the author was one of the editors, probably still living, of the Oxford English Dictionary, which is always undergoing revision. I have a hard copy of the OED, the reduced copy, and now I have the OED on CD. I am a lover of language, so I'm always reading about language. I read *Key Words of the English Language* at least a couple of times. One thing I always remember from that is the statement that the word *nature* is the most complex and the most conflicted in the English language. Think about that. It relates directly to what you are saying here. Think of the way in which nature has been represented, so very often, in terms of binary oppositions: nature is good/evil; beautiful/ugly; bounteous/stingy, etc. Just the fact that we so often represent nature binarily reflects the conflicted semantic history of the word. But I think we're in a remarkable period of time in relation to that word, and it's because of this new generation of people that I'm going to call the postmoderns. Some are physicists, chemists, litterateurs, philosophers, they come from all different areas. One who comes to mind is Ilya Prigogine and the second who comes to mind is David Bohm. Prigogine is a Nobel Laureate. He was educated in Europe, so he has a bit more of an expansive conception of science, and thus of nature, than most natural scientists educated in America, many of whom are my friends, and some do have an expansive conception of nature as well. In the book he coauthored with Isabelle Stengers, *Order Out of Chaos*, he talks about the multiple representations or descriptions of nature that can be made, and then concludes with a detailed passage stating that none of these are privileged and none of these are definitive, and we have entered into a new understanding of this world in which we are embedded. He says the only reason we can know this world, and create these representations, is because we are a part of this world, and created by this world. We are a part of the chaos that turns into order, the evolving complexity of the system. I think that Prigogine's insights are very important. I don't want to privilege them as the last word, though. He goes on, in books like *The End of Certainty*, and develops some nuances to this, but you can put the conflictive, complex nature of the word *nature* into other contexts, like hierarchical sociopolitical systems, and then you can see that certain representations of nature become privileged. They begin to choke out alternative interpretations of nature. Women's bodies are a classic area of study for this.

Q: It's interesting that you bring up the subject of women here. Do you think that this alienation in any way has been more prevalent for women? That is, the majority of those who have written or spoken for or about *nature* have been men. Are women "linguistically enframed" differently than men and do women write about nature differently than men?

A: Just to share a little personal history, I'm fifty-eight now, and lived through the period of the sixties when there was talk of sisterhood as powerful. This was really the first upswelling of feminine consciousness, though, of course, there has been some philosophical writing prior to that period. To tell you the truth, it was hard for me, because I was still in the early phases of my own philosophical training and education to make much headway with that. As critical feminist inquiries became richer and more complicated, I remember reading *The Origin of Patriarchy*, and I said, "Holy cow! This is an awesome argument." It made me realize several things: my own privileged position as a male, and how many things I took for granted, and the realization that there were very significant differences based on class, gender, etc., simply based on the contingencies of our own birth. After that, the world started looking a little bit different to me. I find the writings of people like Terry Tempest Williams, for example, to be incredibly powerful, reflecting a position I can appreciate but can't totally grasp because of my own privileged position. I remember reading Susan Griffin's *Woman and Nature* for the first time. I couldn't read it for more than five minutes. It was so incredibly powerful. I had the same experience with *Pornography and Silence*. I don't think there's a neutral language for anybody. What we need to do to find our way into a viable and sustainable human future is to begin to listen attentively to everybody's stories. Not that they're all the same, but we need to listen, for a start.

Q: In *The Idea of Wilderness* the majority of writers you treat are those whom we typically view as nature writers: Thoreau, Muir, Leopold, Jeffers, Snyder, and others. In *Unweaving the Rainbow: Science, Delusion, and the Appetite for Wonder*, scientist Richard Dawkins argues that "the spirit of wonder which led Blake to Christian mysticism, Keats to Arcadian myth and Yeats to Fenians and fairies, is the very same spirit that moves the great scientists." In your estimation, how do scientists contribute to or affect the philosophy of wilderness? That is, in what ways does their language—their discourses—alienate or reconcile us with nature?

A: I mentioned Ed Wilson as a friend and someone who has inspired me with his writing, and I mentioned Ilya Prigogine. I might mention some-one like C. F. Von Weiszacker. I might mention Schrödinger. There's a number of scientists who, through their writings, have helped us begin to come to grips with the socially constructed circumstances in which we are embedded vis-à-vis the earth, and its ongoing biophysical processes. Unfortunately, these people tend to be exceptions. To deny the serious-ness of the anthropogenic impacts on the global atmosphere is the height of silliness, but it's based on this illusion we've had for three to four hundred years, part of which I talk about in *The Idea of Wilderness*. Many other people have talked about the fact that we cannot act upon the earth and its systems with impunity. We can act without consequences for at least a short period of time, but the earth strikes back. We are caught up in a push-pull system. A book came out three or four years ago, written by a fellow named Daniel Sarewitz called *Frontiers of Illusion*. In that book, in one sense, he's doing the kind of thing that Francis Bacon did, who was a great apologist for science 350 years ago. Sarewitz looks at the apologetics for science at the end of WWII, which is basically known as the Vannevar Bush model. The idea is that, by investing hundreds of millions of dollars on a yearly basis on basic scientific research, we will get all sorts of spin-offs, like transistors, which lead to PCs, and so on and so forth, that are going to make us all rich. We'll all be healthy, wealthy, and wise forevermore. Defense spending was legitimated by this apologetic that we would get this unending stream of social and eco-nomic benefits. With the collapse of the Soviet Union, and that's what Sarewitz is looking at, in 1990 roughly, the Vannevar Bush model falls flat on its face, and everyone in Congress, and the committees that are advising Congress, realizes this. Furthermore, it was a failed model to begin with. Everyone was not getting wealthy and living happily forev-ermore. The rich were getting richer, and the poor were getting poorer. We weren't really solving the fundamental socioeconomic problems that our society faced, and we were totally ignoring other sorts of problems, like environmental problems, many of which were being exacerbated by the very science fueled by the Vannevar Bush model. Sarewitz then goes on to say that we need a new, legitimating narrative, and he suggests here the myth of sustainability as a viable contender. Now that story is to be continued, but it begins to show that scientific communities, and they're very diverse, depend upon large and continuing streams of funding, and that, ultimately, from time to time at least, these funding streams, and the course of science, are subject to criticism. Where is the moral now? We're in one of those periods where the work of people like Wilson, Prigogine, and Bohm, is incredibly important.

Q: Physicist Werner Heisenberg once wrote: "What we observe is not nature itself, but nature exposed to our method of questioning." From a rhetorical standpoint, it's interesting the way Heisenberg approaches this—particularly for those in the humanities who have often been engaged in a postmodern fascination with the way we "build" and "construct" nature, not question it. In short, who do you see as asking the right questions about nature? The wrong questions?

A: Let me subvert that question just a little bit. I'm thinking here of Bacon, whom I continue to think about off and on, and some of the remarkable books written about Bacon, like the one by Leiss. Bacon believed in the domination of nature. If you read his texts, you see that he thinks of nature as a female, and we need to put her to the test, we need to control her. It's this questioning frame that is the vehicle for control. It implies that the human relation to nature, as captured in the very notion of objectivity, is *mono logos,* a monologue that we are putting nature to the test, that we are forcing her to reveal her secrets, in a Baconian sense. Once she has revealed her secrets, then we will control her. What I want to suggest now is that the people who are doing the deepest thinking about the relation between nature and culture are people like Ilya Prigogine. His *The End of Certainty* argues that we are in the middle of a second scientific revolution, and that part of what is going on is that we realize that the *mono logos* is not a viable way of interacting with the earth, that it has to be a *dia logos.* Think of people like Terry Tempest Williams or Mary Oliver and the remarkable piece of poetry at the beginning of Terry's book *Refuge.* We can put ourselves in a place where we can begin to hear nature, we can give voice to nature. But to do that, we have to bracket or control some of the deeply embedded tendencies in the dominant stories. To take just one example—and it's a very important part of what's going on out here in the West with public lands—87 percent of these intermountain western states are public lands, and they are a treasure, not only for our nation but for the entire world. The possibilities are enormous; these are singular sorts of biophysical entities. But the public lands forests are at risk of catastrophic fire. Why? We've had this enormous public relations propaganda campaign that fire is bad—Smokey the Bear: "Only you can prevent forest fires." We had

Gifford Pinchot saying that forest fire is a waste because it destroys valuable timber that we need to harvest so that we can achieve the greatest good for the greatest number. Fire suppression and fire exclusion becomes forest service policy for an entire century. All of a sudden, we're beginning to realize in the intermountain West, particularly in our ponderosa pine ecosystems but also in our mixed conifer ecosystems, that through our own lack of ability to appreciate nature's own evolved processes, we have created the conditions for catastrophe, for stand-reducing catastrophic fires that can also destroy the built environment. Los Alamos, with its $1.5 billion property losses, is just the tip of the iceberg. The community in which I live is 65 percent in the red zone; 65 percent of this community could be snuffed out in a runaway forest fire. From time to time, we live in terror. We created those conditions. By listening to nature's own voice, what we begin to see is that low-intensity ground fires kept the forest open, kept the parks open. That was the way the forest healed itself. That's what we're beginning to do, participate in the *dia logos*, and get over the *mono logos*. This is part of the education of young men and women as they move into the scientific communities; they need to be able to participate in a dialogue with the forests.

Q: In another interview in this book, when asked as to what place he sees for postmodernists in the sciences, Edward O. Wilson has said "Close to zero." He continues to say that postmodern scientists "may be listened to by people in humanities, but scientists are scarcely aware of their existence." You have written extensively about postmodernism, particularly as it intersects with philosophies of wilderness. You have, for instance, written, "the emerging postmodern wilderness philosophy is more than environmentalism in new guise. It represents a convergence of scientific research and reflective thought on the premise that the human and cultural—including the ethical, theological, and philosophical—are linked with the material and organic. In other words, there are no grounds to draw radical distinctions in kind between ends and means, or facts and values, for what is known to exist is known only in relation to something else, and that is most fundamentally an evolutionary continuum." You go on to say that "the postmodern conception might be understood in terms of cosmic synergism. More important, the idea of wilderness in postmodern context is, as Neil Evernden and others imply, a search for meaning—for a new creation story or mythology—that is leading humankind out of a homocentric prison into the cosmic wilderness. And if that new creation story is to ring true in a postmodern age, then it must have both scientific plausibility and religious distinctiveness." How would you respond to

Wilson's claim that scientists don't really pay attention to postmodern thinkers and scientists in the sciences?

A: As I mentioned earlier, Ed is a friend, and we correspond from time to time. When I took this position, he sent me a letter of congratulations. I've studied a lot of major intellectual figures. When they live long, rich, complicated lives, like Ed, they have the opportunity to contradict themselves. Bertrand Russell comes to mind, or Ludwig Wittgenstein, who had several different careers, and they abandoned previously held positions. If you read Ed's work, you'll find when he's grinding his materialist axe, he'll say that religion is bunk, but if you read in another place, he'll say religion has very high survival value. I think that Ed is definitely rooted in an East Coast Ivy League context, where postmodernism is understood in a very truncated way, where it means deconstructive nihilism and relativism. He's not thinking of it in terms of postmodern currents that are critical but also constructive and pragmatic. Ilya Prigogine, for example, is a postmodern scientist. And so, scientifically termed, Ed's sample is too small. It would be like coming to conclusions about ants by maybe studying two or three different species of ants, rather than the thousands of species that he has. Nobody can do it all, of course. I think Ed also has a keen appreciation of the rhetorical value of saying things like that. I mean, there's nothing better for book sales than pissing readers off. This fans the flames. I remember reading a review of Camille Paglia's *Sexual Personae*, and she was described as the bête noir of feminism. It wasn't by accident that *Sexual Personae* achieved a lofty position on the *New York Times* Best-Seller Lists. She irritated a whole lot of people. I think Ed is more than sophisticated enough to do those kinds of things.

I would like to say there are people, like Brian Swimme, who, in collaborating with Thomas Berry, is working toward these kinds of cosmic synergisms, or new creation stories, that you mentioned earlier. There are also a number of people who, though they are not creating or writing new myths, are looking at what is called "the re-enchantment of nature." That is, abandoning the classical and neoclassical scientific view that nature is nothing but material atoms in motion, running into each other, and recognizing the reality of what Ernst Mayr calls the teleonomy of self-organizing, increasingly complicated, kinds of structures. Nature has tendencies or directions. Bohm talks about the qualitative infinity of nature, that we're just in a particular place at a particular time, and we can begin to see a hundred or thousand years, or we can speculate about the Big Bang, but the story is never ending, it goes on and on. I always take Ed seriously, but as an intellectual myself, well, you have to learn the ropes. There's a lot of postmodern scientists out there. If Ed meant that, say, you're a systems ecologist, and you're out studying the ponderosa pines ecosystem, if he meant, are you thinking about Derrida and Foucault. No. They're not thinking about that. They're trying to organize their students and their research team and supervising and coming back over the next year or two, and interpreting their data. But most of the scientists I know around here, for example, are fully aware that they are engaged in acts of interpretation, that there are no brute facts that interpret themselves in the world. A very important book for me was by Allen and Hoekstra, called *Toward a Unified Ecology*. In one sense, it is a postmodern scientific primer for ecologists. It simply says that the scientist or research group that is unaware of its own interpretive framework is one destined to no good end.

Q: Continuing along those same lines, you conclude your book *The Idea of Wilderness* by saying "We, the spoiled children of the Great Mother, we who refuse to see, to hear and heed Her message, Her laws. Is salvation possible? Or have we so fouled this earth, so covered the green world beneath our second world, that no light can penetrate the world's midnight? Is there hope for the plant and animal people? Is there hope for all of us? These are questions that must be answered by the postmodern mind, for only through that exercise of consciousness can our modern dilemma be transcended." You published that conclusion in 1991. Here it is a decade later and a decade deeper into the postmodern era. Has postmodernism begun answering these questions in any substantial ways?

A: I think it has. I think I am more optimistic than pessimistic. Just to name a few examples and tendencies, I think of Donna Haraway's most recent work, *Modest Witness*, or the most recent work of Terry Tempest Williams, *Leap*. These are incredible, rich, different yet similar, postmodern performances. Performativity. Beginning to learn the possibilities of altered awareness, of each other, of the earth, of the processes of the earth, of the spaces in which we exist. What is Hieronymous Bosch's triptych, *The Garden of Earthly Delights*, but a figuration? And what is *Leap* but this incredible interpretation of this figuration that has figured so significantly in Terry Tempest Williams's own life? Her grandmother had Heaven and Hell, two of the three panels, hanging over her bed. Terry grew up with that binary opposition. On the literary front, the artistic, creative front, with the kinds of work done by people like Haraway and Williams, I see some exciting material. Every time I go back to Haraway,

I can't read more than a page without going off; it's just such awesomely powerful stuff. I think there is a many-threaded growing conversation, with a sustainability metaphoric at its very heart, that is playing out in 101 different ways. When Gro Brundtland and others were in the business of organizing the United Nations Conference on Environment and Development (UNCED), they truly meant to leave many things "unsaid." They were attempting to provide some Band-Aids for the hemorrhaging of the earth, to assuage both the concerns of environmental communities, particularly those in the Northern hemisphere, and the economic concerns of the Southern hemisphere. What was interesting is they wanted the unsaid to remain unsaid. Namely, the globalist narrative is essentially anomalous. It's going to either fall apart, or undergo critical imaginative variation. The sustainability narratives that are emerging are the beginnings of alternatives. I mentioned the work of Sarewitz because he's not talking about sustainable development, he's not talking about the new world order, he's not talking about the globalist agenda. The quote you have here, I'm actually making some rhetorical flourishes. I talk about the world's midnight, and there are some contemporary Europeans who talk about that, but I was particularly thinking of Hegel, and his assertion that the owl of Minerva flies only at midnight. We're there. The twentieth century, if nothing else, was a sobering century. Everything was possible, but nothing was done. Masters of space, yet we can't even deal with the basics of living on this planet.

Q: You have also been clear, "Truth is not out there, in a world independent of a community of scientific researchers, but is enabled by the linguistically articulated assumptions and human practices . . . that enable inquiry." You continue, "The crucial question, faintly but unmistakably present on the horizon of our inquiry, is to determine how culture—that is, the continuing process of choice called the West—presently influences science. Yet with recognition of these questions the reflexive paradox appears with a cognitive vengeance, for language is caught in its own circle." You go on, "In other words, recognition that language plays a central role in all knowledge and thought, indeed, in culture and therefore life, has also called into question claims to absolute certitude." If not certitude and truth, what then do we look for in intellectual exploration of human interaction with nature and wilderness?

A: I'm not a relativist, and I'm not willing to abandon cognitive claims. I believe that the quest for truth is fundamentally important. What we've gotten over is what Anthony Damasio calls Descartes' Illusion or Delusion, the belief that we can have sure and certain knowledge through methodological commitments that grind truth out like an assembly line. We've gotten over that. Take an example, the very good scientific research that's going on in the local vicinity in our forests. This research reflects ethical and literary excursions that were taken up 150 years ago by Thoreau, or 100 years ago by Muir, or 50 years ago by Leopold. All those pieces are beginning to come together. We are beginning to grasp and make real the notion that the metaphysical divide between biological ecology, biophysical ecology, and human ecology, is not intellectually tenable and is ecologically dangerous. I see that happening in the communities of people working around here. They realize that the forest is not just a resource for their economic appropriation, which reflects an ethical dimension to these problems. They also realize that the forest, these ponderosa pine ecosystems, need fire, which reflects the changing *dia logos*, as I mentioned earlier, and reflects the notion that forest service policy itself needs to be transformed. All these things are beginning to converge, and we're transitioning. We've had some interesting bipartisan support, politically, in Congress. I'm cautiously optimistic that we might be able to move back to bipartisan ways of dealing with these issues, which transcend class and property interest. We're getting over the illusions that we had Truth about forest policy, forest science, and forest ethics, and we're beginning to see that we have conjectures, which we refine and live out. We're becoming aware of our own evolving nature. I'm not a relativist. Anything but.

NOTES

1. This interview was conducted during the fourth biennial conference of the Association for the Study of Literature and Environment (ASLE) in Flagstaff, Arizona. Just prior to the interview, Janisse Ray had delivered a magnificent talk about her life, her book *Ecology of a Cracker Childhood*, and her involvement with environmental movements.

Mapping Babel

A Response to Max Oelschlaeger

M. Jimmie Killingsworth

There's a war going on in Max Oelschlaeger's provocative comments about environmental philosophy and discourse—or if not a war, certainly a series of border disputes. His metaphors suggest connections that are worth tracing out, even if we end up with a version of truth that he may not have envisioned on his quest. In pursuing rhetoric and composition as ecocomposition, we need to locate key metaphors and interrogate the way they move an audience and how they connect with the texts that we read and write with our students. (By *we*, I mean teachers of ecocomposition. As I'll be talking about identity and the rhetoric of unification, such things are important to say.)

Many of Professor Oelschlaeger's conceptual metaphors have to do with war and land. We shouldn't be surprised to find the language of war after two decades of thinking through Lakoff's and Johnson's *Metaphors We Live By*, which established the prevalence of the metaphor "argument is war," especially in academic or disciplinary discourse. Nor should the language of land surprise us. Look at any text that's conscious of environmental issues, and you'll find an almost neurotic compulsion to repeat variations of the metaphor "texts are landscapes." What happens in Professor Oelschlaeger's commentary is that the two metaphorical trends flow together: Environmental discourse becomes a war over textual landscapes.

The metaphor that links war and land is that of the map. In disciplines such as geography, geology, anthropology, and the agricultural sciences, we expect to find language associated with maps, but now in ethics and rhetoric, mapping and other spatial metaphors appear more frequently as scholars take up issues related to the environment. Studying the permutations of the "land ethic" and the voices that claim to be "speaking for the earth," ethicists and rhetorical analysts come to see themselves as geographers of the human spirit. They have remapped consciousness as biocentric rather than anthropocentric; charted ecology for depth and shallowness; suggested bioregionalism as a substitute for state governance; and extended the concept of rights, once confined to the human sphere, to include animals and indeed all of the natural world. Professor Oelschlaeger joins in as he considers concepts like "the horizon of human possibilities" and spatializes notions of identity and temporality pondering "who we are and where we're going as we enter into postmodernity." He explicitly mentions Charles Taylor's concept of "moral maps," and map-mapping lurks behind many of his complaints about unnatural divisions—the "untenable" or "unsustainable distinction between wilderness and civilization," for example, or the division of literature and philosophy into separate disciplines. Professor Oelschlaeger wants to erase the lines of the map that reinforce such distinctions. But he wants to keep other lines intact. For example, he certainly doesn't want to cross the line into the territory marked by ecofeminist scholars.

Professor Oelschlaeger's comments remind me of another philosopher whose aim has been to eliminate boundaries and take the large view. In the Preface for *Toward Unity among Environmentalists*, Bryan G. Norton writes, "I have tried to provide a map of the countryside of environmentalism in the United States . . . to look not at trees but at forests, to subtract details in the hope of seeing larger patterns, and to look at the world in larger resolution than would be possible within the confines of a single discipline" (vii). Like Professor Oelschlaeger, Norton draws strongly upon neo-pragmatist thinking, though he lacks the interest in language that makes Professor Oelschlaeger appealing to ecocompositionists. But it is Norton's drive for disciplinary unification, something he does share with Professor Oelschlaeger, that leads him to a problem of discourse worth examining further. The absence of a "common interdisciplinary language," Norton says, stands in the way of a "unified theory of environmental stewardship," so that, "If one listens to what environmentalists *say*, one hears a cacophony of programs and explanations"—a veritable "babel of voices" (ix). The task Norton sets for himself is to look beyond the "environmentalists' rhetoric—the explanations they give for what they do" and concentrate instead on "their actions—the policies they pursue—as the fixed points on [his] map" (x).

With his interest in postmodernism and the linguistic turn in philosophy, Professor Oelschlaeger would certainly object to Norton's sweeping dismissal of rhetoric. But let's not rush to dismiss Norton's suggestion that language stands in the way of unification. We can see in the interview some problems having to do with shared language and texts as

Professor Oelschlaeger struggles to qualify what he means by "postmodern" (in contrast to what Professor Wilson means) and dodges questions that involve authors usually absent from his bibliography (such as Kenneth Burke, a central figure for environmental rhetoric if not ecocomposition). So, let's follow the map metaphor a bit further to see where it leads us.

In our book *Ecospeak: Rhetoric and Environmental Politics in America*, Jackie Palmer and I join Bryan Norton in using both the metaphor of the map and the myth of Babel—but with quite different aims. Like Professors Norton and Oelschlaeger, we believe that the field of environmental politics has suffered from unnecessary and often artificial divisions. Our main concern is the inclination of some politicians and reporters in the media to reduce the debate to two sides—environmentalists versus developmentalists—or to simplify the issues to facile contrasts, like jobs versus clean air—and thereby to engage in what we call *ecospeak*, a form of discourse that, like *newspeak* in George Orwell's *1984*, limits thinking and action by reducing linguistic resources to an impoverished minimum. We attempt to replace this oversimplified mapping with finer-grained analyses and thereby to point the way toward clearer positions from which people can speak, act, and cooperate in achieving their common goals.

We differ with Norton primarily on the importance of rhetoric in determining the ultimate character, or ethos, of environmentalism. We believe that how people represent themselves in public debate may provide a critical insight into what values they hold most dear and how they will eventually act. In our view, people's language works like a badge of identity, which they use to form alliances and set up psychological and social boundaries. Their tendency to form exclusive communities of discourse makes rhetoric the study of "the state of Babel after the Fall," as Kenneth Burke has suggested (23). In lamenting the "cacophony" of voices that characterizes *Homo rhetoricus* in the environmental debate, Bryan Norton resists the fallen condition and seeks, by a concentration on action, to construct an ethical platform on which to rise above the noise and confusion. He wants, it seems, to rebuild the Tower. While admiring his liberality and pragmatism, I think we should actively resist the rebuilding.

My worry is that the view from the Tower may prove to be an unfairly privileged perspective, even an instance of oppression. The myth of Babel itself indicates this possibility. You may remember from reading the book of Genesis that the Babelites spoke a single language and, in mounting their Tower, hoped to encompass the world within a single perspective. In this sense, they were mapmakers par excellence, as the

map requires the controlling vision of an aerial view, the perspective of
the overlord (see Dougherty, Chapter 3). This is where the Babelites went
wrong. The Bible says that God was offended by their ambition. "Look,"
He said, "they are one people, and they have all one language; and this
is only the beginning of what they will do; nothing that they propose to
do will now be impossible for them. Come, let us go down, and confuse
their language there, so that they will not understand one another's speech."
"So," we are told, "the Lord scattered them abroad from there over the
face of all the earth, and they left off building the city" (NRSV, Genesis
11.6–9). This jealous God, who would put such limits on His heroic
creatures, holds little appeal for a modern readership, with its technological pride and global vision. But in a world where the values of modernism and globalization have come under attack, we should grasp the divine
wisdom. In undoing the designs of the Babelites and in decreeing that
their descendants will suffer the confusion of different languages, the
God of Genesis undermined the possibility of human totalitarianism and
left people to cultivate smaller corners of the world, each with their own
kind and their own tongue. The myth of Babel rings true in our time
because, despite enjoying access to global networks of communication
and transportation, none of the modern totalitarian powers—neither the
great imperialists nor the Nazis nor the perpetrators of world communism nor yet the powers of the multinational corporations—have proved
capable of sustaining their control too far beyond their own limited
resources and borders in space and time.

Babel after the fall, then, means difference and diversity. Difference
and diversity in human relations give rise to rhetoric, the aim of which is
identification and unification, but the result of which is always limited—
an identity and a unity necessarily temporal, incomplete, and continually
threatened with dissolution back into difference. In a world of small repub-
lics, circumscribed powers, temporary coalitions, special interest groups,
outposts of ethnicity, and lifestyle enclaves, the work of mapping must be
constantly pursued, and the work of rhetoric—the making of appeals across
boundaries of difference—becomes a daily activity. As the political theorist
Ralf Dahrendorf argues, "The politics of liberty is the politics of living with
conflict. Diversity and equality each have their place in a constitution
which seeks the greatest life chances for all" (xi).

The work of the rhetorician in public discourse always involves
identification and a plea for transformation. The work of rhetorical criticism is to sort out the costs and benefits of the proposed changes, to look
at what differences have been reduced and what complications glossed
over. It may well be that the cost of unification is just too high at any

given moment in history. In such a case, scholars in environmental ethics and rhetoric can make their strongest contribution by staying attuned to disaffected voices and keeping alert to positions consigned to the margins or left off the map altogether. We should not be too quick to take literally the notion that any one group or coalition or person "speaks for the earth." The earth has many children, and not all of them have been considered equally in the making of environmental policy and the forming of environmentalist action groups. By retaining and voicing separate identities—whether regional or ideological—environmentalists of various stripes assure themselves a place on the map of policy in the future. They stake out the frontiers of environmental politics.

At this point in the evolution of ecological politics, new voices can be heard more clearly than ever. I am thinking in particular of the calls for environmental justice that arose during the 1990s among our Hispanic, Native American, and African American communities in the United States. These voices present the environmental movement with its greatest challenge yet and put a number of its most cherished points of identity in question.

Consider, for example, Aldo Leopold's justly famous and influential concept of the land ethic. Leopold's argument begins with the point that, over the course of human history, our ethical sense has gradually expanded. People who were once excluded—slaves, women, foreigners— were gradually brought under the protection of our system of right and wrong until finally the whole of humankind was, under Western liberalism, understood to have intrinsic worth. So far so good, says Leopold; but now we need to expand the boundaries yet further, to bring wild nature into the ethical fold, to end our oppression of the land and its nonhuman inhabitants. This extension of the boundaries of ethical behavior would require a new identification. We must identify with the land, become like the beasts of the field and the fowl of the air, just another species of earthlings. As far as ethics is concerned, nature and culture (or "civilization and wilderness," in Professor Oelschlaeger's formulation) would become one.

The problem is, in our hurry toward unification with the earth, we might overlook the somewhat hasty step in Leopold's argument, which suggests that all people actually do enjoy equal status as ethical beings. Even as environmentalists, we need to slow down and notice that racism and discrimination are rampant, and that an uncritical environmentalism can exacerbate inequitable practices and prejudicial attitudes. As the developing nations have pointed out for years now, it is hardly fair for environmentalists from developed countries to set global policy that restricts development for people whose basic needs have not been satisfied. It is easy to admire wild nature and defend biodiversity with a full belly. Environmental stewardship, as environmentalists see it, may thus appear as "green imperialism" to policy makers in the developing countries (see de Onis; also Redclift).

But you don't have to go to the Amazon to hear charges of ecological racism. The last decade of the twentieth century brought a heightened awareness of the inequitable distribution of environmental degradation right here in the United States. From Louisiana's "cancer alley" to the toxic dump sites on Indian reservations across the West, racial and ethnic minorities have begun to organize and defend themselves against threats to human health posed by industrial and agricultural pollution. In some cases, environmentalist organizations have joined this struggle. A notable example is Greenpeace, which has denounced "toxic colonialism" and has cooperated with grassroots activists in East Los Angeles and in Alsen, Louisiana, to resist placement of toxic dumps and incinerators in predominantly Hispanic and African American communities (Bullard, *Confronting* 19, 32). In other cases, environmentalists have offered technical advice and assistance or have contributed money to the grassroots movements.

Still there are cases, however, when mainstream environmentalist groups ignore actions on the front of ecological justice and, through neglect and bad policy, help to perpetuate environmental racism. This problem has received increasing attention in recent years, for example, in the continuing work of sociologist Robert Bullard and his colleagues. Take, for example, the experience of the Hispanic farming community of Ganados de Valle in the Chama River region of Northern New Mexico. Faced with economic decline and the migration of young people away from the community, the Hispanic shepherds and craftspeople in the area began to use common pastures and cooperatives to raise and shear sheep, harvest and butcher lambs, and weave and market woolen products as a community venture. With the influx of tourists and buyers in recent years, this small-scale operation has thrived. Founded on principles of sustainable land care and community development, guided by technical advisors from nearby universities, and committed to earth-wise values, the people of the community were encouraged enough by their early success to attempt a modest expansion. With the help of their advisors, they designed an experimental project that included a request for grazing rights on state lands. But, because the plans included intrusion into a Wildlife Management Area (an elk preserve), the request was refused by the New Mexico Department of Game and Fish. When the people of Ganados pressed the issue, they found themselves up against not only the state agencies but also what they came to call "The Green Wall," the coalition of mainstream environmental interest groups like the Nature Conservancy and the Wilderness Society as well as various hunters' organizations. Thus, while the local group worked to reconcile their community needs with the need to protect and even replenish the natural environment, it was the environmentalists this time who simplified the conflict to a question of people versus the earth and who came down, of course, on the side of the earth (see Pulido).

This position represents a curious inflexibility, what I would call the *habitual no*. It is true that environmentalists have accomplished much by saying no, by setting limits, by redrawing the map of human action with hard lines. But we can only go so far without finally submitting plans for future action. In facing sustainable alternatives, we must be prepared occasionally to grant a *provisional yes*, especially when issues of community revitalization among indigenous and traditionally marginal peoples are at stake. Otherwise, we may well be excluding from environmental politics the very people who will give the movement not only a much needed diversity but also new direction for future developments in human settlement.

Moreover, though the opponents of environmental racism do not have the luxury to pursue protection of the land regardless of human costs, they have in recent years proved themselves quite capable of recognizing economic blackmail when they see it and saying no to development schemes when the occasion demands. We encounter case after case in which victims of environmental degradation rise up to put a stop to practices that threaten the land and the health of the people. These include actions rural and urban, among black, Hispanic, and Indian populations, from Los Angeles to the Midwest and Deep South. In at least one case, an Hispanic community with a development plan much like that of the Ganados wool cooperative has, with some success, waged a blocking operation against a cyanide-leaching gold mine in Colorado's San Luis Valley. The opposition to the mine has used tactics of public relations, media management, technical advice, and community involvement that provide an excellent model for how to resist environmentally damaging practices without alienating the nonenvironmentalist segments of the existing community. When the news media reported that the community was equally divided in the dispute, for example, the opponents of the mine invited a sociologist from Colorado College to carry out a validated public opinion survey. The poll demonstrated that, in fact, only a small minority favored the mine. With this success behind them, the local organizers convinced the newspapers to allow their researcher to write a series of articles on the conflict. They thereby took control of the public discourse on the issue. All the while, they managed to sustain a dialogue with local businesses who stood to benefit from the mine, so that, when the mining company finally defaulted on its local contracts, the disaffected businesspeople could feel good about joining the opposition. Throughout the conflict, then, the community remained relatively undivided and preserved a mutual good will and neighborly respect (see Peña and Gallegos).

With its models of grassroots organization and sustainable development, the environmental justice movement has a great deal to offer to, as well as to gain from, a more inclusive development of the environmentalist ethos. Redefining the character of the movement in broader strokes could bring new hope and energy into the movement. It would mean that, as the mainstream environmental groups map the territory of ecological politics and inquiry, they must not neglect the problem of environmental racism by categorizing it as a social problem or an issue of public health.

As for ecocompositionists, environmental justice links nicely with approaches to teaching writing and reading that recognize cultural diversity and explore the effects of language, literacy, and literature on personal and ethnic identity (see George; Kells and Balester; Brown; Killingsworth and Palmer, "Ecopolitics"). It makes me happy to hear that Professor Oelschlaeger arrives at a new and beautiful state of mind—overcoming "the divide between egoic consciousness and the rest of nature"—when he reads W. S. Merwin's and Gary Snyder's poems meditatively in the western mountains. But I wonder what lines we might cross, what new regions of consciousness we might explore, if we read Gloria Anzaldúa's and Leslie Marmon Silko's borderland writings somewhere near the stink zone of Tex-Mex factories and feedlots. My maps keep leading me back to those sad places.

WORKS CITED

Brown, Stephen G. "The Wilderness Strikes Back: Decolonizing the Imperial Sign in the Borderlands." *Ecocomposition: Theoretical and Pedagogical Approaches.* Ed. Christian R. Weisser and Sidney I. Dobrin. Albany: State U of New York P, 2001: 117–29.

Bullard, Robert D. *Dumping in Dixie: Race, Class, and Environmental Quality.* Boulder, CO: Westview, 1990.

———., ed. *Confronting Environmental Racism: Voices from the Grassroots.* Boston: South End, 1993.

Burke, Kenneth. *A Rhetoric of Motives*. Berkeley: U of California P, 1969.

Dahrendorf, Ralf. *The Modern Social Conflict: An Essay on the Politics of Liberty*. Berkeley: U of California P, 1988.

de Onis, Juan. *The Green Cathedral: Sustainable Development of Amazonia*. New York: Oxford UP, 1992.

Dougherty, James. *The Fivesquare City: The City in the Religious Imagination*. Notre Dame: U of Notre Dame P, 1980.

George, Ann. "Critical Pedagogy: Dreaming of Democracy." A *Guide to Composition Pedagogies*. Ed. Gary Tate, Amy Rupiper, and Kurt Schick. New York: Oxford UP, 2001: 92–112.

Holy Bible, New Revised Standard Version. Oxford: Oxford UP, 1989.

Kells, Michelle Hall, and Valerie Balester, eds. *Attending to the Margins: Writing, Researching, and Teaching on the Front Lines*. Portsmouth, NH: Boynton/Cook, 1999.

Killingsworth, M. Jimmie, and Jacqueline S. Palmer. "Ecopolitics and the Literature of the Borderlands: The Frontiers of Environmental Justice in Latina and Native American Writing." *Writing the Environment: Ecocriticism and Literature*. Ed. Richard Kerridge and Neil Samuells. London: Zed, 1998: 196–207.

———. *Ecospeak: Rhetoric and Environmental Politics in America*. Carbondale: Southern Illinois UP, 1992.

Lakoff, George, and Mark Johnson. *Metaphors We Live By*. Chicago: U of Chicago P, 1980.

Leopold, Aldo. *A Sand County Almanac*. New York: Ballantine, 1966.

Norton, Bryan G. *Toward Unity among Environmentalists*. New York: Oxford UP, 1991.

Peña, Devon, and Joseph Gallegos. "Nature and Chicanos in Southern Colorado." *Confronting Environmental Racism*. Ed. Robert D. Bullard. Boston: South End, 1993. 141–60.

Pulido, Laura. "Sustainable Development at Ganados de Valle." *Confronting Environmental Racism*. Ed. Robert D. Bullard. Boston: South End, 1993. 123–39.

Redclift, Michael. *Development and the Environmental Crisis: Red or Green Alternatives?* London: Metheun, 1984.

———. *Sustainable Development: Exploring the Contradictions*. London: Routledge, 1987.

In Response to Max Oelschlaeger

Derek Owens

I'm compelled to admit a weakness: I don't much care for a lot of so-called nature writing. Unless the language moves in experimental or avant-garde directions, I can't maintain much interest in fiction or poetry or personal essays celebrating nature or wilderness. The language is too often predictably romantic or New Agey or struggling to be quietly moving, aspiring to inspire readers into some altered state of spiritual contemplation, lifting us temporarily from our presumably less interesting immediate locales into imagined vistas conjured by some narrative voice lucky enough to be trekking through the Adirondacks or camping in the outback under the stars. More unsettling to me, such celebrations of "the natural" simply serve as reminders of how far away I am from those (constructed) worlds. Like more than half of all Americans, I live in suburban sprawl, and while I'm sure a great many of us would prefer to live elsewhere, somewhere within walking distance of hiking trails and landscapes absent of traffic and commercialism and people, there are family, professional, and economic factors that keep people like me planted in embarrassing, kitschy, nondescript suburbia. So, I tend to find consecrations of wilderness a little frustrating, a little too show-offy. While I'm glad that somewhere a writer is experiencing contemplative reveries while living in a cabin next to a brook in a deciduous forest, I'm more concerned with what can and can't be done with the view outside my window: crowded, uninspiring ranch homes, perfunctory landscaping, parked cars, and no humans in sight. Instead of being reminded of how great things are elsewhere, what I need—what most of us need—is to reconceptualize my daily surroundings. To know the histories embedded in the places that are "mine," to understand the reasons why these places are in various degrees at risk (which all of them are, given our escalating environmental crises), to envision the probable futures for these places, and to work toward improving them.

Max Oelschlaeger's *The Idea of Wilderness* is not, to be sure, one of the aforementioned indulgences in nature writing, but is rather an extraordinary work of environmental history and philosophy that aids considerably in this kind of reconceptualization of place. Oelschlaeger's mapping of wilderness through paleolithic, neolithic, modernist, and postmodernist ages offers an essential tool for understanding how our cultural construction of wilderness has evolved across millennia. This four-tiered historical strata provides us with a means by which we, and our students, might better understand the long-term historical evolution buried both beneath our feet and within our psyches, and why we now find ourselves at a most critical juncture. While not overtly pedagogical in nature, I read *The Idea of Wilderness* as a companion of sorts to Edmund O'Sullivan's *Transformative Learning: Educational Vision for the 21st Century,* in that both authors situate their environmental hopes in frameworks postmodern and cosmological: Oelschlaeger embraces this current moment where "we are on the edge of articulating a new mythology, a fresh and profound creation story within which humankind can again be at home in a cosmos that . . . is the ground of all that is eternal and sacred" (*Idea* 331). This echoes O'Sullivan's "presentation of a cosmology that can be functionally effective in providing a basis for an educational programme that would engender an ecologically sustainable vision of society in the broadest terms; what can be called a planetary vision" (4).

Because of my own interest in sustainability, this is what I find most intriguing about the implications of Oelschlaeger's work—how his articulation for a rethinking of wilderness in the context of postmodernity complements objectives associated with strong sustainability. As he comments in the interview, this distinction between wilderness and civilization is inherently unsustainable. And while he touches on it only briefly, I was pleased to see Oelschlaeger mention Daniel Sarewitz's proposal for "the myth of sustainability as a viable contender" as "a new, legitimating narrative." In fact, the "sustainability metaphoric" Oelschlaeger refers to is essential to any such new postmodern mythology confronting today's ecological crises, more so I think than the concept of wilderness, an awkward term due to its inescapable association with the leisure class as well as its inherent privileging of wilderness zones over nonwilderness sites.

In "The Trouble with Wilderness" William Cronon writes:

> Ever since the nineteenth century, celebrating wilderness has been an activity mainly for well-to-do city folks. Country people generally know far too much about working the land to regard *un*worked land as their ideal. In contrast, elite urban tourists and wealthy sportsmen projected their leisure-time frontier fantasies

> onto the American landscape and so created wilderness in their
> own image. (94)

Such a critique is not leveled at any attempt to preserve wilderness, but
rather is offered in hopes of more productive terminology. For wilderness
on some level is always associated with privilege. Imagine for a moment
if every person in the United States were permitted to spend one day each
year in some piece of wilderness in the country. With current population
at 287 million, this would mean that on every day of the year those
quiet, open spaces would be populated with more than 787,000 unwanted people, thus effectively transforming wilderness into tourist site.
Herein lies one of the rarely admitted paradoxes of wilderness: those who
passionately, legitimately, and quite understandably defend the virtues of
the wild nevertheless implicitly desire that the majority of their listeners
keep their distance. Spokespersons for wilderness occupy a difficult position in that there is always the potential for their arguments to be
undermined by their own success—the last thing Oelschlaeger probably
wants is for too many of his readers to find their way into his aspen grove
to read their own poetry. It's also interesting to note that, for a scholar
like Oelschlaeger to illustrate that wilderness is more idea than fact, it
helps to *know* that wilderness pretty intimately, and understand it as
something sensory—a phenomenon to be touched, tasted, and inhaled
(the funk of elk, for instance). For the masses, who are likely not prone
to think of wilderness as a social construct, wilderness is actually little else
but a vague, elusive idea—something far away and out there, encountered by others (mostly white, educated, middle class or affluent) with
the necessary geographic and economic access to wilderness settings. In
any case, the idea of wilderness is inextricably compromised by hierar-
chies of class and culture.

    What also concerns me is that the privileging of wilderness inevitably
leads, intentionally or not, to a devaluing of nonwilderness sites—which,
of course, is where most of us humans spend the bulk of our lives. "The
place where we are is the place where nature is not. If this is so—if by
definition wilderness leaves no place for human beings, save perhaps as
contemplative sojourners enjoying their leisurely reverie in God's natural
cathedral—then also by definition it can offer no solution to the environmental and other problems that confront us" (Cronon 97). This is why,
in attempting to help my suburban and urban students better understand
their inherent connectedness to the places they inhabit—to contest that
bifurcation between the self and the "out there," which is one of
Oelschlaeger's goals as well—I've emphasized writings that explore the

phenomenon of *place* over *wilderness*. And when wilderness does enter
our classroom conversations, it's more in the sense of microwildernesses:
abandoned city lots, suburban sumps, thickets sandwiched between strip
malls, reservoirs, condemned tenement buildings, golf courses at night,
dumps, parking garage basements, tracts of phragmite along highway
shoulders. These hardly fit the definitions of wilderness under scrutiny in
Oelschlaeger's study, but they are nonetheless wild in that they are un-
inhabited and forgotten places, and certainly more accessible to most
people than "real" wilderness. In fact, because of works like *The Idea of
Wilderness*, we can now read wilderness with relative ease, whereas the
narrow bands of woods that parallel interstate highways now seem more
mysterious, even wilder in comparison. After all, people can still walk
through true wilderness, but no one visits or thinks much about those
swaths of trees and thickets sprouting in the median. How to contextualize
these invisible points on the map?

If people are going to understand wilderness, arguably they must
have some degree of firsthand contact with it—and not just the occasional weekend of camping, but hands-on encounters over sustained
periods of time. This is not only impossible but ecologically suicidal. To
go back to my example of the 787,000 people showing up in wilderness
zones on a daily basis, the energy expenditure for such daily migrations
would simply be impossible, and even if there were enough energy to
support this kind of leisure act, the effects would be environmentally
catastrophic. I won't go so far as Cronon to argue that "wilderness poses
a serious threat to responsible environmentalism at the end of the twentieth century" (97)—the term seems more conflicted than damaging—
but I will argue that it makes more sense now for all of us to focus on
place rather than wilderness, especially since the former includes the
latter and thus need not imply rejection of that concept. *Place* is a fact
as much as a concept; after all one is never, physically, out of place.
Everyone can relate to place, study it, learn to articulate why some places
are lousy to be in and others desirable, and explore ways of maintaining,
restoring, and preserving place.

What I seek is a means for incorporating Oelschlaeger's invaluable
historical mapping into a larger, more pragmatic and accessible project
for the sustainability of place. This would not reject a preoccupation with
wilderness but rather further expand that term so it can entail a variation
of wildernesses and microwildernesses, characterized in both positive and
pejorative contexts. What can wilderness mean to the majority of our
students, let alone the population, that will never encounter the wild in
anywhere near the manner that writers like Oelschlaeger have? How will

this and subsequent generations come to further reject and redefine concepts of wilderness? What are the different manifestations of urban and suburban wilderness—not just nature reserves but abandoned shopping plazas and seas of parking lots? In what ways is a preoccupation with wilderness potentially at odds with bioregional perspectives (one's watershed need not be located in wilderness)? In light of writers like Donna Haraway, who argues that we're all cyborgs (a rather dated argument now close to two decades old), or Joel de Rosnay, whose cybiont is a planetary superorganism comprising humans, nations, machines, ecosystems, and networks, how do these ideas force us to reconstruct, evolve, or even set aside the idea of wilderness? What does it mean to even write so that readers might "reestablish roots in that fertile soil which nurtures all life" (*Idea* 245) now that the preeminent compositional landscape is digital and virtual, our culture's primary writing workspace the World Wide Web? How do our notions of wilderness, nature, and ecology undergo change when we look not to romantic and modernist poets (like Jeffers and Snyder respectively, whose work is examined in *The Idea of Wilderness*) but to the most active contemporary multimedia writing communities and practices, now found largely on the Web and electronic magazines (epc.buffalo.edu)?

At one point in the interview Oelschlaeger mentions the need for young men and women "to be able to participate in a dialogue with the forests." I would agree, were this possible, but, to return to my earlier point, to help preserve the wilderness sites that remain we can ill afford to shuttle millions into those forests. Only a tiny minority will ever be permitted to experience wilderness on these terms. But everyone experiences place, twenty-four hours a day. What Oelschlaeger's project does for me is to provide some necessary insight into this much larger, pressing, and accessible need to know the idea and evolution of place.

WORKS CITED

Cronon, William. "The Trouble with Wilderness." *The Best American Essays 1996*. Ed. Geoffrey C. Ward. Boston: Houghton Mifflin, 1996: 83–109.

de Rosnay, Joel. *The Symbiotic Man: A New Understanding of the Organization of Life and a Vision of the Future*. New York: McGraw Hill, 2000.

Oelschlaeger, Max. *The Idea of Wilderness. From Prehistory to the Age of Ecology*. New Haven, CT: Yale UP, 1991.

O'Sullivan, Edmund. *Transformative Learning: Educational Vision for the 21ˢᵗ Century*. London: Zed Books, 2001.

A Reconsideration of Wild Discourse

Response to Killingsworth and Owens

Max Oelschlaeger

INTRODUCTION

Where to begin? First, let me cop a plea. I did not choose the original title of the transcribed interview, which was "The Quest for Truth: Max Oelschlaeger on Rhetoric and Wilderness." I'm all right with the "Rhetoric and Wilderness" bit. But the "Quest for Truth" phrase gives me concern. "Truth" has plenty of advocates. I'm more interested in changing the conversation, especially about wildness and wilderness.

Words somehow never convey all that might be conveyed. Then again, words are what make us distinctively human. We are truly and incontrovertibly, as Derek Bickerton makes compellingly clear, language animals. I do not believe in privileged claims, in methods that yield ironclad, eternal verities. I self-identify as a constructive postmodern hiker, not content to camp within the limits of cultural boundaries, yet fully aware that there is no reinvention of self or society ex nihilo. Truth is more and more about the journey, and breaking the cake of custom—as Dewey would say—than the destination. Systematic philosophy, since Parmenides, conveys its message with a capital "T" in truth. Postmodern reflection is a discursive, fallible, and transformative process.

So am I a relativist? Am I implying that the commentaries of Derek Owens and Jimmie Killingsworth are nothing more than postcards from Babel? Am I saying that each of us is entitled to our opinion? And that opinions are all that we have? Shall we all cuddle up with Protagoras?

Not really. The postmodern condition allows many interpretations, for example, Donna Haraway's *Modest Witness* or Jean-François Lyotard's *Postmodern Condition* or Hilary Lawson's *Reflexivity* or Richard Rorty's *Contingency, Irony, and Solidarity*. Yet the linguistic turn allows those who embark on that path to bypass Cartesian anxieties (epistemic worries about absolute truth or the shifting sands of opinion), and set off toward Oz, that is, "communicative rationality."

That said, let me join the conversation.

RESPONSE TO DEREK OWENS

Like Owens, I do not like a lot of nature writing. I once received a fancy fee for reviewing a "big name" nature writer's latest book. The review was not published. Why? Because I wrote that I was tired of writers finding cosmic significance in mouse farts or experiencing an epiphany as the tide rolled in while Earth was aligning with Mars. But I'm not a nature writer, as Owens observes. He terms some of what I've done as "historical mapping," writing chapters of intellectual history that until the latter part of the twentieth century were not considered legitimate areas of scholarship. Owens wants to fold that project into a "larger, more pragmatic and accessible project for the sustainability of place."

Having lived in the Dallas/Ft. Worth metropolitan area for more than twenty years, I share Owens familiarity with "the great sprawl," and his concern for the amenities of nature for those who live there. Old enough to have been present at the beginnings of the post-1950s environmental movement, I cut my teeth on Rachel Carson, Ian McHarg, Gregory Bateson, and so on. "Design with Nature" has been on my mind ever since. I wish Owens would have mentioned McHarg, or some of McHarg's intellectual progeny, like Joan Nassauer, or movements like the New Urbanism.

The "S" word, sustainability itself, Owen's notes, is huge. I agree. He uses the term "strong sustainability," which chimes nicely with Charles Taylor's notion of strong evaluation. The dominant idea of sustainable development, as articulated in, for example, *Our Common Future* and *Agenda 21*, is a weak evaluation, that is, a narrative that perpetuates the problems it purports to solve. All hail wise use. I also like the understated comments that Owens offers concerning myth and mythology. Mythological narratives are architectonic, language at its imaginative, originary issue.

If Owens were sitting across the table from me as we sipped lemonade—by the way, speaking of sustainability, under what conditions is lemonade a bioregional drink? Or beer, for that matter?—I would raise some questions. Under the heading "productive terminology," he takes a stab at a reductio ab absurdum. Namely, wilderness visitation implies socioeconomic privilege, and with 287 million American souls, that would equate with 787,000 people per day, "effectively transforming wilderness into tourist site." Such a rate of visitation, Owens continues a few pages later, would be "ecologically suicidal," just on the basis of the "energy expenditures" required. He's right in some ways. American's are loving wild places to death. We would have problems if the number of daily visitors equaled total population divided by 365. But this hasn't happened, and it won't happen. And it's not in the final analysis a crucial issue when it comes to wilderness. Actual on-site recreation is only one part of a far, far larger complex of issues and ideas. Like avoiding an anthropogenic mass extinction event.

His "reductio" gesture means that he ignores other interpretive possibilities carried by "wild texts." Granted that the overwhelming majority of Americans live in metro areas, is it nonetheless possible to still consider "our places" as having first had a natural history? Does New York City not have channelized rivers and streams running beneath its streets? And Central Park is, indeed, a "wild place." Do the interpretive texts of the built environment conceal as much or more than they reveal? More consequentially, every human on the planet has a profound dependence on biosystem services. And a stake in avoiding irreversible changes in naturally evolved systems, such as the atmosphere, a biophysical system evolved over hundreds of millions of years. Ed Wilson puts the point thus: "An Armageddon is approaching at the beginning of the third millennium. But it is not the cosmic war and fiery collapse of mankind foretold in sacred scripture. It is the wreckage of the planet by an exuberantly plentiful and ingenious humanity" (2002, xxiii). Does Wilson suggest that the terror of recent events, however dreadful, however heinous, could be exceeded by a cascade of catastrophes of our own making?

Consider this. The human species has been around less than 100,000 years (maybe only 50,000 years) since the so-called Great Leap Forward. In that time we have become the scourge of the planet, turning forests into deserts, grasslands into salt flats, and the Pleistocene megafauna into extinct species. We have created a witches' brew of some 70,000 chemicals—none of which existed in the evolutionary environment—which are creating all kinds of havoc, including the depletion of stratospheric ozone by chlorofluorocarbons (CFCs). We have monopolized nearly 70 percent of the planet's freshwater. Our species appropriates nearly 40 percent of the Earth's net biological product. Our planet is perched on the precipice of an anthropogenic—a human caused—mass extinction.

The naturally evolved wild systems to which human beings were loosely coupled until the Neolithic revolution and its aftermath (domestication of animals, cultivation of cereal grasses, conversion of habitat, sedentarism, population growth, writing, organized war, social hierarchy, epidemic disease), are increasingly becoming anthropogenic systems to which human beings are closely coupled. Like the Sorcerer's Apprentice, who bid the broom to do his work and had hell to pay, we don't know what we are doing.

Those who study these issues, from all sides, including the natural sciences, recognize that the most fundamental questions are ethical, that is, entail considerations of human agency. Why do we do what we do? John Firor, a physicist, and former director of research at the National Center for Atmospheric Research, argues that there are no technological solutions for atmospheric dysfunctions. Technology will be part of any solution, but not until humankind fundamentally reconsiders its self-definition. And to quote E. O. Wilson again, from another compelling book written ten years ago, "Environmental problems are innately ethical. They require vision reaching simultaneously into the short and long reaches of time. . . . To choose what is best for both the near and distant futures is a hard task, often seemingly contradictory and requiring knowledge and ethical codes which for the most part are still unwritten" (1992, 312).

My point is simple. Recreation is mostly beside the point, and all the more so in the context of the questions concerning sustainability. Euro-American's have always wanted to dominate nature, to exploit the natural largesse for all that can be had, even while remaining "spiritually close," somehow identifying with the lands and creatures and the purple mountain's majesty. But finding our way into stories that are for the present "still unwritten," which is to say reconnecting ourselves with the wild chaos from which we emerged, will not be easy. One dimension of the challenge is to come to the "wild knowledge" (to use Will Wright's term) that reconnects the stories governing our lives with the evolved natural systems upon which the sustainability of any and all meaningful stories finally depend.

Owens also expresses concerns involving "devaluing of nonwilderness sites," and then quotes Cronon to the effect that by definition wilderness is where we are not. Which is consonant with the language of the Wilderness Act, certainly, as well as the perceived American idea of wilderness. Owens continues, remarking that *place* may be a more useful term than *wilderness*, especially for today's college students, who have little or no opportunity to enjoy relatively wild landscapes. "Microwildernesses," like abandoned city lots and thickets between malls, he implies, are more readily available as tutors than wilder places like Glacier National Park. Which reminds me of Gary Snyder's remark that there is plenty of wildness to be found in a container of yogurt. Rather than talking about wilderness, Owens asserts, we should consider changing the conversation to a more practical one that considers the "sustainability of place," which has the benefit of engaging young men and women who will never have the privilege of living where I live, or wandering the mountain trails that I've wandered, and so on.

Right on, I'd say. Indeed, projects such as the "Chicago Wilderness" and movements like the "New Urbanism" (see Leccese and McCormick) are prime examples of people concerned about the sustainability of place, and questions of how nature can somehow be reconciled with the built environment. Ian McHarg's influence shows in Owens's comments. McHarg reached similar conclusions and made similar recommendations forty years ago. "We need nature as much in the city as in the countryside," he wrote. "It is clear that we must look deep to the values which we hold. . . . We need, not only a better view of man and nature, but a working method by which the least of us can ensure that the product of . . . [our] works is not more despoliation" (5). Which is why, I believe, that wild talk counts. That's what the rhetoric of wilderness is about, isn't it?

Still, I'm not too optimistic about the possibilities of tomorrow. The so-called ecological footprints of the urban-suburban dwelling citizens of the G-7 nations, the global middle class, trod heavily across every corner of the planet. Cultural adaptation has to begin somewhere, and every little bit helps. But it's very hard for anyone to argue credibly that the great sprawling cities of the world, let alone the United States, are consonant with long-term sustainability. We can do more, and are doing more, concerning the sustainability of the places we live. But that will not, in my opinion, slow down the approaching collision between the human species and the rest of life.

Finally, Owens throws some wonderful conversational curves when he raises questions like "How do our notions of wilderness, nature, and ecology undergo change when we look not to romantic and modernist poets (like Jeffers and Snyder . . .) but to the most active contemporary multimedia writing communities and practices, now found largely on the Web and electronic magazines (epc.buffalo.edu)?" Uh, I don't know. Or do I? We remain a naturally evolved species. We have, as it were, Darwinian bodies, a species being cloaked by the narratives of culture (and, of course, talk like *Darwinian bodies* is itself a text). Does "man make himself," as the anthropologist G. Gordon Childe, avows? Are we infinitely plastic, mutable? Does culture overdetermine all aspects of lived experience? If so, then the literary avant-garde, cyborgs inhabiting cyberspace looking at the world and interacting with others only through so many digitized pixels are the way of tomorrow. Or is it possible that the fertile soils, the evolved matter of cosmic, physical, and biological evolution, still nurture our species? Do we still need fresh air and water? The experience of otherness, of the diversity of life? Is biophilia a genetic inheritance? Do the affective (emotional) flows between humans and the rest of nature still matter?

I think so.

RESPONSE TO M. JIMMIE KILLINGSWORTH

Killingsworth, unlike Owens, changes the conversation. More than half of his commentary is an extended discourse on environmental justice (which is a rhetorical gesture, but not about rhetoric). The interview is more or less processed through Killingsworth's "Ecospeak Machine." Whir, grind, and presto, and out comes a shrink-wrapped text. Which is fine. I always like visiting with bright people. And Killingsworth has forgotten more about ecocomposition than I've ever known. So, I always learn a lot when I read his stuff.

But really, I'm not a rookie when it comes to conversations concerning environmental justice and/or racism. I know Bullard's work, much of the literature, and many of the environmental justice issues, beginning with "the letter that shook the movement" to the present moment, as in the issues involving Black Mesa, the Snowbowl, and the Borderlands. And especially from my work in the 1990s, which looked at the toxic Gulf Coast of Texas (Gunter and Oelschlaeger). The Gulf Coast is the petrochemical capital of the world. Big money. Also big problems. Dotted with a couple of dozen "Superfund" sites, there are thousands of people of color who are sick because of petrochemicals. Literally sick, because of chemicals adversely affecting their health, and figuratively sick, because of the indifference and ineptitude of federal and state regulatory agencies.

Processed through the Ecospeak Machine, the "Rhetoric of Wilderness" equates roughly with a prefrontal lobotomy. And, if not classism and racism, indifference. So we "babel on," spewing words about moral maps and the like, sanctimonious and privileged "OF's." Does he really mean it? Whose in denial? Most of Killingsworth's claims were brought into the discursive realm with the 1998 publication of the edited collection, *The Great New Wilderness Debate* (Callicott and Nelson). The text collects a wide array of Americans, as well as numerous Third World and Fourth World commentators, who have explored the anthropocentric, ethnocentric, phallocentric, and androcentric aspects of the received idea of wilderness.

The great new wilderness debate has several threads. One strand deals with the exclusion of Native Americans from traditional landscapes through their designation as national parks or wildernesses. These lands were not, as the enabling legislation implies, *terra nullius*, empty lands devoid of human presence. Another strand has to do with the hypocrisy of First World conservationists and preservationists arguing that the Third World should set aside vast tracts of land in perpetual conservation easements. And a third strand concerns the impact of Third World elites, caught up in their enthusiasm for sustainable development and the new world order, on indigenous groups living in subsistence economies, who are, for example, displaced by massive hydraulic projects.

The main thrust of Killingsworth's commentary appears to be that ol' Max's ardor for the blooming, buzzing confusion of the naturally evolved Earth blinds him to the pain and suffering of politically disempowered and economically exploited people. Which is to say, at least a couple of billion people on the planet and tens of millions of Americans. Such criticisms of the wilderness movement and advocates have been around for two or three decades (see *The Idea of Wilderness*). But here's a thought. *A concern for wild places and creatures does not preclude a caring concern for people.* Here's another. *The exploitation of nature is tied up with the same narratives that legitimate the exploitation of people.* As the conversation concerning sustainability unfolds, one point of agreement is that the desperate social, political, and economic plight of the world's have-nots must be ameliorated. Yet these actions must also be reconciled with the biophysical limits imposed by evolution. Issues of social justice go hand in hand with concerns for ecological integrity. And we will not have either until we find our way into some new stories—narratives of adaptation. The rhetoric of wilderness is, I believe, part of that project. Architectonically. And persuasively.

One further point on this subject (roughly, that tree huggers are, if not misanthropic, blind to human pain, and thus guilty of ecospeak). A century of ecological inquiry spanning an array of natural, social, and human sciences has established at least three premises: That the absolute separation of human ecology and biological ecology is untenable and unsustainable. That ecological inquiry is as much about the human estate and cultural schemes as about nature. That the world which sustains all life may be broken on the wheel of our own misdeeds, turned round and round by hubris, greed, and ignorance. So, Killingsworth is right when he places social issues on the table. But he's more or less wrong if he believes that discourse about wild nature does not also entail discourse about the human condition.

There is another thread in Killingsworth's commentary: the question concerning maps. He implies (at least in my case) that mapmakers make tacit claims to moral superiority. Not that I have a knockdown position, but I think Killingsworth is behind the learning curve on mapping. He's correct insofar as he implies that maps have typically been the province of hierarchical powers, drawing the lines on the paper that signify empire, possession, control, and the like. But what he misses—so far as I can tell—is that the proletariat have learned that maps are like swords (if I might be allowed a warrior metaphor). If the establishment has them, you better get some yourself.

Hence the rebirth of mapping as community building, politically energizing, and socially conscious enterprise, sweeping across the country, indeed, the entire continent. And, ironically, being used by the environmental justice movement itself. Like the black and brown people living along the toxic coast of Texas, who mapped the wind plumes from petrochemical factories, the locales where poor black and brown people lived, and the incidence of respiratory disease. Funny thing, how elevated levels of disease and mortality, neighborhoods of color, and the toxic winds coincided. Indigenous people are mapping as well. Their lands and waters, the flora and fauna, the good places to hunt and fish, and the sacred sites. And they're mapping the consequences of empire upon the lands and waters, flora and fauna, and their ability to sustain themselves.

Finally, let me take up the subject of moral maps. I wish I had been clever enough to originate the conversation concerning moral mapping. But the term reflects the genius of Charles Taylor, and his conceptions of human agency and language, strongly evaluative processes that through comparison-contrast of alternatives weave narratives of legitimacy, webs of interlocution that become cardinal points on a moral map. Ideas with rhetorical legs, as I like to say, narratives that move us, motivate us, guide us in this direction rather than that. Moral maps situate humans in space and time—on Earth, in a region, in this place, for example, smack dab in the wild lands of the intermountain West, and the ongoing history of effects, the many confluent streams of people, with their hopes and dreams, and the creatures and the rivers and mountains. And the trouble that we have today.

Killingsworth spins my talk about moral maps like Ronald Reagan spun liberals. "There they go (Max goes) again." Tacit claims to moral superiority. Selfish concerns about wild places when there are suffering humans. But isn't the rhetoric of wilderness simultaneously architectonic, that is, about humankind's place in the evolved scheme of things, and persuasive, that is, about calling forth appropriate actions, given that positioning in the world? What we do to the world we also do to people.

CONCLUSION

Owens's commentary reminds me of Ian McHarg, specifically and concretely, and Gregory Bateson, generally and philosophically. McHarg's vision of "design with nature" was groundbreaking. When McHarg argues for designing the built environment with nature in mind, he connects with place. So too Bateson when he writes "We are not outside the ecology for which we plan—we are always and inevitably a part of it" (504).

Killingsworth's commentary moves in a different way. Wild talk frightens most people. It certainly frightens me. I sometimes long for the psychic cocoon of civilization, for the notion that we are in control of the planet, and that the force of reason will ultimately triumph over all nincompoopery (to use a philosophical term). Ultimately our human language games, however fond we are of them, face the test of survival. Can we frame wilderness rhetoric not as *ecospeak* but in Kenneth Burke's terms? *"For rhetoric as such is not rooted in any past condition of human society. It is rooted in an essential function of language itself, a function that is wholly realistic, and is continually born anew; the use of language as a symbolic means of inducing cooperation in beings that by nature respond to symbols"* (43). Survival across many species depends on such cooperation.

WORKS CITED

Aberley, D., ed. *Boundaries of Home: Mapping for Local Empowerment.* Philadelphia: New Society Publishers, 1993.

Bateson, G. *Steps to an Ecology of Mind.* New York: Ballantine, 1972.

Bernstein, R. J. *Beyond Objectivism and Relativism: Science, Hermeneutics, and Praxis.* Philadelphia: U of Pennsylvania P, 1983.

Bickerton, D. *Language and Species.* Chicago: U of Chicago P, 1990.

Bruner, M., and Max Oelschlaeger. "Rhetoric, Environmentalism, and Environmental Ethics." *Landmark Essays on Rhetoric and the Environment.* Ed. C. Waddell. Mahwah, NJ: Hermagoras Press, 1998.

Burke, K. *A Rhetoric of Motives.* Berkeley: U of California P, 1950.

Callicott, J. B., and M. P. Nelson, eds. *The Great New Wilderness Debate.* Athens: U of Georgia P, 1998.

Carson, R. *Silent Spring.* Greenwich, Conn.: Fawcett Publications, 1961.

Childe, V. G. *Man Makes Himself.* New York: New American Library, 1951.

Firor, J. *The Changing Atmosphere: A Global Challenge.* New Haven: Yale UP, 1990.

Fisher, A. *Radical Ecopsychology: Psychology in the Service of Life.* Albany: State U of New York P, 2002.

Frodeman, R., ed. *Earth Matters: The Earth Sciences, Philosophy, and Community.* Upper Saddle River, NJ: Prentice-Hall, 2000.

Glacken, C. *Traces on the Rhodian Shore: Nature and Culture in Western Thought from Ancient Times to the End of the Eighteenth Century.* Berkeley: U of California P, 1967.

Gould, E. *Mythical Intentions in Modern Literature.* Princeton: Princeton UP, 1981.

Gunter, P. A. Y., and Max Oelschlaeger. *Texas Land Ethics.* Austin: U of Texas P, 1997.

Haraway, Donna J. Modest_Witness@Second_Millennium. FemaleMan©_Meets_ OncoMouse™: Feminism and TechnoScience. New York: Routledge, 1997.

Lawson, H. *Reflexivity: The Postmodern Predicament.* LaSalle, Ill.: Open Court, 1985.

Leccese, M., and K. McCormick, eds. *Charter of the New Urbanism.* New York: McGraw-Hill, 2000.

Leopold, A. *A Sand County Almanac: With Essays on Conservation from Round River.* 1949. San Francisco: Sierra Club Books, 1970.

Lincoln, B. *Discourse and the Construction of Society: Comparative Studies of Myth, Ritual, and Classification.* New York: Oxford UP, 1989.

Lyotard, J-F. *The Postmodern Condition: A Report on Knowledge.* Minneapolis: U of Minnesota P, 1984.

McHarg, I. L. *Design with Nature.* Garden City, NY: Natural History P, 1969.

Nassauer, J. I., ed. *Placing Nature: Culture and Landscape Ecology.* Washington, DC: Island P, 1997.

Oelschlaeger, M. *The Idea of Wilderness:* From Prehistory to the Age of Ecology. New Haven, CT: Yale UP, 1991.

Rorty, R. *Contingency, Irony, and Solidarity.* New York: Cambridge UP, 1989.

Taylor, C. *Human Agency and Language: Philosophical Papers 1.* Cambridge: Cambridge UP, 1985.

———. *Philosophy and Human Sciences: Philosophical Papers 2.* Cambridge: Cambridge UP, 1985.

———. *Sources of the Self.* Cambridge: Harvard UP, 1989.

Wilkinson, C. *Fire on the Plateau: Conflict and Endurance in the American Southwest.* Washington, DC: Island P, 1999.

Worster, D. *Rivers of Empire: Water, Aridity and Growth of the American West.* New York: Pantheon Books, 1985.

Wright, W. *Wild Knowledge: Science, Language, and Social Life in a Fragile Environment.* Minneapolis: U of Minnesota P, 1992.

Writing the Native American Life

An Interview with Simon Ortiz

Simon J. Ortiz has earned the reputation as not only one of the most important contemporary Native American writers but also as one of the most important poets. His writing, which centers on everyday Native American life, uses language so expertly and provocatively that his work not only reflects the narrative structure of Native American storytelling but also manifests the power of that very language and other languages. Ortiz is aware of the power of language and is able to masterfully use that power both as narrative tool and as a means for creating awareness of that very language.

Ortiz, an Acoma Pueblo Indian, is deeply aware of the role education—both in school systems and in larger cultural systems—plays in maintaining English-language events as the dominant discursive power. English, for Ortiz, is a second language; Acoma is his first language. While he is critical of the ways in which English oppresses, he is also aware of how that power might be used. Here he talks about how the English language functions to bring nonnative speakers into the English-language culture by making English appear to be the only choice for language users: "So the language that I use, the English language, is the language of convenience, the language of the moment, the language of availability." He is rightly critical of how this language use carries over to larger cultural manifestations, such as availability of consumer products and education.

Ortiz, in addition, comments on such things as the place of writing in activism, the purposes and goals of his writing, the responsibilities that writing carries, and the larger epistemological systems in which writing and thought are embedded. Of interest in such issues is Ortiz's discussion of "one's sense of being helped by what is a source of life: the land, culture, and community." Ortiz, nonetheless, argues that such connections between human cultures and the land have been drawn too narrowly between only native peoples and their environments, "whereas it is not only the nature of indigenous peoples of the world who have responsibility because it is ours, universally, to acknowledge and carry out." Ortiz's words below help us better understand these responsibilities—the relationships—between people and places, cultures and places, writing and places, language and places.

Q: In the Introduction to *Earth Power Coming: Short Fiction in Native American Literature*, you write, "There have always been the songs, the prayers, the stories. There have always been the voices. There have always been the people. There have always been those words which evoked meaning and the meaning's magical wonder. There has always been the spirit which inspired the desire for life to go on. And it has been through the words of the songs, the prayers, the stories that the people have found a way to continue, for life to go on." You reiterate this idea several other times in your work, for instance in *Fightin'* you say, "The stories belong to you. Remember that they come from the source of a community: people and people, people and all life. These songs and words of them come from the nature of all life. The stories that come from the source and nature of all life." We are particularly interested in the relationship between storytelling and life. As teachers and students of writing as well as writers, we are fascinated by the ways in which writing, storytelling, narrative affect life. Could you speak for a moment about this relationship, between the telling and the living?

A: In the first case, in *Speaking for the Generations*, I speak about the traditional way of knowledge that native people have in regards to their relationship with the natural world or natural environment. There are ways in which this knowledge is spoken of through prayer, ceremonial ritual, instructions, and ways of behavior, whether they are social or personal, that speak about one's inextricable relationship to the natural world and one could even say to the whole of life. I think that what traditional knowledge really expresses is responsibility, a practice of responsibility that we as social entities, as communities, have with the land, which is the source of all life.

I've spoken about, or used the phrase "land, culture, and community," which is the basis of that responsible relationship that we as a human cultural community have as native people. Beyond just the native American community, of course, is the kind of responsibility that everyone must have and that is what the second quote you offered addresses more specifically. The responsibility is ours, by which I mean the human cultural community, universally, and not just tribally or locally, or regionally, or only within the ethnic community of Native American people, but within the culture of humankind. Because it is our responsibility, it is our sense of existence, that is the basis for how we come to live in an appropriately reciprocal relationship with the natural world. Too often, native people have found themselves as models, or examples, of how human cultures can acknowledge that inextricable relationship between human culture and the environment, whereas it is not only the nature of indigenous peoples of the world who have the responsibility because it is ours, universally, to acknowledge and carry out. Of course, in the local and regional, it is up to the community culture. Where I come from, in New Mexico, the Acoma Pueblo culture is responsible for their own, but this can be applied to the world at large and not just to native or indigenous people. This is what we are all faced with as members of a modern world where culture is transacted on the global scale.

Q: You have often discussed and written about the relationships between oral and written narrative: "Although, obviously, written language is very prominent, and unfortunately prominent in some ways, oral language is still the way we affect each other." We were wondering if you could expand on what you mean by oral and written narrative "affecting" each other?

A: Oral language is the most common way in which people communicate. The individual within a social community expresses himself and is addressed by the group, that is, by the largest cultural unit. Oral language is spoken within what he knows of his family, his clan, his tribal unit. Different languages are spoken throughout the world by many ethnic groups, and the development of writing is relatively recent in the course of human history. Writing is a representation of oral language. Although, it is not always simply a representation but is an act of language in itself, like oral language. I've always been mystified and amazed at the scale of oral culture affecting human events. The power of oral language is very persuasive. One of the ways it is persuasive is that it requires a sense of participation, involvement, and engagement by both the speaker and the community affected by the oral language. By participation and involvement, I mean there's a real sense of commitment because of the immediacy and intimacy that is contained through, or is at the core of, the oral tradition. I feel that oral language is the real language of human and social culture, that oral language is what makes the power of language both possible and real. Written language, on the other hand, is too often seen as the handmaiden of Western culture, because it facilitates Western kinds of knowledge that demand an objective scientific outlook. I've said in two of my works that the written tradition of native peoples, in the

Americas especially, is an extension of the oral tradition. How correct that is, I am not too sure; there might be some linguists who would disagree that written language is simply oral language put into written or graphic and visual form. I know that written language sometimes is a major indicator of the expertise and intellectual objectivity of human society and culture, so that it lacks in some sense the intimacy and immediacy expressed and conveyed through oral communication.

It might seem odd for me as a writer to say or to suggest that written language is not as vibrant as oral language. Sometimes I am uncertain how oral language can be represented in written form. I know I have a preference for written English that has the power, the vitality, and the energy of the oral tradition. I am partial to reading writing that evokes the energy, power, and spirit of the oral tradition. I think that written language can emulate the oral tradition, but this depends on culture insisting that writing maintain the technical facility and integrity of oral tradition.

Q: You have also written, "The tradition of the oral narrative, expressed by the many different Native languages of the indigenous Americas, is at the core of this philosophy of interdependence. Traditional oral stories depict, assert, and confirm the natural evolvement—or the origin and emergence—of Native people from the boundless creative energy of the universe." We hear a lot of conversation—both academic and nonacademic—about diversity, about multiculturalism, about cultures maintaining their voices, their stories. Could you speak to the importance of storytelling for Native Americans not just as cultural artifact but as a means for maintaining this interconnectedness?

A: The oral tradition is so significant for Native communities because it is the principal way in which we are involved with the actual carrying out of our responsibility to the environment. That not only requires the practice of carrying out this responsibility to the land but also requires fulfilling this responsibility among each other, as members of a community. The oral tradition as told through the story actually addresses and focuses on that responsibility, whether it be political, social, cultural, or religious, because certain codes of conduct are expressed through stories, and not just spoken or verbalized but also through practice. What is the work ethic or what kind of socializing behavior is involved? The respect of the young to the elders, and the role of the elders as leaders and as bearers of culture, so that there is a whole sense of community and a dynamic maintained through the story and the oral tradition. It is not just what is said but what is carried out and practiced. This is what keeps a tribal entity intact. Native identity has a lot to do with how one is able to maintain himself as a person with an ethnic background that is Native, or indigenous, and that has to do with the ability and the freedom to be able to be Native. What I mean is that the freedom to be who you are as a Native person has to be in place to truly be able to carry out your responsibility. The story, or knowledge-energy that is carried in the story and maintained through that story, is necessary for that community to function, especially as stewards of the land. I hope that what I am saying will not be interpreted as too abstract, especially in terms that are not comprehended outside of the Native community. I think oftentimes we have felt restricted as Native peoples because we are not recognized for who we are in terms of our indigenous culture, because it is much easier to go along with mainstream American culture. This means that we often find ourselves neglecting our indigenous cultural ways, which must be maintained.

Q: You write: "Using the English language is a dilemma and pretty scary sometimes, because it means letting one's mind go willfully—although with soul and heart in shaky hand, literally—into the Western cultural and intellectual context, a condition and circumstance that one usually avoids at all costs on most occasions. Even though I believe I did not have many overt problems with it, learning to speak, read, and write in English was fraught with considerable tension for me. As a result, years later I admit I have felt uneasy and even disloyal at moments when I've found myself to be more verbally articulate in the English language than in my own native Acoma language. I have to honestly admit that there is a price to pay for selling your soul, if that is what has happened." Many others have written about this dilemma of turning to the English language. Richard Rodriguez's *Hunger of Memory* comes to mind immediately, as do the works of other Latinos/Latinas, Chicanos/Chicanas, Asian Americans, Native Americans, and others who have had to acclimate to and be assimilated in English-language culture. Compositionist Victor Villanueva, who writes about this conflict of languages, has written, "When we demand a certain language, a certain dialect, a certain rhetorical manner in using that dialect and language, we seem to be working counter to the cultural multiplicity we seek." He goes on to say, "The demand for linguistic and rhetorical compliance still smacks of colonialism, practices which reproduce, in effect, the colonial histories of America's people of color. What we need, I'd say, is a greater consciousness of the pervasiveness of the ethnocentricity from which we wish to break away." Could you speak for a moment about this assimilation, the role the English language plays, the role American schools play, and the impact on Native American life?

A: Cultural knowledge, in and of itself, is a state of being. When I speak about myself as a Native Person of Acoma, meaning that I am an Acoma person from Acoma, and speaking of that as a state of being, with a sense of myself in terms of the identity of culture and community morals and habits, customs, and traditions of the people, that is an important matter, which is critical and significant. I think it is vastly important to be the identity that maintains myself as who I am, who I want to be, and how I want to be regarded. However, in the United States, which is a vastly large country with a multitude of populations, a very multicultural society, Native Americans are a very minor population and political entity. No matter how much the people within that cultural group value their identity as natives, whichever tribe they might identify with, they find themselves faced by this larger and more prominent outside world that is massive and overpowering. This is the way of the America that sometimes overwhelms one's sense of being, that you can't be an Indian, because you would feel that you were somehow in the wrong, or out of step, so you will find many people, all ethnic minorities, who find themselves faced by this other massive presence. We find ourselves gravitating toward, stimulated by, mystified by, and attracted to this other force, because it is what gains attention, what provides the educational process, provides the assimilation energy, because even though we may have a great need for our own unique enduring identity, we soon find ourselves wanting and, in some respects, needing what is offered by the larger dominant society. We find that this soon translates into institutions and institutional power, such as educational institutions of the United States. I went to Indian day school at home at McCartys in New Mexico when I was much younger. The Acoma Pueblo reservation had a small day school at McCartys, which was not really that involved with the native community but was run by the Bureau of Indian Affairs. The Bureau of Indian Affairs only offered American educational fare and that was it. It didn't offer anything that dealt with Acoma native culture. It didn't encourage Native American language. The language at home was the Acoma language of Keres, but the school only offered what would Americanize us: how to speak English and seek American ways. With this kind of education, this soon becomes your wants and wishes because you are being indoctrinated to that every way. I think this is what really eventually overcomes us. We permit ourselves to be overcome, and we permit ourselves to be influenced. I was just in Boulder, Colorado. I was looking for some presents for two of my grandchildren. The five year old had her birthday yesterday on the second of July, and my granddaughter will be eleven on the 31st of July. I have two daughters, one is going to be nineteen, and the other is twenty-eight, so I wanted to buy presents. Now, the only choices I have are what is offered by the American marketplace in the usual stores, like Target or Kmart, the choices all Americans too often are limited to. Soon we won't have any choice but to want the kinds of things those stores offer, and soon we end up having those things. This has a lot to do with what kind of identity we allow ourselves to have and this affects the language choices that we make. I wrote that I have often felt disloyal because I end up being more articulate in the English language not because I want to be more articulate in the English language, but because I have no choice. It's almost like this shopping trek. I don't have any choice other than the stores that are out there, so I respond with whatever selections I make in my limited choices. So, the language that I use, the English language, is the language of convenience, the language of the moment, the language of availability. I think it creates quite a dilemma, not only for me as a writer, as an intellectual, but as a situation that faces countless numbers of Native American people.

That's really a dilemma that Native American people and ethnic minorities face, because we know what we want, but is it possible to have what we want and must have to be who we are? I think that until the educational system in the United States, the social and cultural institutions that we have, whether at state or national levels, until that system understands what ethnic minorities want, and addresses that want, I think that we, and especially native peoples, are going to be faced with the situation of having no choice except to make the selections that we do.

Q: In *Woven Stone* you say, "I realized that what I do as a writer, teacher, and storyteller is to demystify language." You go on to say, "Making language familiar and accessible to others, bringing it within their grasp and comprehension, is what a writer, teacher, and storyteller does or tries to do. I've been trying it for over thirty years." Given what you have just discussed regarding the price many pay for enculturation into white-Western culture, what you have said regarding your own hesitations of learning English, and your experiences as a teacher, is there a contradictory role, then, enacted by the teacher as educator and agent of enculturation?

A: Yes and no. Yes, because he or she makes decisions based on what he or she feels is a good choice to make in trying to help or to be a model to people who are forced by the powers of colonialism into this system. Oftentimes, I find that simply repeating the voice of the English teachers I had in school or of reiterating what they said is not the best practice, because that simply continues the model of colonialism that traps people.

What we do then is to try to remake, revoice, or recreate that knowledge process that is within the human cultural spirit universally to try to have people come to their own decisions, their own means of perception and understanding according to their own cultural systems and cultural ways. By creative use of language and artistic use of expression that insists on the people's own indigenous integrity, I think it is possible to do that. However, because we are forced to work within the system of education, within United States cultural institutions, we are caught in a bind: you use the same methods and are in agreement with governmental and social forces that are not comfortable for either you or your people. In regards to English, this is what we end up doing. As native peoples with our own indigenous languages, we use English casually and carelessly, without knowing what the consequences are. We have only recently come to know English as a language to use, for the great majority of people for less than one hundred years. For the Acoma people only since 1950 has there been a much more extensive use of English and the Western cultural system of knowledge that is behind the English language. So, our experience of using English is not extensive, and yet we have found ourselves using it very easily and perhaps very thinly, yet, at the same time very proficiently, very fluently, quite expertly. But I don't think with any real sense of consequence. I wish I were wrong in saying this, but I think this is an honest perception that we do not have any real sense— we as indigenous people who regard English as a second language even though for many of us, it is the only language we know and it is the first language and is the only language we find ourselves dealing with and using—of the power of the English language. I am not just talking about language but also the knowledge system behind the language. I think this is quite a difficult situation, as people trying to decolonize ourselves and it is then a contradiction to use the very language of that system which has colonized us to try and decolonize ourselves and try to be free in the use of the language, which is English for the most part. It is not just English, but Spanish for the peoples of South America and Mexico, and a large number of Hispanic people, who are really Mestizo, here in the United States use Spanish as their first language while in their native spirit, they do have their own languages, even if these are way back in the past.

Q: Recently, conversations in composition studies have engaged what is being called "hybrid" or "mixed" forms of discourse. These new discourses, as Patricia Bizzell has defined them, combine traditional academic discourse with new forms of discourses, often drawing on home or parent discourses, and are being accepted as "doing serious intellectual work and are received and evaluated as such, even though they may violate many of the conventions of traditional academic discourse." The idea, it seems is to provide more access to academic discourses by creating hybrids that value home discourses alongside academic discourse. Yet, some, like Sid [Dobrin] and Victor Villanueva, have warned that hybridity moves toward hegemony. As Villanueva explains it, "Hybridity can mean creative transcendence, an affirmation of cultures and histories that are both of the mainstream and other, but it also tends to include the cultural mimicry that the other is forced to undergo before creative transcendence is allowed expression." As one who has thought and written a good deal about the relationships between home discourses and English-language culture as enacted by language events such as Standard Written English, how would you respond to this idea of hybrid or mixed discourse?

A: The most important thing to have in language use is a firm and substantial sense of self. So that the language you're using expresses who you are and what you are doing internally. So that this is clear to those who are in relation to you but are not of your indigenous community. The identity and the firm stand that you have in that language is most important. I think you can be who you are with an adopted language, and this includes, I think, a hybrid language, as long as you insist on being what and who you are and cognizant of how that empowers you in your relationship to other people. I think there is a hybrid language. That is, we borrow language continuously; language is always in flux, just like culture is in flux. I think there is some danger because of change that may fragment or weaken the firm and substantive base that you start with. But if you insist that you will use that language, whether it is English or Spanish, or any hybrid language, in your own terms, and by way of doing so, maintain who you are and what your traditions are, then you are relatively still within the power of the identity that you choose. However, the danger is that you will either soon forget or not notice the subtle changes that take place. Because sometimes change is a very sly process that is not very apparent; you don't know that you are changing. You may believe you are just as articulate in the Acoma or Native American way of life as you are in your use of English, or in your use of the hybrid language. But, you may also be part of the process or complicit in the change that is taking place. I don't know if I use a hybrid language or not, but I know that I speak a kind of English that still insists on who I am as a Native American, especially of the Acoma Pueblo tribal community. However, I have to be aware that I, too, may suddenly find myself a victim of change that has undermined my identity as a Native

American and especially as an Acoma person. I think use of indigenous languages must be maintained. I have to admit that over the years—I am sixty years old, and have been dealing with the American system of knowledge for quite a few years—I know that we are changed even against our will, whether we realize it immediately or not. But I hope that, even if and when we do change, it's still change on our terms. I would not be so foolishly brave as to say that we don't change, because we do. But we must change so it is still to our benefit, and is still something of our choice.

Q: In an interview with Laura Coltelli you said, "The real America is the Native America of indigenous people and the indigenous principle they represent." Your writings, particularly your poems and short stories present an array of pictures of America and its peoples' relationship with the land. It has also been said that your work "transcends ethnicity and is a universal plea for respect toward individuals and what the land offers them." Could you speak to what it means to you to "transcend ethnicity"?

A: Our responsibility, as people, and how we put that responsibility into practice, is really what transcends. It is not just that Native American way of life, or any particular peoples, but what we have to work toward, and what we are empowered by throughout creation is a sense of respect. Respect and responsibility is to be carried out by everyone. I don't just mean by cultural communities around the world, but through that way of existence that includes all the other parts of life that we know to make up our world, the ocean, the sky, the water, all the elements, because we are in a community with them. We must think beyond the human community; we have a continuing responsibility to the environment that is placed on all of us. I think that indigenous communities insist that we all pay attention to those things that are so important. We must continue life in some manner. We have to insist that life is unending, and that we are very important to the creative energy we are a part of. If we give up, through cynicism or anger, and accept destruction, then we have accepted self-destruction. We must continuously fight against self-destruction. I speak of this in a universal sense; I try to address these issues in my work. I think that if being Native American means anything, it means making environmental responsibility apparent on a much greater level.

Q: In *Speaking for the Generations*, Roberta J. Hill says, "The impulse for my writing was my need to find a way to deal with my anger. . . . My anger is distilled in the writing, and the anger no longer harms my life but instead becomes awareness and social action." In what ways do you see writing as a form of activism? Is contemporary Native written expression now entrenched in social action?

A: Writing is, as I have said in my work, an extension or continuance of the oral tradition. The oral tradition is an expression of form, of participation, of active responsibility. We find ourselves feeling, thinking, and saying things that reflect how we practice everyday life, so that we are continually aware of our relationship to the physical world, and that we are reciprocally responsible. Writing is, to me, a native form of expression. Now, is that the only thing that writing is for Native American people with their activist insistence? No, I don't think that it is, but, it is certainly a part of the Native American tradition to be active participants and practitioners and active in a traditional way. This tradition insists on involvement in issues, concerns, circumstances, and experiences where we do not just speak but are involved. Do we only speak about what we act upon? I think that's true, but I think literature for Native American people is a very reflective and meditative form of expression that is not limited only to activism. I think that is too narrow a division, or too narrow a way to define Native American literature.

Q: To continue for a moment about activism, speaking of the numbers of times you speak publically, you write in *Fightin'*, "Geesus, sometimes, I don't know why I say I will do it. This place is a church, and I know churches are places where you are to bring your tired bones and shredded soul for salvation but, man, I don't know why I say, Yes, sometimes." You seem to be questioning your own activism. Could you speak for a moment about the role of activism, why you might be frustrated with your own position as a public speaker, and what ways others—who do not necessarily have the visible exposure public figures like yourself have—might avoid frustration with their activism?

A: I think that sometimes I do get cynical, particularly when no one's going to listen anyway, and they're just going to go shopping some more, or they'll go speeding down the highway, burning all the fossil fuels as long as they can afford it. I sometimes feel it is pointless to rant and rave. But, I think I go ahead and do it because it is worth it. Life is precious. If you are passionate, you realize what is at stake. Let's see, I have four grandchildren, no five, and three step grandchildren, and I have three children, who range in age from nineteen to thirty-three, and I see the failure of the world at stake not just in the lives of my children and

grandchildren but really in all life, the world, its populations, the animals, and plants. I feel that my sense of existence requires that I must not
be cynical, that I must not get frustrated. I know that life is much more
important. I'm a recovering alcoholic, and I have known moments when
I have given in to those kinds of self-destructive tendencies, and life
could have ended personally in a very unhealthy self-destructive way. But
I also know the misery of that. I know the sickness of that. There is a
quality of life that I think we can have, and I think we can share. How
do we get there? I think part of it is through an activism that says, "Don't
give up!" and that tells the public that we don't have to use water wastefully, or that we don't have to use electricity wastefully. If we have to have
these things, then we must use them judiciously, so that we are not
simply victimizing ourselves and simply exploiting our limited resources.
We must be conscious of our use, and responsible for what we have at
stake. Oftentimes, I feel frustrated and disgusted by people who feel there
is nothing we can do. By that, I mean I sometimes feel frustrated by my
own children and friends and relatives who may feel this way. I don't
want to sound judgmental, though. We need to remind each other that
we need to be much more responsible when it comes to natural resources,
and what we can do to help the Earth. I cannot say enough about
helping. That is one of the ways I think I was raised, culturally, within
the small Native American community of Acoma, to help. Whether this
is through story or poetry or other kinds of writing that I do, or through
my example and voice, my primary mission is to help others.

Q: As a final question, we'd like to ask: as a writer who focuses upon the
exclusion, colonization, and almost invisibility of Native Americans in
the United States, can you tell when your writing has created and achieved
"real" effects and consequences?

A: It makes me feel good if people are able to bring about changes that
are influenced by the Native American insistence on ways of seeing things.
Although I am still faced with difficult problems that writing cannot
immediately solve. I'll provide a local example. Our community is currently working to ensure the cleanup of the Rio de San Jose River, for
example, which was affected by uranium mining from the fifties through
the early eighties. This river was traditionally used for watering our fields
and gardens, our corn and chilé, and our orchard trees and hay pastures.
The river water was, and the groundwater still is, used domestically. But
the water was affected by the industrial changes brought about by the
uranium mining and processing. I know we've been fighting to have that

river recovered somehow. It's like having our lives recovered. Over the years, not too much change has taken place, but still the people insist on speaking about it. What I have written about it, through poetry and short stories, has brought attention to some degree to what has taken place, and to other incidents of land corruption. Does this bring about change? I think this brings about attention, which can bring change. Large-scale changes oftentimes do not occur, but over the years, Native American writings, which have grown in influence since the sixties, have gained attention for their exposition of these problems. This provides a way for people to pay attention to and try to enact change. I think there has been more attention to the environment, more attention to political and human rights concerns demanded by Native people, whether in South Dakota, Arizona, New Mexico, or California, brought about by native writers and native literature. I don't think there's been too many occasions in which I've said to white Americans that I congratulate them for using the Native American model, but they're there and it makes me feel happy and aware that we are creating changes.

On a larger scale, for native people and activists, writing has brought some things to attention. The Maya struggle in Chiapas and in Guatemala has been ongoing for over five hundred years, like the Native American struggle here in the United States. Recently, within the past ten years, the Maya people in Chiapas have taken action against NAFTA by liberating some towns. They have spoken in ways that have been influenced by Maya tradition. In some degree, this has brought about attention not only to the power of the oral tradition. I think that this kind of consciousness will result in America finally coming to grips with its identity. If anything, we hope what will come about is that America as a whole will realize what its identity is, an identity based on a sense of responsibilities for what it maintains itself as and how it maintains itself as an idea and as a nation-state, or a series of nation-states, which includes all the countries of the Americas. I think that change comes about through Native American writings, and the literature that we bring about as a result.

Rethinking Responsibility

A Response to Simon Ortiz

Scott Richard Lyons

Simon Ortiz—who at this point in his life exercises what I'll call the "elder-function," not only among his own people but with readers as well—imparts a particularly indigenous form of wisdom we shouldn't take for granted in the realm of public discourse. After all, while Native Americans have been writing for the public—and writing it in English—for well over two centuries now, it wasn't until the "Native American renaissance" of the sixties and seventies that writers like Ortiz, Gerald Vizenor, Leslie Marmon Silko, Louise Erdrich, N. Scott Momaday, James Welch, and others were actually read in earnest, that is, actually listened to, by a general readership. Only then were Native intellectuals taken seriously as a cultural movement, not because (as some would have it) indigenous people suddenly "gained voice" or grew into culture (that is, became "civilized"), but primarily because non-Indians started paying attention to Indian thoughts. Unlike earlier Native thinkers and writers—Charles Alexander Eastman, say, or Zitkala Sa, who through no fault of their own were received by audiences as something of a curiosity ("The Chief Speaks!" "Come Hear the Indian Princess!")—Ortiz and his generation cannily succeeded in capturing the attention and imaginations of thinking readers who finally saw in them—in us—a meaningful group of people with something important to say, both in and on our own terms. These intellectuals made claims, and they laid claims: to canonical inclusion, to resources in academe, to the very right to exist and be recognized in all of their cultural difference—in short, to rhetorical sovereignty. Of course, this literary movement was coterminous with the Red Power civil rights activity of the sixties and seventies—Alcatraz, the Native American Embassy, the Longest Walk, and Wounded Knee—and should never be abstracted from that political context. But it would be a mistake to connect Native writing only to the civil rights movement. As Ortiz suggests, Native writing is, and has always been, connected to something much deeper and older and wiser and tougher: traditional Native culture. During his career Ortiz has consistently found continuities where one might be tempted to see breaks, witnessed renewal where others had forecasted the end, and, always, pointed to a kind of circle at work: deep connections between past, present, and future; orality and literacy; different generations, peoples, and forms of life. Through this "circular logic" (here, a very good thing indeed), in this particular interview, Ortiz also addresses an apparently new, but actually ancient, and ultimately quite crucial, ethic of responsibility.

Responsibility as a key theme in Ortiz's discussion should come as no surprise considering the concept's importance to Native communities and cultures. In English, the word *responsibility* hearkens back to the Latin *responsum*, "to promise in return," which also gives us the word *response*. Signifying at once a cause, a sense of trustworthiness, a settling of accounts, and the condition of answerability, responsibility ultimately points to a powerful act of language: to be responsible means in part to *say* something, to answer, to *respond*. Silence, then, might be construed as an act of irresponsibility. Responsibility doesn't follow the logic of moral equivalences (that most American of notions, where everything works out in the end with the good rewarded and the bad blamed) so much as it requires the *continuous rebirth* (in Ojibwe, *minobimaatisiwin*) of answers that would renew the economy of life and death. To be responsible is, at least on one level, to honor a call for response. And if there is no answer, if the exchange of language is finished, then so is the discussion and so are the interlocutors; they cease to exist. It is in this way, perhaps, that both humanity and the planet can perish.

Ortiz explains how Native Americans have long understood and lived by this ethic of responsibility:

> I speak about the traditional way of knowledge that native people have in regards to their relationship with the natural world. There are ways in which this knowledge is spoken of through prayer, ceremonial ritual, instructions, and ways of behavior, whether they are social or personal, that speak about one's inextricable relationship to the natural world and one could even say the whole of life. I think that what traditional knowledge really expresses is responsibility, a practice of responsibility that we as social entities, as communities, have with the land which is the source of life.

Tradition expresses both responsibility (characterized here as a *practice*) and response (that which is *spoken*). The two go hand in hand in a distinctively Indian logic. Referring to the ontological basis of ceremony and ritual, Ortiz explains how Native peoples have traditionally used language to communicate not only with each other but also with Mother Earth and the natural processes of time, transmitting knowledge and instructions through the act of ritual and subsequently establishing certain relationships between life forms. In rituals, people use ceremonial language to acknowledge their humility and dependency upon the healthy production of nature, and in so doing socialize themselves into proper ways of acting and being. Contrary to the old stereotype of Indians simplistically "worshipping Nature," this deep ontological activity in truth recognizes and affirms a cooperative relationship between living beings that happens to express itself through spirituality. So, for example, when an Ojibwe family sponsors its annual feast for the wild rice, a ceremony designed to honor and thank the *manoomin* for giving itself through harvest, it articulates and establishes a responsible relationship through word, song, and deed: the humans thank the food for arriving in our lakes each year and promise not to abuse that gift by overharvesting or endangering the plant through other means (like pollution), and the wild rice—understood to speak a different language than us but a language nonetheless—responds in turn by coming back. One speaks, the other answers: it is in this way that responsibility is pursued by way of response.

I remember my grandfather, Aubrey Lyons, who was not a particularly traditional Indian in most respects, honoring the spirit of *waawashkeshii* by performing a simple ceremony each time he shot a deer for food. I asked him once why he did what he did out there in the woods, why he thought his sons and grandchildren should carry on that particular tradition, and my grandfather simply said, "I learned it from my grandpa, and it keeps the deer coming. If we don't do it, they'll stop coming." My grandfather also knew that one honored the spirit of the deer by ensuring that its habitat was protected, so his ceremonial response was accompanied by another, more political, practice of responsibility: the protection of habitat. Likewise, I recall a talk given by Red Lake elder Raining Spears in which he explained, using spiritual language, why Red Lake was fished out. "People stopped having feasts for the fish, so that spirit has now hidden itself until the feasts return." When a younger member of the audience protested that the lake's fish stock was depleted simply because too many people took too many fish, Raining answered, quite unfazed, "That's what I was saying." Built into the ceremony of feasting the spirit is an acknowledgement that one only takes what one needs, responsibility always already built into the act of response. So, yes, that's exactly what Raining was saying.

Relationships and responsibilities are established through the articulation of response in traditional ceremonial language, and people learn how to act. Furthermore, this sense of responsibility is coded not only in the language of ceremony and song but also in the tales of the oral tradition; as Ortiz points out, "codes of conduct are expressed through stories." For instance, there are many Ojibwe stories that explain how key spiritual figures—like the eagle—intercede on behalf of humanity whenever the spirits grow weary of the endless neglect of our responsibilities and consider doing away with us altogether. In such stories, we are taught not only to honor those spiritual benefactors who save us at the last minute, but more importantly to learn the crucial lesson built into the tale: namely, how to live in respectful concert with the processes of the natural world. Dreams, too, which can themselves become stories, are sites of response. The Ojibwe, who have traditionally taken dreams quite seriously, encourage their young to remember their dreams, even to work for them, as a means of guiding individuals into another venue of responsible dialogue with the spiritual/natural world. I'm thinking now of a friend of mine who once dreamed of a mother wolf who suddenly killed one of her four cubs and tossed it out of the den. Later, at ceremony, the dream was discussed and a conclusion drawn: the mother wolf was symbolic of Mother Earth, the cubs being the various life forms inhabiting the world, and the sick one in particular representing that reckless species known as humankind. Because wolf mothers are known to kill a sick cub for fear of it endangering the others, the dreamer interpreted the dream, with the help of the traditional community, to be a dire warning indeed.

When children are raised in this kind of culture of responsibility, they typically become adults who are loathe to waste, endanger, or offend wild rice, deer, fish, or the many other powerful spirits of nature. We may speak in spiritual terms, but that is simply the language we use to understand and describe natural processes and delineate proper action: it is, *in a manner of speaking*, our way of articulating responsibility. In the kind of culture that tells itself these kinds of stories, that sings these songs and dreams these dreams, responsibility and respect become meaningful to one's very self-image: it becomes impossible to conceive of oneself as existing apart from the natural world. In learning how to act, you learn who you are; in formulating response, you become responsible. It becomes an inextricable part of your identity. This is why, as Ortiz says, "if being Native American means anything, it means making environmental responsibility apparent on a much greater level." You live responsibly not only because it's the right thing to do, or because if we don't we will certainly perish, but also because the ethic has been hardwired through socialization into the fabric of your being.

So, it is true that traditional Native cultures are environmentally oriented, that we have long lived in harmony with the natural world out of a deep cultural imperative, and that responsibility is built into our language and socialization processes. Yet, it is also true that many of us have been struggling to retain that culture in the face of colonization, consumerism, and all of their attendant forces. Our kids, like yours, are watching MTV, wanting Nikes, and eating too many Big Macs these days, but at least in the Indian world there still exists a viable alternative in the form of traditional culture. The fight to maintain that culture, with its concomitant values and practices, is in large part a fight to remain responsible. As such, indigenous sovereignty movements—from land claims cases in upstate New York, to hunting and fishing treaty rights struggles practically everywhere, to the ongoing indigenous battle against neoliberalism in Chiapas, Mexico—should be supported by environmentalists who would doubtless find powerful allies emerging from victories in the Fourth World. Indigenous peoples may very well be among the last remaining groups on Earth to retain a strong culture of environmental responsibility, one that fashions the relationship between humanity and the earth so strongly as to become part of Native identity itself, and in that sense we should be in a position to lead the world to sustainable living. But we need support in our fight for sovereignty, our continuing struggle to survive as distinct peoples, which is the ultimate foundation of all indigenous political movements worldwide.

Of course, there is also risk in characterizing Native cultures as leaders in this way. "Too often," as Ortiz points out, "native people have found themselves as models, or examples, of how human cultures can acknowledge that inextricable relationship between human culture and the environment." One danger is that we can become too heavily scripted as natural environmentalists, in stereotypical fashion, thus being denied a basic right to be fully human or to make mistakes. Another danger is the possibility of having our traditional ceremonies or stories taken without permission and without context, which not only results in cultural imperialism but also misses the point of local community action. "Where I come from, in New Mexico," Ortiz says, "the Acoma Pueblo is responsible for their own," that is, for themselves and not others. And how can it be otherwise? The Acoma Pueblo, the Minnesota Ojibwe, and other Native communities cannot be responsible for everyone and everything in the world; to assume as much would be, if anything, a shirking of responsibility. Indeed, we have our hands full simply trying to resist the degradation of life caused by our neighbors—for instance, the sixteen nuclear waste dumps currently planned for Indian reservations, or the more than one hundred federal proposals offered in recent years to dump toxic waste in Native communities (LaDuke 2–3). Communities and peoples need to be responsible not only to the natural world but to each other; it's everyone's responsibility, not simply the Indian thing to do. Still, despite this particular caution, Ortiz is quick to point out that the indigenous way of living responsibly might indeed "be applied to the world at large and not just to native or indigenous people." Perhaps the crucial point here is to think in terms of form rather than content: to appropriate a cultural logic, not the culture itself. How, for example, can nonindigenous cultures develop forms of socialization that would lead their people to see themselves as connected and responsible to the natural world? How might the dominant culture think of new ways of using language to formulate response?

Our best bet may be to consider what local cultures already have to work with. Literacy, for one, seems to be a potentially powerful site for the making of connections—a way to use language to formulate response, refigure subjectivity, and articulate responsibility. Derek Owens has described an approach to reading and writing instruction that both emanates from, and pursues as a goal, the concept of sustainability. Defining sustainability as "meeting today's needs without jeopardizing future generations," Owens actually sounds a little like an Indian describing Seventh Generation thinking, which calls for all decisions to be made only after considering their impact on the seventh generation to come (1). With the value of sustainability guiding his practice, Owens has his students write about their communities as places, thinking reflectively about them, probably for the first time, and considering how places and people interact with each other with greater or lesser degrees of responsibility. These home stories of place are enabled by the creation of "sustained classroom spaces where students can think critically on the past, present, and future of their communities," a crucial "first step" on a walk to a sustainable outlook (76). In addition to place, Owens's students also think and write about work, that most human of activities that perhaps more than anything else in the modern world defines the ways we interact with the places around us. Students reflect on what are quite often their "crummy jobs," and encounter the fact that most work is unsustainable, painful, even bad for you, before considering the possibility of "more enriching and sustainable employment" (104). Finally, Owens has his students consider the future as represented in a diverse range of "future scenarios" they read, and they eventually construct their own through a process of thoughtful dialogue between their desires for the future and the predictions, wishes, and concerns of others. "Future scenarios are inevitably vision statements," Owens writes; by bringing students into the realm of vision seeking, he charts a course toward a culture that might make the "impossible" possible (128). Having students think and write about place, work, and the future in these ways, Owens uses his position as a teacher of literacy, a cultural worker, to help students imagine themselves anew: as products of place, as creative workers in the world, and as seekers of visions. This is one way an individual might use what's already there to create the conditions for the emergence of a responsible culture. Indeed, Owens's students are *responding*.

I don't mean to suggest that the entire content of all Native cultures is somehow completely off-limits to the rest of the world; to the contrary, there is much to be learned from Native people living in cultures of responsibility. But rather than sneaking into someone else's ceremony, it would be better to consider the gifts that have already been given: for instance, the long and venerable tradition of Native writing, which has consistently depicted responsible living and advocated for its importance to the world. This tradition has been available for consideration all along, through the Indian medium of *writing*, which Ortiz calls "a native form of expression." Ortiz's own work definitely fits this bill, as would the first several chapters of a still very relevant text recently under right-wing attack: Rigoberta Menchu's *testimonio*, in which readers are presented with plain-spoken personal descriptions of responsible indigenous life and culture, including childrearing, community making, and sustainable living. *I, Rigoberta Menchu*, spoken by her and written down by another, exists in between the technologies of orality and literacy. For Ortiz, the Native written tradition *always* emanates from the oral one, and it seems to do so by design.

> I know I have a preference for written English that has the power, the vitality, and the energy of the oral tradition. I am partial to reading writing that evokes the energy, power, and spirit of the oral tradition. I think that written language can emulate the oral tradition, but this depends on culture insisting that writing maintain the technical facility and integrity of oral tradition.

It would also depend on the culture carrying over some of its oral themes in writing, which is why I'd like to close with a brief consideration of Dakota writer Charles Alexander Eastman (Ohiyesa). Perhaps Ortiz would agree that Eastman's writing represents exactly the spirit of responsibility found in Native oral cultures and retains an undeniably indigenous character.

In his 1911 philosophical treatise, *The Soul of the Indian: An Interpretation*, Eastman describes the indigenous culture of responsibility in large part, as he puts it, to "emphasize its universal quality, its personal appeal" (xii). Above all, Eastman's people exist in harmony with the world; there is no nature/culture dichotomy in Indian country. "There were no temples or shrines among us save those of nature," Eastman writes in his opening essay, "The Great Mystery":

> Being a natural man, the Indian was intensely poetical. He would deem it sacrilege to build a house for Him who may be met face to face in the mysterious, shadowy aisles of the primeval forest, or on the sunlit bosom of virgin prairies, upon dizzy spires and pinnacles of naked rock, and yonder in the jeweled vault of the night sky! (5)

Anticipating the arguments of anthropologists, who would spend much of the twentieth century reading such statements for evidence of animism, Eastman went on to clarify that Native beliefs and ceremonies "were wholly symbolic, and the Indian no more worshiped the Sun than the Christian adores the Cross" (13). Indians are rational beings who simply—and sustainably—live a relationship with nature we might accurately describe as loving. This relationship isn't "savage"; in fact, it's scientific, as Eastman elaborates.

> The Sun and the Earth, by an obvious parable, holding scarcely more of poetic metaphor than of scientific truth, were in his view the parents of all organic life. From the Sun, as the universal father, proceeds the quickening principle in nature, and in the patient womb of our mother, the Earth, are hidden embryos of plants and men. Therefore our reverence for them was really an imaginative extension of our love for our immediate parents, and with this sentiment of filial piety was joined a willingness to appeal to them, as to a father, for such good gifts as we may desire. (14)

This is not chatting with trees; this is *response* demystified. To further illustrate his point, Eastman also articulates the ceremonial relationship between humans and the spirits of nature in the context of hunting: "He had faith in [animal] instincts, as in a mysterious wisdom given from above; and while he humbly accepted the supposedly voluntary sacrifice of their bodies to preserve his own, he paid homage to their spirits in prescribed prayers and offerings" (15). Although using much plainer English than Eastman, that day in the woods long ago, that's also what my grandfather was saying.

The approach of white "civilization," however, described by Eastman in terms of endless settlements, industrialization, and a rapidly increasing population, marked the arrival of a different kind of culture, one lacking a sense of environmental connection because of its tendency toward alienation.

> To the untutored sage, the concentration of population was the prolific mother of all evils, moral no less than physical . . . and not less dreaded than the pestilence following upon crowded and unsanitary dwellings was the loss of spiritual power inseparable from too close contact with one's fellow-men. All who have lived much out of doors know that there is a magnetic and nervous force that accumulates in solitude and that is quickly dissipated by life in a crowd. (11)

This "force," enabled by nature and threatened by urban life, was for Eastman an integral part of the Indian's "soul": the fabric of one's identity and the power behind responsible living. As such, it was this force (and not the workings of "savagery") that determined the course of Native history up until colonization: "It was not, then, wholly from ignorance or improvidence that he failed to establish permanent towns and to develop a material civilization" (10). To do so would have been to work against one's soul, to betray oneself as a responsible person in the world. In his interpretation, Eastman seems to suggest that to the Indian, "material civilization" must have seemed, well, irresponsible.

And so it has become. But it's true, a better world *is* possible, and Native people, like Eastman, and Ortiz, and Menchu, and even in his quiet way my grandfather, have been depicting that world for quite some time now: in ceremony, in song, in speech, and in writing. And in memory: we remember that world, and our responsibilities, even as we forget them. The better world is something we dream, and encourage our children to dream, with some fear for the future. But also with hope. "If anything," as our elder Simon Ortiz says in his interview, "we hope what will come about is that America as a whole will realize what its identity is, an identity based on a sense of responsibilities."

WORKS CITED

Eastman, Charles Alexander. *The Soul of the Indian: An Interpretation*. Lincoln: U of Nebraska P, 1980.

LaDuke, Winona. *All Our Relations: Native Struggles for Land and Life*. Cambridge: South End P, 1999.

Owens, Derek. *Composition and Sustainability: Teaching for a Threatened Generation*. Urbana, Ill.: NCTE P, 2001.

Dear Simon

A Response to Simon Ortiz

Malea Powell

Dear Simon,[1]

I was sitting in a meeting today, doing those things that get done in academic committee meetings, when the question of language arose. We were working on documents to represent our new Ph.D. in Writing & Rhetoric, working out the language with which we will, at least provisionally, represent ourselves as a program. And, yes, I know, when the subject is language one would assume that the question of language would sit center stage. But we both know how assumptions work. So, there we were, a half dozen Ph.D. professors of varying ranks staring at pages of text, doing that critical reading thing that makes up a large part of the practice of professional academics, all being very, well, collegial. That's pretty much where we were when one word in particular jumped out at me. My reaction was unmediated and visceral—"oh, we can't use that word, that's an awful word, an offensive word"—and immediately answered with an explanation of where the word came from, why it was used, all the institutional and official reasons why it had made it into the drafts we were reading. I continued to protest—"it offends me, and I think it will offend prospective students." My very surprised colleagues had, by that time, recovered enough to say, "it's just a word, we'll change it" and to suggest a different word, equally offensive in its assumptions, but less viscerally so. The word I hated: *examination*; the word we used in compromise: *defense.*

Clearly, here, as in every other rhetorical situation, context matters. As I left that conference room, I thought of you, of your interview with Sid Dobrin and Chris Keller, of other Native elder-scholars, and of how important "just a word" can be. I think, sometimes, that many folks take a statement like "there have always been those words which evoked meaning and meaning's magical wonder" (Dobrin and Keller, 194) as something more stereotypically quaint and less intensely theoretical than it seems to me. And, as much as I enjoy reading and learning from traditional academic theorists of language like Wittgenstein and Lacan and Derrida and Lyotard, I still find myself confused by the refusal of most academics to see and admit that Native people already had an understanding of the way in which language creates the universe, the way in which words matter, the way words and stories hold the world together. That confusion is probably the most naive failing; it is also the thing that encourages me to go forward, though, because I know that even these stories here in this book are full of pedagogical and epistemological power.

I have been charged by the editors collecting these stories with offering a response that will talk about what "we" in composition studies might learn from what you said in your interview. Mostly, Simon, I just want to tell folks to listen, and to do so carefully, caringly, with their hearts as well as their minds. But I also feel that institutional pressure to articulate, once again, the connections between what is important to Native writers, Native scholars, and Native communities with what is important to scholars and teachers of writing. I was taught that my elders are my teachers, so I hope, Simon, that you will forgive me then for the mistakes I'll make here as the weight of story and memory and language bear down on me, and that you will know how deeply I respect your work, and your words. One of the things I've learned from Native scholar-elders is that there are ways to mediate these academic pressures—familiar pressure brought on by familiar questions—so I began thinking about this response in the way that I have been taught to think about any problem—I went to the trees for answers.

There are four maple trees lining the street in front of my yard here in south-central Michigan. When I wrote this response they were loaded with whirly-gigs—my childhood name for those evocative flying seed pods that insure the community of maples' survival. As an insatiably curious child growing up on a small subsistence farm, I spent many a summer day carefully examining every state of whirly-gig development, tearing open the pod to see what the seed looked like, day after day watching for the inevitable changes—from undifferentiated tender green to tightly packaged sprout. I was fascinated by how easily those pods came apart, how easily the world came apart and remade itself every season, especially compared with how much work it took when humans insisted on shaping it into a coherent whole—the preparation and planting and weeding and watering and feeding and harvesting and butchering and preserving that added up into simple survival for another season.

I'm no longer fascinated by how things come apart, though I have been known to be occasionally seduced by theory, especially by deconstruction and psychoanalysis. Mostly, Simon, I am, like you, more interested in how things come together, how we come together as humans, how we remain connected to the place of our birth, how we create and remember ourselves as a community. In the Introduction to *Woven Stone*, you tell a story about introducing yourself to some children at Laguna Elementary. It's a translation story about the significance of knowing, in one's own language, the place where you come from, the places we all come from, and in the middle of the story you say, "I realized that what I do as a writer, teacher, and storyteller is to demystify language. . . . making language familiar and accessible to others, bringing it within their grasp and comprehension" (3–4). Later in that same Introduction, you point out the importance of understanding that our stories continue even when we tell them in a new language, and that this sense of continuity—from tribal languages into what some have called "colonizer's" languages—is "essential to Native American life" (9). We use English because we have no choice—that's what it means to be the language of colonization. And while we must acknowledge there are consequences to using colonizing languages, it doesn't mean that English can't be used by American Indians and other colonized populations to "remake, revoice, or recreate," "to come to their own decisions, their own means of perception and understanding according to their own cultural systems and cultural ways," as you suggest in the interview above.

In "Creating Language," one of the poems from *After and Before the Lightning*, you say, "To use language, / the speaker has to know / its real bones, guts, blood, / spirit, mind, heart. / . . . / And the only way he can / is to know / he is being created / as he speaks it" (110). This crystallizes an important point for me—not only that we create and are created by/ within language but also that this creation is not a solitary act of individual heroism. It is, instead, a communal effort of making and negotiating meaning within a framework that always spills off the page, all over our hands and feet, and onto the landscape. Being a writer, a scholar, a Native person, a human—all are acts of participation that are laden with implied commitments to the existence and continuance of other writers, scholars, Native people, humans. You've said this over and over in your own writing, but I think this is a hard argument to make to teachers and scholars of writing and rhetoric. We get to *be* because we are willing to help others *be*. Like you say, Simon, in "Becoming Human": "We are given permission / by the responsibilities we accept / and carry out. Nothing more, / nothing less" (*After* 64).

I keep thinking here of my charge in this response—to consider what teachers/scholars of writing might learn—and of the ways in which some non-Native scholars in Rhetoric & Composition have begun to consider pieces of what you've expressed here. I think that one of the things that keeps me going is finding assonance in odd places. By this I mean that it's relatively easy to find scholars of color in this discipline like Villanueva and Royster and Mao who are considering language and responsibility in ways very similar to that of Native writers; many of these scholars have, in fact, nurtured me and my work for many years now. What's more difficult is finding the ways in which that work has filtered into other, less predictable arenas in the discipline. I'm thinking here of work being done in the part of the discipline we call "professional and technical writing," specifically of Jim Porter's work on rhetorical ethics and Bob Johnson's theory of "use" that frames his *User-Centered Technology*. In Porter's *Rhetorical Ethics and Internetworked Writing*, he is specifically concerned with ethical rhetorics that do not "derive from print assumptions" (1), and with understanding "values and language use as inextricably bound"; thus writing becomes "an act fraught with ethical issues" (149). Johnson, too, is interested in language as "the most fundamental technology of the human experience," a tool that is "taught, learned, and used in strategic ways, much as we might use hammers, automobiles, or computers" (9). I think it's important for those of us who consider Rhetoric & Composition our scholarly home to realize that these "new" theoretical orientations are the stories by which we compose ourselves as a community. They are the stories through which we articulate and enact our commitments and our responsibilities as teachers and scholars of writing.

You've said it in a million ways, Simon, in this interview, with your essays, your stories, your poems, your presence—our stories come from some place, they are going some place; we come from some place, we are going some place. The "we" here simply defines the community, any human community. What connects us, what connects our stories, is this central idea about responsibility. If we take our responsibilities to story, to the land, seriously, then we see that "story has its own life, its very own, and we are the voices carried with it" (*After* 20). In this interview, you refer to the phrase "land, culture, and community" as signifying the "responsible relationship that we as a human cultural community have" and also signifying "an appropriately reciprocal relationship with the natural world." Later, you cite the "oral tradition" as the central way in which we carry out our responsibilities to the environment, responsibilities that aren't just to the land but which are also responsibilities we have in relation to other humans, to other members of the community. Narration, then, becomes a way in which we teach *and* learn, not just about how to *be*, but about how to be human in a particular way for a particular community.

I think here of three conversations I've had in the past few years—the first, with my then-dissertation chairperson about the use of the word *war* in a draft that would become the theory introduction to my dissertation; the second, with a grad student who was troubled about the current state of "publish or perish" scholarship in academic institutions; the third, a constant one I've had with well-intentioned colleagues who praise me for all the time I devote to students and to service but warn me to keep an eye on "what's really important"—the scholarly publications that are rewarded by the institutions. All of these conversations remind me that taking responsibility for "how we come to live in an appropriately reciprocal relationship with the natural world" and extending that into "a real sense of commitment," "a sense of participation, involvement, and engagement" on the part of the writer/speaker and on the part of the community from/to which she speaks is something that scholars and teachers of writing have only just begun to theorize and understand. We too often ignore the impact of our participation, the importance of our honorable engagement in struggle, the significance of our stories to the life of the community, and we too rarely acknowledge the degree to which our scholarship should be responsible beyond mere publication. Maybe that's what we should work on, we in Rhetoric & Composition Studies, a way to make our discipline, our institutions, our departments, our lives as scholars-teachers more humane, more attenuated to the responsibilities we have to help one another. Maybe every time we stand to speak at a conference, every time we send a manuscript out for publication, every time we write comments on a student paper, every time we begin to speak in some academic committee meeting, we should listen to you, Simon, and remember: "Life is precious. If you are passionate, you realize what is at stake" (18).

Newee,
Malea

NOTES

1. I address Simon Ortiz directly, using his first name, not to be disrespectful but to honor the generosity of such an accomplished elder whose kindness and intelligence are so well-known in Native circles that he is, simply, Simon—our uncle and elder.

WORKS CITED

Ortiz, Simon J. *After and Before the Lightning*. Tucson: U of Arizona P, 1994.

Ortiz, Simon J. *Woven Stone*. Tucson: U of Arizona P, 1992.

Johnson, Robert R. *User-Centered Technology: A Rhetorical Theory for Computers and Other Mundane Artifacts*. Albany: State U of New York P, 1998.

Porter, James. *Rhetorical Ethics and Internetworked Writing*. Greenwich, CT: Ablex Publ. Corp., 1998.

Stories for the Earth

An Interview with Scott Russell Sanders

The writings of Scott Russell Sanders have covered not only a great many concerns, ideas, and issues but have also traversed a number of genres and styles. A glance at the long list of Sanders's writing would certainly include, though not be limited to, such nonfiction works as *Secrets of the Universe: Scenes from the Journey Home* (1992), *The Paradise of Bombs* (1993), *Staying Put: Making a Home in a Restless World* (1994), *Writing from the Center* (1995), *The Country of Language* (1999), and *Hunting for Hope: A Father's Journeys* (1999), his novel *Terrarium* (1995), and a number of children's books including *Warm as Wool* (1998) and *The Floating House* (1999). In addition to his career as a prolific and influential writer, Sanders is also a professor of English at Indiana University in Bloomington, where he teaches a variety of courses in literature, creative writing, and composition.

Much of Sanders's writing centers on nature and environment as well as literature and science, but Sanders's words are also enmeshed deeply in his understandings of family and community, particularly the responsibilities that he believes humans should share in caring for the earth. This is manifest in his own view of himself as a writer with certain responsibilities, which he comments on in the interview below: "If we don't have ways of carrying the land inside us—through stories, images, and names—then we lose touch, we lose the possibility of affectionate regard for the land. . . . One of my tasks as a writer is to provide stories for the portions of the earth that I've had the chance to know in some depth." Sanders cultivates this personal knowledge of places with discursive skill, sincerity, and care.

Sanders, in addition, provides great insight in this interview into the ways that nature and place are viewed and dealt with in composition, in English departments, and in universities in general, suggesting that "The current desire for nature writing also reflects a desire for literature that is relevant to the actual world. So much contemporary fiction and poetry, like most films and television programs, pay little or no regard to nature." Furthermore, readers should be interested in the ways Sanders touches on the current and future roles of ecocriticism for composition and literature specialists, noting, for instance, that "There's . . . a danger that ecocriticism will simply become another academic mill for cranking out papers and books. However, because so many of the people involved in teaching and writing about nature recognize the pettiness of academic specialization, there is a good chance that ecocriticism may remain open and big-spirited." Writing, according to Sanders, is a conversation he carries on with readers, and readers here see once more why so many are listening to what he says and reading what he writes.

Q: You write in "Letter to a Reader" that "In 1971 I brought back with me from England a fresh Ph.D. and a suitcase of manuscripts. The degree earned me several offers of teaching jobs. (I never considered trying to write without holding a job. The unemployed men I had known while growing up were miserable, humiliated, broken.)" As the rest of "Letter to a Reader" attests, you've produced a great amount of fiction and nonfiction, as well as some literary criticism since 1971, but you've also been an English professor at Indiana University most of this time. Can you comment for a moment on the relationship between writing and teaching? For instance, do you see yourself as a writer first and foremost? Do you feel that you teach because you are a writer, or is writing one part of being a professor? In what sense has writing created your identity?

A: Early on, I would have answered that I am first of all a teacher, and only secondarily a writer. In those days I was a beginner, I hadn't published much, and I felt that until one manages to publish regularly, one shouldn't call oneself a writer. I also didn't yet realize how much writing would matter to me. Within half a dozen years or so, I was deeply committed to writing and I was publishing often, so I began to think of myself as a writer who taught. I love teaching, but if I had to choose between writing and teaching, I would choose writing without hesitation.

Q: More specifically, you've been labeled by many a *nature writer*. You've written many essays that examine the natural world in relation to your own life and culture at large. You've been invited as guest speaker to this ASLE conference, an organization devoted to the analysis and facilitation of nature writing. The back cover of your novel *Terrarium* designates it as a work of fiction *and* environmental writing. Yet, you've published numerous works of fiction, nonfiction, and books for children that are not solely about nature per se. Is it accurate to label you a nature writer? Are you comfortable with this designation?

A: Sometimes the label makes me restless because it suggests that nature is a specialized interest. But nature is the universe, the context within which everything occurs. Humans are entirely and inescapably embedded in nature. Therefore, the fact that my books pay a great deal of attention to our planetary home shouldn't be treated as some sort of parochial interest, as if I wrote about sports or politics or film. Besides, I write about a great many other things—family and community, science and work, travel and art—yet I always understand these smaller realities to be encompassed by the greater reality of nature.

Q: Could you offer your own definition of nature writing?

A: Nature writing is simply any work of poetry, fiction, or nonfiction that recognizes our true home, placing us within the cycles of the earth, within the rhythms of the universe, among our fellow creatures. It honors the human world, but sees it as derived from and dependent on the primary world of nature.

Q: In the faculty biography page of your departmental Web site, you're listed as teaching Twentieth-Century American Literature, Writing about Nature, Science Fiction, History of the Novel, Creative Writing (Fiction), and Expository Writing. We're interested in the latter course: expository writing. These courses have been areas of scrutiny for administrators and other departments for many years now because many claim they do not adequately teach students to write correct academic discourse. Some have complained they are apolitical, while others believe they've become too political. Could you spend a few minutes discussing your own approaches to teaching expository writing? What do you see as your pedagogical agenda and approaches? In particular, do you include nature writing or ask students to write about nature in expository writing courses?

A: I often use nature writing in expository writing courses. I do so not only because I want my students to think about their place in the natural world but also because these literary models have inspired some splendid writing in my classes. I might ask students to write about a wild place that has mattered to them. I might ask them to write about a powerful encounter with nature—and nature here could mean an animal, a storm, an illness, a death, ferns curling out of the ground in spring, or the icy spikes of winter stars. I appreciate the fact that students need to learn to write clear, clean, functional prose. They need to be able to write research reports, summaries, proposals, and reviews. I'm committed to helping them develop those skills, but I also want students to see writing as a mode of discovery, a way of finding out something about themselves or the world that they would not otherwise know. Unless they experience writing as a way of discovery, unless it matters to them *personally*, then prose will remain for them a dutiful, mechanical medium.

Q: Following up on the last question, you suggest in "Beneath the Smooth Skin of America" that "Most of our children spend a year in grade school studying the history of their home states. Shouldn't they spend as much time studying their home ground? Let them take walks, handle stones and leaves and dirt, watch squirrels and bats and bugs, pore over photographs and fossils and maps, feel the land in their bones." Many compositionists believe that it is not just grade-school children who need direct contact with the natural world, but college students as well. What benefits and/or problems do you see in a pedagogy that asks students, in a sense, to explore nature and write about it for graded assignments?

A: Sending students outdoors to observe the life of the planet, or bringing pieces of wildness into the classroom, can be tremendously beneficial. Such contact reminds us that language arises out of the world. We start by naming things. Children begin by learning the names of everything they can touch and taste and smell. And it's good to recall that connection between language and the world. Putting students back in touch with nature is also a healthy way of turning them outward from their own emotions. Young writers can become caught up in their own psychic states, as though private feelings and notions were the only subjects worthy of art. By inviting them to pay attention to something outside themselves, you help free them from this preoccupation with the self. So, I'm a firm believer in making assignments that require students to go look at things, particularly things not made by human beings.

Q: Stephen Kellert writes in *The Value of Life: Biological Diversity and Human Society* that "The higher a person's education, the more likely that person is to express greater concern, affection, interest, and knowledge (and less exploitative and authoritarian attitudes) toward animals and the natural world. This tendency is especially pronounced among the college-educated." Could you comment on this quote, answering the following: What roles do you see the university playing in regard to environmental learning? Do you share any of Kellert's optimism about university education regarding the future of our natural environment?

A: First of all I would be wary of assuming that people with less formal education are therefore less likely to feel a strong attachment to the natural world. I can think of many contrary examples among people whom I've met on the back roads and in wild places in this country and abroad. I also know a good many people with Ph.D.s who behave callously toward other species and toward the earth. So I resist Kellert's generalization. However, I do agree with the positive claim he is making, which is that a university education can foster a deeper understanding of and sympathy with the natural world. Such an outcome is not inevitable. In most universities, the business curriculum will not foster a regard for nature, nor will economics, sociology, political science, or many other standard subjects. One can graduate from our best universities without knowing why the ozone layer matters, without understanding the greenhouse effect or the extinction crisis, without recognizing the impact of human population growth. On the other hand, students can certainly learn about the fundamentals of ecology in environmental studies courses, and they often explore our relations with nature in courses on anthropology, biology, literature, and art. Such learning can occur in any course, in any discipline, if the teacher is committed to helping students recognize that we all belong to this greater community, that we humans are merely one tribe among the host of living tribes. We're not born feeling compassion and love toward other organisms. Those feelings must be nurtured, and they can be nurtured in a number of ways—through school, through family outings, through solo rambles in woods and fields, through reading, through the practice of writing.

Q: In "The Common Life" you say that "For us [you and your wife], loving America had little to do with politicians and even less with soldiers, but very much to do with what I have been calling the common life: useful work, ordinary sights, family, neighbors, ancestors, our fellow creatures, and the rivers and woods and fields that make up our mutual home. . . . I still believe that loving your country or city or neighborhood may require you to resist, to call for change, to speak on behalf of what you believe in, especially if what you believe in has been neglected." Numerous composition scholars see the writing classroom as a place to learn how oppressive structures function, and a place to begin resisting these forces. In particular, some have written about the writing classroom as a place to not only learn about nature and environmental problems, but a place to facilitate activism. Can you offer any opinions about the classroom as a space to begin resistance and call for change?

A: I believe in urging students to reflect on our environmental and social dilemmas, but I don't believe I should tell students how to act on those dilemmas. I'm a teacher, not a political organizer. Obviously, one's own values and concerns will affect everything one does in teaching, from the selection of reading material to the conduct of discussion. While acknowledging this inevitable bias, I still feel it's crucial to respect the students' own judgment and vision. So, in my classes I try to raise fundamental questions about how we lead our lives, how we shape our communities, how we treat the planet, but I don't supply the answers. I want students to think critically about our "consumer" culture. It's the only culture that most of them have ever known, so I want them to realize that the world doesn't have to be this way—filled with war, strife, pollution, and waste. It hasn't always been this way and doesn't have to continue this way. Either because of deliberate action or because of ecological collapse, things will change, so let's examine our way of life and ask how it could be improved. I don't want to dictate what conclusions my students should draw when they ask those questions. Unless students feel they're being invited to undertake genuine inquiry, in class discussions as well as in their writing, they're unlikely to become good writers or tough-minded citizens. My goal is to energize their writing and thinking, rather than to imprint them with my views.

Q: Many in composition have argued that we need to examine our relationships with the environment of the classroom as much as we need to examine our relationships with natural environments. In what ways do you think of the classroom as an environment, a place?

A: Clearly, every part of a university, from classroom to dormitory, has a pedagogical effect. The whole campus is part of the curriculum. Unfortunately, most campuses I have visited do not demonstrate good environmental stewardship. The buildings are usually designed for appearance or economy, with little regard for energy efficiency or harmony with the surrounding landscape. The grounds are usually sprayed with herbicides, mowed obsessively, and planted with exotic species that require extra water and fertilizer. In many places the dining halls have been given over to the same fast-food chains that blight our highways and ruin our health. Such campuses teach that the human world is an autonomous realm superimposed on nature. No matter the time of the day or the season, the typical classroom feels cut off from the planet. If there are windows at all, they usually don't open. Fans blow heated or cooled air and fluorescent lights sizzle overhead. The only sounds one hears are foot-

steps, human voices, and the grumbling of machines. The simplest way
of escaping from this envelope is to move the class outside, take walks,
sit on the grass and feel the wind, listen to the birds, and weave these
wild threads into discussions. Sometimes I take my class to the library,
sometimes to a museum, sometimes to my home, which is near campus.
Those, too, are artificial environments, but they're governed by slightly
different values than the ones governing the classroom.

Q: You write in "Landscape and Imagination" that "It is never a simple
matter actually to see what is before your eyes. You notice what memory
and knowledge and imagination have prepared you to see." This suggests
to some degree that we are *culturally* conditioned to see nature in certain
ways. In your Afterword to the second edition of *Terrarium*, you say, "No
matter how far we have retreated indoors, we are inseparably bound to
the earth through our senses, through our flesh, through the yearnings
and pleasures of sex, through the cycles of birth and death." Do you see
humans, on the whole, losing their desire to affiliate with nature? Do you
agree with Edward O. Wilson's use of the popular term *biophilia* to
describe a deep *biological* need for humans to affiliate with the natural
world? Or, must humans *learn* to love nature and care for it?

A: I agree with Wilson's claim that we carry into the world an inherent
fascination with other life forms. Anyone who has spent much time
around young children will recognize this intense curiosity, this craving
for contact. Unless they are discouraged by jittery adults, children are
drawn to other animals, they're mesmerized by the spectacle of seeds
sprouting in a pot, fish circling in a bowl, birds pecking seeds on a
windowsill, worms slithering across a sidewalk. While I believe this
impulse is inborn, I also believe it needs to be nurtured as children
grow up. If children never have a chance to see other living things—
if they pass their days in sealed-up rooms, spend every spare moment
gazing at electronic screens, ride about in air-conditioned cars—then
their craving for contact with wildness may wither away and die. The
naturalist Robert Michael Pyle warns that we are suffering from
"the extinction of experience," by which he means that we are losing
the chance for encounters with nonhuman creatures as we retreat ever
farther inside human enclosures. Certain crucial experiences are vanishing as species and open lands are vanishing. If we're going to nurture
biophilia, then we'll need to preserve wildlands, we'll need to quit
spraying poisons, we'll need to turn away from our electronic toys and
open our sealed rooms and go outside.

Q: Let's talk for a minute about exposure and vulnerability and writing. Nature writing often introduces readers to beautiful places they have never been before. Nature writing also presents a reverence for those places. It seems one of the central tenets of nature writing, or a characteristic of the genre (if we can call it so), is to encourage a respect for natural places. But, at the same time, nature writing also encourages readers to experience nature for themselves. In essence, this writing invites readers to *wild* places. And even if readers don't visit the exact places a writer describes, nature writing is often inspirational and readers may want to visit some place similar. In a lot of ways, nature writing exposes nature. Even if a writer is adamant as to why that place must be protected, does that exposure make that place and other places vulnerable?

A: Writing about wild places may certainly expose them to risks. I always bear that in mind, especially when describing my journeys in fragile and already overused habitats, such as the Boundary Waters or the Great Smoky Mountains. Edward Abbey hated the idea of crowds tramping through the wilderness, and yet his *Desert Solitaire* has attracted thousands and thousands of people to his beloved Arches and Canyonlands areas in Utah. He must have recognized the savage irony in that outcome. Unlike Abbey, I believe that humans can learn to dwell responsibly in wild places, but I know that we can also love the natural world to death by visiting in excessive numbers, as we are doing in many state and national parks. It's a quandary. If we don't inspire a love for nature in our readers, if we don't invite them outdoors, then how will they be moved to resist the human assault on the natural world? On the other hand, by inviting people outdoors, we risk smothering the last wild lands. Clearly, we need to protect more land so there are more places to visit. We need to create parks and reserves in every community, so that people can greet the earth close to home and not have to flock to distant and glamorous places. And in the long run we have to reduce the human population, to bring our numbers into balance with the carrying capacity of the planet.

Q: Similarly, although the Enclosures you describe in your novel *Terrarium* are only fiction, do you ever feel that nature might be better off if those humans who would potentially do it harm were living entirely separate from it, while those who truly care for the wild are the only ones brave enough and willing to escape into it? Or, like Teeg Passio, do you feel it is the duty of some to help cultivate others' (the Phoenix Marshalls of the world) relationships to the earth?

A: I end up siding with my character, Teeg, who tries to share her passion for the earth with those who feel only indifference or fear. It would be arrogant for anyone to claim that "I know how to behave in the natural world and, therefore, I should be able to enjoy it. And you don't know how to behave, so you should stay indoors." We're all animals, made for life outdoors. We're all capable of recovering, or of learning for the first time, a love for the earth. My central work as a writer and a teacher is to cultivate that love, in myself and in others. Of course, if it turns out that humans simply can't be restrained from damaging the web of life, if no amount of education or science or art will change our ways, then we'll vanish from the scene, and new life will take our place. The earth will pass final judgment on our behavior.

Q: In "The Writer in the University" you say that "The university has become a still more hazardous home for writers because of the Great Awakening now spreading from campus to campus under the banner of Theory." There are a few questions we'd like to ask you about this assessment. First, you continue in this essay, "Rightly or wrongly, many of us who make stories and poems feel that the net effect of recent theorizing has been to turn the writer into a puppet, one whose strings are jerked by some higher power—by ideology or the unconscious, by genetics, by ethnic allegiance, by sexual proclivities, by gender, by language itself. . . . [W]e learn that to regard ourselves as conscious, purposeful, responsible artists is a delusion." Is this criticism of theory solely a critique from the vantage point of a creative writer, someone whose main intent is to produce texts instead of interpret them? Could you speak of any other problems you see with the Theory Boom that still continues in English departments?

A: I began by speaking from my own feelings as a writer, as someone trying to carry on difficult work in an intellectual environment that is often hostile to art. Of course I'm partly defined by my gender, race, class, age, and other sociological factors. But I reject the view that my writing, or anybody's writing, can be reduced to such lumpy generalizations. I wouldn't be a writer if I felt I were a puppet, if I felt I were being manipulated by external conditions. Nor would I be a reader of books by other authors if I felt that they, too, were puppets. I may seem to be caricaturing the aims of theory, but I have heard enough trendy lectures, read enough jargon-filled papers, to see that there are certain theorists out there who make such claims. So, I raise questions about theory as a working writer, but I also voice my concerns as a teacher. If I can't assure my students that literature is a source of pleasure and wisdom and insight, then I wonder why they should bother reading it. If novels and poems and plays are only storage places for bad ideology—containers for unacceptable views that need to be unmasked and corrected by a critic—then why don't we stop reading literature? Let's just read the critics, so we can get the correct ideas from the outset. Clearly, I don't believe that literature is only a storehouse for defective ideology, or I wouldn't read it, and I wouldn't try to make it.

Q: Nature writing in the academy has become quite popular in the last decade. The number of university faculty members teaching nature writing has increased drastically in the 1990s. This has come about in relationship to a large number of university instructors who see the need for ecologically literate students, as evidenced by such textbooks as *The Norton Book of Nature Writing*, *A Forest of Voices: Reading and Writing the Environment*, Fredrick O. Waage's *Teaching Environmental Literature*, and numerous others. Could you speak for a moment about any changes, for better or worse, in nature writing since it has become a more established part of academic teaching and scholarship?

A: The rise of interest in nature writing as an academic subject partly reflects the ecological concerns of the teachers who take up these tasks, and partly reflects the ecological concerns of students. Many students bring to campus an affection for the wilds and a concern for the planet, and so colleges are responding by offering more and more courses on nature, ecology, and the environment. The current hunger for nature writing also reflects a desire for literature that is relevant to the actual world. So much contemporary fiction and poetry, like most films and television programs, pays little or no regard to nature. Much literary theory ignores the world outside the text. So, anyone who is aware that our lives are woven through and through with nature is likely to welcome honest, eloquent writing about living on a wild planet. The emergence of environmental studies programs on campus after campus seems to me a hopeful sign. Whether these academic programs have affected nature writing is harder for me to judge. In my own case, I have kept on pursuing the same few burning questions about our way of life and our place in the natural order, but I do find it encouraging that so many teachers are bringing this green literature into their classrooms and into their scholarly work.

Q: In relation to the prior question, and to touch on theory again for a second, the growing number of nature writing texts taught in the university has risen in direct relationship to the growing number of *ecocritics* and *ecocriticism*, which sees the need for examinations of the interrelatedness of a human cultural activity like literature and the natural world surrounding it. Ecocriticism, of course, cannot be limited to a single methodology. It is an umbrella term for scholars who approach literature and the environment with the same feminist, Marxist, cultural studies, and poststructuralist approaches found elsewhere. Have these theoretical approaches, in a sense, helped legitimize the teaching of nature writing in the academy? Meaning, for example, have these theories drawn attention to authors like Edward Abbey, Annie Dillard, Wendell Berry, as well as yourself, and helped give their works a place on English course syllabi?

A: Probably so. Ecological criticism has made it easier to create undergraduate- and graduate-level courses centered on nature writing. Such criticism gives teachers pathways into the works, although, as with any form of criticism, it also raises the danger of a single-minded approach. As the country saying goes, "If the only tool you have is a hammer, you treat everything like a nail." There is the same risk with a literary theory that uses one tool—interpreting everything in light of one factor, such as race or gender or class. There's also a danger that ecocriticism will simply become another academic mill for cranking out papers and books. However, because so many of the people involved in teaching and writing about nature recognize the pettiness of academic specialization, there is a good chance that ecocriticism may remain open and big-spirited.

Q: Do you see ecocriticism in any way working against the literature that it is trying to promote?

A: No. I don't see that happening yet. It could happen, though, in the same way that deconstruction sets out to dismantle everything it looks at. I haven't detected that sort of impulse in the ecocritical work that I'm aware of.

Q: In your essay "Beneath the Smooth Skin of America," you write, "We need a richer vocabulary of place. On average, according to geographers, there are fewer place names per square mile in the United States than anywhere else on earth. In long-settled countries such as Ireland, and in the few portions of our country where memory has been sustained over

centuries—as in the Hopi mesas and Mohawk Valley of the Iroquois—
every water-course, every bluff or butte, every prominent rock bears a name
and a story. In the same way, we need to be able to speak about the
particulars, the subtleties, the varieties of all our places." Could you speak
a bit more about the notion of naming? That is, why is it so crucial to
ascribe vocabulary to place? And, does naming a place construct that place?

A: By naming a place, we define it in human terms. That's inevitable. We
can't use language about the world without shaping and, therefore, de-
limiting the world. Language opens up perception, but it also closes off
certain possibilities. We don't have the option of dwelling in the world
without imposing names because we're verbal creatures. But we can certainly strive to make our names responsive to places. If we don't have
ways of carrying the land inside us—through stories, images, and names—
then we lose touch, we lose the possibility of affectionate regard for the
land. So naming means not only applying labels to places but also telling
stories about those places, saturating them with meanings and emotions,
so that we can bear the land in our hearts and minds. One of my tasks
as a writer is to provide stories for the portions of the earth that I've had
the chance to know in some depth.

Q: In "The Naming of Names" in *Wilderness Plots*, you write, "Except for
barbaric Indian words, which did not count, the map of Ohio was as
bald of names when the first white people settled there as it had been on
the day of creation. Without titles for the creeks and swamps and hills,
nobody could be sure where they were when they arrived somewhere."
You conclude this tale by writing, "But for all their struggle to imprint
their own names on the Ohio wilderness, the white settlers could not
eradicate the Indian words. Those haunting syllables crept back out of
the soil, sang in the rivers: Miami, Ottawa, Pickawillany, Chillicothe,
Cuyahoga, Tuscarawas, Shenandoah, Ohio." You express optimism here
that certain place names will continue thriving, but does naming risk
conquering, taming, and colonizing?

A: Sure it does. Even if we take over the old names—Ohio, Erie, Sen-
eca—that doesn't guarantee those words will carry the same meaning for
us as they carried for the Shawnee, the Miami, or the Iroquois. And we
shouldn't forget that long before there were Shawnee in the Ohio Valley,
say, or Iroquois in the Mohawk Valley, there were earlier cultures that had
their own languages and place names. Think of the people who fashioned
the Serpent Mound in Ohio, or those who built the amazing complex at

Chaco Canyon. Over the past ten thousand years or so, the continent has been layered with one set of names after another. There's always the danger that when you impose a new name you will colonize a place, you will assume that the mere act of naming gives you control. But naming the Mississippi River will not keep it from flooding. Even building levees and dams will not keep it from flooding. Names and concrete give us the illusion of control, but finally the river is bigger and stronger than our inventions. I'm aware of the danger that naming entails, but as I said before, I don't think we have an alternative, except to be respectful of places, to learn from our ancestors, to listen to the land. It's healthy to debate how we use names, to question the truth of stories, but we shouldn't imagine that we could live without language.

Q: Much of your writing expresses ideas that we all hold certain places "sacred," despite the fact that all creation is "holy." In the Preface to *Staying Put: Making a Home in a Restless World*, you write that "This book is my own tasting of the dirt, my effort to find out where I am. It records my attempt to fashion a life that is firmly grounded—in household and community, in knowledge of place, in awareness of nature, and in contact with that source from which all things rise." In other essays you lament the erasure of regional differences, the homogenization of America by technology, commerce, the media, and our "feverish mobility." Though it is important to note that you say regional differences must flourish without "old regional markers, such as those 'Colored' and 'White' signs over toilets, or the statues of black jockeys faithfully holding lanterns beside front doors, or cigar store Indians." You admire "wisdom worked out in relation to place." Many might say that there is too much nostalgia in your writing? How would you respond to such a criticism?

A: I've certainly heard that criticism. Sometimes the charge of nostalgia arises from the feeling that the artificial world—the enclaves that humans have constructed within nature—is the inevitable future, and thus to write about the nonhuman world seems backward. Such critics imply that I should go with the flow, move to a big city, hang out in the mall, celebrate cell phones, rhapsodize about virtual reality. Well, nothing is inevitable about the future. The future is something we collectively fashion by the way we choose to lead our lives, and I want to have my own say about how we ought to lead our lives. As for thinking in terms of regions, that is a way of respecting natural differences. No matter how homogeneous the human veneer becomes, the land itself is not homogeneous—the tropics, the deserts, the prairies, the hardwood forests, the tundra are different places, and they need to be treated differently. What makes sense in the Sierras would be nonsense in the Everglades. The culture that is appropriate to a given region is one that pays attention to the place itself and not just to the images beamed in from elsewhere. There's nothing nostalgic about respecting the natural order on which the human order ultimately depends. That strikes me as the sanest form of realism.

Q: As residents of the state of Florida, we were curious about your use of "disneys" in *Terrarium*, those artificial zoos that hold artificial animals for the inhabitants of the Enclosure. We were interested in how the word *Disney* as a proper name became the lowercase *disney*, to signify a more common type of park. Most recently, Disney opened Animal Kingdom in Orlando: not a zoo, but a natural habitat for the animals. Disney claimed Animal Kingdom would be "better than nature" because viewers would not be exposed to the hazards of the real thing and would not have to witness animals killing other animals. Could you offer any thoughts on Disney and where you see it heading in the future?

A: Well, I know that the Disney empire has made some effort to acknowledge the ecological worldview in recent displays, and I'm glad they're doing that. At the same time I'm disturbed by their habit of making the world cozy and safe—mechanical alligators, pump-driven rivers, spotless Main Streets, lions that never kill the lovely gazelles. Actual nature, outside amusement parks and video screens, is not always pretty or tidy or safe. So Disney is fostering an illusion. I understand the attraction. It's like watching nature shows on TV: you're not going to get bitten by a mosquito or snake, not going to break your leg, not going to sweat or shiver, not going to risk your neck. Such make-believe is appealing, but we shouldn't confuse it with the real thing. Above all, we shouldn't let these nature surrogates delude us into thinking we no longer need the real thing, the messy, unpredictable, wild planet beyond the walls of the amusement park. Real nature does not obey our rhythms, does not take account of our needs. It follows its own rules, and our task is to adjust our lives to those fundamental patterns. Insofar as the Disney exhibits inspire people to study and respect those natural patterns, well and good. Insofar as they are merely trading on our desire for a cute, clean, controlled fantasy land, then they are only compounding our problem by alienating us further from nature.

The Grounded Voice

A Response to Scott Russell Sanders

Lezlie Laws

April Mallory, fresh out of graduate school, sits in my tiny office, enduring yet another interview she hopes will lead to a position teaching
college English. I could add that we're both enduring the interview. She
looks so young, and to assure myself she is indeed a viable candidate for
our position, I glance again at her vita. She has a modest collection of
publications. She has presented at several NCTE conferences. She has
taught Freshman Composition for two years during her graduate studies
under the able supervision of a leading compositionist at a large, state
university. If not a star in the pantheon of new writing teachers hitting
the market this year, she is certainly a reliable supporting actor, a player
whose future in the profession looks secure.

As our interview winds down, I ask my eager candidate, "What do
you want most for your students to accomplish in your writing class?"

"Well, the main thing I want is for my students to find their own
voice." She brushes a bouncy wisp of tawny hair away from her forehead,
then nervously twists the silver hoop of her earring.

"Voice?" I ask. "Can you tell me a bit more about what that means
to you?"

"Well, you know, I want to have a student-centered classroom where
the kids feel free to express themselves honestly, where they can write
authentically, where their unique personalities can be heard in the
classroom."

I listen patiently, if not amiably, to this inexperienced and oh-so-
eager young woman. Honesty—authenticity—voice. Seems you can't
interview a prospective writing teacher without hearing something about
these ideas; and yet, even after thirty-two years of teaching, I'm still
wondering, just what does "finding your voice" or "having a voice" mean?

I've certainly tried to talk about it a lot over the years. I've been able to point to voice, but I'm not sure I've come close to teaching voice or imparting voice to my students. Still, I share April Mallory's interest in leading students to "voice," and her comments have led me to ponder yet again this elusive notion.

After April's departure, I sat in my office and stared out the window toward Lake Virginia. The sun was setting, but it was still warm and bright in Central Florida. I let myself be distracted by a water skier whose back-arching dips were sending sprays of sun-flecked glitter into the air, like a fireworks display erupting out of the depths of the lake. I wondered what I wanted to hear from April Mallory on the topic of voice. What kind of answer would have been acceptable to me, and instructive to students in our small liberal arts college?

I do not intend here to give an overview of the literature on voice. Peter Elbow and many others have done this sufficiently, and I recommend heartily Dona J. Hickey's *Developing a Written Voice* for classroom practices in the study of voice. I'd also rather not comment on the failure of our Ms. Mallory to explain in any consequential manner the value and importance of seeking voice in writing, much less what voice *is*, though I wondered whether her collection of catch phrases would equip her to do much more than beseech her students to write honestly. I'm certainly no stranger to the pedagogical technique of beseeching. Been reduced to it plenty of times. And sometimes, when I manage to display the appropriate combination of desperation and encouragement, it even works with my students. Still, it's not a technique I want to rely on. So, I was led back to my question: just what, Lezlie, would you have had her say about voice? Or maybe more truly, just what, Lezlie, would *you* like to say about the concept of voice?

Before the Mallory interview, I had been reading Sid Dobrin's and Chris Keller's interview with Scott Russell Sanders, and so the writings of this enormously talented essayist were on my mind. In a post-interview reverie, I pulled my copy of *The Force of Spirit* from my bookshelves and read Pattiann Rogers's blurb on the back cover: "Sanders' voice is honest and witty and rich with the joy of storytelling; he confronts gently, but with determination, many of the dilemmas of our time and the enigmatic nature of our worlds." Rogers is right. Sanders is a writer possessed of a wonderful voice, and "honest, witty, rich" are great words to apply to that voice. But what do I know about Sanders's style once I've labeled him in this way? Is merely describing voice the best we can do? Is there a better way to point to what voice is?

I've come at the topic of voice in a number of ways, sometimes head-on with definitions and exercises—examining tone, perspective, level of intimacy, and other elements of authorial stance—sometimes sidling up to it at an angle. Looking at it askew, the way you sometimes observe a constellation in the night sky by looking slightly away from it rather than straight at it, I've tried to look away and see, or rather, hear voice in writing. I've learned lately that all my rushing toward it has been part of the problem; my attempts to define and demarcate and fix the concept have only left me with fine adjectives like "honest" and "witty" and "rich." In reading Sanders, I've decided voice is not something you go out and get, a technique you add to your growing bag of writerly tricks. No, it's something much deeper and more subtle than that, more like something you receive. Or even better, maybe it's a quality you deeply possess and somehow, when you stop pretending to be someone else, you finally let it emerge in your writing. Could voice be something as simple (and as complex) as letting go? Is it like falling into what Sanders would call "the ground of being"?

I went back to Sanders's essays and listened again. I heard details, I heard stories, I heard laughter, I heard love, I heard his many, many keen observations about the earth and his place in it. But on this reading, provoked as I was by Ms. Mallory's proclamations, I heard something else in his essays: an unrelenting willingness to ask the big questions.

"What abides?"

"Does anything persist?"

"What are we called to do?"

"What do I fear?"

"What is my true home? Is there solid footing anywhere? If so, how can I reach it? If not, on what shall I stand?"

"Is there a pattern in our striving, a moral to be drawn from this history of breath?"

I could go on. The essays are riddled with the big questions of existence. They are the defining quality of his voice, this yearning, this seeking, this desire to understand from whence he came. You cannot talk about Sanders's voice, much less his body of work, without paying attention to the pattern of his questions, for they form the very ground of his work. In "Ground Notes" he says, "These questions are the ground notes of my life, playing beneath everything I do, like the steady bass notes in Bach's music that underlie the surface melodies. They are also questions *about* the ground, a reaching toward the outmost circumference and innermost core of things" (128).

Sanders is what I would call a lyrical essayist. Though his writing is driven in many ways—by a need to inform, by a strong sense of social responsibility, by a joy in observing the natural world, by a desire to tell a passionate story—beneath his explicit rhetorical purpose lies a tacit lyrical purpose, writing marked by melody, image, and emotion that creates a single, unified impression. That impression is almost always linked to Sanders's obsession with the big questions. In essay after essay he unabashedly probes his inner universe to seek answers about the outer universe; he sees these two universes inextricably bound to one another. In "Wayland," he describes "an unshakable hunger to know who I am, where I am, and into what sort of cosmos I have been so briefly and astonishingly sprung" (190). Again and again he ponders his own presence in the universe, a questioning that possibly began when his ninth-grade botany teacher, giving him a handful of foxtail seeds, told him: "That's the universe unfolding right there in your hands. The same as in every cell of our bodies. Now *why*? That's the question I can't ever get behind. Why should the universe be alive? Why does it obey laws? And why these particular laws? For that matter, why is there a universe at all?" (185).

Indeed, why at all? That's the question Sanders can't ever get behind either, but one he never puts down. His subjects change, his stories range widely, his intentions clarify, but he never drops those seeds from his fourteen-year-old hands, nor does he release the mind-blowing notion of a universe unfolding within his own body as well as in every kernel of nature around him. How to wrap human mind, heart, bones, skin, blood, breath around such a thought? But that's just what his essays push us to do. And his relentless attention to the big questions mark, shape, and give power to his voice. We begin to know who he is by the questions he asks. Could the nature of the writer's questions be a primary determiner of voice?

In the introduction to *The Force of Spirit*, Sanders says,

> I have reached the time in life when I can no longer put off asking the ultimate questions. Where are we, in what sort of universe? Is there a pattern in the confusion of details? How did we come to be here, and why? What is our place among the other creatures? How should we spend our modest allowance of time? The obvious risk is that my answer will be too small, too clumsy, an amateur's raid on mystery; but that is less of a risk than to leave the questions unasked. (2)

In Dobrin's and Keller's interview, Sanders explains how he brings these questions into his teaching. He lures his students toward the powerful "I" in their writing, insisting on "hearing what they themselves think about the hard questions," forcing them to "climb onto the page and risk their own necks" ("Who Speaks on the Page" 115). He is, of course, no stranger to risk. Though carefully attentive to the physicality of his world—he is, in fact, known for his beautifully descriptive and imagistic language, his keenly attentive delineations of the natural world—he simultaneously explores realms of consciousness and spirituality not easy to define or describe. Alongside his passionate environmental admonishments, he intermingles the wisdom of Christian scripture, Eastern concepts of enlightenment, New Age notions of ultimate source, and ancient mystical notions of divinity. He is not afraid to confront the mystery: "By 'mystery' I do not mean simply the blank places on our maps. I mean the divine source—not a void, not a darkness, but an uncapturable fullness. We are sustained by processes and powers that we can neither fathom nor do without" ("Telling the Holy" 162). He raises fundamental questions for his students to ponder—how we lead our lives, how we shape our communities, how we treat the planet—but he doesn't supply answers. He wants them to feel "they're being invited to undertake a genuine inquiry" (Dobrin and Keller interview). It is that spirit of inquiry that most powerfully marks Sanders's own writing, and his voice. In his questions we hear not the anguished bleatings of a lost soul, but the grounded yearnings of a man seeking the force of spirit in his own breath. Speaking of the art of memoir, in a recent article in *Poets & Writers Magazine*, Vivian Gornick says

> A memoir is a work of sustained narrative prose controlled by an idea of the self under obligation to lift from the raw material of life a tale that will shape experience, transform event, deliver wisdom. Truth in a memoir is achieved not through a recital of actual events; it is achieved when the reader comes to believe that the writer is working hard to engage with the experience at hand. . . . The question clearly being asked in an exemplary memoir is "Who am I?" Who exactly is this "I" upon whom turns the significance of this story-taken-directly-from-life? On that question the writer of a memoir must deliver. Not with an answer but with a depth of inquiry. (13)

Sanders delivers. His is the voice of a penitent, a seeker, and an apostle all at once, a body who yearns to know what he is, that his presence on the earth is evidence of a larger purpose. Why am I here, how might I lead, where do I find grace? These huge, unfathomable, insistent questions come barreling off the pages of his essays. They appear explicitly and implicitly. They rise, again and again, like a fine scent of musky soil out of the visions of his world and the yearnings of his heart. What he knows, the contours of both land and heart, mind and emotion, emerges from these primal questions. What we hear in those questions is the voice of Scott Russell Sanders.

And here's the paradox, the writer's love–hate relationship with the known and the unknown, the spoken and the silent, the doing and the being, the leaving home and the staying put, the world that's inside me and the world that's outside me. The paradox that hovers just beneath the surface of his writing is that even in the midst of these overarching wonderings, these tentative beseechings for meaning, we *can* be led to a presence, a mindfulness, a grounding in time and space. Sanders refers often to that presence as an opportunity "to slip out of my own small self and meet the great Self, the nameless mystery at the core of being" ("Silence" 159). That "presence" gives Sanders many things—a clarity of being, a connection with source, a footing on the earth. It also gives him a voice with which to speak.

WORKS CITED

Gornick, Vivian. "The Situation and the Story: The Art of Personal Narrative." *Poets & Writers Magazine* September–October 2001: 12–17.

Hickey, Dona J. *Developing a Written Voice*. Mountainview, CA: Mayfield Publishing, 1993.

Sanders, Scott Russell. Introduction. *The Force of Spirit*. Boston: Beacon Press, 2000. 1–3.

———. "Ground Notes." *Staying Put: Making a Home in a Restless World*. Boston: Beacon Press, 1993.

———. "Telling the Holy." *Staying Put: Making a Home in a Restless World*. Boston: Beacon Press, 1993.

———. "Wayland." *Staying Put: Making a Home in a Restless World*. Boston: Beacon Press, 1993.

———. "Who Speaks on the Page?" *The Force of Spirit*. Boston: Beacon Press, 2000.

One Tribe among the Host of Living Tribes

A Response to Scott Russell Sanders

Sushil K. Oswal

The Destruction of our planet is not based on some mythical law of nature but on a conflict, a very human conflict, arising from the domination of some people over other people. But what men and women have done, they can undo or do again differently.

—Thijs de la Court, 1990

Compositionists have championed various social and political causes from time to time. These range from issues of basic civil rights for select ethnic minorities to gender issues that cut across American society. They have also included topical issues, such as the Vietnam War, pornography, and freedom of the press. As time passed, many of these issues became integrated in the common curriculum of Composition Studies. A casual survey of the tables of contents of the first-year composition textbooks reveals that a majority of these issues and topics are the standard fare in our reading curriculum. Whether we are personally invested in any one or more of these causes, we develop our reading and writing assignments around these issues and topics from these textbook chapters to teach narration, argumentation, and analysis.

It is curious then that we delegate environment-related issues to an entirely separate domain—the domain of activism—and the task of teaching reading, thinking, and writing about the environment becomes the responsibility of a different class of teachers—teachers who are either interested in nature writing, or who participate in environment-related activities. At a small private university such as where I teach, such people are sometimes also associated with radical politics and are bestowed upon with additional titles, such as environmentalists, Greens, or just plain activists.

The situation outside the Rhetoric and Composition departments is not so different from what Scott Russell Sanders suggests in the preceding interview. He explains, "In most universities, the business curriculum will not foster a regard for nature, nor will economics, sociology, political science, or many other standard subjects. One can graduate from our best universities without knowing why the ozone layer matters, without understanding the greenhouse effect or the extinction crisis, without recognizing the impact of human population growth."

I will visit the Composition Studies-related points of Sanders's interview, question the limited attention nature writing and environment receive in the composition courses, and interpret our current focus on ecological issues from a postcolonial perspective. The study of, or compositioning about, nature writing may not be as isolated in all the writing departments around the country as my opening remarks may have sounded. After all, many of us foray into environmentalism from time to time and place a piece or two of nature writing on our syllabi by well-known names, such as John Muir, Aldo Leopold, Rachel Carson, Wendell Berry, or someone controversial like Edward Abbey or Dave Foreman. It's also not unusual for us to come across a student or two in our courses who elect to write research papers on topics such as recycling, fuel-cell cars, or something more philosophical such as Gaia Theory or Eco-Feminism.

Likewise, Sanders sounds an optimistic note about the rise of interest in nature writing among English faculty. In terms of composition theory, the work on ecocomposition coming out of the SUNY Press alone is sufficient to exemplify this recent growth of interest in ecological issues.

Nevertheless, the widespread use of the label *nature writing* is itself a good indicator of how we as producers and propagators of letters isolate nature writing from all other types of writing by boxing it into a separate category. In response to a question about his writing being labeled as nature writing, Sanders brings to our attention the myopic view we take of our natural surroundings when we indulge in compartmentalizing these all-embracing planetary issues. In Sanders's own words, "Sometimes the label makes me restless because it suggests that 'nature' is a specialized interest. But nature is the universe, the context within which everything occurs. Humans are entirely and inescapably embedded in nature. Therefore, the fact that my books pay a great deal of attention to our planetary home shouldn't be treated as some sort of parochial interest, as if I wrote about sports or politics or film. Besides, I write about a great many other things—family and community, science and work, travel and art—yet I always understand these smaller realities to be encompassed by the greater reality of nature."

When I was reading these words in Sanders's interview, I was reminded of a first-year-writing program administrator's comments on a tenure-track faculty member in his department dedicating both the semesters of a first year writing sequence to environment-related issues. In this WPA's view, the guilty faculty's rationale that "one semester was focused on the 'history of the American lands,' whereas the second semester dealt with the more recent effects of industrialism and consumerism on our planet during the last one hundred years" did not make sense. According to this administrator, "the earth talk" did not warrant so much attention; students could deal with environment and nature only so long. His position was that "environment" was one topic, and one could only teach so much about it. Our students, in his opinion, should not be put through it more than once, and this topic must be abandoned after one semester in favor of something more interesting, such as "Beauty and the Beast," "fashion," or "high-school experience."

Sanders speaks of a number of environmental issues in this interview. His is a poetic and sincere voice that portrays our environmental predicament through carefully selected phrases, metaphors, and images. Sanders does not invoke environmental disasters to draw on our reserves of sympathy for the downtrodden Mother Nature because he has no doubts about the blue planet's ability to survive any level of stupidity, greed, arrogance, or outright assault by its human inhabitants. Sanders wisely, and rather solemnly, declares, "Of course, if it turns out that humans simply can't be restrained from damaging the web of life, if no amount of education or science or art will change our ways, then we'll vanish from the scene, and new life will take our place. The earth will pass final judgment on our behavior." Sanders has greater faith in Nature's intelligence than that of human beings; however, he remains concerned for humans, as well as for the millions of other species that collectively formulate this Earth's ecosystem and depend on this planet's biosphere for sustenance.

Sanders perceives the classroom as valid a ground for teaching about nature as he sees nature a fit space for teaching, learning, and literacy. While tackling Sid Dobrin's and Chris Keller's question about apolitical/political classroom controversy, he points out, "Such contact [with the natural world] reminds us that language arises out of the world. We start by naming things. Children begin by learning the names of everything they can touch and taste and smell. And it's good to recall that connection between language and the world." Equally vital is Sanders's stress on firsthand contact with the "real world." "Putting students back in touch with nature is also a healthy way of turning them outward from their own emotions. Young writers can become caught up in their own psychic states, as though private feelings and notions were the only subjects worthy of art. By inviting them to pay attention to something outside themselves, you help free them from this preoccupation with the self." Any composition teacher with the experience of having read a significant number of personal narratives over the past decade would appreciate this antidote to the all-consuming megalomania that pervades most student writing in the name of self-discovery. By reminding us of this basic language acquisition skill—naming, which children seem to crave from some innate urge—Sanders underscores the inseparability of nature from the academic world for those who might view writing about the world outside as somehow undermining the goals of the writing classroom.

Sanders emphasis on the centrality of nature to our planetary existence does not arise out of sentimentalism or nostalgia for a bygone age even though a significant percent of his writings dwell upon the questions of land and nature. In *Bad Man Ballad*, a novel set in the preindustrial Midwest, Sanders's protagonist, Owen, finds it "impossible to believe that nature worked without malice." Overwhelmed by an unusually strong rainstorm, Owen begins to question the very idea of founding a European-style civilization in America. He asks rhetorically, "How could you build a civilization in the face of such elemental hostility?" (60).

Most of Sanders's historical and fictional characters are preoccupied with the acquisition or construction of material objects. It is particularly obvious in his children's stories, such as *Warm as Wool*. By concentrating on these material obsessions of his characters, Sanders highlights the struggles and suffering these earlier people had to go through to acquire even the basic amenities of life. While narrating these tales of hardship and suffering, he does not shelter his young readers from the bitter truths about the exploitation and disaster these new Americans brought to the Indians and their native lands. In an endnote to *Warm as Wool*, Sanders wrote, "Suffering is part of the truth about the frontier. The settlers suffered; the native people suffered; the woods and soils and wild beasts suffered. Children can understand this, I believe, if we are honest with them. Children enter the past, as we all do, not through names and dates but through the feelings and thoughts of those who lived in that past" (26). We can see that the characters in his historical works, who lived close to that bounty of pristine nature on this continent, are no less motivated than the inhabitants of our own times to reshape the natural world to their material ends. Sanders, however, equips these characters with a worldview in which the surrogate world of human creation is never independent of the other world—the parent from which it must draw sustenance for its existence.

I would like to go back to Sanders's remarks about coaxing our students out of their personal cocoons—the cocoons that are often enough entangled with issues of self-image and material consumption—by introducing them to the outside world of nature so that I could underline the view that ours is probably the least materialistic society. As compared with the earlier generations of Americans, we tend to value nothing because everything, in our opinion, is disposable and replaceable. Earlier generations were far more materialistic in that they were strongly attached to whatever few possessions they could attain.

This point about taking the bounty of our times for granted is just as true for us as academicians as it is for our students. We need to question the way we compositionists in particular, and university academicians in general, assume the First World lifestyle—a lifestyle structured around mindless consumption of goods and services—as a norm in a "civilized" and "democratic" society rather than an exception. Instead of taking the roles of pathfinding and trendsetting as leaders of the society, we seem to be dragging around behind the various market forces. While teaching reading, critical thinking, and writing skills, we maintain a total silence about the role of our curricula, our assignments, the physical spaces of our classrooms, and our own lifestyles in promoting consumerism. Our day-to-day acts of academic efficacy provide consumerism an easy center stage, and we yield to the administrative pressures to insert little-tested technologies between ourselves and our students. In one of my recent composition courses, one student rather cogently argued that I would not have assigned them four major papers if I were serious about solving the problem of deforestation. Another student in my Environmental Science class reflected in an appendix to his assignment on the audit of personal possessions, "I don't like video games, and I don't like the Internet. I would not even own a computer if my professors didn't require me to take electronic quizzes on the Blackboard and force me to take part in online discussions."

I can perceive some crucial connections between the technological developments in the field of reading and writing and the parallel developments in the consumption of goods and services going back to the early Indian and Chinese romance with the written word. The introduction of the printing press and the ninteenth-century developments in office systems have been systematically connected to the start of European colonialism and the beginning of automation of American industry, respectively. The more recent developments related to information systems also seem to be driven by the forces of production and geographic expansion. We need to remember, however, that no virtual technology can fuel the consumer economies of scale—economies that remain the primary danger to the health of our ecosystems. For keeping the wheels of these industrialized economies turning involves the stockpiling of a vast array of resources for production and distribution of goods and services—agricultural and forest lands, cheap labor, reserves of nonrenewable oil and other minerals, and renewable but relatively localized raw materials, such as cotton, jute, spices, or even bananas.

In his response to Dobrin's and Keller's question about taking activism to the composition classroom, Sanders resists the temptation to become an ideologue. Instead, he describes a choice-based pedagogy that informs students about the major challenges facing their generation and lets them make up their own minds about the necessary action. Sanders describes these challenges thus, "I want students to think critically about our 'consumer' culture. It's the only culture that most of them have ever known, so I want them to realize that the world doesn't have to be this way—filled with war, strife, pollution, and waste. It hasn't always been this way and doesn't have to continue this way."

What Sanders has outlined above needs some elucidation and elaboration because here lies the crux of our ecological problems. For this purpose, I turn to Ramachandra Guha's Third World perspective on the American radical environmental movement, which is also associated with the Deep Ecology movement.

Guha begins by defining the four fundamental tenets of American Deep Ecology—a shift from an *anthropocentric* to a *biocentric* perspective, an obsession with preservation of unspoiled nature and restoration of degraded areas to their original state, an attempt to locate an authentic lineage for Deep Ecology both in the early Eastern and in Western religious traditions, and an effort to represent themselves as the spiritual, philosophical, and political vanguard of American and world environmentalism. While unpacking these characteristics, Guha critiques each of these four traits and describes their effects on the Third World poor, as well as their political implications in terms of extending American hegemony around the globe.

Guha explains how the agenda of these American radical environmentalists focuses on population reduction, rain forests, and national parks while it overlooks the two biggest culprits behind the worldwide ecological degradation, which, according to him, are: (1) First World consumerism—which is also mindlessly imitated by the urban elite in the Third World, and (2) worldwide militarism in the form of global and regional arms races and ongoing territorial conflicts. Such militarism deploys both systematically organized national or regional military forces and random insurgent guerrilla groups. Most of these violent conflicts could be considered as the corollaries of the endless military interventions around the globe by the two superpowers during the second half of the twentieth century.

Guha points out that neither the biocentric perspective of these American Deep Ecologists, nor their concern for the preservation and restoration of the wilderness, deals with these two bigger menaces to the health and integrity of the natural world. Instead, the agenda of these environmentalists has made it possible to appropriate the meager natural resources of the Third World countries for the recreation of the First World rich. For example, World Wildlife Fund, World Bank, and International Monetary Fund have dictated this radical agenda in determining the terms of loans to the developing countries. Furthermore, setting these natural resources apart in the form of pristine nature reserves and national parks, such as India's Corbett Tiger Park, has uprooted the forest-dwelling natives from their homes while making room for tourists from the industrialized countries.

Coming back to my original purpose for introducing Guha's critique, I invite compositionists to link their understanding of our environmental problems to these two issues—First World consumerism and worldwide militarism. Unless we gather the courage to confront our consumeristic tendencies and these expansionist forces, we cannot expect an end to our current environmental and political predicaments.

While providing his assessment of ecocriticism, Sanders cautions us about the risk of it becoming, like other theories, a "single-minded" method for analyzing texts and churning out research papers. Sanders's concern is a real one, but a more real threat is our somnolence about our own appetites. Our well-intentioned efforts at reconnecting with nature are bound to fail if we are not honest with ourselves in assessing the threats we face. As the following example will illustrate, many of our academic attempts at grappling with today's environmental problems might ultimately be an extension of the same consumeristic urge that has alienated us from nature and wrought havoc in this world.

A recent issue of the newsletter of an environmentally inclined academic organization to which I belong published a well-written announcement of its upcoming international meeting (for 2003). The announcement begins with a comment about the choice of an urban locale for the conference and a university dormitory for accommodations. Then, it goes on to describe some nature-centered activities—a trip to Henry David Thoreau's residence, bus tours to the local urban renewal projects, and many other scenic locations. Included in the same issue of the newsletter is a note advertising a guided tour—led by Edward Abbey's own guide and thus adding some historical significance—to the Grand Canyon country for the benefit of the members of this literary organization. Guha is again pertinent here. Discussing the American radical environmentalists' fascination with pristine wilderness, Guha writes, "the function of wilderness is to provide a temporary antidote to modern civilization." As a special institution within an industrialized society, the national park "provides an opportunity for respite, contrast, contemplation, and affirmation of values for those who live most of their lives in the workaday world" (301).

The choice of a college dormitory for lodging the attendees is certainly an improvement on those overchilled, and of course overpriced, three-, four-, or five-star hotels we are regularly offered for national meetings. Simple sorties into the host city and its surroundings by the conference attendees appear innocent enough even if they have some impact on the local ecosystems. The outdoors agenda of this relatively small conference is refreshing in comparison with the litany of facilities— cocktail lounges, palatial ballrooms, Olympic-size swimming pools, temperature-controlled indoor gardens, and myriad other opportunities for social and commercial transactions—that all of us routinely come across in the brochures for the larger conferences.

If we try to understand the nature of our interest in these outdoor activities in light of Guha's critique, we might find ourselves redefining our motives for such actions and readjusting our attitudes toward the current state of the environment. Viewed in a wider context, we would notice that these simple acts of nature gazing, historical or otherwise, can slowly build to damaging trends and lead to chronic destruction of a local environment. When Edward Abbey was writing *Desert Solitaire*, I wonder if he realized that his work, with all its warnings against what he scornfully calls, "industrial tourism," would be responsible for attracting perhaps just as many ecotourists as the park roads and automobiles have done for all other categories of tourists.

We, as educators, researchers, and writers, may want to heed Guha's critique of the elite environmentalism of the First World. With all our good intentions, we might be actually causing further harm to the environment by descending down on places of historical or literary interest and by participating in such nature-related consumption from all over the country. We could, instead, establish an example for others by questioning centralized organizational structures, and strengthen local and regional organizations to achieve goals similar to what national and international meetings achieve. Such meetings, because of their smaller scale, and because of their localized venues, could also allow the development of research agenda for meaningful community action by the participants.

On a closing note, I argue that the basic issues of critical thinking, literacy, and equality are not as apolitical as they first appear. If we are talking about literacy, do we ask whose literacy are we teaching? Could oral literacy be of more value to some of our students than others? Could written literacy alienate some of them from their families, their communities, and their oral cultures? Where does ecoliteracy fit in all of this? Are we somehow assuming that our students are above or beyond ecology, free of the environment and above the matters of this earth? Do we consider ourselves belonging to some surrogate world that could truly claim itself to be independent of the earthly demands? If the answers to these rhetorical questions, at least at the moment, happen to be *nays*, then how is it that we, as the educated elite, we, as the "most" civilized society in this world, and we, the harbingers of the "most" advanced century in human history, don't feel the need for "universal" ecoliteracy in this country?

Our assessment practices also favor one kind of literacy over all other literacies. Rarely do our literacy courses reward oral skills—necessary skills for functioning effectively in small localized groups and for relating to the natural world—at the same level as we reward the written skills—particularly the analytical and organizational skills that are essential for economies of mass production. Bias for the written word is deep-seated and widespread. Even when f-yc courses are labeled as "reading and writing courses," the orality is just a by-product of reading and its sources are invariably written texts. We might encourage discussion in our classes but ultimately we want that discussion to translate into "good" papers. (The erstwhile English classroom pedagogy—lecture from the podium—was no more logocentric because the ethos of a speaker was nevertheless rooted in a professor's writing/publication record.) In the same vein, while teaching the most academic of all—the research paper or essay—we favor written evidence over oral evidence. And scholarly articles over firsthand interviews, even when we know from our experience that, irrespective of the standing of the journal, most scholarly articles, like any other body of writing, have dubious value as far as the contribution to overall human knowledge is concerned.

Anthropologists tell us that the societies with close ties to the land cherish, cultivate, and pass down the cultural tradition of oral storytelling. Albeit literate and urbanized societies view such oral cultures as backward and primitive, oddly enough those cultures often bestow the skill and authority of storytelling on all and sundry. Common people in these societies have the opportunity to share their feelings and experiences just as freely as the professional storytellers do. The societies distanced from the land, however, tend to undermine the oral storytelling by overemphasizing the significance of the written word. These societies bestow more authority and power in the hands of those who can write than those who can only tell.

Just as Sanders feels that one of his responsibilities as a writer is "to provide stories for the portions of the earth" he had the opportunity to know well, one of our tasks as compositionists ought to be to inspire our students to learn in some depth about the portions of the earth they traverse. Furthermore, it should be one of the primary goals of composition studies to cultivate in students the discursive skills, curiosity, and care for this planet so they can begin to study and see firsthand beyond the perspective of the human-made, surrogate world—the perspective of the manufactured environment—which views nature and the environment merely as a source of raw materials. Only then can we expect them to aspire to tell and retell those stories of their estrangement with the land, the corollaries of their insulated existence, their early efforts at confronting this rift with nature, the battles their psyche had to fight while negotiating between the human-made binaries of the natural and the surrogate world, and their novel discoveries about their much-neglected, immediate surroundings—stories that are crucial for forming a thinking, living, and loving community on this planet. Only then can we hope that the human inhabitants of this planet will learn their proper place among the community of species and recognize what Sanders calls "our true home."

WORKS CITED

Abbey, Edward. *Desert Solitaire: A Season in the Wilderness*. New York: Ballantine Books, 1977.

de la Court, Thijs. Quoted in *Reading Our Histories, Understanding Our Cultures*. Ed. Kathleen McCormick. New York: Allyn & Bacon, 1999. 530.

Dobrin, Sidney I. "Writing Takes Place." *Ecocomposition: Theoretical and Pedagogical Approaches*. Albany: State U of New York P, 2001. 11–26.

Guha, Ramachandra. "Radical American Environmentalism and Wilderness Preservation: A Third World Critique." *Environmental Ethics: Divergence and Convergence, 2nd Edition*. Ed. Richard G. Botzler and Susan J. Armstrong. Boston: McGraw-Hill, 1998. 296–305.

Naess, Arne. "The Shallow and the Deep, Long-Range Ecology Movement: A Summary." *Inquiry* 16 (1973): 96.

Sanders, Scott Russell. *Bad Man Ballad*. New York: Bradbury Press, 1986.

Sanders, Scott Russell. *Warm as Wool*. New York: Bradbury Press, 1992.

Weisser, Christian R., and Sidney Dobrin. "Breaking New Ground in Ecocomposition: An Introduction." *Ecocomposition: Theoretical and Pedagogical Approaches*. Albany: State U of New York P, 2001.

Ecocriticism, Writing, and Academia

An Interview with Cheryll Glotfelty

Cheryll Glotfelty is a pioneer. Though the term *ecocriticism* is most often attributed to being introduced by William Rueckert in his 1978 article "Literature and Ecology: An Experiment in Ecocriticism," Glotfelty is the person most frequently associated with the ecocritical school of thought. Her definitions of the term stand as seminal in the field. She was, by all accounts, the first individual to be hired to a faculty position devoted to the study and teaching of environment and literature—at the University of Nevada at Reno. Her work has been the cornerstone in the formation of the Association for the Study of Literature and Environment (ASLE) and the disciplinary journal linked to this organization: *Interdisciplinary Studies in Literature and Environment* (*ISLE*), which Patrick Murphy established in 1993. Along with Harold Fromm, Glotfelty edited in 1996 the first collection addressing ecocriticism, *The Ecocriticism Reader: Landmarks in Literary Ecology*, which has become the definitive text on the subject. For those unfamiliar with ecocriticism, it is best described succinctly by Glotfelty in her Introduction to *The Ecocriticism Reader* as "the study of the relationship between literature and the physical environment." Since the early 1990s, this school of literary criticism has become one of the most important in literary studies and has been at the forefront of not only the "greening of the humanities" movement but of the entire greening of the American university, primarily because of the work and initiative of Cheryll Glotfelty.

In the interview that follows, Glotfelty talks about the development of ASLE and the future of work in ecological criticism. She discusses what has happened to ecocriticism as it has become more entrenched as an academic endeavor. What readers may find most interesting about Glotfelty's words is her understanding of the way ecocritical theories and methodologies have influenced English departments—both literature and composition studies—and other academic departments as well. Glotfelty posits a number of nuanced thoughts about the teaching of environmental texts and makes an important charge that we might broaden our "understanding of nature writing, perhaps even changing it to something like environmental writing," in order to provide a more inclusive understanding of different worlds and worldviews. Glotfelty, furthermore, makes numerous insightful comments about the production of nature or environmental writing, the ways in which writers create "a story for nature rather than reading a story that's already in nature." Glotfelty, in addition, remarks about the complicated relationship between discourse and place, a relationship that has become especially relevant to compositionists and their studies of the ways that environments affect writing and the ways that writing affects environments.

Glotfelty's cogent observations about ecotheories and pedagogies remind us that we are only at the forefront of new ways of thinking about higher education in general and English departments and composition studies in particular. Her words will certainly help guide the way.

Q: In the Introduction to *The Ecocriticism Reader*, you write "the claim that literary scholarship has responded to contemporary pressures becomes difficult to defend. Until very recently there has been no sign that the institution of literary studies has even been aware of the environmental crisis." You wrote that a little over five years ago; in that time have any changes occurred for better or worse?

A: Yes, significant changes have occurred. ASLE was formed in 1992; so, it was formed before my book came out, but the book was in process before ASLE was formed. As you know ASLE stands now at about 1,000 members, and that is an institution in a sense. It is an institutional response to the environment in conjunction with literary studies, and it's a group primarily of literary scholars. It does include some authors; it does include some publishers and some general readers. But primarily, it's academics. I'm attempting to find ways to bring the study of literature to bear on environmental concerns. I would say that institutionally now there is a presence, and I could no longer write the same kind of introduction. There are also now chapters of ASLE in Japan and the UK, with others brewing in Western Europe and Australia. This is quickly becoming international. In addition, the MLA accepted ASLE as an allied organization, so ASLE now has an institutional presence there. ASLE is guaranteed two paper sessions at each MLA convention. That's another sign of the institutionalizing of literary study and environment. In addition, there is now a professional journal called *ISLE* [Interdisciplinary Studies in Literature and Environment]. In a way I now see all the institutional accoutrements or signs that this is a presence. You find words like ecocriticism, green cultural studies, much more in parlance than they were when *The Ecocriticism Reader* came out. Also, I just learned today that there is an environmental caucus that has formed with the American Studies Association. So, different kinds of disciplinary connections are pursuing environmental studies. I know CCCC has its own environmental wing now. So, I don't think I could say the same thing, although I would say that in terms of mainstream academics, environmental study still is not nearly as visible or as powerful of an approach as something like, for example, feminist studies, gay/lesbian studies, minority studies. There was a forum in a recent *PMLA* called something like "Literatures of the Environment," to which many scholars wrote, which indicates that it really has made it into the major journals. Still, I think it's regarded as kind of a fringe group; it hasn't been mainstreamed. You don't see too many environmental articles appearing in the major central literary journals. I think it has a ways to go.

Q: Has ecocriticism in any way become "neutralized" since achieving recognition in English Departments as a valid area of study? That is, ecocriticism is "the study of the relationships between literature and the physical environment"; how much, if at all, has ecocriticism become "academic"? Academic, as you note in your Introduction to *The Ecocriticism Reader*, means "scholarly to the point of being unaware of the outside world." This is to say, by becoming more and more accepted in the academy, has ecocriticism lost or gained any emphasis as an activist endeavor?

A: That's a really great question, and there are very differing answers on this. In fact, *ISLE* 2.1 (Spring 1994) ran a forum session on "Ecocriticism and Institutionalization" that Michael Branch introduced, noting all the ways in which it could in fact become neutralized by becoming institutionalized. And then a number of us were invited to write responses to that. My take on it was that institutionalization gives you a voice, and without that you have no power in the profession. But, certainly, I'm sensitive to the dangers of becoming merely academic, of becoming careerist, and in fact in my own life, sometimes I question "What is the relationship between my own scholarship in this field and the way I actually live my life?" Does the fact that I work in this area make me participate in more activist efforts, or is this some form of something I do to placate my conscience and actually excuse me from being more of an activist? I think all of us have to answer that question for ourselves. I see the benefit of institutionalization mainly in providing jobs for people. In this recent MLA Job List there are actually a couple of jobs that are

asking for people with a specialty in literature and environment. I'm
thrilled when I see those ads. Because that means someone who is concerned about these things is going to be put in a classroom, getting to
teach some books that are going to reach people, getting to work with
students. And so ultimately, I think whether it becomes neutralized or
not is up to the individual instructor and the individual practitioner. And
certainly for some it's going to become an academic endeavor, and personally, I don't even see that as a tragedy. My standard line is "there's
many voices in the choir." I think we each have a talent, and we each
have a role. Pure academic studies, in a way, can lay the groundwork for
more activist-oriented things. So, I think the answer ultimately depends
on who it is that goes into this field and what they decide to do with the
leverage that they're given.

Q: Would you consider those roles in, say, the classroom and writing
books that you've mentioned a form of activism?

A: I personally do. Absolutely. Teaching is activism. Even if you don't
come in there with an ideological line, but rather you come in there just
exposing students to arguments, which is what I do. I like to always have
every side of an issue, or as many sides as I can, presented. Students hear
them; they make up their own minds. My students have changed my
mind on a number of issues. But the fact that these issues, environmental
issues, are even being talked about at all, to me that's what needs to
happen in a classroom, and teaching is a form of activism in that it's
raising awareness and changing consciousness.

Q: When you say that about your students, you learning from your
students, it resonates that great line from Rick Bass, when he says, "I love
it when the lines between being a student and a teacher blur and you
can't tell who's teaching whom."

A: Yes, that's ideal.

Q: You've already brought up ASLE. The mission statement of ASLE is
to promote the exchange of ideas and information pertaining to literature
that considers the relationship between human beings and the natural
world and to encourage new nature writing, traditional and innovative
scholarly approaches to environmental literature and interdisciplinary
environmental research. As you mentioned, ASLE has been enormously
successful in the 1990s in promoting these agendas. And, while we want

to recognize that ASLE's organizational journal, *ISLE*, claims to be an interdisciplinary journal, we'd also like to ask, has the success of ASLE in English departments in any way isolated it as in an area of study that primarily engages literary scholars? That is, has it become specialized and in what ways do you see ASLE taking strides, if at all, to become more interdisciplinary?

A: Yes, I think in fact it has become mostly a literary organization. Scott Slovic, editor of *ISLE*, actively invites people outside of literary studies to contribute articles, but such articles don't often come floating in over the transom without some kind of recruitment. Similarly, if you go to some of the conferences you'll see almost exclusively papers by literary scholars and creative writers. So, I actually think there's more interdisciplinary work going on in an organization like the American Studies Association than in ASLE, and much more of a diversity in ethnic mix. That conference just occurred last week and Scott reported on it to me; I'm thinking about it. In fact, ASLE has become a sort of home for people who didn't have a home. But it also hasn't become an organization that, for example, a lot of scientists are attending, or that a lot of historians are attending. Historians go to the Environmental History Conference.

Q: Scientists go to SLS: the Society for Literature and Science now.

A: Yes, or they go to science conferences. I remember one geographer came to the 1999 ASLE conference in Kalamazoo, and at the end he kind of piped up and said, "You know, there's just no place for me here. You guys are pursuing a really rigidly literary line, and in fact you often end up discounting the perspective of science." I think it's hard. I think interdisciplinarity is inherently difficult because there's so much knowledge. Even mastering more than one subfield within literary studies is very challenging. I'm now thinking about some aging issues, and it's amounted to an incredible curriculum in reading for me. So, I think it's kind of built in to be difficult. Although maybe activists and activism might be a good link between many disciplines.

Q: Let's throw this into the mix of that answer: In a 1998 panel at the Conference on College Composition and Communication Convention in Chicago, Randall Roorda (now President of ASLE) called for the Association for the Study of Literature and Environment to redirect their focus from "literature" to "literacy." In this call, Roorda offered a definition of "ecological literacy" based on David W. Orr's definition of the same term. Roorda then moved to establish the ASLE-CCCC special interest group, which met for the first time the following year at CCCC in Atlanta, sparking some of the most exciting conversations of the conference. Similarly, Sid [Dobrin] has argued that the organization might consider becoming the Association for Study of Language and Environment to include a broader notion of production and interpretation. You have also noted that "ecocriticism takes as its subject the interconnections between nature and culture, specifically the cultural artifacts of language and literature." How would you respond to either Roorda's or Sid's suggestions regarding the expanded direction of ASLE?

A: I think it sounds great. I think it's a really good idea. Look, for example, at the Modern Language Association; so that group, which is the primary organization for literary scholars, does have a more broad understanding of itself. Yes, I have to agree. I think it's a great direction to move in. I don't see any reason to have one group studying literature and another group studying language when in fact they're part of the same larger project.

Q: One of the goals of this collection is to explore the relationship between discourse and the "making of nature." A majority of the work done in ecocriticism takes on a similar task of examining how nature is represented in text. As you explain it, "ecocriticism is the study of the relationship between literature and the physical environment. Just as feminist criticism examines language and literature from a gender-conscious perspective, and Marxist criticism brings an awareness of modes of production and economic class to its readings of texts, ecocriticism takes an earth-centered approach to literary studies." In his essay "Writing Takes Place," Sid argues that "if ecocriticism is a literary criticism that focuses on textual interpretation, ecocomposition is the flip side of the same coin, concentrating on textual production and the environments that affect and are affected by the production of discourse." While the relationship between ecocritics and ecocompositionists has yet to be discussed as both seek to establish identity, we are curious as to why you feel that ecological methodologies made their way into English departments through the vehicle of literary criticism as opposed to the many other avenues that lead into contemporary English departments, such as cultural studies, film studies, or composition, to name but a few.

A: That's an interesting question. I guess, I don't know; perhaps it was just coincidence really. When I think of how ASLE came into existence there were just sort of a few people who had been working independently, Scott Slovic would be one, I was another, Mike Branch was another, and we just sort of said, "it's really time to get something together." And none of the three of us had had much training in composition or in thinking about that end of things, so maybe it was just coincidence. I guess if you actually do a bibliographical search, you will find individual scholars have been working in many of these areas long before the organization is formed, long before an institutionalization, so it could very easily I would say have arisen from some of these other sister approaches. I don't know if you looked at feminist studies if it would have a similar genealogy.

Q: The parallels between the development of ecofeminism and ecocriticism make for an interesting point of departure, also.

A: Ecofeminism actually seems to have originated more from philosophy. And in fact still is dominated by philosophers and activists, I would say, even more than literary scholars.

Q: Sure, someone like Dorcetta E. Taylor, who is much more of a social scientist activist.

A: Yes. So maybe ecocriticism's origins in literary criticism just happens to be a little bit coincidental.

Q: Many have argued—Kenneth Burke, for instance—that what sets humans apart from nature is language and ultimately language's formation of culture. Of course, this position lends itself to further bifurcation of human from nature. Others, such as David Abram in *The Spell of the Sensuous*, argue that nature has its own languages, but that humans simply don't pay attention to those languages anymore. And of course, the catch phrase "who speaks for nature" also suggests that nature has been silenced. Does nature have a language?

A: (laughter) Well, certainly it does. Certainly it does. Whether it has a political language that we can understand is another question.

Q: What a great distinction—political language.

A: Yes; I think absolutely it does. I mean, bees have their dance that tells the other bees where the honey is. All kinds of vocalizations and all kinds

of body language and sense. Yes, absolutely, nature has a language. I think
the extent to which we can converse with nature is questionable. The
extent to which we can say what nature wants, in other words speak for
nature, I think that is really problematic. But I do think nature has a
language—or languages—and I think there have been certain human
beings throughout time who seem to be more tuned into nature's languages than others.

Q: You've said it would be difficult for us to understand that language,
or to communicate in that language. There have been a lot of people who
have also said that we can read nature as text. How does an ecocritic read
the text of nature?

A: In this case, I think so often reading amounts to projection onto
nature, creating a story for nature rather than reading a story that's already in nature. For me, maybe, the people who are actually reading the
text of nature would be the scientists who are figuring out how it works.
I don't know how ecocritics would read nature itself. They're really reading cultural constructions of nature. They're looking at language and
written work rather than nature itself. Nature writers, I guess you could
say, are creating a way to view nature, but I don't know if even they
would say "I'm reading nature" so much as "I'm interacting with nature.
I'm presenting one way to think about nature."

Q: Nature writing—and nature writers, such as Scott Russell Sanders,
John McPhee, Rick Bass, Terry Tempest Williams, to name but a few—
is experiencing a good deal of popularity these days. Most magazines that
publish essays now include large numbers of nature writing essays each
year. Nature writing collections and single-authored books are very popular. How do you account for the growing popularity of nature writing,
not just among readers but among writers as well?

A: Yes. Both readers and writers. Well, some of the stuff is just really
good. And so, its own merit probably sells it. I think the audience,
though, for nature writing is typically an urban audience. You really don't
find, I suspect, a lot of rural people gravitating toward this particular
genre. So, I think in some cases nature writing becomes a kind of vicari-
ous way to identify with nature. You don't have the time to go there
perhaps, you're not living a lifestyle intimately connected to nature. But
by reading nature writing, thinking about it, it gives you some kind of
a spiritual or intellectual connection. So, I think among readers, first of

all, a lot of it is just really good stuff and interesting. And furthermore, I think it helps people maintain an identification with something they don't want to lose. As for popularity among writers, I would say, probably that success breeds practitioners. I think that the really high profile success of people like Barry Lopez, Terry Tempest Williams, and Rick Bass becomes very inspiring for aspiring writers. And they think, "well, shoot, if they can do it, maybe I can, too." And also the success of the high profile writers creates a market for this material, so there's lots of publishers out there who are actually clamoring for good nature writing manuscripts. When there's a market, you are going to find writers to fill it. It's kind of a pragmatic answer, but I think we're seeing that. You know, I think once these people get in the public eye, go on the lecture circuit, there will be aspiring writers in the audience who think, "wow, you know, I could do this."

Q: Along the same lines, as you know, publishers of composition textbooks quite often put together anthologies of essays for first-year composition students. We've noticed over the years that a large number of these anthologies are filled with essayists who are considered nature writers: Scott Russell Sanders, Rick Bass, Terry Tempest Williams, John McPhee, Aldo Leopold, Annie Dillard, N. Scott Momaday, Edward Abbey, and Sue Hubbell, for instance. Can you speculate as to why essays by such authors might make good readings for first-year writers?

A: I guess it depends what purpose these essays are being taught for. I mean, there are these thematic composition courses where nature in fact will be the whole theme of the course, so naturally such a book would be suitable for those courses. In a more general course where students would be exposed to just maybe a couple of these types of essays, perhaps some of them are chosen simply for their rhetorical form, maybe it happens to be argumentative or expository or something like that. It provides a nice model. Also I think composition teachers are often trying to help students get beyond the predicted essay—you know the my-first-kiss or what-I-did-last-summer kind of thing. So, probably by exposing students to writing about nature will help them to find material beyond just themselves and start thinking about things that extend beyond their own limited experience.

Q: While we're talking about nature writing and anthologies, it seems important to note that the litany of authors just mentioned seem to be part of what is rapidly becoming a canon of nature writers. In fact, when

Sid received reviews of early drafts of his textbook anthology called *Saving Place*, one of the most common critiques was that too many of these core authors were not featured. Do you believe that nature writing is a canon forming? And if so, has ecocriticism and the formation of ASLE led to a rapid canonization of nature writing? Are there dangers is creating such a canon?

A: That's a great question. I want to have one little addendum to the last question, before I go on. I think another reason nature writing is included in composition readers is it's so often nonfiction, and a lot of the beginning composition classes are trying to teach students to write nonfiction, so it provides a nice model for that.

Back to the canonization question: yes, there's no doubt that canons are being formed. And I think each anthology, in fact, proposes its own canon. In a sense to me, an anthology is a canon, creates a canon, and so you'll find all these rival anthologies out there, and it's really interesting to compare them to see what criteria have been used. There are all kinds of forms of discrimination, I guess you could say, a lot of anthologies that will be regionally slanted in one way or another, or ethnically slanted in one way or another, or generically slanted, maybe honoring nonfiction more than some others. So, I think the canon wars are taking place virtually in every field of literary studies, and I find the canon wars quite exciting because what we're doing is trying to argue for writers we feel are important and by the argument itself bringing attention, making ourselves more conscious of why we teach what we teach. When I went to college, and I'm sure many of us were this way, you took an American Literature course and you knew beforehand exactly who was going to be in that course because these were the great American writers and everyone agreed with that. I think there are a lot of built-in assumptions that are not being recognized in that automatic canon. So, canons have always been formed. It's just that now we're being a little more self-conscious and contentious about the way we form them. So, I see this kind of debate as exciting and healthy.

Q: In their essay "Ecology, Alienation, and Literacy: Constraints and Possibilities in Ecocomposition," M. Jimmie Killingsworth and John Krajicek contend that "nature writing as it has become canonized, largely in the woodsy and wordy tradition of Thoreau" excludes people of color. Similarly, Chris has argued in his essay "The Ecology of Writerly Voice: Authorship, Ethos, and Persona," that "Cultural, social, and discursive constructions of nature tend to exclude African Americans and other peoples of color." How do you respond to the critique that nature writing and the construction of nature has been, for the most part, exclusionary?

A: I think it's a good charge. And the environmental justice movement is starting to really put some of these issues into some forceful arguments. People who write about nature, people who recreate in nature, tend to be from a certain socioeconomic class and if we understand nature writing to be that kind of writing "I go to nature and I appreciate the waterfall" kind of thing, that is going to limit it culturally to who produces this kind of stuff, and really who reads it. These things can be profoundly irrelevant to certain types of readers. I'm all in favor of broadening understanding of nature writing, perhaps even changing it to something like environmental writing, to admit that we can write about urban issues and still have it be environmental writing. So, just by using that term nature, you are automatically then kind of setting it opposed to culture or urban spaces, and it's going to exclude writers of color in many cases. Maybe we should move toward a more inclusive term for *nature*, such as *environment* perhaps, a term under which different kinds of writing could still be considered in that purview. I am trying to say that I pretty much agree with that charge that it has been exclusionary. I don't think that it's been a closed door, "no, we won't accept what you're writing"; I think it's more that people of color are not writing nature writing because it's not relevant to them. We need to actually expand what we're willing to consider as writing that grapples with the natural world and environment.

Q: Is there a difference between writing nature and nature writing?

A: (laughter) These are fun questions. Well, nature writing—I think that term now has almost become a generic term. It's being argued about: Will it include fiction? Will it include poetry? But it is now a technical term within literary studies, *nature writing*. Whereas writing nature is certainly not. Writing nature sounds like a more broad and amorphous concept. And I wouldn't think they're the same. Because of the fact that nature writing is now this generic category used by publishers and scholars and teachers. Whereas writing nature is not.

Q: In "Cultivating the American Garden," Frederick Turner writes: "Gardens, music, landscape painting, cooking: each mediates between culture and nature in a fertile and inventive way." We are interested in the ways in which you see *writing* as a mediator between culture and nature, or if you even do see writing as a mediator. However, we are also interested in the ways that writing doesn't just mediate between culture and nature but constructs those separate realms. In particular, how has the rise of ecocriticism mediated or constructed nature and culture in the academy?

A: These are hard questions; one could spend a lifetime thinking about some of these questions. I think, personally, writing can be a mediator between nature and culture. In order to write something, you have to pay attention. You have to pay attention to what you are writing about, you have to find words. There's a great essay, something called "Watching Crows" about a man who sits in a tree watching crows all day. He's studying crows, and he finds himself getting bored after about ten minutes. And then he decides, "okay, I'm going to take a little notebook up, and I'll just jot down some of my observations," and he fills up that notebook and stays attentive all day. So, I think writing is something we do that is active rather than passive, and it's participatory for us rather than merely passive. The act of writing itself can be a mediator, helping us discover things in nature that we wouldn't have discovered unless we'd been writing about them. I have some other friends who keep journals; when they see the first flower of the spring, they'll note it in their journal, when they see the first chickadees returning, they'll note it in a journal, and that act of recording actually makes them more attentive to the natural world. So, the first answer is yes, I think it clearly can be a mediator between nature and culture.

Q: And does writing not just mediate between culture and nature, but does it help construct those separate realms?

A: In fact that's what all these debates are doing right now. They're arguing over the constructions of nature and culture that people feel are most useful or enlightened. The debate is on right now, and it's taking place via writing and I doubt it will ever be settled. I think it might not only reinforce or construct certain understandings, it also causes understandings that we have taken for granted to be called into question and rethought so I think it could probably do both, it could entrench certain kinds of understandings and it could also take entrenched concepts and open them all up again for reconsideration.

Q: Do you see media constructions of nature in any way working against what ecocritics are trying to accomplish? That is, commercials and movies represent nature as idyllic as often as they either vilify nature (as news coverage of natural disasters seems to do) or as conquerable by technology.

Should ecocriticism see as one of its goals not simply to interpret texts but to combat popular images of nature that exist beyond academy walls?

A: Certainly. There really should be some ecocritical media studies, and I'm sure there are. I've seen articles on Disney films, for example, critiquing Disney films. There really should be someone devoting their attention to television as well. And newspapers, too. As you say, nature can be demonized in these natural disaster reports, but I think it could also be cast as victim. And ecocritics themselves, I think, tend to often cast nature as victim in a way that it probably really isn't. Certainly an ecocritical project should be to study the way media represent nature. I've seen so many of these public television stations featuring endangered animals trying to cause us to care and send money somewhere. Maybe this is necessary. Maybe it does raise consciousness. But at the same time, we're so saturated with these kinds of programs that it becomes rather deadening, I think.

Q: Can students learn about nature without somehow being immersed in it? And, in what ways is it, if at all, our responsibility to push students beyond texts and into the physical and material worlds of nature?

A: Well, for me there really is no substitute for personal experience. So, I do feel that field courses that take students out, not necessarily on a hike but just to a place, or a cleanup trip, trail-building trips, have a kind of an impact on a student's values and allegiances that a book can never have. I try to avoid "shoulds" a lot; I try to leave it up to the inspiration of the individual instructor. I would never tell someone they ought to do something as opposed to something else. Now, introducing them to books though could make them desire for the first time to go out and experience these things for themselves. It could change their voting patterns even if they never go out. We also have a problem in America of loving it to death. There's an article in a recent *National Geographic* talking about just the problem of huge numbers of tourists, particularly ecotourists really threatening the very thing that we're trying to save.

Q: That's a serious problem here in Florida.

A: Is that true?

Q: One of the examples we use regularly in our classes is that Crystal River in the winter is one of the most popular sites for visitors because it's a warm water river—all of our rivers are warm water rivers—and the manatees come in the winter. Viewing manatees has become such a huge industry. In fact, Sid used to guide wildlife trips but won't do it anymore because on any given day we may have 1,500 manatees in an area of the river, but we have 2,000 boats trying to deliver folks to look at them. It's just crushing the manatees out.

A: It's just heartbreaking. And I know, you know. Look at Moab, Utah, after Edward Abbey's *Desert Solitaire.*

Q: That actually brings up an interesting sideline to this. One of the things that we've always talked about with nature writing and ecocriticism is this notion that you mentioned in terms of creating an awareness so at least our students think about these things, are aware of places and nature and environment, but does that awareness make, say, a place like Moab vulnerable?

A: Yes, it does. It certainly does. This is why I think we need to start teaching wider varieties of books. Sometimes when you have a narrow canon that means you have a narrow set of places that people are going to start tromping to. My own work now has gone from ecocriticism in general to Nevada writing. I am putting together an anthology of literature of Nevada and am thinking about Nevada. So, my push now is toward the regional and the bioregional, introducing people to the literature of their own place instead of these charismatic places halfway across the country. To me, that can really inspire students to take care of where they actually live instead of wanting to journey toward the Sierras so they can be like John Muir or something like that.

Q: That's an important argument; it's one we've seen Scott Russell Sanders emphasize in some of his writing. The thing that is odd about that is that if you take a place like Moab or Florida—places that have huge amounts of literature produced about them—bioregionalism becomes not only a project of local awareness but also a larger public project of either countering or continuing work that has created these initial text images and perceptions of those places.

A: Yes, yes. In sort of a bioregional approach, you might not have these great figures, these really high-profile figures speaking for a place because really that place is made up of the responses of everyone that's there. It's sort of a whole discourse community where one voice is not necessarily privileged over another. I really like this returning to one's own place approach.

Q: How much of that kind of writing, both the kind you were talking about and, say, the kind that Aldo Leopold did or Muir did or, here locally we would think of Archie Carr, where we do have those bigger names describing a place, how much do either of those kinds of writings actually make a place?

A: Right. It comes down to what is a place? And I think that people are starting to understand that a place is a really complicated concept. A place is a relationship of land and stories about land. A place is a dynamic concept. Places are always being made. So, in that sense, I think these more classic texts certainly create place. Create an understanding of place. I know that the first time I went to Nebraska, after I had read some Willa Cather novels, I know I understood that place and responded to it entirely different than I would have had I not been exposed to her work.

Q: The University of Nevada at Reno, it seems, has been very open and sympathetic to studies of literature and the environment. However, many scholars interested in this kind of work at other institutions are still viewed as pariahs in their own departments. Can you explain in any way why UNR has been so successful in promoting ecocriticism, and do you have any advice for those of us trying to make these methodologies more influential and accepted in our own departments?

A: That's a great question. I remember when I was inclined to imagine myself as a professor of literature and environment before I was hired anywhere. I sent out a whole bunch of letters trying to articulate my dream and saying, "Do you have any suggestions?" And a couple of these letters said, "Go West." So there was some sense that the West might be more receptive to a place-based approach or an environmental approach, nature-oriented approach, than the East. Perhaps because the West was newer, and it wasn't so entrenched with the Ivy League type of scholarship, perhaps because a lot of people regard the West as still wilder, much more public land, open space. I don't know what it was. But perhaps part of UNR's receptivity to ecocriticism is just that it is in the West. I think another part of it is that when I was first hired, I was the first person hired to create the literature and environment program that we now have that includes Ann Ronald, Scott Slovic, and Michael Branch, and now Michael Cohen as well. When I was hired Ann Ronald was dean of the

College of Arts and Science at UNR. She's a longtime Sierra Club member, she wrote the first literary study of Edward Abbey. She's a longtime member of Western American Literature Association. She very strategically built environmental expertise in a variety of fields at UNR. We have several environmental historians and a really strong geography department. And so I think actually the fact that UNR became a place receptive to this approach may owe itself to Ann Ronald's effort. After we were all hired, she decided not to be dean anymore, and so she now is back in the English department and is a member of the literature and environment faculty.

Another possible reason UNR became a place where ecocriticism is an accepted and even welcomed approach is the foresight of the English department. As a Ph.D.-granting program at a relatively small state university, the UNR English department must be smart to attract good graduate students and to place them upon graduation. As a department, we decided that is would be wise to develop some particular areas of strength, building on the expertise of our faculty. In our case, two areas— Rhetoric and Composition and Literature and Environment—became magnet programs, attracting excellent students from all over the nation and even internationally. We drew upon existing faculty strengths and eventually hired new faculty to build upon these flagship programs. In the case of ecocriticism, then, UNR's decision to develop a strength in this area was due both to existing faculty interests and to its desire to stay competitive in the academic market of graduate programs.

In terms of advice to one's colleagues, I do feel sorry for people viewed as pariahs. I think sometimes people who can manage to offer courses in literature and environment or nature writing will find that these courses fill quite well. So just showing those high enrollment figures to a department can be quite persuasive. Also, you can start using the "keeping up with the Joneses" argument to your departments, because increasingly, places are hiring specialists in literature and environment, and pretty soon places that don't have programs like that are going to start to seem behind the times. Maybe it's just a matter of waiting, maybe it's just a matter of teaching some good courses that fill well, maybe giving a few public lectures so colleagues can actually see what you're doing. In my case, I tried to convince my department that they already *were* interested in this area, and I pointed to a number of people: one person who was studying eighteenth-century landscape architecture, another person who's interested in rivers, things like that. Try to show them that, actually, they're already doing this stuff if they would only realize it.

Q: We'd like to wrap up the interview by returning to discussions of ASLE for a few more questions. ASLE members, through its well-attended conferences, its journal *ISLE*, and its rather prolific Listserv have engaged a wide range of discussion topics and scholarly pursuits. What do you consider the most important conversations ASLE members have had of recent? That is, what discussions among the ASLE community excite you the most?

A: Well, I am quite interested in the diversity conversation that's been taking place in a strong way. I'm looking forward to the next conference this summer in Flagstaff to see how much that diversity mandate has actually been carried out in the creation of the program. I, too, would like to see ASLE become much more responsive to urban issues. That's another area that excites me greatly, an attention to urban issues. Michael Bennett and David Teague have that anthology out now called *The Nature of Cities*. Great anthology. Really interesting things to think about. The ways to describe nature in which a much broader population could find a toehold. I know some other people who are really starting to focus on weather a lot, people's perceptions of weather, weather in literature. This, too, would seem quite promising to me to attract a larger audience. So, I guess urban studies to me holds so much potential that is untapped. Diversity studies, quite exciting. I like this media idea, and film studies. Looking at some of popular media. Really thinking about them in a critical way. I'm also very excited, incidentally, with the composition wing of ASLE, and I really look forward to seeing more panels at ASLE devoted to writing. I think you reach such a larger constituency with ecocomp than you do with ecolit because every single student has to have a composition class. You're going to reach everybody with an ecocomposition approach. Ecolit tends to be maybe English majors or upper-division students. So, it's a really exciting movement. I also am interested in any kind of international discussion. Or, comparative literature approaches. I think we have a lot to learn from people around the world and many more problems and issues to consider than those that are in the United States. Anything that has any kind of a Marxist slant or socioeconomic concern is very interesting to me, too. I think there's so much still to be done.

Q: As a final question, what do you see as the future of ASLE as an organization?

A: Hard to say; hard to say. It seems quite stable now, so I do see that it will probably continue to exist, which in the early days was always a question. We're getting people to run for the different offices, so it seems like a viable organization. I think really that the active membership will determine the future. It's not up to some graybeard to say where it should be going. I guess if I predict where it will go, I do predict greater internationalization. There's a lot of energy in these other countries wanting to get together groups, and it's really interesting how different the different international groups become. Very different slants, very different sort of patron saint type of figures. Kind of fascinating there. I don't know that I would necessarily predict greater interdisciplinarity. I don't know that that's going to happen even though it would be desirable for it to happen. ASLE has been viewed as kind of a Western American phenomenon, and most of the early conferences were in the West. I think that's going to change; I think it's going to be much more of a national kind of an organization probably. Hard to say. I would hope that it would move in the direction of ecocomposition. Because there's a lot of interest in ecocomp and I hope these people are not going to get frustrated. I hope there will always be a way for ASLE to respond to the interests of its members and never get too narrow of an understanding of itself. Otherwise what we're going to see is a bunch of separate groups forming because their interests are simply not served by ASLE. So, I guess I hope it stays inclusive and stays welcoming of new energies and new ideas.

Writing, Nature, and Composing Bridges

A Response to Cheryll Glotfelty

Kaye Adkins

As I read the conversation with Cheryll Glotfelty, I am struck by how often old fissures—composition/literature, science/humanities, academia/ the "real" world, and nature/human culture—still appear in the conversation. In some ways this is not surprising, because these fissures divide us, although the distances between them are becoming less chasmic. Glotfelty recognizes the ways in which ecocriticism has helped close these gaps, but I believe that understanding the ecology of writing may bridge them more completely, and I welcome her enthusiasm for ecocomposition.

Glotfelty explains that the Association for the Study of Literature and Environment (ASLE) began as a group of literary scholars, and has thus been primarily concerned with literary questions. She suggests that it may be "coincidental" that environmental concerns entered English departments through literary studies because of who was doing the first work and how the group first met. While that is one possibility, this history is natural in an atmosphere that has traditionally privileged literary studies, especially in large, theory-building universities. Instead, many of those who are actively practicing ecocomposition, who are presenting papers about it, and who are regular participants in conversations about it teach in two- and four-year colleges, or are members of composition staffs of larger colleges and universities, often as part-time or nontenure track faculty. There is nothing particularly sinister about this, no particular oppression on the part of our ecocritic colleagues. Instead, this is a reflection of the environment in which many compositionists work.

If we recognize rhetorical studies as part of composition studies, ecocomposition has also had a presence since the early years of ASLE. The first ASLE conference in Fort Collins included sessions of rhetorical analyses of environmental texts, and from the earliest years of the ASLE discussion list, rhetorical issues have been part of the conversation. Killingsworth's and Palmer's *Ecospeak*, published in 1992 (the same year ASLE was formed), showed those of us with interests in composition and environmental concerns one way of combining these interests.

Green rhetorical studies illustrates how rhetorical studies in general have helped blur the line between literary studies and composition studies. As we apply rhetorical analyses to literary texts, and include literary nonfiction in freshman composition readers, the barrier between the two fields becomes more and more permeable. As Glotfelty observes, more discussions of nature writing are appearing in composition journals. Nature writing is also appearing more regularly on composition syllabi, whether from collections dedicated to environmental writing, or as entries in other freshman readers. While this serves as one of the ways to link literary concerns and composition interests, compositionists must also ask what value nature writing has as a pedagogical tool in composition classes. Certainly, as Glotfelty points out, we admire the style of nature writers, and wish that our students would write as well, but what would happen if our students wrote in essays that followed the model of Dillard, Abbey, or Thoreau for a biology professor? Or even as a humanities seminar project? Why include environmental writings in composition classes, and why teach an ecology of writing? Not because of their value as models for argument or expository forms, but because they help bridge the gaps that I referred to in the opening of this response.

The science/humanities gap remains a gulf, at least for ASLE, as Glotfelty readily admits. And she clearly identifies the ways in which ASLE has failed to make scientists feel welcome. Scientists, indeed, are among those who are "reading the text of nature," and organizations like the American Studies Association are making those connections more successfully. She reports that scientists have been disappointed by ASLE conferences, and they have not contributed to the journal of *Interdisciplinary Studies in Literature and Environment (ISLE)*. Perhaps the problem springs from how ecocritics present our work to those outside our field. We have been so concerned with convincing our literature colleagues that environmental approaches to literature are as valuable as other critical approaches that we have focused narrowly on "literary" texts and concerns. The great irony here is that many ecocritics enjoy reading scientific writing. We want to know how the world works. Consider the authors whose work we admire. Writers like Rachel Carson, Aldo Leopold, and Lewis Thomas are scientists, writing about scientific subjects, yet ecocritics spend much of our time convincing our colleagues (and ourselves) that this writing is humanistic, even literary.

Thus, ASLE's lack of appeal to scientists may be a problem of persona building more than anything else, and this is a problem that composition theorists address regularly. Ecocompositionists could examine our own texts, our journal, our conference programs, and our Web site to evaluate how others see us and to think about how we can appeal to this other audience. The scientific audience is ready to listen. At the last ASLE conference there were a few presentations from teaching teams that paired ecocritics and scientists. I've had conversations with biology teachers about how we approach "The Land Ethic" in my composition classes, and this semester, a student told me that her father, a wildlife sanctuary manager, can't wait for her to read *Silent Spring* because it's one of his favorite books. One of the contributions ecocompositionists can make to ecocriticism is to define the field in ways that invite broader interdisciplinary participation.

Another way of broadening the appeal of ASLE and ecocriticism would be to look beyond our traditional texts, beyond nature writing and the occasional philosophical treatise, to scientific writing. Tools for this kind of work can be found in studies of scientific and technical communication, studies that have their roots in composition studies, and that share many of the same concerns and practices. In technical writing, we talk about content providers or subject matter experts, the people who provide the information that technical writers turn into documentation, reports, and Web sites. Perhaps ecocritics can learn from this kind of relationship with scientists, to see them as partners, with valuable information to contribute to environmental approaches to literature. Already a few rhetorical studies of environmental impact statements have been published by specialists in technical communication, and ecocritics should welcome discussions of the science in our favorite natural history texts. This combination can make it easier for us to connect ecocriticism to the world beyond academia.

Ecocomposition asks us to look at the real world environments in which writing takes place—how those environments affect texts and how the texts affect environments. This may be the most important divide between ecocriticism and ecocomposition, and the biggest contribution of an ecological approach to composition—bringing together academic and "real world" concerns. This is not a new concern for composition studies. Studies of discourse communities are similar in many ways to studies of biological communities. The researcher observes, records, analyzes, and theorizes about the interrelationships, about actions and reactions, about context and behavior. In this way, ecocomposition carries on the work of theorists like James Kinneavy, Patricia Bizzell, and Linda

Flower by considering the impact of environment on writing and by studying communities of writers.

This is an important way to address the questions that Glotfelty raises about the relationship between activism and academics. This is a difficult problem, and Glotfelty's approach—allowing students to see all sides of an issue before making up their minds—is one that most composition teachers are comfortable with. For ecocritics who want to make more direct connections with the real world, who seek activist connections between the literature they are studying and environmental problems, there are composition teachers who model radically activist pedagogies. These may be carried out through service learning, a growing area of interest in composition studies, through the cleanup or trail-building trips that Glotfelty mentions. Activities like these can indeed have an impact "on a student's values and allegiances."

But ecocomposition also offers ways to ease students into environmental awareness and activism. Glotfelty rightly suggests that "pure academic studies, in a way, can lay the groundwork for more activist-oriented things." Ecocomposition also asks students to pay close attention to the world around them. This is one of the values of asking students to read nature writing, and to use nature writing as a kind of model in place-based writing of the kind that Randall Roorda has described. This writing has pedagogical value because it asks students to observe and include concrete details, addressing a common weakness in freshman writing. As students begin to approach academic subjects, their writing becomes more abstract. Composition teachers often find themselves urging their students to use concrete examples and descriptions to support their "glittering generalities," and asking students to write descriptions of physical places is a good way of countering this tendency.

Place-based writing has another value, one that brings us back to the issue of activism. If students write about places they care about, they begin to see that these places have value—they are worth preserving and nurturing. And ecocomposition asks students to look at all kinds of environments—where they write, where they learn, where they work, and what the impact of those environments is on their inhabitants. Students can then be asked to apply these habits of mind to a variety of texts, and begin to consider the value of both familiar and exotic places.

Finally, the examination of the ways texts are influenced by, and influence, their environments leads us to an examination of cultures, and the rift between nature and culture. Perhaps most important to composition specialists is the way socioeconomic class seems to affect the way students respond to nature writing and the natural world. It does often seem that the audience for nature writing is an urban audience, as Glotfelty observes. The classic assumption is that urban audiences (and urban students) are cushioned from the harshness of nature, see it only as an escape from the city, and thus respond more romantically to nature writing. But if we look at the kinds of writings that all students respond to, we begin to see the value of *environmental* writing over *nature* writing. Some of our students do, indeed, come from urban environments that make any other environment seem an improvement. They may hope to live in the suburbs some day, or rural life may seem idyllic to them. Our rural students, however, often question writers like Wendell Berry who idealize the farmer and land connection. Some of these students' fiercest criticism is not of the cities, but of the suburbs, whose malls and cul de sacs are driving their families out of farming. Bringing all of these students together, the composition classroom gives critics and students alike an opportunity to look closely at how cultural backgrounds affect responses to nature.

One of the things that many composition teachers find when they bring environmental issues into the classroom is that the divide between human culture and nature is not as great as we often imagine it, at least not for our students. Pedagogies of place give students a stake in what they are writing about. As they try to understand why particular places are important to them, and why those places should matter to others, they begin to see how the presence or absence of natural elements affects the quality of the environment. They find that, as Glotfelty suggests, this importance can best be communicated in stories about these places. They can begin to consider how complicated and dynamic the relationship of culture and nature is.

It may be this potential that has made Glotfelty so enthusiastic about ecocomposition. By examining the connections between writing and its environments, by encouraging environmental literacy, ecocomposition bridges these traditional gulfs, prepares students to observe and respond to the world around them. Literate in the language of environmental influence, students can carry these tools with them to their other courses, to their workplaces, to their recreation, and even to their political lives.

Where the Fusang Grows

A Response to Cheryll Glotfelty

Dean Swinford

In *The Following Story*, a recent novel by the Dutch author Cees Nooteboom, Herman Mussert, a teacher of Latin and Greek, finds himself sailing on a boat to a faraway land. The late-night water crossing, for Mussert, is a constitutive component of an infernal, and recognizably Greco-Roman, geography. The destination is the land of the dead. He is, of course, crossing the Styx.

Or so it seems. One night, Mussert and another traveler, Professor Deng, watch the stars as their ship passes over the phosphorescent-tinged ocean. For Mussert, "the blackboard of the sky was inscribed in Latin" (Nooteboom 79), but Professor Deng recognizes a different series of stories moving through the skies. The charioteer that Mussert calls "Perseus" is, to Deng, something else altogether. The constellation is not a figure, but the pool of the gods. The Chinese scholar recites lines from Qu Yuan's epic poem, which situates the pool of the gods near the "Fusang tree, an enormous tree at the westernmost tip of the earth" (Nooteboom 81). Deng remarks that, at the end of Qu Yuan's epic, "he announces his intention to quit this corrupt world to seek the company of the holy dead" (Nooteboom 83). Each character recognizes the trajectory of the water journey within a specific cultural context. But Mussert and Deng resign themselves to the same fate through different stories and different geographies.

After the two compare perspectives, Mussert comments that "we had all wanted something from those cooly sparkling points of light—something they would never give us" (Nooteboom 83). This tale of competing stories and frustrated desires speaks of people seeking stories and placing themselves within these stories in order to understand disconcerting experiences.

I bring up Nooteboom's *The Following Story* to discuss the possibilities available to ecocriticism as a form of inquiry that reflects the needs of various disciplinary, cultural, and international communities. For ecocritics to achieve the goals Cheryll Glotfelty recommends in "Ecocriticism, Writing, and Academia: An Interview With Cheryll Glotfelty," these communities must converge. More important, they must compare stories and share methodologies.

Glotfelty's "Literary Studies in an Age of Environmental Crisis" is such a significant essay because of her identification of an area of analysis missing (at the time of its publication) from literary discussion. The essay is also crucial because of her identification of the global environmental crisis as "the most pressing contemporary issue of all" (Glotfelty xv). This generalization cannot hold true for any other issue. Indeed, various world leaders, from Mikhail Gorbachev to Ernst Ulrich von Weizsäcker, have declared the environment the most important priority of the twenty-first century. The significance of ecocriticism, then, is strangely at odds with its current status as a marginalized field of interest within the academy. The sheer urgency and volume of environmental problems currently besetting human culture renders the environment a key issue for humanists. Indeed, as Glotfelty points out in this essay, "current environmental problems are largely of our own making, are, in other words, a by-product of culture" (Glotfelty xxi). Because the environmental crisis is a human crisis, it is a legitimate area of concern for humanists. Furthermore, unlike many of the areas of concern currently problematized by the academy, the environmental crisis is an earth crisis: environmental degradation knows no national or cultural boundaries.

In this interview, Glotfelty grounds the principles of ecocriticism that she first outlined in *The Ecocriticism Reader* with strategies for the composition classroom. While her discussion in "Literary Studies in an Age of Environmental Crisis" focuses on the urgent state of global environmental problems and critiques the academy for its denial of life beyond culture, in this interview, Glotfelty is much more invested in the pragmatic issues affecting ecocritics. She discusses the professional viability of the Association for the Study of Literature and Environment (ASLE); the institutional significance of the journal *Interdisciplinary Studies in Literature and Environment (ISLE)*; the burgeoning market for both nature writing and environmentally oriented composition anthologies. While Glotfelty acknowledges the success of this institutionalization, commenting that "I could no longer write the same kind of introduction," she also states that "I still think it has a ways to go. . . . I think it's regarded as a kind of a fringe group; it hasn't been mainstreamed." Her apparent dismissal of her own academic success seems linked to her desire "to find ways to bring the study of literature to bear on environmental concerns."

While ASLE has had very real professional successes, Glotfelty's primary purpose involves practical success. Institutional acceptance is only the first stage in a much larger project. Glotfelty's concern with pragmatic issues relates to her desire to merge intellectual inquiry and activism. The realization of such a synthesis, however, is problematic. The activist must take direct action; the humanist is often viewed as someone who takes no direct action. Glotfelty points out her own sensitivity to this disjunction: "Does the fact that I work in this area make me participate in more activist efforts, or is this some form of something I do to placate my conscience and actually excuse me from being more of an activist?" The motive behind the action is not secondary to the action itself.

But Glotfelty is not preoccupied with identifying her role on the academic–activist continuum. Instead, she is quite emphatic that "teaching is activism." The professional success of studies of literature and environment is significant because "that means someone who is concerned about these things is going to be put in a classroom." Her discussion of the variety of classes taught by the credentialed professor of literature and environment indicates ways to directly influence environmental concerns through the study of literature. For example, Glotfelty suggests that the composition classroom provides the professor with an advantage unavailable in higher-level literature classes.

Her point here is of particular interest to compositionists. The composition classroom is an advantageous site for activism: "you reach such a larger constituency with ecocomp than you do with ecolit because every single student has to have a composition class." The extraliterary aspects of ecocriticism—engaging with the community, analyzing public discourse, understanding how cultures compose nature—lend themselves to the tasks of college-level composition. While the content of introductory college composition classes is subject to endless debate, the tasks of these classes lend themselves to the concern with contemporary issues and with the synthesis of cultural and natural underlying studies of the environment.

Ecocriticism, then, becomes a tool useful for mapping geographies of place. It operates as a tool for understanding "how nature is represented in literature" (Glotfelty xxiii). To some extent, a purely academic examination of environment might situate a specific writer in relation to place. Consider, for example, Henry Thoreau's development of the contrast between city and country in "Walking":

> Eastward I go only by force; but westward I go free. . . . Let me live where I will, on this side is the city, on that the wilderness, and I am ever leaving the city more and more, and withdrawing into the wilderness. I should not lay so much stress on this fact, if I did not believe that something like this is the prevailing tendency of my countrymen. I must walk toward Oregon, and not toward Europe. (Thoreau 668)

For Thoreau, this movement is linked to his conception of the relationship between America and the Old World. Thoreau links American culture to the westward journey, embodied here through the motif of the wilderness hike. For Thoreau, America is a particular kind of wilderness: it is wilderness that deliberately contrasts the urban, manicured European landscape.

An examination of Thoreau's work, then, must also consider his relation to other writers helping to construct a cultural view toward nature. Thoreau's central position within the developing canon of American nature writing relies on his attitude toward place. This canonization process reflects, quite literally, the westward walk that Thoreau praises in "Walking": Edward Abbey, Rick Bass, and Terry Tempest Williams are, among others, writers whose writing also walks west, and walks, very deliberately, away from Europe.

As James C. McKusick points out in *Green Writing: Romanticism and Ecology*, however, Thoreau declares the independence of American writers from the European literary tradition while, at the same time, relying extensively on quotations from an English tradition ranging from Chaucer to Wordsworth (McKusick 4). Indeed, Thoreau's rejection of a European literary tradition that is explicitly textual relies on Wordsworth's own emphatic rejection of book learning in favor of direct contact with nature: "When a traveler asked Wordsworth's servant to show him her master's study, she answered, 'Here is his library, but his study is out of doors' " (Thoreau 663). McKusick connects his discussion of Thoreau's geographic and literary positioning to D. H. Lawrence's argument in *Studies in Classic American Literature* (1923) that "the essential symbolic act of the American is the murder of Father Europe, and another is re-baptism in the Wilderness. Wilderness is thus mentally constituted by an act of forgetting" (McKusick 3). These two symbolic acts, taken from the Bible and Freud, signify two poles of a cultural trajectory arcing from Jerusalem to Vienna by way of Greece and Italy. Lawrence's analysis attempts to establish a paradigm that will govern the mythological quest of the American seeking identity through an exploration of the natural.

This paradigm, however, is still constituted through a linear conception of cultural influence. As Thoreau remarks in "Walking":

> We go eastward to realize history and study the works of art and literature, retracing the steps of the race; we go westward as into the future, with a spirit of enterprise and adventure. The Atlantic is a Lethean stream, in our passage over which we have had an opportunity to forget the Old World and its institutions. (Thoreau 668)

An actual forgetting would involve forgetting the Lethe itself. In this instance, for Thoreau, the Atlantic operates as a component of a Western European typology. The cultural components of this mythopoeic landscape situate America, itself a process created as Thoreau and others "walk toward Oregon," as a series of points on a specific cultural itinerary. Thoreau, like Mussert in *The Following Story*, imagines his quest with geographic markers taken from a specifically Western tradition. But, as we all know from our experiences in the classroom, this is not the only tradition shaping contemporary American experience.

Indeed, this example hints at the complexity facing those of us interested in ecocriticism. The classes we teach, and the America they represent, are increasingly stratified in ways that diverge explosively from the single arc of Western influence guiding even Thoreau's rejection of Western influence. As Joel L. Swerdlow remarks in "Changing America," a recent article on immigration and education, "since [1965] more than 60 percent of immigrants [to the United States] have come from Asia, Africa, the Caribbean, the Middle East, and Latin America" (Swerdlow 46). Contemporary America is constructed from a vast panoply of cultural traditions and expectations. Glotfelty's discussion of the canon of nature writing reflects her awareness of this diversity. Nature writing is not the only type of writing that helps to construct place. For her, "people who write about nature, people who recreate in nature, tend to be from a certain socioeconomic class and if we understand nature writing to be that kind of writing . . . that is going to limit it culturally to who produces this kind of stuff, and really who reads it." The conception of place is linked, with writing about the environment, to different cultural perceptions of that environment: these perceptions are reflected not only in the selection of a subject (what part of the environment is written about) but also in the selection of a mode (how does the writer respond to that environment). Glotfelty notes that certain kinds of nature writing, however, "can be profoundly irrelevant to certain types of readers." For her, the consideration of mode and subject affects the usefulness of writing about the environment.

Glotfelty's charge to broaden our understanding of nature writing, perhaps "even changing it to something like environmental writing" to provide a more inclusive understanding of different worlds and worldviews, indicates that our discussion of the boundaries of the field allow it a cultural and political relevance lacking from more parochial studies of nature writing. This reconceptualization of generic boundaries applies to the methodologies used to create environmental writing as well. The interdisciplinary approach is key to the success of true analysis of the ecosystem. Indeed, as Neil Evernden points out in "Beyond Ecology: Self, Place, and the Pathetic Fallacy," the concept of ecology itself implies this "genuine intermingling of parts of the ecosystem" (Glotfelty 93).

However, Glotfelty's comment regarding the geographer at the 1999 ASLE conference in Kalamazoo suggests a problem that could hinder the transdisciplinary success of the ecocriticism movement. The geographer's complaint that the literary critics discounted the purely scientific perspective plagues interdisciplinarity, particularly when that interdisciplinarity is given professional credence through journals and organizations. C. P. Snow's "The Two Cultures" most famously probes the wide gap separating the arts and the sciences. But Glotfelty suggests a solution that seems likely to diminish the antagonism that tends to characterize alliances of the humanities and the sciences. Activism, or the pursuit of common, tangible goals, necessitates the synthesis of disciplinary approaches. Many roles are necessary in order to solve regional environmental issues. The writer, the soil scientist, the urban planner, and the systems ecologist are enmeshed in their own stories. But, like the characters of *The Following Story*, they are united by the same journey.

WORKS CITED

Evernden, Neil. "Beyond Ecology: Self, Place, and the Pathetic Fallacy." *The Ecocriticism Reader: Landmarks in Literary Ecology*. Ed. Cheryll Glotfelty and Harold Fromm. Athens: U of Georgia P, 1995. 92–104.

Glotfelty, Cheryll. "Literary Studies in an Age of Environmental Crisis." *The Ecocriticism Reader: Landmarks in Literary Ecology*. Ed. Cheryll Glotfelty and Harold Fromm. Athens: U of Georgia P, 1995. xv–xxxvii.

McKusick, James C. *Green Writing: Romanticism and Ecology*. New York: St. Martin's P, 2000.

Nooteboom, Cees. *The Following Story*. Trans. Ina Rilke. New York: Harvest, 1996.

Snow, C. P. "The Two Cultures: And the Scientific Revolution." London: Cambridge UP, 1993.

Swerdlow, Joel L. "Changing America." *National Geographic* Sept. 2001: 42–61.

Thoreau, Henry David. *The Works of Thoreau*. Ed. Henry S. Canby. Boston: Houghton Mifflin, 1937.

Response to Adkins and Swinford

Cheryll Glotfelty

As I reread my interview and consider the responses by Kaye Adkins and Dean Swinford, I am struck by our mutual desire to bridge gaps, heal rifts, and join perspectives in the larger purpose of caring for our world. Adkins perceptively identifies fissures that still crop up in our conversation—composition/literature, science/humanities, academia/ the "real" world, and nature/human culture—and she points out that ecocomposition is ideally positioned to bridge these gaps. Swinford acknowledges the differences in perspective that often separate diverse disciplinary, cultural, and international communities, and he looks to activism to encourage people to exchange stories and share methodologies in our common journey. And my original motive in promoting ecocriticism in the mid-1990s was to bridge the gap between literary studies and environmental issues. It appears, then, that not only do we share a desire to address environmental problems—which, as Swinford points out, are both regional and global—but also we are all concerned with the fragmentation of knowledge and seek ways to heal rifts in communication itself. E. M. Forster's injunction in *Howards End* to "Only connect!" seems to animate us all.

A further traditional gulf that I think we all try to bridge is the one between the theoretical and the practical. It seems to me that we all seek solid theoretical ground, but that, once found, rather than just standing there, we want to run. Thus, Adkins thoughtfully articulates a theory of how nature writing bridges the traditional gaps identified above and how ecocomposition helps to connect ecocriticism to the world beyond. Once this theoretical groundwork is in place, however, Adkins goes on to discuss activist pedagogies, such as service learning, and to propose the project of persona building for ASLE to help the organization invite broader interdisciplinary participation. Swinford, too, unites theory with practice as he first explores the conceptual metaphor of different story-tellers on the same ship and then suggests that activism—solving regional environmental issues, pursuing tangible goals—not only stimulates but necessitates a synthesis of disciplinary approaches. I, too, like to think of ecocriticism as both a promising theoretical construct and a useful political tool, and I am as interested in getting ecocritics *hired* as I am in pushing ecocriticism to *higher* levels of analysis.

I have learned from this exchange that my own conception of ecocriticism has inadvertently privileged literary studies over composition studies. When we used to say *mankind* to refer to *humankind* or *mail man* instead of *letter carrier,* we effectively rendered women invisible. So, too, to speak of ecocriticism as the study of "literature and environment" rather than, say, "language and environment" does tend to efface many kinds of writing and composition. So, I have been educated by this forum into the methodologies, sophistication, and promise of ecocomposition, and I hope that, whether we come to regard ecocomposition as a subset of ecocriticism or as a parallel movement, ASLE and *ISLE* will continue to welcome studies of both interpretation *and production* of writing and environment.

Writing Natural History

An Interview with Ann Zwinger

For the past thirty years, Ann Zwinger has been recognized as one of the most important natural history writers writing in America. Her writing is often exciting, though marked primarily by its quiet, contemplative moments. Much of Zwinger's writing is accompanied by her drawings, giving her texts a visual facet that enhances her writing. Her drawing can be characterized as sketches of objects she observes: plants, rocks, insects, and animals. Zwinger wrote her award-winning *Beyond the Aspen Grove*, which focuses on the natural history and ecology of her family property in the mountains outside of Colorado Springs, a place she calls "Constant Friendship," named after an ancestor's farm in West Virginia. Marie Rodell, a literary agent specializing in natural history (who was Rachel Carson's agent), visited Constant Friendship and was taken by Zwinger's drawings, which decorated the walls of the cabin. She asked Zwinger if she had considered writing about Constant Friendship, and later admitted that it was Zwinger's artwork that had sparked the query. Rodell saw *Beyond the Aspen Grove* published in 1970 and handled Zwinger's books until Rodell's death in 1975.

This interview was recorded at Constant Friendship, and we are grateful to Zwinger for inviting us to see the setting that inspired her first book. After *Beyond the Aspen Grove*, Zwinger's writing earned a good number of awards, including a National Book Award nomination in 1972 for her book coauthored with Dr. Beatrice Willard, an alpine ecologist, *Land above the Trees: A Guide to American Alpine Tundra*. She was awarded the John Burroughs Memorial Association award—the most prestigious award given for nature writing—in 1976 for *Run, River, Run: A Naturalist's Journey Down One of the Great Rivers of the West*. She received a WESTAF (Western Arts Federation) for *Downcanyon,* and the John Hay award (for writing, teaching, and conservation) from the Orion Society. Without question, Zwinger is one of the foremost writers of natural history.

In the interview that follows, Zwinger discusses not only her thoughts on writing, on the production of writing, and the role of the writer, but also on how writers should engage in the production of natural history. Her remarks about the ways in which culture and nature are both enmeshed in written discourse will raise interest among theorists and practitioners whose work centers on discourse, science, and cultural studies. Zwinger, who characterizes herself as "a *very* adjunct professor" at Colorado College in Colorado Springs and whose writing is often described as didactic, here, too, turns to teaching and pedagogy as a subject for conversation. Zwinger articulates directly her thoughts and concerns about environmental education—in English departments and elsewhere—which are now some of the primary conversations in the modern university and secondary schools.

One could not summarize Zwinger and her writing better than she does below when she comments, "I think there are saltwater people and freshwater people, plant people and animal people. I'm a plant people."

Q: You have been a very prolific writer over the last three decades, beginning with *Beyond the Aspen Grove* (1970). You have, in a sense, dedicated much of your life to understanding nature, but you have also dedicated much to the written word. Let us ask you first why you have chosen writing as the medium in which you work.

A: I don't think I had any choice—it just worked out that way. I'm not sure that I chose it. The way I wrote *Beyond the Aspen Grove* has been characteristic of my career. I keep falling into a mud puddle and coming out smelling like a rose. Have you seen the edition of *Beyond the Aspen Grove* with the aphid-green cover from the University of Arizona Press?

Q: Yes.

A: The introduction to that edition explains how it all started with a chance meeting with Marie Rodell. I think from that it's apparent that I didn't start out to be a writer; I started out to be an artist. But, once I began writing, I found it the ideal medium for what I wanted to do. And writing one book is like eating one potato chip—you just can't stop at one.

Q: In the Preface to *A Nearsighted Naturalist* you write, "Compiling these essays reinforced my sense of the rich cross-disciplinary quality of writing natural history. It is a healthy and appealing discipline that continues to lead those of us who practice it to tromp through streams, chase dragonflies, count snowflakes, row rivers in windstorms, travel to faraway places with strange sounding names, host spiders in our boots, cherish the pure sweet descant of a canyon wren, and acknowledge the healing power of a lapping tide and a sea-smoothed pebble." We were wondering if you would expand on your notion of cross-disciplinary writing. Certainly your writing is cross-disciplinary in that it uses the traditional scientific disciplines, such as ornithology, biology, geology, and entomology, to name but a few, as well as social scientific disciplines, such as history, anthropology, and sociology. What benefits do you see in this hybridization of disciplines?

A: From my point of view, it is a very salubrious thing to have a natural history writer's view of the world. The way that most of higher-education learning situations are structured stresses specialization, becoming more focused; the risk is losing the richness of the larger patterns. I find it exhilarating to have a speaking knowledge in all of the varied disciplines involved in natural history. You gain a very basic acquaintance with them just from reading all the various periodicals involved with natural history, and that acquaintanceship grants you an at-homeness with a wide variety of sources. I love reading bibliographies and lists of references, and I love the learning involved in natural history writing. I could maybe do away with the writing, but doubt that I could survive without the learning.

Q: From a rhetorical standpoint, what would you like your reader to do or get out of your books and essays? Do you have a goal in mind when you write?

A: Yes, although it's often a subliminal and kind of a simplistic one. It's one that arrived after I wrote *Beyond the Aspen Grove.* In my newly glorious state of having learned so much about our land, I was surprised that other people knew so little about the natural world. They think spiders are insects, and some city kids think that milk comes in cartons. If you think that, you are alienated from the natural world.

But if you can get somebody interested in a plant or an animal, talk about it in a nonconfrontive way, make it interesting and fun—the "what's that?" and "what's that funny-looking golf ball?," which you then cut open and find it's a puffball mushroom—all of a sudden people may get curious. If people get curious, they learn the right questions to ask, and maybe they will go look up a plant in a field guide. Pretty soon, they know something about something. And the only way that you own something is when you can hold it in your mind. The minute you know about something, you become involved, and if you're involved, you may begin to care. And if you care, you won't destroy what it is you know about. It may take months, years, a long time to do, but such slow self-learning sticks with you. Then if someone wants to cut old growth forest, you won't think, "OK, go ahead, it's all right." You'll know why it's *not* all right.

I think that's what natural history does at its best. It says, "take a moment to stop and *look* at what's out here." For most people, I'm sorry to say, natural history is not number one on their best-seller list. It's not a discipline that appeals to a great many people. I think it's a little more intellectual, just as nonfiction is not everybody's cup of tea. But it's part of the process of trying to get other people to look and to care. If you care, you won't destroy. Heaven knows we need a lot of that.

Q: To follow up on that, it would seem that you agree that one of the primary goals of writing about nature, of providing detailed natural histories of places is a way to create an awareness of place, a way for readers to better know that place and, in turn, to be conscious of protecting that place. You have written, "One of the things natural historians have done over the decades is to put into words an appreciation of the natural world and by so doing, lead others to care." We often assume that such an awareness comes from exposure to a place. Certainly we could account for the large number of environmental magazines, television programs, and other publications as an attempt to expose more people to places with the hope that they then learn to care for those places. Yet, at the same time, such exposure also causes a good deal of vulnerability; the more people who know of a place, the more likely more people will visit that place. For instance, writing about *the* aspen grove makes it a place readers would want to go, thus writing exposes it. We'd like to ask about that relationship between writing, exposure, and vulnerability, and to what you see your writing exposes readers.

A: Well, I would agree with that. Of course when talking about *the* aspen grove, essentially we have sequestered and so "control" this forty acres. So, we do have a say who comes and goes here; beavers and pasqueflowers have a bigger say. It's different in other books I've written about public lands. If you follow any of the directions that I wrote in *Wind in the Rock* to where the archaeological sites are, you will be woefully lost and quite likely rimrocked. I purposefully don't give accurate enough directions that anyone can follow. With the deserts, there's the sense that these are quite openly traveled by a lot of people. There are some protections that you can build in. You can misname places. That's the only time when I am deliberately inaccurate in my writing. I think natural history writing must be accurate, accurate, accurate. But intentionally misleading to protect a place is an instance in which I can let go of accuracy. I don't think anyone is so crazy that they'd take off for the Robinson Crusoe Islands just to see that landscape—you'd have to be nuts to go that far away for that reason.

Q: Many have attempted to delineate what characterizes nature writing as a genre. You label yourself a *natural historian* more often than a *nature writer*. Do natural historians write "nature writing?" Do you see differences between the two? How would you define nature writing?

A: This is a personal semantic prejudice on my part, but nature writing smacks of little old ladies in tennis shoes smelling the flowers, whereas natural historian, has, I think, a little more dignified sound. No one has ever been able to give a satisfactory name to natural history writing. Many people describe nature writing as creative nonfiction. That will have to do until someone comes up with a better name.

Q: Many people see natural history as an attempt to document the outer world of nature and see nature writing—like that of Thoreau—as being directed more inward and reflective of the writer.

A: That's a good point. I come down clearly on the side of the outside world. Pure scientific writing eschews using first person singular. In natural history writing you *do* use *I*. I have had several excellent editors tell me that if you're going to write fairly dense informational material, you have to carry your reader along with you or they will close the book. The way you do this is to use the almighty *I* to ask the reader to share in your experience of the moment. But it can never be an ego trip. When you finish a natural history book, you have to be able to say that the focus was on natural history, not that the focus was on the writer. That's why natural history is such a healthy discipline. It avoids the eternal moaning and groaning about "my angst," which makes it more a personal memoir. There's a healthy world out there, and it's a good place to be. So, I try to make my observations to a particular moment that is as brief as possible and concentrate on place. If someone can recall that they too have been out in a wet sleeping bag, he or she is going to follow you in your experience because they've had one in common. Or if they think that crazy idiot is out there in a wet sleeping bag in December, they're going to read on because they can't believe anyone's that silly, or to find out how you coped and kept your sanity. I've learned a lot in the last thirty years from my daughter Susan, who's a natural history writer, too, about storytelling and the universals we plug into: life, death, hunger, the basic human needs. And it's the universals that will entice your reader to follow your text.

The most personal essay I think I've ever written was "Of Pebbles and Place," which I wrote for *Audubon* about a trip to Whidbey Island to see Susan after she had had surgery. I had a wonderful editor at *Audubon* who preferred the more emotional aspect end of the spectrum and kept pushing me in this piece. I kept protesting that *that* wasn't my kind of writing. But he was right, and the essay was well-received. I think I tend to be a little aloof from the more emotional and personal mode, and that's just personal predilection and my personality.

Q: That does seem to be a trend throughout natural history writing. If you look at, say, Bartram's writing versus Audubon's writing, you see that every other sentence in Bartram's writing starts with *I*. It's much more a heroic tale of his exploits in nature than the cataloging that he suggests was what he was really doing. There seems to be that want to put *me* in nature when observing it.

A: I always had the feeling that he wanted to say, "Look what I'm doing; I'm making history!"

Q: And always heroically, too. Don't forget he single-handedly dispatched twenty or so crocodiles with a canoe paddle.

A: A *very* vivid picture! John Muir had much the same kind of travel in the South, but there's such a difference. With Muir I can put up with a lot of *I* because that exuberant personality of his comes through. It's not the *I* he's focused on, but the "I am here, this is for *real*."

Q: In your presidential address to the Thoreau Society, entitled "Thoreau and Women," printed in the *Thoreau Society Bulletin* (and reprinted in *Nearsighted Naturalist*), you start out by noting Thoreau's misogyny and then measure his writing against ten passages written by nature-observing women from Dorothy Wordsworth to Rachel Carson. We are curious as to whether you see men and women viewing nature similarly or differently.

A: Some of us in the field have chatted about this from time to time. I'll refer you to a book that Gary Nabhan edited called *Counting Sheep*. It is an anthology of people who have written about the bighorn sheep count conducted annually in the Cabeza Prieta, a preserve in Arizona on the Mexican border. The genesis of the book was the contrast between Chuck Bowden's essay and mine as opposite poles of the same experience. Chuck is an intelligent and literate writer who can also have a very macho style. He starts by stumbling down a hill, gashing his leg, streaming blood, and railing at the world. It's a wonderful, vigorous masculine beginning. My essay begins with the humor in trying to get there, what I expected, and what I found when I settled in for a week alone in the desert. It's a quiet essay. I think you could tell the gender of those two essays without knowing the authors' names. But most of the time, I think the power of place subjugates a lot of the differences, and if it's very good writing, you *can't* tell gender.

Q: John Burroughs wrote, "The literary naturalist does not take liberties with facts; facts are the flora upon which he lives. The more and fresher the facts the better. I can do nothing without them, but I must give them my own flavor. I must impart to them a quality which heightens and intensifies them." You are often labeled a *naturalist* by yourself and others—a writer who bases her work on keen observation. Is there a literary quality to your work in the way Burroughs describes? And, is there a certain flavor to your natural history writings that you can put into words?

A: That's an interesting question. Mr. Burroughs is not one of my favorite writers, but I would agree exactly with what he says. I think you can't help but put your own stamp on it because if you don't, then the style becomes scientific. That personal intrusion is one of the charms of natural history writing, that there should be a connection established between you and the reader, and how you do it depends upon your own personality, like it or not.

Q: Traditionally, natural historians have attempted to represent in the writing a literal, objective image of their subjects, as opposed to nature writers like Thoreau who rely heavily on figurative language. Your own writing seems more aligned with the former in that you sparingly use figures, schemes, and tropes. Do you feel that nature is characterized more precisely and completely without the use of figurative language?

A: Is this a question of style or substance? I don't think I avoid figurative language in my own work, but I think you're a better judge of that than

I. Thoreau was undeniably one of the most superb observers of the natural world, and I think that his journals are his great contribution to natural history writing. To digress for a moment, one way of defining natural history writing is the way the Burroughs Award does it. To qualify for the award, a book should consist of three things: first, actual, on-the-spot field work. You can't write about it if you ain't been there, cold, wet, tired, and hungry. You can't fake that. And there are some nature writers who have—nobody we know. Second, it has to be backed with superb research, that's accurate, so that when somebody calls you on what they feel is an erroneous statement, you can go back to your note cards and confirm your source. The words *natural history* on the cover imply a contract with the reader that assures them that what they read is as accurate as the writer can make it, with no fudging to slide entertainment over fact. The third facet is to put experience and research together in a literary way. You can't just say, "I had a week in the Grand Canyon counting eagles in winter," and then on the next page list what the eagles are doing. I doubt anybody would continue reading it. It's that synthesis, that "literary" part of it, that makes a coherent and harmonious book. And it's the hard part, and that's where good writing comes in, figurative or not. The first two parts are relatively easy, but the third is murder. You use every literary device at your disposal—simile, trope, metaphor, humor, irony, and maybe a few more devices that you think of in moments of panic, and then edit and re-edit and re-re-edit at least ninety-three times.

Q: It seems that when humans began writing and began writing about nature, so too began the move from living within nature to living separate from it. That is, the very activity of writing seems to be an activity that recorded nature as something separate from those doing the writing. That is, writing seems to have always played a large role in how humans respond to and interact with nature. How would you categorize the relationship between writing and nature?

A: True—when you're trying to wrest some farmland from a dark and threatening forest, nature is *not* a friendly place. Only when you're separate can you look at the forest with an objective (or even romantic) eye. I'd like to think that current natural history writing introduces the reader to the magnificence of the forest and helps her or him to understand its worth and fascination and internal workings.

Q: That sounds a lot like the argument that environmentalism can only be an upper- and middle-class endeavor.

A: I think that's proving to be largely true, don't you?

Q: That might be true in that that is how environmentalism has developed economically, but if you look at some underdeveloped countries where, for instance, killing an animal or even an endangered animal is much more of a survival tactic, you are dealing with a larger ideological position than just economics. There are larger cultural questions of how people are enculturated to see the interaction and a single moment's decision can be very different than thinking about such issues long-term.

A: Many native peoples make some kind of communication with the animal, wish it a good death, understand that when they eat it they are consuming and taking into themselves the animal's spirit. Richard Nelson and Dave Petersen express this point of view beautifully. There are also those wonderful lines of appreciation that have come down to us from medieval times, spoken by the monk before he plucked the healing herb.

Q: There's a great book by James A. Swan called *In Defense of Hunting* in which Swan writes about that very hunter's ethic. He writes a good deal about the apology, about how when he hunts he makes an offering of corn meal by spreading it on the ground before he hunts to put some energy back into the place he's going to take from.

A: I suspect that's the exception today. Native peoples are superb observers of nature, but let's not forget that their ancestors hunted animals like mammoths to extinction, driving them off cliffs, from the lack of an overall view.

Q: Perhaps the exceptions are occurring because we've only begun to talk about such issues.

A: Good point. Coming back to your earlier question about alienation from the natural world, could it be because of an urban society where people don't normally grow their own food, observe where what we eat comes from. It may be a matter of economics where if you don't have an SUV you can't buzz up to the mountains and go back happy. Equipment is expensive. Still, I think back to when I grew up during the Depression. We never did any camping. I had never even heard of it (and Indiana has enough mosquitoes in the summer to make sleeping out a misery). But there were so many things that parents did do with their children, and a lot of it consisted of going on a picnic or going on a walk. In the letters that I got after *Beyond the Aspen Grove* was published, one theme came through over and over: "It reminds me how my parents took me by the hand and showed me"—a tree, a butterfly, a whatever. One of the best ways to teach children about nature is one-on-one, the little hand in the big hand. I know it sounds corny, but it can be scary out there for a little one. If you have somebody to gently lead you to and through the experience, the strange becomes familiar. What we lack is the communicative opportunity to acquaint children with nature *before* they get to school. My children remember—and it was pure desperation on my part at the time, with Herman in the Air Force and away on TRY a lot of the time, and with three lively ankle-biters—I used to take them out for walks in the meadows when we lived in the country in Arkansas. They still remember that place. There was no real thought on my part. I didn't know anything about the meadow. I knew there were sometimes cows in the meadow, but that was about as far as I got. But just being out-of-doors gave them something. Here they were, grass above their heads—what a mysterious world that must have been. And all we did was just go out and plod around. And I remember too that that quiet acquaintance with nature was a very enticing thing for me.

I occasionally speak for organizations that are drumming up support and conducting fund appeals. Recently, a young fund-raiser said that he was having a hard time raising funds not because the money wasn't there, but because it was difficult to persuade his contemporaries, who are successful young entrepreneurs, to give money or time to charitable causes. He said his job first began with trying to persuade them not to buy the second Mercedes or Ferrari but to make a donation instead. He thought it was often because they didn't have a sense of making contributions to society, and to do so was perhaps inherited from their parents. There was a time when parents had more time in their lives to give back to their communities. Now it seems that the press of simply keeping current with the bills has eaten into contribution time, and along with that has gone less time to do things with their children, too. If you work all day and then come home and cook meals, help children with homework—I don't know how parents today accomplish it all. But there may be a price in the fraying connections. It just seems to be something that now has happened, now we're aware of it, and we look back and nostalgically feel we're missing something.

Q: Yes, and now more than ever, all of the state and national parks are overflowing. When you bring up the Mercedes or Ferrari, we also have to note that often it's the stuff that makes the excursion into nature important now, not nature itself. The opportunity to try out the new SUV or fishing rod or boots or whatever gear seems to be the thing that brings people into nature rather than the experience itself. It seems to be a desire to see how well gear can function in nature rather than seeing how well one gets along in nature. That is, excursions seem to be guided by the artificial; adventures seem to be conducted as acts of tourism rather than acts of experience. Obligation seems to be lost if places are simply places to visit, not to be linked with. The experience doesn't seem to be as much an issue of getting one's hands dirty, of getting in the wet sleeping bag, of being cold, tired, hungry, and bug-bitten, but of experiencing nature at a safe distance. The experience seems to be reduced to staying in the lodge, taking a one-hour cart tour around the park, and being able to then say, "I'm home safe and I've done nature."

A: That's why zoos are so successful. They are crowded with people in ways they didn't used to be.

Q: Particularly now since zoos have moved from the 1970s caged-animal experience to the habitat zoos we see today.

A: They certainly are a lot more attractive.

Q: It may look better, but what an ideological fraud for the animals. It used to be that the animals knew they were caged; now they are oppressed without knowing it.

A: That's an interesting way of putting it.

Q: That's actually a metaphor Todd Taylor at the University of North Carolina uses to explain feminist and women's movements in the late 1990s. When his students complain about talking about feminist issues because "we aren't oppressed anymore," he explains the condition of being trapped in a new zoo much like the position of women in the 1990s—you may not see the bars, but they have been constructed to keep you in place, nonetheless. You may not see the boundaries, but they are subtly there.

A: Mercy! That's a depressing approach to feminism!

Q: Let's turn back to your writing. Much of your writing is accompanied by your very detailed illustrations. You write about drawing, "that's when the learning begins: on a nondescript plant with nondescript flowers, that I soon discover to be both fascinating and beautiful." Could you talk about the relationship between writing and drawing for you in a text? How does that visual rhetoric work for you? Is one more important than the other? And is one more expressive for you?

A: I have drawn for as long as I can remember. My mother always saw to it that I had art lessons. I never knew that there was another way to spend your Saturday mornings when I was a kid. When I went away to college, I had this wonderful notion that I was going to be a two-dimensional artist. Well, Wellesley didn't have courses in pure studio art then as they do now. But they had something that was even better for me. They pioneered a system by which you had two classes of art history lecture followed by a lab class in which you learned the techniques of the artists you'd been studying. And I fell in love with art history.

I quit doing artwork after I married and had children. There just weren't the blocks of peaceful time. I went back to drawing when both my parents were ill and I lived faraway. Drawing became therapy. About the same time we found our forty acres in the mountains. I was a city girl who didn't know any of those bright flowers, and there weren't many good field guides available thirty years ago. But I could cement the size, colors, textures, by drawing them. That's when I started drawing seriously again, and drawing became learning. I was interested primarily in plants. I think that there are saltwater people and freshwater people; there are dog people and cat people. There are plant people and animal people. I'm definitely a plant people. I think drawing plants is one of the greatest, most peaceful, pleasant things to do, the simple coordination between eye, arm, hand, and pencil. It's like listening to a Gregorian chant and feeling all of your molecules lining up and celebrating.

Q: In *The Mysterious Lands,* you write: "There must be thousands of bushes of Texas silverleaf, loaded with big lavender flowers. Where many flowers cluster at the top of the bush the name becomes understandable as they haze the desert with a silvery lavender. Local lore has it that this is Zane Grey's 'purple sage.' The only trouble is, silverleaf is neither purple nor true sage, which belongs to the Mint Family, or sagebrush, which has tiny yellow flowers and belongs to the Daisy Family, but a figwort, cousin to snapdragons and penstemons and Indian paintbrush. If so, Zane Grey has forever and indelibly fixed this figwort in literature by the wrong name and the wrong color—so much for the power of the printed word." Actually, it would seem a more accurate assessment to say, "what power has the printed word." What does this suggest to you about the power of a writer to shape thinking about nature?

A: The writing word sometimes has huge psychological power in our society. We learn everything as little children by listening, and I bet you can still sing all of the songs from your growing-up days. We pick those up orally. *And then we learn to read.* Somehow when we learn to read, we stop listening so intently (unless it's repetitively played for us). When I'm working, say, on the river, and I'm drawing, people will come up and ask if they can watch. Heavens, yes, I don't mind because all I'm doing is rubbing the paper and bringing out the lines as though they were emerging out of the paper and not out of my hand. You can carry on wonderful conversations while drawing, but the minute you pick up a notebook and start writing, it's all over: you can't talk and write at the same time. There is that kind of little mystical moment, like that old TV show, *Get Smart,* and the cone of silence. You have raised your own cone of silence that shuts everyone else out—and putting down words becomes (unfortunately) something separating and therefore carrying a kind of indefinable power.

Q: Which is interesting that we think of that kind of writing as a solitary activity, but the act of writing itself is social, particularly if we're writing for a specific audience.

A: The *act* of writing is, has to be, solitary; we're not yet evolved to where we can carry on a conversation, think clearly in another mode, and write sentient sentences, all at the same time. It's only social in terms of its later forms. Perhaps people are a little in awe of the act of writing, and I can understand that a little bit, the magic of putting little black characters on paper that someone years hence can read. In my situation, people often wonder if I'm writing about them and that makes them uncomfortable. Of course, I never do that in the field; if I do so, it's only later.

There must be a mystique about writing—I'm always curious about people who express themselves so handsomely in speech but become so unglued when faced with a blank sheet of white paper. I'm not sure I understand this, having had diarrhea of the typewriter ever since I can remember. Perhaps it's because, like it or not, writing is so self-revelatory. Whether I am reticent or not, people think they know things about me that I am just as sure they wouldn't bother about. The same is true for any fiction or nonfiction writer. It's a very exposed position. You're standing on the end of your precipice of privacy, watching it crumble beneath your feet.

Q: That goes back to what we discussed a moment ago about making things vulnerable when you write about them. It seems that the number one thing that you expose is the author, yourself. Authors make some very critical choices about what they're willing to expose and what should be kept safe.

A: There are some choices that are beyond you as author that readers will relate to, that you never intended in a thousand years. They may be way off the mark, or they may be right on. Do you, as a writer, have people who say to you when they've read things you've written, "Oh, I know you!" And of course, my reaction is utter horror, what do they know that I don't know?

Q: Yes, so, let us ask then when in *Beyond the Aspen Grove* you write, "Herman catches just enough [trout for] dinner and cleans them. I put a sprig of fresh tarragon and a chunk of butter into the cavities, drizzle them with lemon juice, wrap each one individually in foil and steam them in the oven. We often have a baked potato, slightly charred from the head of the wood stove, or perhaps a thick slide of homemade bread. A green salad with watercress fresh from the stream, a beautiful pale Sancerre or Riesling, raspberries picked that afternoon (if there are any left after Jane and Sara have exercised collectors' rights): one of the favorite late-summer meals at Constant Friendship." We offer this quote because it presented an interesting moment in one of Sid's ecocriticism and nature writing courses. A student referred to this passage when he suggested that parts of *Beyond the Aspen Grove* "just seemed too perfect and idyllic." Do you intentionally strive for idyllic, or even pastoral, moments in your work? Is that what you want readers to know? And if so, can you explain why?

A: Obviously I'm a romantic. But that moment *was* true, and one of many memorable times we've had over the years up here. Living where we do, at high altitude in Colorado, we may have opportunities that you sea-level Floridians don't, and I speak as someone who lived in Florida for several years. I cannot imagine cooking on a woodstove in Florida! And that's exactly what I was doing in Colorado, cooking on a woodstove. We did have trout in the lake because we'd stocked it. I used to sprout watercress at home and bring it up and plant it in the chilly south stream where we also chilled the wine, which probably cost three bucks in those days. Same with tarragon, brought it up from downtown. We had a lot of times like that, halcyon times. My daughters will probably deny it, but for us as parents they were at that wonderful, wide-eyed age of "What's this?," and "What's that?," full of curiosity and imagination and energy.

You're here today with snow on the ground. The magic of this place in the summertime is just not to be believed. Clearly, I could have said, "Herman hacked the head of the fish, I slapped it in a pan, popped a beer while the children pulled the legs off spiders." It would have been patently untrue, but would that have made better reading by your generation's lights? Maybe it's younger readers' reactions to things that my generation values, to what for me was a fairly straightforward narration about a simple meal.

As Edwin Way Teale said, writing natural history is like preserving a fly in amber—we can always go back to examine it, every bristle and wing vein intact. And so I feel about that passage: it's a time and place that will not come again. But I can always revisit it—because it's written down as it happened. And if that's nostalgia, so be it.

Q: That, then, becomes the site for your audience to say, "I know you. I feel like I've had dinner with you and Herman."

A: And they didn't have to prime the pump, heat the water, and wash the dishes either.

Q: In "A World of Infinite Variety," you write: "It is impossible to write natural history without getting involved in history history, and especially so in a book about historical letters." We're curious about the relationship between natural history and history history. Both seem to be narratives that tell a kind of story for people and by people. It has, of course, been argued, that when history history is written, the stories that are told are often biased, flawed, oppressive, or empowering. Simply because natural history has been "written," it would seem that its telling is equally problematic. We were wondering if you could talk about the politics of writing natural history. That is, Heidegger said that language both reveals and conceals; what do you see the writing of natural history revealing and concealing?

A: Just as with history history, it is almost impossible to keep your own personality, your own prejudices and understandings, out of it. It is my intent to be accurate, honest (and honest about what I don't know), and informative. Those are ideals. I recognize that someday I'm going to base an essay on a piece of scientific information that is revealed as false between the time the essay is in type and before publication, and I'll be powerless to do anything about it and will be ridiculed for it. Those are the risks of the game.

I have no doubt that natural history has often been biased and flawed. For instance, the "Mother West Wind Stories" taught children about nasty little Jimmy Skunk who ate birds' eggs or adorable baby cottontail rabbits. The author did not acknowledge that if somebody didn't eat those rabbits we'd be up to our eyeballs in rabbits. As I understand it (secondhand information), over time a lot of natural history information has been flawed or downright inaccurate, knowingly or unknowingly.

So you come down, as you do with history history, to asking if you trust the writer? Has he been trustworthy in the past or has he played fast and loose with facts in such a fascinating way that you'll forgive them anything and keep on reading?

Heidegger's statement that language both reveals and conceals is true of natural history writing. What the writer isn't interested in or finds too difficult to understand is never revealed. What the writer does *not* want the reader to know is deliberately concealed. And so what else is new? I've always thought that writers were first and foremost writers, but it may be that they are first and foremost *people* and writers *second*. So, you do the best you can under the circumstances, trying to fill in the lacunae in your knowledge, telling it like it is while realizing how you see it may not be how it is at all, and muddle through, acknowledging your imperfections and being pleased if once in a while you write a sentence worth retaining. I suppose if you thought about it too much you'd never write another word.

Q: In the Transcriber's Notes in *John Xántus: The Fort Tejon Letters*, you write about Xántus's mechanics, spelling, margin use, and paper space. What did you learn about the activity of writing from working with these letters?

A: The same things you learn from your students when you look at handwritten papers. You can see an organized mind at work. You can see a precise mind at work. You can see a sloppy mind at work. You can see the stamina of the writer, the breadth of their interests. I find the analysis of handwriting is absolutely fascinating, and a very useful skill.

Q: Did working with these letters help you reexamine your own writing?

A: Not particularly—Xántus was such a different personality: although hardworking, he was bombastic, willing to fabricate, etc., and writing letters is a different ball game than writing a book. I found in reading them another facet of a character that's represented in a different way. Instead of the words themselves, it's the neural connection between head and hand and how that represents what's going on in a writer's head. I respected him for the good work he did do under very difficult circumstances, but he was not primarily the kind of writer from whom one learns style or technique or whatever.

Q: Let's talk for a moment about the scientific aspects of your work. Does a scientific or natural historic knowledge of nature enhance your appreciation of it? That is, does reading what others have written about it enhance the hands-on experience? Similarly, in "Annals of an Insect Collector" you write, "I care about recording, over the years, as many species as possible that occur on this quarter of a quarter section, and to learn their scientific names." Would you expand on the importance of learning names? That is, can nature be known just as well without knowing all the scientific designation?

A: You can "know" a lot without knowing a plant or animal's name but you can never know as much as if you do because that's the only way you can discover what's already known about it. For some, pure observation is enough. It's not for me.

This is an ongoing discussion I'm having with a couple of friends of mine. One believes that knowing names is important, the other one says, "Who *cares*?" To me, it's the same as knowing your names or those of your students: I owe you that honor. If I kept calling you two, for instance, John and Jim, we'd have a problem here. A name is what sets something apart, gives you a handle on looking something up, finding out what it does in its spare time, what it prefers for lunch. A Steller's jay is NOT a red-winged blackbird. For me, it enhances a great deal of what I know about the natural world. To know a name allows you all of a sudden to start seeing families and genera and, over time, gain a familiarity so that when you go into a strange habitat you have clues as to what's there, a basic recognition. Recognition is one of the things that makes up home, a sense of knowing what and who's there, what they're doing. Are they going to bite? Are they going to sing? Are they going to sit there and smile calmly like a Pacific tree frog? That may be terribly important just in the housekeeping sense in a new place and may keep you from making a stupid error, like picking up a velvet ant because it looks like an ant.

Q: When writing about places, you often turn to other writers who wrote about those places. Do those other writers help you to see those places better? That is, do those writers help write those places for you? Are there any particular writers who help you define certain places?

A: Yes, it's lovely to read what somebody else has written, and often it will corroborate something that you've felt and often it doesn't. But it doesn't really matter if it's a good piece of writing. If it's a good piece of writing, it enriches the way you see because each of us has a distinct and unique reaction that they put on paper. If you are a writer, you ultimately have to see a place in your own terms. If you get all of your information from another source, you are missing out on the most important relationship, one between you and place. But if you discover someone else who reacts in much the same way, there's a reassurance in good company.

My students frequently worry that they'll be copying if they "write that way" when reading other authors. If sometimes we have students read so much that they forget to see things for themselves, we end up with essays that look like what Thoreau or Abbey or McPhee wrote. Especially if students aren't sure of themselves yet, not sure of their own voice. When they are, they will recognize even if they commit to memory every word written by William Wordsworth that they will never write like William Wordsworth. They will write out of what they see and know. It becomes a matter of confidence. Writing *is* a matter of self-confidence.

As to a writer who helps me think about places, certainly Edward Abbey. It's difficult to think about Moab and the places he wrote about without thinking about what he wrote. And Rachel Carson's *The Edge of the Sea* is my idea of the perfect book; she made it possible for this timid Midwesterner, afraid of the sea, to walk into the ocean. The fact that she made it so fascinating made the difference. Many of the nature writers that I admire may not tie to a particular place, although I can't think of butterflies without thinking of Bob Pyle, and insects without thinking of Sue Hubbell, or the Arctic without thinking of Barry Lopez. Susan Zwinger has introduced me to places that I associate with her, like Alaska and the North Country.

Q: You've explained through your writing that as you walk around places, like the Chihuahuan Desert, you pause from time to time to take notes or to sketch. That is, you explain that part of the way you write about a place is to write in that place. You even have written in *The Mysterious Lands* that sometimes you concentrate so hard on taking notes that "when a cicada lets off a five-second burst like a bandsaw going through metal, I jump." That seems like some real concentration in the writing. How does place affect your writing and, in turn, how does your writing about a place affect how you see or know that place.

A: First of all, let's not get taking field notes and compositional writing mixed up. Field notes have little literary quality, they are an extremely concentrated-on-the-moment recording because if you don't get it down then, you may find yourself in deep trouble a week or a month later when you're actually writing text.

When I'm working on a book, there's a lot of back and forth. When I first go out into the field, I know very little. I keep the last page of my field notebook for questions, and come home with an arm-long list. I answer as many as I can in the library. The next time I go out, I am much more sophisticated in the way I look, so I come back with *another* list of questions. So, there is this back-and-forth that comprises a growing knowledge of place. That's the way it works for me anyway, and revisiting different areas is more characteristic of writing a book than a magazine piece. When you ask, "how does writing affect place," I don't think writing affects place at all. I am simply trying to understand what's going on; I'm not sure that nature gives a hoot about understanding my point of view. If you are a writer who is so effective that you save, say, a mountainside from being clear-cut, then you *would* have changed the environment but that's not generally what I do.

Q: In *Beyond the Aspen Grove* you write, "This is invigorating country for walking; it is varied and unfrequented, and full of treasures for the bright-eyed. Jane finds a porcupine skull, complete with long yellow ponderosa-scraping incisors. Sara discovers a nest, tumbled to the ground in a recent storm, lying beside an unfamiliar wildflower. Susan picks up a weathered tree knot that looks like a bird. Or perhaps a whale, depending upon which way you hold it." It often seems that the biography of your family is completely enmeshed with the biography of Constant Friendship. You have written, "Both physiology and limited mobility bind desert reptiles to their region, and their distribution closely reflects the influence of both ecology and history." It seems that these are the same kinds of connections you identify between the growth of your family and its region. Could you discuss the relationships between places and individual and familial growth? That is, how influential is a place on the people who live there?

A: I never thought of it that way, but I find your comment a knowing and perceptive way of characterizing our relationships to this place. I still get letters from dear people saying, "I wish you'd write another book like *Beyond the Aspen Grove*," and I bite my lip because clearly that was a time and place that will never come again. Because my daughters are grown-up young women, I cannot write about them as contemporary children. I think I have come less and less to write about family because I respect their privacy, and I feel strongly that what I want people to remember is the natural world, *not* my family's peccadilloes. And let's be honest, inserting family is also a great ploy. Richard Shelton, a superb poet, wrote a delightful autobiographical book called *Going Back to Bisbee,* and he speaks about "my wife" all the time. I said, "Richard, here's this wonderfully talented woman. She's an opera singer. She was the head of the poetry center at the University of Arizona for years. And yet all you have to say about her is 'my wife?' Not even her *name?*" He replied, "You have to understand, she's a ploy. She brings in a live, breathing person that makes it easier for people to stomach more or less objective writing, and on whom I can hang ideas." He's right. And so in that sentence above with the three children in it, they are obviously ploys. And I trust they forgive me.

Q: Stephen Kellert writes in *The Value of Life: Biological Diversity and Human Society* that "The higher a person's education, the more likely that person is to express greater concern, affection, interest, and knowledge (and less exploitative and authoritarian attitudes) toward animals and the natural world. This tendency is especially pronounced among the college-educated." Could you comment on this quote, answering the following: What roles do you see the university playing in regard to environmental learning? Do you share any of Kellert's optimism in university education regarding the future of our natural environment? Do you see environmental studies taking a more influential role in university curriculums in the future?

A: I agree with that quote, and I think it goes back to your earlier question about upper- and middle-class people being those predominantly interested in environmental concerns. It's in situations where working people are running up against someone (e.g., an immigrant) who is taking their job away that you get the worst prejudice. Or just being threatened with losing their job. Remember the bumper sticker, "If you're cold and starving, eat an environmentalist?" People who have had broader exposure, who have been able to see other peoples and environments, walk in their habitat footsteps as it were. As a result there is a greater understanding, a greater empathy. I also wonder if indeed more educated people are only those interested in preserving the environment, if that is not a product of increasing numbers of solid environmental studies. If you don't know what's going on out there in any sense, you're not going to care what happens, but if you have some education about it, I think you're a little more open to protecting habitats because maybe you can "afford to," but more important, you can understand the long-term reasons for *not* doing so. If there's a serious financial pinch—e.g., burning down rain forests to clear land for farming—you won't be able to see the long-term advantage for the short-term gain. Same for the Monarch butterflies wintering in forests in Michoacan that are being cut for fuel and farm land. I believe that education *does* have a lot to do with how we treat the world we live in.

As to why my students take my "writing-the-natural-history-essay" class, I think they often take them for reasons other than advertised. A few of them, one or two, take it as a pipe course and are woefully disappointed in the workload. Biology or other science majors nearly always want to learn how to write. Then there are those who think it sounds like something fun to do and, oddly enough, they are the ones who come out with a real sense of not so much becoming environmental activists, but with a real sense of a natural world that is important to their survival. That's good to see.

Q: For ecocompositionists, those of us interested in studying the relationship between writing and environment, writing is crucial for both the activity of writing and what it conveys about a place. Your writing is instructive in that it helps readers appreciate and, we hope, come to love the natural world. It instructs readers toward a way of seeing. As teachers of writing, our goal in teaching natural history and nature writing—your own included—is to teach students awareness and concern for nature, and to be better writers as well. Your writing certainly lends itself toward the former, but how, if at all, do you envision students of your work learning about the latter? That is, does reading Ann Zwinger teach readers how to write natural history?

A: First of all, I do not teach my own writing. If students want to read what I've written, that's fine, and I don't discourage it for there is an advantage in having the author there to question. My primary goal is to draw out of students what they didn't know they could do. To that end, I have them read as many nature writers as possible. Reading natural history writers *does* give students ideas of what they like and don't like, develops their critical sense, I hope gives them some pleasure.

When I teach writing, I teach the literature along with it. I usually assign either John Elder's and Robert Finch's comprehensive *Writing Nature* published by Norton, or Scribner's two big volumes, *American Nature Writers*. I ask them to skim the book, look for a writer or subject that catches their eye, then pick one nature writer that they really like, read more of that writer's work, and be prepared to speak to the class about their choice. They need to read something that they think is the epitome of how they perceive this writer writes. Later we come back and look at first paragraphs and last paragraphs, which is extremely instructive. So, they're really looking at someone's writing as both natural history writing and as writing writing. They run parallel.

I also teach lots of editing. The first time I taught, I realized that students seldom vet their papers before handing them in. In my experience, editing is what refines and makes good writing into fine writing. Students also read their writing aloud in class if they're comfortable doing that. A great method to help them see their own writing is to have someone else read their words to them—a fantastic revelation of phrasing and thought patterns. If the reader stumbles over a word or phrase, you know it needs to be revised.

Of course students keep field notes/journals all the time. "Field notes" is a useful objective term; journals suggests a more personal kind of writing, and I don't want them to slip into the "Dear Diary" mode. Because Colorado College is on the block system (a $3^1/2$-week block during which you teach only one class and they take only one class), I can take them out into the field. This is when I can monitor their attention to their observations. I take half their notes one night (I limit the class to twelve to fourteen students), write detailed comments on a laptop, and print them off so they have their notes back first thing the next morning. These notes will furnish the basis of their essays, and they won't be able to write a competent essay if they don't take competent notes. It means a couple of nights with an hour or two of sleep, but it's necessary, in the compressed time frame, to provide instant feedback because there's not a lot of time to fiddle around if you get off track. It also says in a very practical way that I'm willing to make the same extra effort that I require of them.

Q: You write in "Remembering Indiana," "Writing natural history—which is what I have done for the past twenty years—is an esoteric field. Ideal nature writing combines a love of research, a devotion to scientific accuracy, and personal experience in the field. The first two one can learn, in varying degrees of success; the third totally depends on one's willingness to set foot out of one's dooryard, or to explore one's dooryard with the same tenacity with which some writers explore the whole world. The best nature writers I know have a real sense of being at peace with the natural world, and this is often true of other people involved in outdoor work, whether they be foresters who study how trees grow and forests work, or lichenologists who spend most of their time on hands and knees observing the world through a hand lens." Both of us have taught writing courses in which we ask students to write what Randall Roorda has called "retreat narratives"—narratives that document a writer's literal movement from the cultural to the natural. Of the three conditions you list for writing natural history, students have the imposed motivation toward the third, but not necessarily the first two. We have found that this holds great potential for teaching students to write; however, we are curious as to what benefits, if any, you see in moving students from traditional classrooms "into the field." That is, has education become too much of an indoor activity?

A: Yes, *yes*, and *YES!* I personally think many subjects can be taught outdoors, but that's another topic. I see a lot of classes where teachers take students out on the lawn while they lecture, which is *not* the point—that's very distracting. That's not really taking students out to participate in nature. If you're going to teach natural history writing, you have to get them out into the field as soon as possible, period, full stop. That's where Colorado College's block system is a great advantage. You cannot teach without being in the field. It's that old business about if you ain't been cold, wet, tired, hungry, bitten, miserable, you haven't recognized what the natural world imposes on you (of course the other side of that coin is feeling exhilarated, awed, and delighted by a buttercup or a sky flowered with stars). Ironically, that discomfort heightens your sensitivity to the natural world. Being out *alone* also changes your attitude; if you're smart, you start being careful in ways you never were before. It changes one's outlook. It influences your whole relationship with the world about you. I try to make that experience possible, if only in a limited way, for students. You just can't get that experience in any other way—not in the classroom, not in the lab. However, this is not "retreat writing" in your sense of the word, useful concept that may be. I want students to bring their cultural background with them to illuminate the new world they're discovering because in that way their new world illumines the familiar one and gives them a storytelling base with which to work.

Q: In *The Mysterious Lands* you write the wonderful sentence, "Desert is where I want to be when there are not more questions to ask," and in "A World of Infinite Variety" you write, "there is the joy of discovery and the sense of wonder." When does Ann Zwinger stop wondering, discovering, and just go to the desert?

A: [laughing] Well, I'm going to Greece in a couple of months, will that do? I don't think I'll ever stop wondering or discovering, it's just part and parcel of this peculiar genetically and environmentally driven personality I walk around in. For me, writing is one of those professions from which you never have to retire. You just hope that you're going to get better at stringing words together while growing more human and understanding. If you keep your wits I would hope you could keep on writing forever and ever and ever. I actually can't answer your question but know that I won't ever quit *asking* questions. Not having questions means having no more hope. But that statement in *TML is* cryptic, and I probably meant it to be so. Let's just say it works for me.

Rambling

A Response to Ann Zwinger

Randall Roorda

In his much-cited taxonomy of nature writing, Thomas J. Lyon includes among subheadings of the genre a category of texts he calls "rambles." This is the nature essay in which the author-naturalist "goes forth into nature . . . and records the walk as observer-participant," moving in leisurely, peripatetic fashion across the terrain and remarking on such features, tangible and associative, as he or she happens across. The ramble contrasts, though mildly, with the natural history essay per se, "the main burden of [which] is to convey pointed instruction in the facts of nature," whereas the ramble gives the author's own presence "an equal or almost equal place with the facts themselves" (5). To Lyon, John Burroughs is the quintessential exemplar of this genteel discursive mode—Burroughs after whom the prestigious Burroughs Award is named, which Ann Zwinger has won—and despite her confessing in this interview to a certain coolness toward Burroughs, the ramble is a form in which Zwinger too works, wonderfully so, albeit with a pronounced tilt toward the natural history side of the scale. Her characteristic procedure is to position herself in a wild place, set up a bare frame of narrative in her movement about it, then festoon the frame with observations, mostly detailing the natural features of the place but also dipping into its human history and including spare asides on her state of mind and body as experienced there—her aversion to the personal (also expressed in this interview) notwithstanding. "Rambling" in this sense has an honored place in environmental writing, as in the essayistic tradition it extends from, and Zwinger is among its most accomplished practitioners.

In exposition and argument, though—the realm of the thesis-driven and systematic—rambling has altogether another valence. It connotes digression, distraction, rifts in coherence, an inability to fix upon and stick to a point. When writing evaluators huddle to hash out traits and matrices, rambling ranks high among their bêtes noires—a vestige of the dreaded "writer-based prose," a chatting to oneself on paper. For rambling is manifest more often in impromptu speech than in cold type, in which tangents and evasions protrude like burrs on smooth surfaces—irruptions that would recede in the warm warp of conversational exchange.

Whatever else might be said of her remarks in this interview, it must be allowed that Ann Zwinger rambles. In expository terms, she is all over the lot, in ways I will suggest and be tempted, as a critic, to assail. Given this temptation, I want to move swiftly if not to dismiss at least to reduce the charges. It's unfair to transcribe what Zwinger treats as a conversation and scrutinize it as if it were a composed, deliberate performance, from which compositionists might expect to elicit insights and applications. What we read here is a cheerful woman thinking or rather chatting out loud. It's written down but can't be treated as writ.

The oral aspect of Zwinger's comments opens an avenue to considering them. If, discounting objections and qualifications,[1] we follow accounts of oral-literate distinctions to the extent of noting that oral performance is more likely than written to depend on verbal formulae—slogans and proverbs, fixed expressions, reiterable utterances memorably phrased—we can detect in Zwinger's comments elements of such formulae. We can discern scraps of phrase, assertion, and anecdote that seem played out before by a writer who, given her success, gets called upon routinely to hold forth in this impromptu manner, before audiences and interviewers and students. (Zwinger refers in passing, for instance, to her frequent speaking engagements on behalf of preservationist causes—few, I'd suppose, requiring pre-scripted remarks.) Any number of word-workers are self-scripted in this way, of course—some more gifted than others at pronouncing on their feet but all bearing repertoires of verbal tape loops, set to play out as occasion demands. In Zwinger's remarks, we can discern some such elements, most already evident a decade ago in an occasion like this one, an on-stage interview conversation with Gary Nabhan, moderated by Ed Lueders and published in his *Writing Natural History*. Present there and notable here is her formulaic response to the stock "purpose" question: Why do you write? Her rejoinder: so people will know a place and thereby own it, for if they know it, they will care about and thus protect it (or at least not destroy it).[2] This is so memorable and airtight a sentiment, I'm loathe to wade into the ways it might be complicated and disputed.[3] For subject as it may be to corrosion through critical scrutiny, the knowledge-care-protection formula has a creed's durable patina. Readers in the genre who accept it are unlikely to invite dissensus. And even if it could be induced or forced, I'm not certain critical headway would effect more good than harm. Who knows what vulnerable recesses of allegiance and belief lie below such verbal shells, like heartwood below bark? Critical lightning, if impressive and pleasurable to wield, can do damage, as we teachers come to recognize.

The scripted expressions a verbal performer falls back on, at any rate, indicate what matters she has dwelled upon and rehearsed. Conversely, the absence of such formulae may delineate topics, discursive locales, where little rehearsal and reflection have taken place. In this respect it seems clear that on many of the topics composition professionals obsess over, the accomplished writer interviewed here has nothing really to tell us—nothing, at least, she can draw off the cuff. The pattern in this interview is glaring: on one topic after another—writerly purpose, interdisciplinarity, gender, class and privilege, literary technique, visual rhetoric, the social nature of language, and so on—our comp-aligned interviewers pose a question, the interviewee rambles around or right past it, and the interviewers proceed to suggest a version of what they were after, which version the interviewee may seize upon as a welcome and arresting recognition. A case in point is the question of the provenance of the genre term *nature writing,* as distinct from *natural history.* Zwinger responds by equating the former with "little old ladies in tennis shoes," an association this proudly impersonal writer allows may be strictly personal; and when the interviewers, for whom genre questions are butter and bread, propose a distinction of their own, Zwinger seems happy to ratify it, as if no such thoughts had ever strayed across her radar. The pattern holds with the topic of interdisciplinarity, a question about which elicits from the writer a free associative circle that begins in embracing "a writer's view of the world" and concludes by musing that one "could maybe do away with the writing." Ditto with such questions of social class, consumption, and privileged access to landscape as crop up, on which the naturalist avers that some urbanites may be "alienated" from nature because "if you don't have an SUV [or, she might have added, a husband with an airplane] you can't buzz up to the mountains and go back happy," and breathtakingly acquiesces to a proposition the interviewers lob up, that "environmentalism can only be an upper- and middle-class endeavor." Her ramblings on these matters—with their reiterated motifs of health, happiness, discomfort (the "wet sleeping bag"), insecurities over being found laughable or "dumb," and so forth—are ripe for analysis in rhetorical not to mention sociohistorical veins. They are an easy mark, altogether—one she seems rarely to have drawn a bead on herself, if these unformed, offhand emissions are any sign.

In some cases, on such unfamiliar ground as the interviewers present, such scripting as Zwinger has recourse to consists in the arch-oral practice of narrating personal history. Prompted, for instance, to comment on her "visual rhetoric," the "relationship of writing and drawing . . . in a text," she resorts to relating the story of her drawing, how she took it up as a child, relinquished it for a while under the demands of parenthood, and came to it again with pleasure later in life—a key episode in her tale of good fortune and dumb luck, her "falling in a mud puddle and coming out smelling like a rose" (or in the second iteration of this formula, a lily). It's a personable, affecting tale, though it does not in the least address the question posed—in this respect not unlike responses writing teachers are used to receiving from students unready to tackle analysis of the sort requested. It might seem odd that a writer so suspicious of the personal should indulge so routinely in anecdotes of family and past— or would seem so, if there were evidence to suggest that the questions were not foreign to her, that she had rehearsed to address them in any other way. On topic after topic, no such evidence is forthcoming; one question after another leads to another blind alley, another box canyon.

It may well be that analysis of the sort the interviewers are angling for—such reflections as comp pros would invite and hope to discern in the talk of accomplished writers—would strike Zwinger as foreign to her enterprise. Though enamored of education and research, she has little penchant for critical inquiry. She might well regard talk of "rhetorics" visual or otherwise, musings over language's social construction, cogitation over epistemology, ideology, subjectivity, genre-parsing, race/class/ gender and the like as so much "moaning and groaning," angst-ridden hand-wringing that distracts from the fundamentally "healthy" endeavor of fixing on the particulars of the place itself. If we liked, we critics could seize on and press further the tangled rhetoric her remarks betray, these notions of health, fitness, discipline, leisure, introspection, fortune, and otherwise, exposing their continuity with Anglo worldviews dating at least to the American fin de siècle, fostering beloved Burroughs and bigoted Ford alike—whites like me. Moaning and groaning, indeed. Belaboring her remarks to the extent I have is making me feel distinctly unhealthy. After all, I *like* Ann Zwinger. She's a fine writer, a crack naturalist, apparently an open, generous person. It must have been fun to talk with her. I wish her more readers than she has already, more than *I* have (an easy wish). I'm not eager to tar her (or powder her) with associations my critical impulses and professional allegiances press upon me. I'm not sure that in my moaning and groaning I hadn't better just leave her alone. But doing so, I'd have nothing to say pertinent to this occasion, for a compositionist intent on gleaning much from these sunny ramblings seems bound to resort to deconstructing, reading across gaps and against intentions, into inadvertencies, juxtapositions, tropes, and associative trains. Such disjuncture between text and treatment, between the spirits of small talk and critique—it's bloody wearisome.

So, I'll bail out with some morals. First, a windup. A common expression (more spoken than written) has it that those who can't *do, teach.* Let's take this as a vernacular version, more or less, of Gilbert Ryle's old distinction between knowing *how* and knowing *that.* This distinction, and the doing-teaching divide, is something composition encounters time and again, with the process movement, for instance, originating largely in a recognition that "knowing *that*" approaches to teaching, by models and formalist nostrums, weren't much touching the *how* of a writer's doing. The doing-teaching slogan won't do, of course—at least for the purposes of the eggheads it disparages. Yet there's something instructive to the expression even so, if not in the mutual exclusiveness at least in the relation between the doing, or rather *writing*, and teaching roles, such that reversing the slogan may be just as instructive: those who can't *teach, do.* Or, those who *do,* can't *teach*—or rather, aren't enabled to teach by specific dint of their proficiency at doing, at knowing *how.* Or, those who do, can't teach about teaching.

Ann Zwinger can *do* like crazy—a consummate pro. What then in these transcribed ramblings can teaching professionals gather? That a writer first registers "information" and "reaction" and only *then* gets it down. That "literary technique" is a sort of overlay applied to information for the sole purpose of hanging on to one's readers. That questions of politics and disclosure in writing come down to whether writers "play fast and loose with the facts." That attention to a writer's working drafts leads as much as anything to a fascination with handwriting. Questions on teaching in particular yield such principles as reading one's work aloud, studying reading along with writing, and going outdoors in order to write about outdoors. What's not unobjectionable here might be actively disputed by folks in our field. If this is what comes from knowing *how,* while knowing *that* may not be knowing *better,* it sure is knowing *different* from the knowing we comp people espouse.

I derive one reassuring lesson from this and one troubling one. I am reassured to be reminded, if I needed to be, that we *have* modes of knowing about writing and teaching that writerly know-how in the close sense does not equip one to practice or profess. I am troubled, though, to have a suspicion dramatized: that close attention to the workings of ecology in natural landscapes, at which Zwinger is unsurpassed, does not in itself predispose a person to apprehend or even begin to reflect on the *discursive* ecologies that a nascent ecocomposition would attend to. It may even be that natural history, generically unmitigated (that is, un-crossed by genres with different presumptions and expectations), tends to discourage or thwart such reflection—that it functions (following the remark by Heidegger that frames the question posed here on politics) as a mode of concealment, a terministic screen, with respect to such affairs as ecocomposition would dwell on. This fixity of attention to natural detail—the occupational psychosis of a "plant person"—seems the flip side to Marilyn Cooper's influential "ecology of writing," which on inspection appears to consist solely of paper and talk, admitting no ecology at all in the sense that Zwinger exercises, no plants not already mulched up. Natural history cross-pollinated by genres of discursive self-consciousness, though—*that's* the sort of thing that nature writing might be or become, with the narrative of retreat an exhibit in a shuttling between modes of "ecology." Or so it seems to me, in speculation and critique. What seems demonstrated here is that study of nature and a practice of writing do not in themselves conduce to critical acumen—at least as construed by an in-group devoted to its cultivation. That's as far as *this* moral goes; what to make of it is another story.

NOTES

1. For more on such qualifications, my "Great Divides: Rhetorics of Literacy and Orality" is a place to start.

2. Here is Zwinger in the present interview: "And the only way that you can own something is what you hold in your head. The minute you know about something, you begin to care. And if you care, you won't destroy it." Here she is in the 1988 appearance with Nabhan and Lueders: "My theory is that we should try to get the reader to really *look* at the natural world. If you once look at something, really *see* it, it becomes yours. And once it becomes yours, you'll never destroy it" (Lueders 72).

3. A bare start: first, there's the question of audience, with Zwinger assuming that natural history expands the circle of knowledge/care, yet conceding immediately that the genre's sway is small and select, "a little more intellectual," an audience of the converted and, implicitly, the cultivated. Then there's the presumption that familiarity breeds care and protection, which John R. Gillis, for instance, in ruminating on "the remote," disputes, positing that preservationist care comes rather from distance: that "it is people 'from away' who have the strongest sense of a place" and "that the greater the perceived distance the stronger the attraction" (39). This is distance of a sort, it might be added, that literate productions may traverse yet reinforce, again by fostering a "cultivation"

divorced from the literal cultivation, the extractive practices of bona fide locals more attached to the place. This distance and the sense of the remote Gillis meditates on is certainly a factor in Zwinger's writerly appeal, despite (or, let's face it, because of) her insistence that the far-flung, exceedingly remote field sites she accesses by airplane, SUV, aching feet, and wet sleeping bag are all "home . . . *really* home" (Lueders 73).

WORKS CITED

Cooper, Marilyn. "The Ecology of Writing." *College English* 48 (1986): 364–75.

Gillis, John R. "Places Remote and Islanded." *Michigan Quarterly Review* 40.1 (Winter 2001): 39–58.

Lyon, Thomas J. *This Incomperable Lande: A Book of American Nature Writing.* Boston: Houghton Mifflin, 1989.

Lueders, Edward, ed. *Writing Natural History: Dialogues with Authors.* Salt Lake City: U of Utah P, 1989.

Roorda, Randall. "Great Divides: Rhetorics of Literacy and Orality." *Ecocomposition: Theoretical and Pedagogical Approaches.* Ed. Christian Weisser and Sidney I. Dobrin. Albany: State U of New York P, 2001. 97–116.

The Mud Puddle and the Rose

A Response to Ann Zwinger

Annie Merrill Ingram

As Sid Dobrin and Chris Keller observe in one of their questions, Zwinger "sparingly use[s] figures, schemes, and tropes" in her writing. When she does use figurative language, however, we pay attention. Twice during her interview, she repeats the expression "Falling in a mud puddle and coming out smelling like a rose [or lily]." Zwinger uses the expression to describe those times in her life when she was just beginning to write and to draw, and she took a significant risk that paid off in the sweet smell of artistic success. For an acknowledged "plant person," the attraction of emerging like a rose or lily makes sense—but so does the mud puddle. Zwinger asserts that in order to produce accurate and engaging natural history, the writer must be willing to take physical risks out in the field, to get cold and wet, to fall into the occasional bit of mud. But somewhere between the "falling in" and the "coming out," the alchemy of writing transforms the raw experience into the polished form.

Although "falling in" connotes an accidental movement, Zwinger's insistence on direct experience of the natural world is quite deliberate. Connecting to the natural world gives people a sense of community, with the environment as well as with each other. When she muses, "I can't help but feel that people, if not completely alienated, are very distant from nature," she counters this observation of the present with a memory from her past: growing up during the Depression in a family that never went camping but nonetheless went on picnics or for walks. Zwinger continued this tradition with her own small children, taking them out to plod around in an Arkansas meadow. What is significant here is not the grandeur or remoteness of the natural environment, but the person's immediate contact with whatever nature is at hand.

Composition theorists have lauded the importance of community for some time now, in the form of collaborative learning environments, discourse communities whose similarities and shared cultural assumptions can be analyzed, and writing-for-the-community projects. The writing community, like the community that forms as a result of tromping through the meadow together, nurtures its members while fostering individual talent. When Zwinger emphasizes the importance of learning scientific names and of achieving scientific accuracy, she acknowledges that natural history and its faithful readers are themselves one kind of discourse community. She writes to introduce her own readers to the natural environments she has come to know, to awaken the care that results in wanting to preserve and protect the natural world. With such a broad community to write for, Zwinger has taken on an ambitious lifework, one that has already succeeded in bringing a number of converts to the wild.

Zwinger obviously cares deeply for the natural world, and her writing can be seen as a form of activism. Instead of focusing on the current events in the newspaper, as some activist writers might, Zwinger proposes "another exhilarating way to understand the world"—by focusing closely on nature and by having "a speaking knowledge in all of those different disciplines," such as biology, geology, or entomology. Her goal of getting people "connected" to nature and their surrounding environments recalls the oft-used trope of the ecological web. In the web, where everything is interconnected, one cannot affect a part of the web without affecting the whole. Before her readers can connect to the natural world, there has to be a "connection between you [the writer] and the reader." The resulting ecology of her writing links author and reader, life and work, voice and text into an interdependent whole. Zwinger places herself as a writer within several different but ultimately inseparable physical, personal, and discursive environments: natural history, scientific accuracy, mother and wife, meadow, aspen grove, Constant Friendship, university classroom, river expedition. The overarching role that binds these specific sites to her work is not so much that of the writer as the learner.

Ann Zwinger makes it sound like she just "fell into" being a writer, but she has the successful writer's most important characteristic: an insatiable appetite for learning. "I love to learn," she says; "I could maybe do away with the writing, but I sure love to learn." She possesses the naturalist's attention to detail and patience for observation; she also has the natural historian's curiosity for scientific fact. When asked how she would differentiate between natural history and nature writing, she notes that the latter "smacks of little old ladies in tennis shoes smelling the flowers," while natural history is "more accurate." For Zwinger, natural history is also "a healthy discipline," one that focuses on the outside world, not the writer's "angst" or "moaning and groaning." Her refreshing rejection of the personal in favor of "universals" distinguishes her writing from much of the creative nonfiction available today. By situating her writing within a larger context of community and activism, she brings not only herself as writer but also her readers into the world *outside*: both the natural environment and what exists outside the self.

Although she notes, "I may tend to be a little colder than the touchy-feely mode that a lot of writers are in right now," her very objectivity and commitment to precision mark her work as worthy of emulation. Too often in college-level writing classes, the personal essay is the primary (or only) form that is taught. And while I certainly value the form (and teach it), I've also found it to be one of the most difficult genres for young writers to do well. Traditional-age college students often have trouble getting *beyond* the personal: they are at a stage in their lives when they are fascinated by their feelings, their roles in society, their achievements, and their struggles. Scott Russell Sanders, in his essay "The Singular First Person," states that "I choose to write about my experience not because it is mine, but because it seems to me a door though which others might pass." The problem I have encountered is that students don't even know there is a door, let alone a world outside of it.

To inspire students to acknowledge and then engage the world out-side, we must encourage them to discover their connections and their community—which returns us to the discussion above of both writing communities and the interdependent ecology of life and work, experience and discourse. To counteract the isolation of the self-centered writer—whose parallel is the "outdoor gear"-driven, SUV-driving nature enthu-siast—we can offer learners the experience of what Zwinger calls "that quiet acquaintance with nature." Significantly, she uses this phrase when talking about how she introduced her own young daughters to appreciate the natural environment.

Zwinger's experience as wife and mother has obviously affected her work. Even in her spoken remarks during the interview, domestic meta-phors occasionally surface. When asked about the importance of learning scientific terms, she responds that knowing names "allows you to all of a sudden start seeing families" of plants and animals. Furthermore, "rec-ognition is one of the things that makes up home," and [knowing the scientific names] "is terribly important just in the housekeeping sense." Families, home, housekeeping: although her writing ranges far beyond the confines of her domestic environment, she remains connected to it at least figuratively, if not always literally. An attention to process may also be the result of her roles as mother and wife—for example, because of the necessity of focusing on the immediate exigencies of Herman's hacking the head off the fish and her children's pulling each other's hair. Yet even these mundane details become transformed into a passage whose simplicity of presentation and style mirror the deliciously fresh and wholesome meal that she is describing.

As a writer of natural history, Zwinger identifies her process as a heuristic of alternating observation, inquiry, and discovery. "I go out in the field, and the last page of my field notebook is for questions. . . . I answer some of them. The next time I go out, I am much more sophisticated in the way I look. Then I come back with another list of questions. So, there is this back and forth that comprises a growing knowledge of place." Composition theory similarly asserts that the writing process is nonlinear—yet Zwinger's vivid example concretizes the theory for us. In the end, she "come[s] down clearly and cleanly on the side of the natural world," an advocate for what the natural world can teach us, especially when we are quiet enough to listen and observe carefully, and when we are curious enough to ask the right questions.

As we ecocompositionists look for ways to transform the academy, we would do well to follow Zwinger's advice, both the implicit and the explicit. Implicitly, the genre of natural history provides a "healthy" antidote to solipsistic, self-oriented discourse. When we take our students outside for class, we need to venture beyond the distractions of teaching "out on the lawn." As Zwinger explicitly suggests, we need to get "cold, wet, tired, hungry, bitten, scratched," to "heighten [our] sensitivity to the natural world" by confronting its power directly. But experience alone cannot substitute for equally important other disciplines. As Zwinger writes in "Remembering Indiana" (as quoted by the editors), "ideal nature writing combines a love of research, a devotion to scientific accuracy, and personal experience in the field." Here, then, are the equivalents of the philosopher's stone that alchemists sought in their search for transmuting base metals into gold, that solve the mystery of what happens between falling into the mud puddle and coming out smelling like a rose: *love* of research and *devotion* to accuracy. The terms love and devotion may seem incongruous to a discussion of composition and its role in the university, but they signal the crucial importance of passion for one's work. What Zwinger leaves us with, at the end of her interview, is a clear sense of her passion for learning and writing, and the inspiring notion that continuing to ask the questions means continuing to have hope.

Response to Roorda and Ingram

Ann Zwinger

Reading the responses to this interview with Sid and Chris left me feeling as if I were lying naked in my coffin, staring up at a circle of unfamiliar faces who had mistakenly wandered into the wrong memorial service. As a writer, I'm used to reviews; you cherish the nice ones and learn from the tough ones. But reviews are a direct reaction, one person's opinion, usually intelligently founded, to inform a reader about the quality and character of a book, which they may recommend or pan. "Responses" are something else again, not tied to a particular book, but to what you've said in an interview, the agenda of which is essentially set by someone else's purposes and biases. It's like judging the personality of someone you don't know by a snippet of thirdhand gossip overheard at a cocktail party, said with a mouthful of smoked salmon and a little too much libation.

It concerns me that the two responses have not been made to original work but to what was focused on by the interviewers. Both responders picked up on the same two items that are so minor in my work that they strike me as nonsensical: an ill-advised, smart-ass division between nature writing and natural history writing (see below), and a summer supper, taken out of context, that I described more than thirty years ago in *Beyond the Aspen Grove*.

That summer dinner did exist, and more than once. The reaction of Chris's and Sid's students as well as the responders has made me realize that we are talking about the difference in Eastern (where I lived for many years) and Western lifestyle, and two very different generations.

No matter how carefully and thoughtfully crafted, as this one truly was, interviews are still in the interviewers' (if they're worth their salt) hands. Unfortunately, intelligent questions can get dumb answers. One of my regrettable answers is the distinction that I made, in a giddy moment, between nature writing and natural history writing. Actually, I've been chided by many friends and colleagues on this same point since, who sensibly find there is no difference. My off-the-cuff attempt to separate the kind of writing that lacks structure and scientific support from that which does, has nothing to do with whether you're a "little old lady in tennis shoes" (as I am, except it's hiking boots), or not. To me, one of the real charms of natural history writing is that wide spectrum that permits gushing over a primrose at the river's brim and nothing more, to writing with an intent to widen the vision of the reader with factual input, to educate without being pedantic. My comment was a useful distinction that does not need the befuddlement of a meaningless quip. That a foolish statement can be so tenaciously haunting is a warning, dear friends: what you set in print you can repent at leisure. So, please let me lay that to rest with the little dignity that it deserves, and accept that the two categories are one and the same.

I found the responses of the two teachers to differ widely in aspect and direction, and also to differ from my experience as a teacher. Annie Ingram's gentle comments lead me to imagine that she is a careful and insightful teacher. She writes clearly and simply ("clearly and simply" is a real compliment, Annie), and her concerns as a teacher come through. She speaks of young writers' inability to handle "the personal essay" well because of a lack of experience at that stage in their lives.

Teaching courses about writing the natural history essay as I do, I've found that the connection to childhood is a wonderfully valid key; students are still closer to childhood in many ways than adulthood, and it is often the universal door through which they may enter a larger world. Students can and do wander back in memory and tie some of the happenings of years past, good or bad, to their immediate experience in the natural world, which may be reminiscent, evocative, healing, or all of the above. Some then write stunning essays, anchored in their own experience. Such an essay, done well, is a reassuring and heartwarming accomplishment, and the praise they receive from their peers and their professor is a solid encouragement to keep on writing, and writing well, and to use their personal experience not as an end but as a beginning to introduce others to a rich natural world.

I'm not as sure that Ms. Ingram's *family* as metaphor holds, as that word is also used in a scientific sense. Certainly *family* appears underlined in my vocabulary for all the obvious reasons. I have been a mother for longer than I have been a writer. I never set out to consciously teach my children appreciation but simply to share my enjoyment of an out-of-doors that gave me and them pleasure. Taking them out to explore a meadow was something to do with three lively children, and because it appealed to them I kept doing it. Fortunately, these interests have carried over into their adult lives: all three of them are at home out-of-doors, and carry a healthy understanding of its working in their everyday lives.

Those similes that Ms. Ingram cites of family life are simply a part of my experience, an unavoidable part, and if one writes what one is, that is what I "is." But it's also important to remember that family is one of the levels of classification of both plants and animals. When Linnaeus figured out an efficient way of organizing a world, prophetically one of the words he used was *family*.

I must be an exceedingly plain-minded pragmatist but I got lost when Mr. Roorda begins on the "honored place in environmental writing" that "rambling" has; when he writes that it has "altogether another valence," I realize how far I've departed from the vocabulary of literary criticism into the nuts and bolts of pragmatism. I believe the hours that we spend rambling or wandering are productive in many ways. Indeed, the change of attitude spawned by getting away from the computer, allowing and respecting the ability of the mind to wander on its own, provides a solution in an essential segment of the creative process.

An interview invites wandering. Writers write because they're often *not* good on their feet, and writing gives them a chance to refine, condense, correct, and at least fashion copper out of dross. An interview is the rough draft, the wandering/searching that eventually congeals a bunch of unruly thoughts into conciseness. So, he's right about profiling me as "a cheerful woman thinking or rather chatting out loud." I sense my responsibility is to be alert, courteous, sentient, and to answer the questions as posed, and to admit that I do not have the predilection for sesquipedalian words in a spoken interview in which I can indulge when I'm quietly alone at the computer.

My response to why I write is not formulaic as Mr. Roorda would have it, but a deeply felt conviction, my own honest-to-God truth, and shame on him for not discerning that. The fact that I have repeated that thought—that it takes time to develop a devotion that gets started through curiosity and questions—testifies to its endurance in my belief system, one formed through experience and time. To have uttered differently on different occasions would presuppose a will-o'-the-wisp mentality, a lack of dedication and assurance, a value system quickly altered to fit the latest academic fad.

Actually, from then on, I got lost in obfuscation. His sentences are like scrambling through a briar patch: once you've gotten into one, you spend a lot of painful moments wondering how on earth you're going to extract yourself with only minor damage. Briars scratch and trap but offer no solutions in return. My writer daughter, who's a lot sharper than I and has the Ph.D. to prove it, who also teaches English composition on occasion and is familiar with the jargon, noted in the margin beside the following sentence of Mr. Roorda's account that it belonged "in the top ten of most baffling sentences in English ever written." I quote: "If this is what comes from knowing how, while knowing that may not be knowing better, it sure is different from the knowing we comp people espouse." He may know what he's saying but I sure don't. My reaction is, "Who's on first?" I admit to not being a deconstructionist, nor do I intend to become one, and I find such esoteric vocabulary and sentence structure one of the ways in which we create an elitism that keeps out the hoi polloi. As a respected teacher and published writer, Mr. Roorda might well reconsider the importance of clarity and the value of reaching a broader audience for those ideas that are important to him.

I simply want to share with my students some basic, essential writing skills, and introduce them to a fascinating natural world, secure in the belief that if they become interested in nature, they will never be bored. They will have a clue about what to do with the rest of their lives, which is precisely what college ought to teach.

I sincerely appreciate both Ms. Ingram's and Mr. Roorda's taking the time to write what I would guess might be one of the less fascinating challenges in their busy teaching and writing worlds, and I thank them for their generosity. Yet, I wish I had the sense that they had read *Beyond the Aspen Grove* so that their judgments could be formed on solid text, not the peripheral prattlings of a pragmatic and "cheerful woman." But hey, in today's world, a little cheerful goes a long way.

Writing the Scientific Life

An Interview with Edward O. Wilson

Scientist Edward O. Wilson is clear, "Most children have a bug period. I never outgrew mine." To say that Wilson has had a bug period is an understatement. This two-time Pulitzer prizewinning author has been one of the most important figures in contemporary science, and a good deal of his work has involved insects and his childhood fascination with all living things.

Wilson earned a B.S. and M.A. in biology from the University of Alabama and a Ph.D. from Harvard, where he currently serves as Pellegrino University Research Professor and Honorary Curator in Entomology of the Museum of Comparative Zoology. He has, in addition, been awarded both of Harvard's most prestigious teaching awards. Coupled with his success as an academic, he writes that his true passion lies in field research, being out in wild places studying the indigenous organisms. His autobiography, *Naturalist,* recounts much of his experience as a field researcher and the discoveries he made that have changed the way we think about the organisms of the world. His contributions to entomology, myrmecology, and biology have been not only some of the most important of the century but in the history of science.

Wilson was awarded the Pulitzer Prize in 1978 for his landmark book *On Human Nature* in which he examines the relationships between biology and behavior. Though a few critics rebutted Wilson's argument as a reductionist approach to understanding human behavior as simple, uncontrollable biological processes, many more saw the value in what Wilson was teaching. Wilson was awarded a second Pulitzer Prize in 1990 for *The Ants,* which he coauthored with Bert Holldobler. The award of these two prizes signified not only Wilson's contribution to science but also his ability as a writer.

For those of us working in the humanities, Wilson's more recent groundbreaking projects of building links between the sciences and humanities make him a figure of deep interest. Wilson has claimed that "the linkage of science and literature is the premier challenge of the twenty-first century." In the interview below, Wilson addresses in detail the importance of this linkage and discusses the importance of writing, not just in the sciences but as a communicative tool for all knowledge makers and storytellers. What many interested in discourse studies will find fascinating in what Wilson has to say is his deep understanding of the activity of writing and the connections he envisions for writing and the sciences. Wilson is certainly a theorist of biology and ecology, but many will be intrigued to find that he is also a theorist of discourse. He has spent a good deal of time reflecting on what it means to write, to be a writer, and what the activity of writing encompasses. Few figures in contemporary thinking about ecology, biology, and environment have given as much thought to the role writing has played in human existence in the Earth's biosphere. In the following interview, he addresses such subjects and, as in most of his writing, asks us to learn a little about science, about writing, about life.

Q: In the Foreword to Archie Carr's *A Naturalist in Florida: A Celebration of Eden*, you note some similarities between your life, particularly your childhood in Alabama, and Carr's. You also write of his writing that "Like all major writers, Carr can be read at two levels. His stories are to be enjoyed straight and simple as adventure. But, more deeply, he speaks for the generation that saw its perception of nature profoundly change." Of course, your own writing could be characterized similarly: *Naturalist* is without a doubt a phenomenal adventure story, but, like your other books, it also teaches a good deal about that very perception of nature you mentioned regarding Carr's writing. What role do you see your own writing play? That is, how do you characterize your own writing?

A: My writing style is designed to combine science with literature, and it is meant to probe as deeply as I'm able as a scientist into the substance of the subject and its meaning in terms of cause-and-effect explanations while at the same time using language that can be varied in a literary manner to run from somber to celebratory and inspirational.

Q: Essentially speaking, your writing has been directed to two kinds of audiences: the scientific world through what you characterize as "technical articles" and to a larger, more diverse audience through books like *Consilience, Biophilia, Naturalist*, and *Biodiversity*. *The Ants*, for example, is "not a book one casually purchases and reads cover to cover, nor does it try in any direct manner the adventure of research on these astonishing insects." *Journey to the Ants*, on the other hand, "condenses myrmecology to a more manageable length with less technical language with an admitted and unavoidable bias." You obviously have different agendas when addressing different audiences; how do you envision different audiences when you write? And, how do certain audiences affect your writing?

A: Technical scientific writing, the kind that one finds in research reports and peer-reviewed technical journals has to be the opposite of literary writing in that it is intended to present the bare bones of factual information. Of course, it's meant to report results that can be repeated by the person—usually an expert—who's reading them, and it allows only a kind of a homeopathic dose here and there of personal emotional expression. It is suspicious of metaphor. Everyone who does scientific technical reporting knows that those are the rules you play by.

In the case of literature, in many respects you have the opposite. There the power and originality of metaphor is everything. The subject, if it's nonfiction, has to be truthfully reported, of course, but it doesn't need to be reported in a manner that the reader can repeat for themselves. They can expect it to be honest, but also they're going to be reading it more for the imagery and the poetry than the raw and testable theory.

Q: Over the years, you've established quite a bit of credibility as a writer and a scientist. With that in mind, how do you envision audiences, knowing that you have both loyal supporters and critical detractors just waiting to comment on your articles and books as soon as they come off the press? Is your writing influenced at all by the fact that your work will receive extended and immediate critique both by academic and popular audiences?

A: No, not in the usual sense. I always write the very best I can, as if I expect to get a Pulitzer. One of my favorite mottoes is by the physically smallish heavyweight champion Floyd Patterson who very admirably won the world championship back in the days when it meant something. He said, "You try for the impossible in order to achieve the unusual."

Q: In writing about the first Martian landing of the Viking probe on July 20, 1976, you recount the events of the landing and then write: "Then it was over. A giddying potential had been reduced to the merely known. The cold dust of the desert plain was committed to photographs in magazines, then to technical monographs, textbooks, and encyclopedias. The adventure became a set of facts, somehow mundane, to be looked up by students and recalled during leisure reading." You have also written

that "At the age of twenty-nine, I had fifty-five technical articles published or in press. Being thoroughly professional in attitude by that time,
I knew that every young scientist needs such proof of productivity." We
find it intriguing that you characterize the transfer of knowledge to textual representation a "reduction," and are curious as to how you think
about the act of transferring historical/scientific moments into text. And,
we are curious as to whether you see writing technical articles as a sign
of productivity or an act of productivity.

A: Let me start from the back and move forward. I see scientific writing
as both a product of and act of productivity meant for special consumption. The results of scientific research have to be presented in a manner that
will attract the attention of other scientists. And something you learn from
a scientific culture is that unless you can impress upon your colleagues the
importance of what you have found, it will very likely be ignored or at best
quickly forgotten. Scientists are for the most part journeymen. They're
hacking away at one particular short segment of the frontier, and they are
not inclined to pay attention to what others are doing around them unless
their associates make a connection to what they themselves are doing. It's
in the introduction or the discussion of a scientific paper where an author
can best present an overview that reaches out to others. So, writing is
extremely important even in rather technical scientific reports. In the quality of the writing and in the sweep of imagination it contains, therefore,
scientific reporting is very much an act of creativity.

Q: You have recently collaborated on a multimedia textbook project
called *Conserving Earth's Biodiversity with E. O. Wilson* that features written text, video clips, and CD-ROM integrations. You also mention in
Naturalist that there was a time when you were hesitant about the use of
computer technology in the field of biology. We're curious as to how you
see the role of technology, particularly new medias like the World Wide
Web, streaming video, and hypertext in both the continuation of scientific
study and the dissemination or making of knowledge.

A: Well, the only reason I would be suspicious of it is where scientist and
public alike might be captured by it as a technology that in some manner
diminishes any part of human imagination. Once we appreciate that
creativity in science is very much a product of the human brain, we can
better understand technology for what it is. Technology is first of all the
key driver of scientific research. It's an enabling activity that allows us to
see more finely, to see farther, to see more quickly, and to compute

complex simulations swiftly enough to make predictions deeper and more powerful than is possible by the unaided human mind. One of the subjects in which technology is now about to play a revolutionary role is the one I started with and still work in, which is systematics—the exploration of biodiversity and the formal description of it down to the species level. Until fairly recently, a lot of the work on systematics was a laborious process of examining specimens, then comparing them to reference specimens, often in museums difficult to reach. This has resulted in a relatively slow pace of systematics to the present time; as a consequence we may have only described a little more than one-tenth of all of the actual species on earth. Now revolutionary and accelerating advances in computer technology and communications services, along with the ability to transmit by satellite, the World Wide Web, and the digital imaging of specimens, even microscopic specimens, with unprecedented clarity and exactitude, have together jacked up the potential pace of systematics by as much as one hundredfold. But this technological advance does not in any way replace the initiative and imagination and ambition of the human mind.

Q: There is a recurring idea throughout your work that emphasizes the importance of theoretical speculation in the biological sciences. Biology has had its own versions of the theory wars, as has composition studies. You are a theorist of evolutionary biology and of ecology; we are theorists of a different kind, intrigued by theories that attempt to explain the functions and facets of written discourse. Richard Dawkins suggests in *The Blind Watchmaker* that "biology is the study of complicated things that give the appearance of having been designed for a purpose. At first sight, man-made artifacts like computers and cars will seem to provide exceptions. They are complicated and obviously designed for a purpose, yet they are not alive, and they are made of metal and plastic rather than of flesh and blood. Yet in this book they will be firmly treated as biological objects." Theorists of writing often see text as "complicated things that give the appearance of having been designed for a purpose." In Dawkins's sense, is writing biological? Are evolutionary biologists and writing theorists working on the same kinds of projects?

A: I believe Dawkins may have misapplied the term *biological. Biological* also implies self-assembly and reproduction. Writing is very biological, however, in the sense that it is a product of an organism and a very advanced organism at that. It's an expression of the activity of the human brain and is meant to reflect directly the activity of the human brain. It's not a machine that has a purpose beyond a capacity to do certain things. Writing, it seems to me, is a reflection of the goal and the means and the most complicated functioning of the organism itself. It also reproduces itself, and mutates while doing so in the minds of readers. Let me just try to clarify that by making one other observation. The automobile sitting there has a function; it carries you. But, it has no goal or purpose beyond that. The writing that's sitting there has a function of communicating to you everything in the organism, including its goals and its reasons for the writing itself. There's a profound gulf between the two kinds of artifices.

Q: In "The Writing Life," a short essay recently published in *Book World*, you write that "Thanks to the continuing exponential growth of scientific knowledge as well as the innovative thrust of the creative arts, the bridging of the two cultures is now in sight as a frontier of its own. Among its greatest challenges, still largely unmet, is the conversion of the scientific creative process and world view into literature." You go on to posit that "To wring literature from science is to join two radically different modes of thought. The technical reports of pure science are not meant to be and cannot be reader-friendly. They are humanity's tested factual knowledge. Open to verification, framed by theory, couched in specialized language for exactitude, trimmed for brevity, and delivered raw. Metaphor is unwelcome except in cautious, homeopathic doses. Hyperbole, no matter how brilliant, is anathema. In pure science, discovery counts for everything, and personal style next to nothing." You have tried both in your own writing and the message of your work to overcome the bifurcation between sciences and literature. Your books are ripe with personal narrative and argue for the very sorts of disciplinary border crossing identified here. Could you speak to why you see "the linkage of science and literature is the premier challenge of the twenty-first century"?

A: For one thing, science, conducted in the manner characterized in that statement, has turned out by great good fortune to be the most powerful information gathering and verification procedure that humanity has ever devised. It really gave us liftoff power for exploring the universe. Now we're approaching an era when science focuses on the human mind and human creativity. Up until this time, those seemed to be two different realms in the epistemology of truthseeking. They've collaborated and remained pretty much that way to the present. The time has come, I think, for the two branches to develop a theory of all the creative arts from choreography and music to literature. Namely, we need a systematic consideration of what human creativity is, why we consider art to be art and great art to be great art, and why we think of them that way and why we resonate to them. To put that in more biological terms, explaining how the brain works and further, why it works that way. Where the creative activity of the human brain came from in evolution. Not to diminish by objectifying and breaking down the components of the creative process, but rather to provide explanations of exactly what it means to be human, and especially the expression of our humanness in the arts.

Q: You have written, "The aim of art is not to show how or why an effect is produced (that would be science) but literally to produce it." Art, however, is typically associated with humanities studies—the kind of epistemological search for meaning you were just talking about—which you have also criticized for focusing on one point: the human species without reference to the space of all possible species' natures in which the human species is embedded. If, as you suggest, "Ideally art is powerful enough to cross cultures; it reads the code of human nature." Can science be art or art science?

A: No, I see a distinction as follows: the creative arts use artifices that transmit emotion directly from creator to audience, and the idea is to provide detail and metaphor with an originality and power that evoke clarity of perception and emotional response. The core of the creative art effort is: direct, person-to-person, without explanation except where the explanation is part of the effort to transmit feeling itself. Science can provide a theory of the arts. The effort would be true theory when it achieves the systematic exploration and eventual understanding of why works of art perform their role and what makes their best efforts so general and powerful.

Q: Have you begun to theorize what that theory of the arts might be?

A: I think it will come substantially out of cognitive psychology and neuroscience, focused on what pushes the buttons in the emotive centers of the human brain directly. It will identify the circuits involved and the neuroendocrinological responses triggered. That may sound kind of cold and mechanical, but by the time we work it out, creative art and science are going to be seen as the richest and most enthralling mechanism we know of in the universe. So to speak of it in broad reductionist language doesn't mean that's the way it's going to be expressed ultimately or even in the near future in simple mechanical metaphors. Another spearhead for the theory of the arts is the recreation of the evolutionary history of humankind. I've just today been writing the account of the Savannah Hypothesis which attempts to explain, and I think with increasing effectiveness and accumulation of evidence, why it is that we like certain environments and almost unconsciously gravitate toward them. And why we like flowers, another universal response. Subsidiary to it is the way we plan our habitations, if allowed to place them the way we choose and build them the way we want to build them. And what we consider to be beauty in landscape architecture and gardening. This already is a fairly solid branch of evolutionary biology called ecological psychology, which is beginning to get some traction in making clearer why we have certain aesthetic responses about nature. So, in sum, it's the evolutionary approach, combined with an understanding of how the human sensory and nervous systems work that will provide the most rapid and immediate progress in the theory of the arts. We will grasp the particularity of our aesthetic sensibility. For example, we do not find as a highly intelligent termite would (if there were such a creature), by which I mean we don't find fungi and deep, damp, dark recesses of the earth endearing. Thus, one bridge I think is beginning to cross the mostly unexplored domain between the arts and science.

Q: It's intriguing that you begin that explanation with the notion of cognitive psychology, because as our discipline of composition theory began to evolve in the 1960s, our first research turns were to cognitive psychology to map writing processes. We looked toward individual writers and cognitive thinking about how writing takes place. To make that link, then, also to a theory of the arts seems to be a fascinating direction. We're also excited to hear that you're writing more about the Savanah Gestalt, because that seems to be one of the most exciting theories that links environmental studies with aesthetics.

A: I'm pleased to hear that. It's invigorating to hear someone in the humanities speak in those terms.

Q: We're actually working in an area of ecocomposition that's bridging ecology and composition studies. So, we're going to ask you some questions about those links.

A: I have grown used to, over the years, getting responses from humanities scholars who have said, "No, no, you can't do this. This is reductionism; you're melting the Inca gold." You're collapsing something that is too membranous and refined and emergent ever to be treated in such biological terms. That objection is, in my opinion, wrong, wrong, wrong.

Q: Let's start breaking all those barriers down. Recently several composition scholars, such as Patricia Bizzell, have begun to attribute metaphors of hybridization to discourses that blend traditional discourses—such as the discourse of the academy—with less traditional discourse—such as personal narrative. A good deal of your writing seems to be exactly this kind of hybrid discourse. You have also done a fair amount of theorizing both hybridization and displacement in terms of biodiversity. If compositionists are beginning to use notions of hybridization in discussing discourse, what advice might you give about theorizing hybridization and displacement in terms of writing? Or more directly, how would you forward a theory of hybrid discourse?

A: In discourse between the humanities and science we need an intermediate body of literature, genuine literature, that combines the best of both enterprises. The way it's to be achieved in my opinion is to recognize that the arts and sciences employ different modes of thinking and expression that can be made explicit, and that the reader needs to know which mode the writer is using. Also, there are the extreme modes, of pure science and pure literature, then there is the one in between. In this hybrid mode the writer is exact and truthful in describing a material entity or process but at the same time uses metaphors, an exposition of the innovative process itself. How did the author arrive at this particular scientific discovery? Or how did the explorer feel upon finding something very new? How can one explain the impact of a rain forest in more than just purely poetic terms? The hybrid mode is the one that I think we are talking about here. This mode has enormous possibilities for creating original thought, and it can be made legitimate by recognizing it as a mode. That is what I started doing, I suppose, as far back as my book *The Insect Societies*. I had some chapters and paragraphs from the book in 1971 that shifted into it. Later, in parts of *Sociobiology*, and then entirely in the book *On Human Nature* in 1978, I shifted into the middle mode. In the last work, incidentally, I was careful to say that the book is *about* science and not *of* science.

Q: That's one of the things that we want to continue to talk about, and I'm wondering, based on what you just said, what your response would be to writing theorists borrowing metaphors like hybridity from science. Are these beginning to make those kinds of border crossings that you're interested in? Not just in terms of science using the literary metaphors that you're talking about, but in terms of writers who study writing.

A: Returning the favor? Yeah, sure, I like it. I think it's quite legitimate and potentially productive.

Q: In your autobiography, *Naturalist*, you write a good deal about academic life. At one point you mention that a good deal of your time was spent "doing research, reading, and talking with faculty and other students, usually about evolutionary biology but ranging widely into subjects as diverse as geography, philosophy, and the techniques of creative writing." Your work manifests a long-held interest in writing as you address the subject regularly through your own work. Many doing work now in what is being called "ecocomposition"—that is, looking at writing as part of larger systems and in relationship to larger physical and historical environments—are attempting to bring ecological inquiries to the study of writing and discourse. Do you see any of your own work both in ecology and in the study of writing making these connections?

A: Do you mean the theory of composition and strategic planning in writing as drawing elements from science.?

Q: Or either way. Does ecology fall into your theories about writing?

A: Yes. In many ways. In one of them, to understand an ecosystem is potentially to produce a vastly richer and more authoritative background in many types of writing, not just nature writing. Nature writing is obviously a nonfiction beneficiary, but there is also a wide range of fiction in which the setting is the natural environment. The same is true of epic narratives where evolutionary themes from simplicity to complexity, form chaos or chaotic perceptions of what's happening around them and lead to a more orderly understanding of how our environment originated. Let me just give you one example of this. My book *Diversity of Life*, which I published in 1992, is a book that, in addition to explaining richness of the living world, tries to explain what we know about that richness and how fast it's eroding, and why we're going to pay a heavy price for our negligence of it, both materially and spiritually. I organized *Diversity of Life* with the aid of a series of mythic themes. In the early chapters I try to build tension by escalating crises of global ecosystems, and especially the tropical rain forest. I tell a personal story of the Amazon rain forest struck by a storm, from which it almost instantly rebounds because it is composed of species that have evolved over millions of years, during which each species acquired resiliency to just that kind of a physical blow. And then I go on to the more dangerous explosions of Krakatau, and next to the cataclysmic meteorite strike that ended the Mesozoic era. But even then life eventually recovered. Finally, I move to the catastrophe that humanity is creating from which the natural world may never recover. I try for tension and mystery against detailed natural history descriptions of ecosystems and evolutionary processes. The sequence is an example of how one can transport biological information into literary expressions and then of course the other way around.

Q: We keep using this word, this prefix *eco-*, in ecology. Ernst Haeckel first defined "oecologie" in 1866 as "the total relations of the animal both to its organic and to its inorganic environment" and as "the study of all the complex interrelationships referred to by Darwin as the conditions of the struggle for existence." We also know that ecology has undergone quite a few shifts since the 1950s. How would you define the contemporary science of ecology?

A: I would call it in early adolescence. I would put it about where physics was in the mid-nineteen century, which was pretty well along. I would call it one of the sciences, a discipline that deals with one of the most complex systems imaginable in the universe and comparable in this respect to the human brain. I'd say that it's growing exponentially in terms of people entering it, journals and articles published, and the quality and sophistication of the work. I would say that when they get their act together, ecologists will see that they have one of the major intellectual challenges of the twenty-first century; theirs is the task of the rules, principles, maybe even laws that govern the assembly of plant, animal, and microorganism communities. The underlying phenomena, the dynamics, the equilibria, and the evolution of the constituent species, are largely unexplored. To be sure, we talk about them all the time. I've been writing on them since my work on island biogeography in the 1960s. Yet, we're just in the very earliest stages of opening the subject up. So, those who are working on your kind of theory would do well to handle ecological theory carefully because you won't be dealing with a static body of knowledge but instead with what will become one of the most rapidly moving and enlarging disciplines of twenty-first-century science.

Q: You recount that once Elso Barghoorn, one of the world's foremost botanists, said to you, "Ed, I don't think we should use 'ecology' as an expression anymore. It's become a dirty word."

A: Yes. Isn't that amazing? That was back during the molecular wars when to the molecular biologists we were the new boys on the block and not smart or sophisticated enough to be members of the gang.

Q: Our next sentence in fact is that you've also written about these early critiques of "ecology as a non-rigorous science, especially from the Harvard molecular biology crowd."

A: That's the point. They had all the advantages of the physical sciences because they'd hooked up with the best of the physical sciences to explore macromolecular phenomena. They had all sorts of sophisticated methodology, experimental procedures, and proof techniques that they'd transported directly in from the physical sciences. At the other end of biology, we didn't have that kind of foundation to connect to, so we were still moving along pretty much in the natural history mode, and it was a very unequal contest. Now biology has become consilient, all the way from molecules to ecosystems. And some of the friendliest people I know these days are molecular biologists who see that a great deal of their future is going to come from molecular evolution, the study of biodiversity at the molecular and cellular levels. Meanwhile, the evolutionary biologists are discovering new phenomena all over the place, and by evolutionary biologists I'm including ecologists. I might add that starting about three years ago I had more and more contact with Jim Watson, the key player in that period in Harvard's molecular revolution, and that we've become quite friendly; I've given two lectures at his invitation, including one keynote at Cold Spring Harbor. On that occasion he introduced me by stating how important evolutionary biology was for what it can contribute in new ideas and problems for other biologists, including molecular biologists. Of course, I turned right around and praised Watson, deservedly, as a key figure in the greatest biological advance of the twentieth century.

Q: Ecology is now being adopted by many in the humanities as a door into the sciences. For instance, in English studies we are seeing the rapid growth of ecocriticism, ecocomposition, ecofeminism, and the likes. Is ecology a good science for the humanities to turn to in these initial cross-disciplinary steps? Or should we be looking to other sciences and developing biocriticism or geocomposition?

A: I think ecology is a very good subject for the bridging of science and the humanities. I think that cognitive psychology is another. Neuroscience is a third, although perhaps a bit further down the line. I would also include biodiversity studies, which are currently linking up with ecology.

Q: One of the major criticisms that we have is that people have been adopting this prefix *eco* as a simple understanding of some kind of environmentalism without making any links to the scientific study of ecology.

A: It tends to be more ideological, using rather vague metaphors about stability and naturalness and sustainability without understanding what's going on as the ecologists themselves understand it.

Q: In *The Betrayal of Science and Reason,* Paul and Ann Ehrlich write that "anti-science rhetoric has been particularly effective in promoting a series of erroneous notions" that distort the findings of environmental scientists. In large part the Ehrlichs are referring to writers in the media and the social sciences as the "brownlashers" who rhetorically manipulate the findings of environmental science. In fact, they mention several brownlashers whose rhetoric misrepresented your own work—Stephen Budiansky, just to name one. We're interested in the Ehrlich's use of the word *rhetoric.* Is this a word that always has negative connotations for scientists?

A: Yes. It probably should not, but generally when scientists say someone is engaging in rhetoric, it's meant to be pejorative about their style. That is, twisting words by engaging in logical arguments with false premises.

Q: You have written that you are cautious in your work and theorizing about nature to "never betray nature." Betrayal, in some ways, suggests not only a turn in loyalty, but a possession of a kind of knowledge that renders betrayal possible. Coming back to Paul and Ann Ehrlich's *Betrayal of Science and Reason,* they suggest that the brownlashers attempt to minimize the seriousness of environmental problems. "Brownlash," they write, "has been generated by a diverse group of individuals and organizations, doubtless often with differing motives and backgrounds. . . . With strong appealing messages, they have successfully sowed seeds of doubt among journalists, policy makers, and the public at large about the reality and importance of such phenomena as overpopulation, global climate change, ozone depletion, and losses of biodiversity." Does our work as theorists, as naturalists, as writers place us in a position that somehow dialectically calls forth these brownlashers? Or, do you agree with Paul and Ann Ehrlich that these people are doing this in the first place? Is this really going on to the extent that the Ehrlichs say it is?

A: Oh, there's no question that it is. Budiansky is an example. When he was a writer from *US News and World Report* several years ago, he questioned the mass extinction of species, and I felt compelled to rebut him. I had the feeling at that time, just to use him as an example, that he was determined to fulfill what appeared to have been given as an assignment to him, which was to present a critical—and I'll use the word *rhetorical*—statement of what he labeled the article "The Myths of Environmentalism." And in order to do that he had to find a few cases here and there that were in doubt about rates of extinction and to play those up and say, "Well, you know, there is plenty of evidence that this does not occur," while ignoring all of the mass of evidence that it does occur and at the rates we've been saying it occurs. So, that's the kind of practice brownlashers use. Another is to say that extinction is a normal process and it's always been replenished by evolution of new species, so not to worry. This is true, of course, but they leave out the fact that extinction rate through human action is now up to 10,000 times faster than the birthrate, which if continued will drive biodiversity down close to about zero. That's something you can present in quite exact documented terms. Another example is the one that we must continue logging in our national forests because this job is an essential function for the country. Here the brownlashers overlook the inconvenient fact that about 75 percent of the contributions of the Gross National Domestic Product of the United States contributed from the national forests comes from recreation, and less than 4 percent comes from logging. That inconvenient fact is seldom mentioned. Then so on down the line with both economics and ecological principles by misstating them, by selecting evidence, and sometimes by just sheer ignorance. The brownlashers manage to provoke a lot of response from the people who want to dismiss unwelcome findings from science.

Q: It seems that the mediums in which brownlashers write tend to be much larger and much more widespread than what academics use.

A: That's the problem.

Q: So, do you see brownlashers, in this sense, kind of winning?

A: No. They're losing. People are listening to the evidence more carefully. They respect science. I've just been invited to go down and give an address at the American Enterprise Institute, for example. It appears that conservative organizations and institutes are opening up a little bit to hearing environmental arguments. Ecologists have won decisively in a number of venues whenever open debate is promoted in journals, including the major news magazines, with the aid of editors who are sympathetic. For example, *Time* has been very pro-environment, and the editors are very well informed. Also, much of current public television is carefully researched and effectively presented. And so gradually the weight shifts, the tide turns.

Q: In *Consilience* you offer a brief "Salute to postmodernity," suggesting that "they enrich culture." And, you say that "we will always need postmodernists or their rebellious equivalents. For what better way to strengthen organized knowledge than continually defend it from hostile forces?" Postmodernists have been more accepted in the humanities than in the sciences; however, the work of postmodern scientists such as Sandra Harding and Donna Haraway still persist in the sciences. What place do you see for postmodernism in the sciences in the future?

A: Close to zero. Donna Haraway, Sandra Harding, and similar writers may be listened to by people in humanities, but scientists are scarcely aware of their existence. Incidentally, most are historians and sociologists rather than practicing scientists.

Q: You have written in *Biophilia*: "The audaciously destructive tendencies of our species run deep and are poorly understood. They are so difficult to probe and manage as to suggest an archaic biological origin. We run a risk if we continue to diagnose them as by-products of history and suppose that they can be erased with simple economic and political remedies. At the very least Sophoclean flaws of human nature cannot be avoided by an escape to the stars. If people perform so badly on Earth, how can they be expected to survive in the biologically reduced and more demanding conditions of space?" You add later, "on Earth no less than in space, lawn grass, potted plants, caged parakeets, puppies, and rubber snakes are not enough." You argue here for a connectedness to nature. Stephen Kellert argues "people have employed nature's rich tapestry of forms for expressing ideas and emotions for perhaps as long as humans have spoken. Through story, fantasy, and dream, the natural world offers raw material for building our species' seemingly unique and arguably most treasured capacities: the ability to use language to exchange information among ourselves." Does language—the way humans use and interpret language—help make or break humans' connections with nature?

A: Emphatically. One wishes that our Norman Mailers and John Updikes all understood ecology. We need more writers of highest caliber who have the background and the training and the inclination to turn to the natural environment for inspiration. But that's not been the case. In fact, literary lions tend to be blinkered in their worldview to an extent that will, I think, in the long run diminish their reputations.

Q: What writers do you see making those connections now? Who do you like?

A: Well, I'm not widely enough read in fiction, for example, to make a judgment, but I just simply haven't run across or heard of distinguished fiction writers of that kind. We have a number of nonfiction writers of very good quality, people like David Quammen, Jonathan Wiener, and Barry Lopez, and a dozen or so others of major talent. There are, on the other hand, extremely few such writers coming out of science as opposed to the humanities.

Q: In *The Value of Life: Biological Diversity and Human Society,* Stephen Kellert writes that "the higher a person's education, the more likely that person is to express a greater concern, affection, interest, knowledge (and less exploitative and authoritarian attitudes) toward animals and the natural world. This tendency is especially pronounced among the college educated." You have written about biophilic learning rules. How much influence do you see a college education nowadays having upon these biophilic learning rules?

A: That's hard to judge, but I have detected some encouraging signs while visiting around colleges and universities. I tend to concentrate on liberal arts colleges and honors programs within all major universities. I sense increasing interest and sophistication in environmental matters in these places. I believe that students, college-aged people, particularly those who are actually in higher education and trying to learn and expand their minds, need a goal, a lifetime crusade of some kind, and they don't have any compelling ones right now. A lot of them can pick up on environment, but not anywhere close in numbers and commitment as, for example, opposition to the Vietnam War, or before that, support of the Kennedy Peace Corps. I've often thought that the environment, with all of its ramifications and enormous importance to humanity, is a logical subject for youthful engagement. Maybe we'll see that happen.

Q: As a final question and continuation of that, you've written that "both teachers and learners fall asleep at their posts when there is no enemy in their field."

A: John Stuart Mills.

Q: Who do you see as our current enemy? Who is keeping us awake in education?

A: Oh, they're all over the place. You may not want the full list, but they certainly include the brownlashers. They include the religious conservatives, and they include the great majority of postmodernists. These are the intellectual enemy in the field. I say, bless them, so long as they don't overwhelm us.

Contradictory Stances
toward Interdisciplinarity

A Response to E. O. Wilson from a
Rhetorician of Science

J. Blake Scott

Edward O. Wilson has indeed been a pioneer in proposing links between the natural sciences on the one hand and the social sciences and humanities on the other. His provocative books *Sociobiology: The New Synthesis* and *Consilience: The Unity of Knowledge*—categorized by rhetorician of science Leah Ceccarelli as "interdisciplinary inspirational" works of science—have indeed inspired many biologists to view the "human condition" as "the most important frontier of the natural scientists" (*Consilience* 267) and have sparked lively debates about the roles of the disciplines and the viability of linkages among them. As Wilson himself laments in his autobiography, however, his calls for interdisciplinarity were not wholly successful, eliciting hostility and resistance from many of his readers, including fellow biologists.

Rhetoricians of science have also responded to Wilson in differing ways. In *Writing Biology*, Greg Myers seeks to explain Wilson's rhetorical prowess in *Sociobiology*, focusing on the way he incorporates a narrative of natural history within a grand narrative of evolutionary adaptation (194–95). Although Myers contextualizes his reading of *Sociobiology* in the larger controversy it fueled, he stops short of evaluating the arguments in the controversy, content instead to explain the participants' citational moves based on their social and institutional positioning. Ceccarelli also adopts an explanatory stance, only she starts from the premise that Wilson's *Sociobiology* and *Consilience* were rhetorical failures. Ceccarelli attributes this failure to Wilson's overreliance on metaphors of disciplinary conquest. In *Sociobiology*, as Myers also points out, Wilson

attempts to bring social scientific disciplines, such as psychology, into the
frame of sociobiology by warning that they are "destined to be cannibal-
ized" by biological sciences (6). Ceccarelli documents Wilson's predomi-
nant use of geopolitical metaphors in *Consilience*, metaphors that tell a
story of the natural sciences dominating the social sciences and humanities in an expansionist war (129).

Given the contradictory receptions Wilson has inspired, it should
not be surprising, perhaps, that his interview for this collection betrays
contradictory stances toward interdisciplinarity, in this case interdisciplinary links between the natural sciences and writing (including literature
and composition). In what follows I tease out two such contradictions in
an effort to diagnose possible challenges to interdisciplinary exchange
between the sciences and humanities and to suggest possible responses to
these challenges. At the same time he advocates—indeed, embodies—the
importance of literary writing to science, Wilson reifies opposing views
of scientific writing and literature. At the same time he encourages exchange between the sciences and the arts, Wilson mainly depicts this
exchange as a limited, one-way enterprise. My aim is not to fault Wilson
for expressing understandable contradictions but to further enable approaches to writing and science that benefit from cross-pollination. My
reading of Wilson's interview ultimately suggests that the lack of exchange between the sciences and humanities is not the result of imperi-
alist attitudes by scientists but the failure of compositionists and others
in the humanities to educate scholars in other disciplines about what we
do (e.g., our objects of study, our methods, our theoretical underpinnings) and how our work might draw on and contribute (however mod-
estly) to science.

One noticeable thematic thread running through Wilson's interview
is his endorsement of literature as crucial to science. Wilson depicts the
scientist as a storyteller who must sometimes combine science with literature, particularly when targeting a broader audience. At one point,
Wilson even describes technical scientific reporting as an "act of creativity," especially in the "framing" sections of a report. In the introduction
and discussion sections, Wilson explains, the scientist must convince
peers of the significance of his or her findings. Later in the interview, in
discussing the possibility of hybrid discourses, Wilson argues that we
need an "intermediate body of literature" that combines the precision
and straightforwardness of scientific writing with a figurative description
of the scientist's creative process. This intermediate discourse would be
about science rather than *of* science, he explains. Although Wilson argues
that literature is valuable to science, this argument presents literary writ-

ing as a useful communicative tool for scientists rather than something that helps shape scientific research.

In conjunction with this call for hybridity, however, Wilson presents scientific writing and literature as being inherently different from and even in many respects opposite of each other. "Technical scientific writing," Wilson argues, "is only concerned with presenting the 'bare bones of factual information' " and is therefore "suspicious of metaphor." Later, Wilson describes scientific technical reports as "raw" descriptions in which metaphor is mostly "unwelcome." Here, Wilson invokes what James Kinneavy has called a windowpane notion of language: good scientific language clearly and directly transmits scientific knowledge, while figurative language obscures it. The windowpane notion of language is tied, of course, to a positivist view of science as a discrete, specialized set of practices for objectively discovering the truths of nature.

Yet transmitting and embellishing reality are not the only functions we can attribute to science-related writing. Rhetoricians of science (not to mention some scientists) have shown science to be thoroughly shaped by language, including metaphoric expressions of it. In *Refiguring Life*, for example, rhetorician and former scientist Evelyn Fox Keller explains how metaphors of gene action have helped shape the scientific practices of molecular biologists starting in the 1930s. This discourse, Keller demonstrates, helped frame the questions scientists could meaningfully ask, the organisms they selected to study, the methods and experiments that made sense to perform, and the explanations that were appropriate (11). For Keller and other rhetoricians, language plays a constitutive though not the determining role in scientific thought and practice. Language works with other "actors," such as cultural norms and technologies to condition scientific practices.

According to Wilson, the project of linking science and literature is so difficult because the two disciplines employ "radically different modes of thought." Wilson's demarcation of science as a distinct enterprise radically different from literature, composition, and other areas in the humanities may explain why he misinterprets the interviewers' description of ecocomposition. As the interviewers point out, ecocomposition is not primarily concerned with writing about nature but about reconceiving writing as part of an ever-changing ecological system that includes textual forms, channels of distribution, interpersonal interactions, cultural norms, and institutional arrangements. Even after repeated prompting by the interviewers, however, Wilson interprets ecological theories of writing to mean theories of nature writing and "fiction in which the setting is the natural environment." Rather than taking up the interviewers' proposition of using ecology to rethink writing practices, Wilson continues to describe writing as a way to increase awareness of science. Wilson is not alone in interpreting ecocomposition as writing about nature; many compositionists and rhetoricians similarly limit the exchange between writing and ecology, as Sid Dobrin has pointed out ("Writing" 13). Stopping short of an interdisciplinary exchange, these compositionists treat environmental concerns as exigency for writing and ecology as a new subject matter for writing instruction.

A second, related contradiction in Wilson's discussion of interdisciplinarity can be found in his descriptions of possible projects linking science and the humanities. At different points Wilson responds favorably to the interviewers' examples of how composition has drawn on the sciences of cognitive psychology and ecology to retheorize the writing process and writing environments, respectively. Yet the conceptual traffic Wilson describes moves largely one direction—from science to the humanities.

This second contradiction is encapsulated in Wilson's response to why he sees connecting science to the arts as the most important interdisciplinary project of the twenty-first century. Instead of discussing what both science and the humanities might have to teach each other, Wilson focuses on how science, as the "most powerful information gathering and verification procedure that humanity has ever devised," can develop a theory of the creative arts, a "systematic consideration of what human creativity is." Echoing the metaphors of scientific conquest that shaped his arguments in *Sociobiology*, Wilson describes the human mind and human creativity as a frontier awaiting scientific exploration. Science has already given us "liftoff power for exploring the universe," Wilson explains, and so now it must help us chart this new internal "space." Wilson's proposed "science of the arts" might indeed be a productive pursuit, even as it reduces aesthetic responses to evolutionary biological processes. This focus on science's conquest of the arts may overlook a range of other productive cross-disciplinary contributions, however, including those initiated by humanities scholars and social scientists.

Toward the end of the interview, Wilson moves past indifference to explicitly reject the idea that postmodern scholars of science studies might contribute to scientific practice. When the interviewers ask Wilson about the work of Donna Haraway, Sandra Harding, and other postmodern feminist scholars, he replies that "scientists are scarcely aware of their existence" and that their influence within science is "close to zero." Later, Wilson includes most postmodernists among the intellectual enemies of environmentalists and ecologists. This stance is strange given that ecology, one of the sciences Wilson champions, can be considered postmodern in several key ways: its foregrounding of networks of relations rather than discrete entities, its emphasis on transformation though not necessarily progress, its rejection of fixed boundaries, its recognition of the scientist's own situatedness. This stance is also unfortunate because postmodern science studies scholars have a great deal to contribute to science, as I will later elaborate. Although Wilson doesn't specify why he views postmodernists as the enemy, it may be because he reads postmodernism's relativism as an attack on science. Many postmodern critics of science, however, share Wilson's commitment to systematically studying the mechanisms of the material world. As Haraway has explained, a postmodern approach to science can combine a recognition of the contingency of knowledge and a self-reflexivity about producing knowledge with a "no-nonsense commitment to faithful accounts of the 'real' world" ("Situated" 187).

My critique of Wilson's apparent positions and contradictions should not be read as an indictment of him but as a reminder of the work rhetoricians, compositionists, literary critics, and others in the humanities have done before us. Wilson and other scientists have done a splendid job of teaching nonscientists about what they study and how they study it. We need to follow their example, to more actively and accessibly share our theorizing about language and writing and to humbly explain how this theorizing might contribute to scientific pedagogy and practice. In addition, we need to ask for guidance from scientists like Wilson in applying and adapting scientific concepts to what we study; following the lead of the interviewers, ecocompositionists could ask for ecologists' help in understanding specific ecological principles and relationships, and this, in turn, might help us enrich our adaptations of ecology.

A thicker interchange between science and composition could lead to richer, more nuanced theorizing in both areas. Ecocompositionists have begun to demonstrate how such an exchange can benefit writing theory and pedagogy. For one, ecological approaches to writing give us a notion of context as a shifting set of organic and inorganic (e.g., technological, ideological) relations of which texts are a part (see Dobrin 12–13). One possible pedagogical extension of ecocomposition is service-learning, which dramatically situates student writers in real-world environments, highlighting interconnections among writers and readers, academic and nonacademic sites, individual and institutional values, texts and technologies, economic constraints, and other conditions for writing. In addition, service-learning writing assignments require students to track transformations of their texts through the processes of production, distribution, and consumption.

A thicker exchange in the other direction might lead to a more nuanced understanding among scientists of science's rhetorical elements and how these elements are connected to extra-rhetorical, material elements. It might also curb scientists' impulse to demarcate science from other types of knowledge building and to be more open to accepting new definitions and applications of science. Science itself might be viewed in more ecological terms. In recognizing the dynamic interplay among language, institutional and social communities and norms, technologies, and nature, Keller moves toward a more ecological and less positivistic rendering of science. Haraway goes even further in her description of technoscience as a heterogeneous tissue comprising interwoven economic, ideological, political, technological, historical, mythic, textual, and organic threads (*Modest* 66–68).

Viewing science as rhetorical and ecological could also lead to more effective pedagogies for scientific and science writing. This training could move beyond the dichotomy of mechanical reporting versus figurative embellishment to more fully account for the rhetorical situatedness, intertextuality, and effects of all such writing. Myers and other rhetoricians offer students of science rich and useful analyses of the rhetorical strategies and conventions of scientific writing processes, reinterpreting such processes as rhetorical adaptation, social interaction, and acculturation. Cultural critics of science, such as Haraway, can help extend rhetoricians' focus on writing in scientific discourse communities by situating such writing in larger cultural networks involving extra-scientific actors. Beyond a discrete and static backdrop for writing, context would be treated as a dynamic interface in which writing is linked to other cultural nodes, from media to bodies to institutional structures to cultural narratives.

WORKS CITED

Ceccarelli, Leah. "Edward O. Wilson's *Consilience: The Unity of Knowledge.*" *Shaping Science with Rhetoric: The Cases of Dobzhansky, Schrodinger, and Wilson.* Chicago: U of Chicago P, 2001.

Dobrin, Sidney I. "Writing Takes Place." *Ecocomposition: Theoretical and Pedagogical Approaches.* Ed. Christian R. Weisser and Sidney I. Dobrin. Albany: State U of New York P, 2001. 11–25.

Haraway, Donna J. "Situated Knowledges: The Science Question in Feminism and the Privilege of Partial Perspective." *Simians, Cyborgs, and Women: The Reinvention of Nature.* New York: Routledge, 1991.

Haraway, Donna J. Modest_Witness@Second_Millennium. FemaleMan©_Meets_ OncoMouse™: Feminism and Technoscience. New York: Routledge, 1997.

Keller, Evelyn Fox. *Refiguring Life: Metaphors of Twentieth-Century Biology.* New York: Columbia UP, 1995.

———. *Secrets of Life, Secrets of Death: Essays on Language, Gender, and Science.* New York: Routledge, 1992.

Myers, Greg. "Narrative and Interpretation in the *Sociobiology* Controversy." *Writing Biology: Texts in the Social Construction of Scientific Knowledge.* Madison: U of Wisconsin P, 1990.

Weisser, Christian R., and Sidney I. Dobrin, eds. *Ecocomposition: Theoretical and Pedagogical Approaches.* Albany: State U of New York P, 2001.

Science, the Humanities, and the Public Intellectual

A Response to E. O. Wilson

Christian R. Weisser

It is important for intellectuals to work through books and then through the media to reach a large number of people. Once this is accomplished, activists can then elevate the problem to the status of public issue. And if enough people are persuaded, it creates the type of pressure that moves political leaders in a democracy. It's very simple: 1 . . . 2 . . . 3.

Interview: E. O. Wilson

This interview with scientist, author, environmental advocate, and two-time Pulitzer prizewinner E. O. Wilson speaks to what may be the most important set of issues in academia today: the relationships we have with the public at large—if there is such a thing—and the responsibilities and obligations we have to make our work publicly relevant and comprehensible. While the urge to connect with public audiences has touched nearly every discipline within the last twenty or so years, many question whether or not intellectuals are capable of moving beyond disciplinary and academic borders to engage in deliberation and communication with larger public audiences. Interestingly enough, Wilson's thoughts concerning his own public writing and activism offer a unique vista from which to survey our own efforts and discussions on this subject. The sciences and humanities alike have felt increasing pressure to justify exactly what it is we do, aside from teaching, and Wilson has been among the most successful in taking his message beyond that of "special consumption" by an exclusive group of biologists to an audience of millions through speaking engagements, TV documentaries, CD-ROMs, and of course books such as *Naturalist, Consilience*, and his most recent best seller, *The Future of Life*. Wilson is, in short, the archetypical public intellectual.

But what exactly is a public intellectual?[1] It would be easy to suggest that only those who have the frequent attention of vast segments of a society can be considered effective public intellectuals, and that this elite circle cannot be easily entered from the stage of the academy. Some scholars have suggested that academic work has little effect on public issues and opinions, and that only those to whom "the public" as a whole turn to often and repeatedly can be truly considered public intellectuals. While it may be true that few academics can hope for the sort of public import that Wilson has attained, I believe—and Wilson's thoughts on the issue published here and elsewhere seem to concur—that most intellectuals have both the capacity and the responsibility to effectively address public audiences. Exercising this capacity, though, requires that we move beyond the traditional sense of public intellectual work. It requires that we reconsider what it means to be a public intellectual, where such activity might take place, and to whom and about what we are capable of speaking.

Early in this interview, Wilson stresses the importance of "intermediate bodies of literature" or "hybrid modes" that an author might produce. This notion gets to the heart of a useful and important reconception of writing meant for public consumption: that it need not speak to an amorphous audience comprising a diverse cross section of the general population. Wilson recognizes and stresses the importance of speaking to various audiences rather than expecting to address all members of society using the same discursive styles and contexts at all times. Wilson's work runs the gamut from "technical writing, the kind that one finds in research reports and peer-reviewed journals," to combinations of "science and literature," and even to what he has called at a recent colloquium of scientists, writers, and educators as "a sort of Homeric narrative" (*Arousing Biophilia*). Intellectuals can and should utilize a number of different avenues and discourses when attempting to spread information and knowledge—not just scholarly books and journals designed for consumption by like-minded peers.

To be sure, though, Wilson thinks carefully and deeply about the audiences he addresses. His voice has been particularly vocal in recent environmental and ecological issues, and a careful study of his writing shows a clear understanding of speaking to and crafting language for specific groups—what Nancy Fraser calls "subaltern counterpublics." Fraser suggests that these subaltern counterpublics emerge in response to exclusions and omissions within dominant publics, and as such they help expand discursive space. The relative lack of attention to environmental degradation, the loss of plant and animal habitiats, and other such issues have led to a proliferation of books, magazines, conventions, conferences, and Listserv discussions that attempt to compensate for the lack of discussion on these important subjects in dominant discourse. The newly emerging field of ecocomposition might be seen as a subaltern counterpublic that is developing as a response to the relative lack of discussion about relationships between discourse and location within the broader field of rhetoric and composition. As such, it draws upon those larger discussions but incorporates issues, ideas, and discourses from fields as seemingly diverse as environmental science, linguistics, biology, literary studies, and ecology. Much like Wilson's own work, particularly that found in his 1998 *Consilience: The Unity of Knowledge*, ecocompositionists hope to discover links between the sciences and the humanities, and, by extension, links with groups, individuals, and discourse communities outside of academia. Ecocompositionists hope to speak not just to themselves but to others in their classrooms, disciplines, universities, and communities. By example, Wilson seems to prod us out of the safe confines of our offices, our disciplines, and our discursive communities to speak to and with others about issues of common concern.

In fact, stepping outside of our disciplinary boundaries is crucial, according to Wilson. He stresses the importance of this move, arguing that intellectuals should do more to "spread the word" about environmental and social issues by recognizing that "the media are all-important . . . intermediaries in spreading information and developing movements, especially in a democracy" ("Interview"). While at times Wilson has been able to capture the attention of large portions of society, that has not kept him from employing other smaller avenues of discourse. He devotes equal vigor to gatherings of five or five thousand, and seeks to cultivate intimate connections with each member of his audience; Wilson has utilized a plethora of discourse communities to voice his opinion on environmental and ecological issues. He envisions his own public writing style as protean, employing "language that can be varied in a literary manner to run from somber to celebratory and inspirational" in accordance with the constraints of his audience. While differences in discursive styles, genres, and audiences do exist, Wilson seems to suggest that creating discourse that bridges the gaps between discrete discursive styles to connect with audiences outside of them is imperative. He states here that "there are the extreme modes, of pure science and pure literature, then there is the one between. In this hybrid mode the writer is exact and truthful in describing a material entity or process but at the same time uses metaphors in an exposition of the innovative process itself." Quite obviously, Wilson devotes a lot of time to thinking about his own writing and the ways in which he might use his expertise to reach outside of his narrow field of study. Intellectuals can take part in discourse in larger public spheres, but we must also look for alternative sites in which to voice our opinions on social and political issues. Obviously, public discourse need not be limited to a single discursive arena that reaches a huge cross section of society.

Wilson's body of work highlights another important aspect of public intellectualism that deserves attention: the willingness to problematize or question the notion that some issues are best decided and acted on by private groups, committees, organizations, or individuals, without the participation of "outsiders." This notion is particularly widespread in current environmental debates, where land-use management and other policy issues are designated as legal, commercial, or governmental matters and as such are labeled as private issues. The terms *public* and *private* are not simply absolute definitions of two basic spheres in a society; they are rhetorical labels that often work to reinforce the boundaries of public discourse in ways that disadvantage subordinate groups and individuals. With this in mind, Wilson speaks out on land-use policy in much of his work, often citing the loss of biodiversity as a public reason to change or modify private regulations that diminish the number of plant and animal species. Thanks in part to Wilson and others like him, some of the relegation of particular environmental issues as private and separate from public discussion and debate is changing, and (according to this interview) it "appears that conservative organizations and institutes are opening up a little bit to hearing environmental arguments."

Wilson seems to suggest that one place to begin erasing the boundaries between discourses and discursive spheres is to begin making connections between seemingly unrelated disciplines. In fact, according to Wilson, making connections between disciplines is the most pressing issue for higher education today. By looking at disciplines not as discrete specializations but instead as interconnecting, shifting hybrid domains moves us closer to truly integrating specialized knowledge in a way that might help shape public opinion. He writes:

> Most of the issues that vex humanity daily . . . cannot be solved without integrating knowledge from the natural sciences with that of the social sciences and humanities. . . . Yet the vast majority

of our political leaders are trained exclusively in the social sciences and humanities, and have little or no knowledge of the natural sciences. The same is true of the public intellectuals, the columnists, the media interrogators, and think-tank gurus. . . . Every college student should be able to answer the following question: What is the relation between science and the humanities, and how is it important for human welfare? Every public intellectual and political leader should be able to answer that question as well. (*Consilience* 13–14)

Clearly, Wilson sees the unification of disciplinary knowledge, discourse, and epistemology as a first step toward a larger goal: making connections with groups and individuals outside of academia to help shape opinion and policy on any number of important public issues.

Of course, as I have mentioned, few of us can hope to get the attention of the sheer number of individuals that Wilson has. But, by seeking out specific public groups in which our discourse can be heard, by carefully crafting language for those groups, by working toward greater understanding with intellectuals in other disciplines, and by using our disciplinary knowledge in ways that benefit our students, our communities, and our biospheres, we might arrive at a new definition of public intellectualism. This new definition would be one that takes into account the smaller roles and opportunities that are more readily available to us than the narrow definition of reaching vast audiences in short periods of time. We might begin to extend our definitions of public intellectualism to accommodate the variety of opportunities we have to foster cooperative public connections. Public intellectuals might be then, quite simply, members of academe who take steps to bring more voices, more discourse, and a greater degree of communication to public debates, and in turn bring about social change. While immediate sweeping changes in society may be unattainable, imagine our satisfaction as "gradually the weight shifts, the tide turns."

NOTES

1. For fuller explications on public writing and public intellectualism, see *Moving Beyond Academic Discourse: Composition Studies and the Public Sphere* and *Natural Discourse: Toward Ecocomposition*.

WORKS CITED

"Arousing Biophilia: A Conversation with E. O. Wilson." 25 Jan. 2002 <http://arts.envirolink.org/interviews_and_conversations/EOWilson.html>.

Dobrin, Sidney I. and Christian R. Weisser. *Natural Discourse: Toward Ecocomposition*. Albany: State U of New York P, 2002.

"Interview: E. O. Wilson." 25 Jan. 2002. <http://www.wildglobe.com/resources/interview_eowilson. html>.

Weisser, Christian R. *Moving Beyond Academic Discourse: Composition Studies and the Public Sphere*. Carbondale: Southern Illinois UP, 2002.

Wilson, Edward O. *Consilience: The Unity of Knowledge*. New York: Vintage Books, 1999.

———. *Naturalist*. New York: Warner Books, 1991.

———. *The Future of Life*. New York: Knopf Press, 2002.

Contributors

Kaye Adkins is an Assistant Professor of English at Missouri Western State College where she teaches essay writing, composition theory, technical writing, and composition. Her research interests include environmental rhetoric, the preservationist movement, and ecocomposition. She has presented papers on these subjects at a number of national conferences, and organizes the ecocomposition Special Interest Group for the Conference on College Composition and Communication. She has been a contributing editor to the Association for the Study of Literature and Environment's annual bibliography. She received her Ph.D. in composition and rhetoric from the University of Kansas in 1998.

Sidney I. Dobrin is Associate Professor and Director of Writing Programs at the University of Florida. He serves on the faculty of the University of Florida College of Natural Resources and Environmental Studies. He is the author and editor of numerous articles and books including *Saving Place: An Ecocomposition Reader, Constructing Knowledges: The Politics of Theory-Building and Pedagogy in Composition* (1997), *The Kinneavy Papers: Theory and the Study of Discourse* (with Lynn Worsham and Gary A. Olson) (2000), *Ecocomposition: Theoretical and Pedagogical Approaches* (with Christian Weisser) (2001), and *Natural Discourse: Toward Ecocomposition* (with Christian Weisser) (2002). He is also the author of *Distance Casting: Words and Ways of the Saltwater Fishing Life* (2000). He is a PADI dive instructor, a licensed boat captain, and a fanatic angler. When not in, on, or under the water, Sid can be found hunting in various bars and grills in search of the perfect grouper sandwich, the perfect cheeseburger, and the perfect glass of rum punch.

Julie Drew is Associate Professor of English at the University of Akron where she teaches writing and cultural studies and complains that nobody in their right mind would choose to live where temperatures reach twenty below. Oddly enough, she lives there anyway.

Elizabeth A. Flynn is a professor in the Department of Humanities at Michigan Technological Universities where she teaches courses in rhetoric and composition, gender studies, and literature. She is author of *Feminism Beyond Modernism* (2002), coeditor of *Reading Sites: Social Difference and Reader Response* (forthcoming 2003), coeditor of *Gender and Reading: Essays on Readers, Texts, and Contexts* (1986), and of numerous articles and book chapters. She has held elected positions in the National Council of Teachers of English, the Conference on College Composition and Communication, and the Modern Language Association of America.

Annie Merrill Ingram is Associate Professor of English and Director of the Center for Interdisciplinary Studies at Davidson College in North Carolina. She teaches courses in ecocomposition, environmental literature, Native American literature, and nineteenth-century American fiction. Her commitment to experiential pedagogies has resulted in several service-learning courses and some falling into mud puddles, too. She has published on ecocomposition and service-learning, contemporary environmental justice literature by women, and nineteenth-century American women writers.

Christopher J. Keller is Assistant Professor of English at the University of Texas-Pan American. He is completing two other books with SUNY Press: a monograph entitled *Topographies of Power* and a collection entitled *The Locations of Composition* (with Christian Weisser). He is active in community theater.

M. Jimmie Killingsworth, Professor of English at Texas A&M University, teaches writing, rhetoric, and American literature. Many of his books and articles deal with issues of environmental rhetoric, ecocomposition, and ecocriticism. With coauthor (and wife), Jacqueline Palmer, he is the author of the critical study *Ecospeak: Rhetoric and Environmental Politics in America* (1992) and the textbook *Information in Action: A Guide to Technical Communication* (2nd edition, 1999). In addition, he has published two books on Walt Whitman and numerous articles and chapters. He is currently pursuing an interest in creative nonfiction with a focus on war and nature.

Lezlie Laws is professor of English at Rollins College in Winter Park, Florida, where she has taught for thirteen years. In addition to directing the Writing Program there, she teaches courses in composition and rhetoric, as well as writing and literature courses in creative nonfiction—autobiography and the personal essay. She is currently writing a collection of essays that explore the intermingling and reversing of roles among teacher and students; right now, she's calling the collection *When the Students Arrive, the Teacher Will Appear.* She received her Ph.D. from the University of Missouri-Columbia.

Scott Richard Lyons (Leech Lake Ojibwe) is Assistant Professor of Writing and Rhetoric at Syracuse University.

Sushil K. Oswal is an interdisciplinary faculty with research interests in the issues of organizational change related to the application of environmental technologies, effects of technology transfer on indigenous cultures, and study of pre-European indigenous technologies. He teaches Professional and Technical Communication, Environmental Science, and Postcolonial Theory at the University of Hartford.

Eric Otto, a graduate teaching assistant and Ph.D. candidate in English at the University of Florida, received his B.A. from Florida Gulf Coast University in May of 2000 and his M.A. from the University of Florida in December of 2002. While at FGCU he worked as a teaching assistant in the school's university-wide colloquium on environmental sustainability. His research interests include the representation of the natural world in popular art and the connections between environmentalist thinking and contemporary science fiction.

Derek Owens is the author of *Composition and Sustainability: Teaching for a Threatened Generation* (2001). He is Associate Professor and Director of the Writing Center at St. John's University, and lives with his wife and son somewhere in the center of Long Island.

Malea Powell is a mixed-blood of Indiana Miami, Eastern Shawnee, and Euro-American ancestry. She is an Associate Professor of Writing, Rhetoric, and American Culture and American Indian Studies at Michigan State University where she teaches graduate and undergraduate courses in writing, rhetoric, critical theory, and American Indian Studies. Her research focuses on examining the rhetorics of survivance used by nineteenth-century American Indian intellectuals, and has published essays in *CCCC, Paradoxa, Race, Rhetoric & Composition, ALTDIS*, and other essay collections. She is editor of *Of Color: Native American Literatures* (forthcoming) as well as editor of *SAIL: Studies in American Indian Literatures*, a quarterly journal devoted to the study of American Indian writing.

Randall Roorda, an Associate Professor of English at the University of Kentucky, is the author of *Dramas of Solitude: Narratives of Retreat in American Nature Writing* (1998). He is the current (2001) president of ASLE, the Association for the Study of Literature and Environment, and the founder of ASLE-CCCC, a group devoted to the study of ecology and composition.

Christopher Schroeder is an Assistant Professor of English at Northeastern Illinois University where he teaches undergraduate and graduate courses in composition and literature. His most recent publications include *ALT DIS: Alternative Discourses and the Academy*, which he proposed to and coedited with Helen Fox and Patricia Bizzell, and *ReInventing the University: Literacies and Legitimacy in the Postmodern Academy*.

J. Blake Scott is an Assistant Professor of English at the University of Central Florida where he teaches courses in technical and professional writing and the rhetorics of science and medicine. Along with Melody Bowdon, he has written *Service-Learning in Technical and Professional Communication* (2002). He is author of *Risky Rhetoric: AIDS, and the Cultural Practices of HIV Testing* (2003).

Dean Swinford is a Ph.D. candidate in the English department at the University of Florida. His areas of interest include medieval cosmological allegories, science history, and constructions of nature. He is currently working on *The Irreal Effect: Allegory, Technology, Exploration*, a study of allegory in relation to cultural transformation enacted through exploration and technological innovation.

Christian R. Weisser is an Associate Professor of Rhetoric and Composition at Florida Atlantic University's Honors College. Christian is the author of *Moving Beyond Academic Discourse: Composition Studies and the Public Sphere* (2002). He has coauthored *Natural Discourse: Toward Ecocomposition* (2002), and coedited *Ecocomposition: Theoretical and Pedagogical Perspectives* (2001), both with Sidney I. Dobrin. With the editors of this collection, Christian is currently writing *Technical Communication for the Twenty-First Century* (forthcoming). Christian lives just a few blocks from the Jupiter Inlet Lighthouse, in Palm Beach County, Florida, and he looks forward to spending time on the beach and in the ocean with his newborn son, Cole.

Lynn Worsham is Professor of English at the Illinois State University where she teaches graduate courses in rhetorical theory and cultural studies and undergraduate courses in women's and African American literature. She is editor of the *JAC: A Journal of Composition Theory,* a quarterly journal for the interdisciplinary study of rhetoric, discourse, and culture.

Index